On the Shore of Nothingness

Ce n'est point avec les idées, mon cher Dégas,
que l'on fait les vers, c'est avec des mots

(Stéphan Mallarmé)

On the Shore of Nothingness

Space, rhythm, and semantic structure in religious poetry
and its mystic-secular counterpart

A Study in Cognitive Poetics

Reuven Tsur

with contributions by Motti Benari

ia

IMPRINT ACADEMIC

Published in the UK by Imprint Academic
PO Box 200, Exeter EX5 5HY, UK

www.imprint-academic.com

Published in the USA by Imprint Academic
Philosophy Documentation Center
PO Box 7147, Charlottesville, VA 22906-7147, USA

ISBN 9780907845447 (cloth)
ISBN 9781845401368 (pbk)

A CIP catalogue record for this book is available from the
British Library and US Library of Congress

This work was supported by grant No. 717.99-2
of the Israel Science Foundation

Table of Contents

Preface

When I was a young high-school teacher in a youth-village near Jerusalem, I said during a discussion of Tchernichovsky's poem "Nocturno" that the poet expressed in it his wish to integrate with nature. One of the students asked "What does he mean by 'integrating with nature'? Does he want to sleep among the rocks?". It may have been intended as a mischievous, teasing question. But I decided not to handle it as such. I suddenly realised that I had been making unquestioning use of a Romantic cliché acquired at the university. It took me decades to come up with what I could accept as a fairly satisfactory answer. Years later I met that student at a students' reunion, and told him that now I had an answer to his question. But he did not remember that he had ever asked it. This book is for people who want to know what we mean when, by way of reading poems, we use such clichés as "The poet wants to integrate with nature", or "dissolve in eternity, or in nothingness"; or "this poem displays an ecstatic quality", "this poem conveys the union of a human ego with a non-ego", "the 'I' in this poem is deeply drown'd in self-oblivion" or "the poet has got a glimpse of an inaccessible reality", or "of the beyond", or "this poem conveys a mystic insight".

This is a book by a practicing nonbeliever who feels that he has had significant intuitions concerning religious and mystic poems, and who believes that it is worthwhile to try to account for them in a principled manner. It is not a monograph on the varieties of religious or mystic poetry. It has no claims for comprehensiveness of any sort. Rather, it explores selected strategies of coping with certain kinds of religious and mystic experiences in a limited area of religious and mystic poetry. Rather than offering a wide scope and a wide variety of texts, I shall go into minute details of a small number of poems. The choice of such a strategy may be justified by the purpose of my inquiry.

As the motto of this book suggests, it is not at all with ideas that one writes poetry; it is with words. This study does not try to explore religious ideas for their own sake, but rather how religious ideas are turned into verbal imitations of religious experience by poetic structure. We face a domain replete with paradoxes. It is not only the great paradoxes of religion and mysticism, but also those involved in the literary endeavour. We explore how poets attempt to express the ineffable by using words; and some of them are quite successful in doing this. Meditation aims at the voluntary surrender of voluntary control. Some meditative poems attempt to convey the resulting nonconceptual state of mind by using conceptual language.

The issue at stake here is how does the poet induce his readers to perceive a non-conceptual state of mind emerging from a stretch of conceptual language. In other words, we are dealing with the translation of perceived qualities from reality to some semiotic system, or from one semiotic system to another. Such semiotic systems not only open possibilities, but, at the same time, impose constraints. The precision of translation depends on how fine-grained the sign-units of the target system are. What we are after is the conditions which arouse an illusion that the experience suggested by the stretch of words is authentic. I have isolated four conditions the presence of which may induce a reader to perceive a group of signs (such as, e.g., a stretch of words) as displaying some nonconceptual, ineffable quality, that is, evoke a perception that the two are somehow "equivalent":

* the most salient features of the source phenomenon are represented;
* a relatively large number of distinguishing characteristics of the source phenomenon are sampled for representation;
* the target system is sufficiently fine-grained to capture the most salient features of the source phenomenon;
* the nearest options of the target system are chosen to represent features of a source phenomenon.

These conditions would apply to compact disks rendering music as well as to mystic poetry conveying mystic qualities. A meditative or mystic poem does not *arouse* a meditative or mystic state of mind; it can only convey certain theological ideas or, at best, *display* some perceptual quality that may be perceived as equivalent to a meditative or mystic experience. It is the afore-mentioned four conditions that govern the conversion of ideas of religious or mystic interest into the verbal imitation of some meditative or mystic quality and evoke a perception that the experience and its verbal imitation are somehow "equivalent". To paraphrase Gérard Genette on Rimbaud's "Voyelles", the global correspondence creates the illusion of a feature-by-feature analogy (Genette, 1966: 152; cf. Tsur, 1992b: 120): we detect, so to speak, a subjective mystic or meditative experience in the text. Moreover, the poetic codes of romantic and symbolistic poetry, for instance, are more fine-grained regarding the features required for conveying subjective experience than many other poetic codes. Consequently I found, paradoxically enough, that some of my best examples for the present conception of mystic and meditative poetry were secular poems—romantic or symbolistic.

Much discussion of mystic poetry translates the poems into their own terms, that is, using and elucidating the terms of a conceptual system developed by the mystics themselves. Yeats's poems are frequently discussed in terms of his *A Vision,* or by invoking Swedenborg. Blake's poems are frequently interpreted in terms of a conceptual system abstracted from his visionary works. The same happens to Ibn Gabirol's philosophical and devotional poetry, in which his poetic ideas are traced back to his philosophical treatise *Fons Vitae,* consisting of a series of Platonic dialogues between Master and Disciple. Such an approach frequently obscures the uniqueness of poetic expression. The present endeavour is radically different: it attempts to use a conceptual system involving cognitive, linguistic, and stylistic terms, to describe the interaction of verbal structures with their contents in a poem; and to account, systematically, for the perceived subjective quality regularly associated with such interactions between contents and verbal structures.

The present study was conducted at a relatively advanced stage of my professional career. This had both an advantage and disadvantage. On the one hand, over the years I have developed a conceptual system that may yield significant insights into the nature of religious and mystic poetry. On the other hand, I have already "used up" some of my most illuminating examples in earlier discussions. Much that I wrote on hypnotic-ecstatic poetry and the poetry of altered states of consciousness in my earlier publications, mainly in my *Toward A Theory of Cognitive Poetics* (1992 a) and *The Road to "Kubla Khan"* (1987b), should have been reproduced here. I particularly regret that I could not reproduce here my discussion of Baudelaire's "Correspondances" (Tsur, 1992a: 455–470) along with Rimbaud's "Voyelles" (Tsur, 1992b: 111–135), the ecstatic rhythms and mystic visions yielded by Colerdige's "Kubla Khan" (Tsur, 1987b), and the stylistic distinctions between Whitman's "illustrative" and "meditative" catalogues (Tsur, 1992a: 416–428). I have contributed a chapter on Cognitive Poetics to a recent book, *Cognitive Stylistics—Language and Cognition in Text Analysis;* it includes a detailed close reading of Keats's "On Seeing the Elgin Marbles" as a poem whose structure suggests an altered state of consiousness. Here I have only reproduced in Chapter 1 part of my discussion of Wordsworth's "Daffodils" (from Tsur, 1992a: 447–450). At the infernal pole, I regrettably had to leave out two of my favourite passages from Milton's *Paradise Lost,* on the Hellish perspectives suggested by "At once as far as Angels' ken he views / The dismal situation waste and wild," etc. (I: 59–64), and on Satan's endless fall, headlong, "from the'etherial sky [...] to bottomless perdition" (I: 44–49). Elsewhere I have offered a close reading of the former passage (Tsur 1977: 180–185; 1992: 85–91), and discussed at considerable length the "perceptual forces" generated by gestalt and prosodic resources in the latter (Tsur 1977: 207–212; 1992: 148–153; 1998: 256–264). The last-mentioned reference also includes an empirical study of the rhythmical performance of that "endless" run-on sentence. I have published during the years three Hebrew books and a number of articles on mediaeval Hebrew poetry, a vast section of which is devotional. I could include only a very small part of this in the present book.

The paper that constitutes Chapter 11 was written back in 1972–1973, and has not been previously published in English. In time, I took from it the comparison of Milton's "Nativity Ode" to corresponding passages in *Paradise Lost,* and included it in another book (Tsur, 1992a: 97–100); I thought, however, that that would not be sufficient reason to omit it from here. The paper that constitutes Chapter 13 was Chapter 3 in an earlier book of mine (Tsur, 1987a); I felt however, that the present book would be incomplete without it. Much of the theoretical machinery of this book has been developed earlier, and is reproduced here from earlier publications. Some chapters of this book have already been published in learned journals separately. The Chapter "Poem, Prayer and Meditation" was published in *Style* 1974. Chapter 12 has been published in *PSYART: A Hyperlink Journal for the Psychological Study of the Arts,* http://www.clas.ufl.edu/ipsa/journal/articles/tsur02.htm (1998). A drastically abbreviated version of Chapter 4 has been published in *Pragmatics and Cognition* (2002). The Hieronymus Bosch part of Chapter 10 is going to be published in a special volume on the grotesque of the *Psychotherapy Patient* series; an abbreviated version of Chapter 8 will be published in a special issue on literature and consciousness in *Journal of Consciousness Studies.*

Motti Benari co-operated with me during part of the project and made valuable contributions throughout the study; in Chapters 1 and 4 he is outright co-author.

Jerusalem, January, 2003.

This research was supported by grant No. 717.99-2 of the Israel Science Foundation.

Synopsis

Chapter 1

"Introduction: Means, Effects, and Assumptions". The first section of this introductory chapter offers an overview of attempts to define varieties of religious, mystic and meditative experiences. The second section points out that there is a religious and a secular variety of mystic poetry. A close reading of Wordsworth's "Daffodils" is proposed as an instance of a romantic ecstatic poem. The third section raises the problem of adequacy in the conversion of perceived qualities from reality to some semiotic system, or from one semiotic system to another. The issue is introduced via an excursus on onomatopoeia. A sound imitation is *perceived as* equivalent to the imitated reality if the target semiotic system is sufficiently fine-grained in the relevant respects, if as many salient features of the source phenomenon are represented as possible, and if the most relevant options of the target system are chosen. Different semiotic systems may represent different salient features of the source phenomenon. The same applies, with the necessary changes, to representing the salient features of mystic experiences in the verbal medium. This may explain why some of the best examples for my conception of mystic poetry are secular, romantic or symbolistic, poems. Poetic codes developed by romantic and symbolistic poetry are more fine-grained than some other poetic codes precisely in those respects that can best convey the salient features of a mystic experience, or display a mystic quality. Finally the problem of ineffability is addressed.

Chapter 2

"Poem, Prayer and Meditation". Is the devotional poem a poem, a prayer, or a meditation? This chapter offers a distinction between these three notions in terms of Roman Jakobson's model of language functions (Jakobson, 1960). In *poem* the poetic function is dominant, in *prayer* it is the "conative" function, whereas in *meditation* the "emotive" function. It is argued that these differences in the dominant function entail further logical, semantic, and structural differences. It also demonstrates that one and the same Holy Sonnet by Donne can be read as a poem, a prayer or a meditation at different times, following up the changing implications of the changing dominant functions. This chapter quotes the article "Aesthetic Ambiguity" by the psychoanalyst Ernst Kris and the logician Abraham Kaplan, who argue that ambiguity is beneficial for an aesthetic object, but detrimental to a liturgical one.

Chapter 3

"The Ultimate Limit—Transcendence and Appresentation". This chapter adopts from Gordon D. Kaufman an archetypal situation in which, he says, people use "Godtalk", that is, language in which such terms as *God,* or *the gods, angels, demons, the other world,* and so on, occur. "In this respect the idea of God functions as a *lim-*

iting concept, that is, a concept that does not primarily have content in its own right drawn directly out of a specific experience, but refers to that which we do *not* know but which is the ultimate limit of all our experiences. What literary movements as different as Metaphysical poetry, Romantic poetry and Absurd drama or literature of extreme situations (e.g., Kafka) have in common is a feeling of human limitedness, being confined to the "here and now"; but against this common background of shared feeling illuminating distinctions can be made. Metaphysical and Romantic poetry strive, with different emphases, to transcend the absolute limit, whereas the Absurd assumes that "God is dead", and that any attempt at transcendence is doomed to failure. Kaufman also puts forward two models of transcendence (and of God): the *interpersonal* and the *teleological*. These two models of transcendence lead to quite diverse theological conceptions, and different kinds of poetry.

Chapter 4.
"'Composition of Place', Experiential Set, and the Meditative Poem". This chapter discusses two crucial aspects of Jesuit meditation and what Louis Martz calls "Poetry of Meditation". Martz and some seventeenth century Jesuits claim that on the "well-making" of "seeing the place" or "the composition of place" depends all the success of meditation. We raise the question of what is the relationship between "seeing the place" and the success of meditation. Meditation involves an essential paradox: it requires that one abandon voluntary control voluntarily. This is the problem solved by "composition of place". Ornstein (1975) argued that both meditation and orientation are typically right-hemisphere activities of the brain. "Seeing the place" activates the orientation mechanism and puts the brain into an operative mode which conforms with meditation. This hypothesis was supported by a recent SPECT-imaging study of the brain during meditation (Newberg et al., 2001). This issue is crucial for an understanding of a paradox in poetic communication, too: How does conceptual and sequential language communicate nonconceptual experiences? It will thus loom large in most chapters of this book. We also have to face the apparently unexplained fact that the "Composition of Place" is more meticulously observed in romantic nature poetry than in the "meditative poem" proper (Martz suggests that some of the best romantic nature poems belong to the meditative genre). It is in this context that we analyse Donne's Holy Sonnet 7 ("At the round earths imagin'd corners, blow"). The other aspect discussed is that of mental set. Tellegen devised a test to assess the personality variable "absorption". This is the personality variable that predicts hypnotisability. He distinguishes between "instrumental set" and "experiential set". Absorption is defined as a propensity to adopt the experiential set. Again, for most people it is not easy to relinquish the instrumental in favour of the experiential set. Both hypnosis and meditation presuppose an experiential set. In the anonymous Spanish sonnet "To Christ Crucified" we follow the process by which it switches from an instrumental to an experiential set. We do not attempt to encompass meditation as a whole, only to point out certain cognitive links between structure and perceived effects.

Chapter 5.

"Mystic Poetry—Metaphysical, Baroque and Romantic". An important assumption of the present study is that devotional, meditative, or mystic poetry is first of all poetry, shaped and constrained by the possibilities and constraints inherent in the various poetic styles. This chapter adopts from John Crowe Ransom (1951) a distinction between three "ontological" models: Physical, Platonic and Metaphysical poetry, of which I shall be using the last two only. In Platonic poetry, a variety of images illustrate one idea; in metaphysical poetry, the various aspects of one image may each suggest a different idea. Both neoclassical and romantic poetry are "Platonic"; but the former focuses on the ideas as represented by highly general images, whereas the latter typically subsumes the concrete images in a particular, coherent landscape. The orientation mechanism evoked by the landscape renders the compact abstractions diffuse, which may be perceived as an intense, supersensuous presence. This chapter discusses the handling of a metaphysical image in a very minor seventeenth century poem by Quarles (Metaphysical poetry at its height is discussed in chapters 2, 4, 6 and 8) and two exquisite pieces of "Platonic" poetry by the German baroque poet Andreas Gryphius, and the English romantic William Wordsworth. In both sonnets, the octet offers a landscape description in which the abstractions are perceived as some supersensuous presence; the sestet offers a "colloquy" that leads to an insight into the human significance of the preceding landscape description.

Chapter 6.

"The Sublime and the Absolute Limit". This chapter takes up the issue of the ultimate limit and its transcendence from chapter 3, and the issue of orientation from chapter 4. The notion of the "sublime" is introduced as a means for rendering the ultimate limit apprehensible: that which is sublime exceeds the observer's ability to perceive it in one intuition. In this chapter I first explore the sublime in biblical poetry. Then I examine how romantic and metaphysical poetry handle these problems. I discuss a quatrain from Keats's sonnet "When I have fears", and Donne's Holy Sonnet 5 ("I am a little world"). In the former I examine how "Huge cloudy symbols of a high romance" and "to trace / their shadow with the magic hand of chance" arouse a vivid intuition of having had a glimpse of the world beyond the ultimate limit. In Donne's sonnet, the apostrophe "You which beyond that heaven which was most high / found new worlds" reflects the crisis and disorientation when the ultimate limit turns out not to be the ultimate limit; when beyond the "ultimate" limit new worlds are discovered (we are in the seventeenth century). In another poem, Donne writes: "The New Philosophy calls all in doubt"—the same crisis is presented in the abstract. In Holy Sonnet 5, the self-specifying information of the orientation space is destroyed. Nonetheless, the numinous is revealed *within* the ultimate limits: the poem ends with a verbal allusion to a verse from *Psalms* which Rudolf Otto quotes as an instance of the numinous. This point is reached not through transcendence, but a painful psychological process: the fire of "envie and lust" is turned into a fire purifying the heart.

Chapter 7.

"Rhythmic Structure and Religious Poetry—The Numinous, the Infernal, and *Agnus Dei"*. This chapter attempts to establish reasoned, systematic relationships between poetic structures on the one hand, and, on the other, poetic qualities of religious interest, regularly attributed to them by generations of poets, readers and critics. It offers a theoretical framework which may account for perceived qualities of poems by relying on an interaction between the rhythm, stanza structure, and semantic, syntactic and thematic elements. It draws upon two notions: "convergent and divergent poetry", and "double-edgedness". Two poetic strategies are considered: that which evokes a stable world, and that which indicates a vague, unstable world; and both are "double edged". By achieving cognitive stability, you irrecoverably lose evasive, undifferentiated precategorial information, which is crucial for adequate adjustment to a world-in-flux. And conversely, by abandoning cognitive stability, evasive precategorial information essential for adequate adaptation becomes accessible; but the sense of control and security is weakened or lost. The same holds true, mutatis mutandis, of prosodic structures. A fairly predictable meter may be perceived as rational, "trance-inductive", or imposing a simplifying structure on reality. When meter is less predictable, and the clear-cut contrasts between prominent and non-prominent events become blurred, it may arouse awe, apprehension, and anxiety, owing to the undermining of security; or the sequence of blurred shapes and contrasts may be perceived as isomorphic with emotional processes and mystic experiences. According to Tennyson, it is the vagueness of Milton's hell that renders it awful; it is vague on all levels: thematic, semantic, syntactic, and prosodic. In a nightmare passage from Tennyson's *In Memoriam,* by contrast, the symmetrical stanza and the all-too-regular rhythm appear to undermine the infernal atmosphere. The numinous, "spell-weaving", potential of regular rhythms—as opposed to their simplifying, naive potential—is explored in Blake's "The Tyger" and "The Lamb".

Chapter 8.

"Visual and Auditory Ingenuities in Mystic Poetry". One of the central assumptions of the present study is that mystic or religious poetry reaches the less rational layers of the mind by interfering with the smooth functioning of the cognitive system. In this way, the experience is affected not only by its contents, but also by the perceived quality of the structure of the underlying mental process. Mystic or religious poetry occurs in vastly different styles. The present study distinguishes between two prototypes of such styles, based on drastic and on smooth interference, respectively. The present chapter examines poems based on a very special kind of drastic disruption, of which George Herbert was the grand master. It considers the relationship between mystic poetry and "typographic foregrounding". In this relationship both mystic and aesthetic principles are involved. At the same time I also explore certain psychoanalytic and cognitive mechanisms underlying the mystic and aesthetic effects. Two opposite tendencies are pointed out. On the one hand, the letters of the alphabet may induce magic and mystic processes of enormous force. On the other hand, human society may apply defense mechanisms against such processes, fossilising them into stylistic mannerisms and ingenuities. A wide range of ingenuities are discussed in George Herbert's poetry: visual, as in the following less well-known poem,

$$\text{Ana-}\left\{\begin{array}{l}\text{MARY}\\\text{ARMY}\end{array}\right\}\textit{gram}$$

> How well her name and *Army* doth present,
> In whom the *Lord of Hosts* did pitch his tent!

and auditory ingenuities, as, e.g., echo plays, or his "pruned rhymes", in which it is uncertain whether the mannerism is visual or auditory; and, eventually, such notoriously ingenious devices as

$$\text{For who can look for lesse, that loveth }\left\{\begin{array}{l}\text{Life?}\\\text{Strife?}\end{array}\right.$$

or Herbert's famous "Easter Wings".

Chapter 9.
"Oceanic Dedifferentiation, 'Thing Destruction' and Mystic Poetry". This chapter takes its point of departure from Anton Ehrenzweig (1970: 135), who speaks of "a creative ego rhythm that swings between focussed gestalt and an oceanic undifferentiation. [...] The London psychoanalysts D.W. Winnicott and Marion Milner, have stressed the importance for a creative ego to be able to suspend the boundaries between self and not-self in order to become more at home in the world of reality where the objects and self are clearly held apart. [...] Seen in this way, the oceanic experience of fusion, of a "return to the womb", represents the minimum content of all art; Freud saw in it only the basic religious experience. But it seems now that it belongs to all creativity". To illustrate what I *don't* mean by oceanic dedifferentiation, I quote Ehrenzweig on the Homunkulus episode in *Faust*. He claims that Homunkulus encased in a glass womb is a perfect image of oceanic dedifferentiation. I claim that, on the contrary, the focused gestalt of this image may be, at best, an allegory of this state. By contrast, Faust's "immersion in an abstraction" image, "Disciple, up! untiring, hasten! / to bathe thy breast in morning-red!", does evoke the detection of such an experience. Indeed, traditional *Faust* criticism claimed that these lines indicated that Faust had had a momentary mystic experience. The main bulk of the chapter is a close reading of three poems from three different cultural periods in three languages: a Hebrew text from the early Middle Ages, from the so-called Mercabah mysticism; a poem by the seventeenth century English poet Richard Crashaw; and a love poem by Baudelaire ("Hymne"). The chapter demonstrates that all three texts are based on strategies of dissolving focussed gestalts into thing-free and gestalt-free qualities and suspending the boundaries between self and not-self or, at least, between the objects. Most astonishing is the finding that the three texts tend to have recourse to similar grammatical manipulations for achieving these perceptual qualities.

Chapter 10

"The Infernal and the Hybrid—Bosch and Dante". I assume that not only numinous, mystic, and meditative qualities can be conveyed in poetry by interference with the smooth functioning of cognitive and psychodynamic processes, but demonic and infernal qualities as well. These principles are applied here, in the visual medium, to traditional representations of the devil and Hieronymus Bosch's infernal creatures; and, in poetry, to Dante's Inferno. Hell can be rendered awful not only through threat of some painful punishment, but also by suspending the sense of intelligibility, control, comfort and security afforded by ordinary consciousness, that is, by suspending the clear-cut boundaries of objects, thought categories, and blurring the divisions into which the world is marked off. This, in the final resort, may evoke a response of "exasperated helplessness", and "emotional disorientation". The key term is the "grotesque". In the devil's image, the boundaries between man and goat are suspended; in Bosch's tree-man between human, plant, eggshell, etc. In Bosch taboos related to excretions are flouted, too. In Dante we encounter plants or flames that reveal "the anguished workings of a human mind and heart". In relation to both Bosch and Dante the weaknesses of source-hunting scholarship are pointed out, as compared to cognitive and stylistic studies.

Chapter 11.

"Let There be Light and the Emanation of Light—The Act of Creation in Ibn Gabirol and Milton". This chapter has a thematic and a stylistic focus. From the thematic point of view I am taking up a problem of great theological interest: the fusion of the personal and the Neo-Platonic conception of the Creator. However, it is not the theological issue which I address here, but the stylistic problem of fusion. I make use of two dichotomies: "split and integrated focus" and "convergent and divergent style". The terms "focus" and "convergent and divergent" have been imported into literary criticism from optics, suggesting that they refer to perceptual qualities. The two central texts in this chapter are one section from Ibn Gabirol's "Kingly Crown" and the creation in Milton by the Son=Word. To use Dr. Johnson's words, in both works "the most heterogeneous ideas are yoked together with violence"; but whereas in the former attention is focussed on their incompatibility, in the latter the transition is made, by linguistic manipulations, as smooth as possible. Finally, I present Milton versus Milton. *Paradise Lost* is usually categorised by traditional scholars as a baroque poem; Herbert Grierson included "On the Morning of Christ's Nativity" in his anthology of Metaphysical poets. In this last section of the chapter I compare strikingly similar passages from the two poems, pointing out the elusive cues the cumulative effect of which is to integrate focus in the former poem, and split it in the latter.

Chapter 12.

"Light, Fire, Prison: A Cognitive Analysis of Religious Imagery in Poetry". This chapter explores the cognitive foundations and the literary applications of spatial imagery. There seem to be several good reasons to have recourse to spatial imagery; this chapter explores two of them. On the one hand, concrete visual images constitute a bundle of features and, as such, allow for the efficient coding of information. This, in turn, grants the cognitive system great flexibility and efficiency both in creative thinking and in poetry. A single image encoding a variety of meaning units can be regarded as an instance of the aesthetic principle "unity-in-variety". This also can be said to save considerable mental energy and, according to a Freudian conception, one possible source of pleasure is the saving of mental energy. On the other hand, the recoding of information into spatial imagery may help the cognitive system to overcome some of its inherent limitations. Thus, fast-changing or lowly-differentiated information may be recoded into a more stable and differentiated spatial template, as in the case of sound pitch recoded into musical scales; or conceptually presented information may become less differentiated in perception, owing to recoding into Gestalt-free and thing-free imagery. Such lowly-differentiated qualities may be reinforced by the mechanisms of spatial orientation, or the mechanisms for alleviating cognitive overload. From such a perspective, the Lakoffean conception of conceptual metaphor based on spatial imagery appears to be congenial to human cognition, but only a small part of a complex situation. This chapter recapitulates two stylistic modes, "Metaphysical" and "Mystic-Romantic". Surprisingly, the techniques by which these opposite effects are achieved are quite similar. The Metaphysical mode seeks to yield an insight into matters of religious significance in a flash, through a sudden transition from complexity to unity. The phenomenological quality of this kind of insight is typically witty. The "Romantic" or "Mystic" mode seeks to achieve the verbal imitation of some experiential contact, of an intuitive rather than conceptual nature, with some reality that lies beyond the *absolute limit* of our experience. Some poems, at least, are remarkably successful in translating those mystic ideas into verbal imitations of mystic experiences. We shall discuss at great length the handling of the images of light, fire and prison in Akhnaton's old Egyptian inscription, in the works of four English poets, Sir Philip Sidney, John Donne, William Wordsworth and T.S. Eliot, and of two Mediaeval poets, Hebrew and Armenian, Shlomo Ibn Gabirol and Kostandin of Erznka. Ibn Gabirol's and Kostandin's texts also touch upon the problem of fusing the personalistic and Light-emanation conceptions of creation.

Chapter 13.
"The Asymmetry of Sacred, Sexual, and Filial Love in Figurative Language". Speaking of sacred love in terms of sexual and filial love is more natural than the other way around; they give rise, therefore, to opposite stylistic effects, emotional and witty respectively. Some sixteenth and seventeenth century poets, such as Michael Drayton and John Donne, do indeed achieve a witty effect by speaking of sexual love in terms of sacred love. After many small-scale examples from English and Hebrew poetry, a whole sonnet is discussed, Spenser's "Most glorious Lord of Life". The first twelve lines elaborate on the love of Christ who sacrificed himself for humanity. In the final couplet there is a surprise: "So, let us love, dear love, like

as we ought / Love is the lesson which our Lord us taught". Such a punch line would be more appropriate in one of Donne's libertine poems than in Spenser's love poem. Two literary traditions are relevant to this sonnet. Viewed in these different traditions, two opposite effects arise in the poem. According to the Platonic conception, love between the sexes is the first step toward the higher harmonies that govern the world (this Platonic principle is reflected in Ibn Gabirol's verses as well, quoted above, in chapter 3). In such a reading wit is rather moderate. By contrast, according to the conventions of the English sonnet, the final couplet should effect a surprise ending, even a reversal of all that's said in the preceding lines. In such a reading the poem offers some extreme metaphysical wit.

Chapter 1

Introduction: Means, Effects, and Assumptions

Means, Effects and Themes

Religious poetry is often analysed via its sources and generic influences, through its historical and social implications, or by its symbolism and religious attitudes.[1] The present study explores how stylistic resources are exploited for turning theological ideas and religious attitudes into poetry, into the verbal imitation of some religious experience. By the same token, it explores how the effects of certain well-known poetic devices are qualified when they enter into a religious context. Our concern is mainly with the effects and qualities perceived in the text, when stylistic and poetic means combine with a religious context.

In this paragraph we will try to present some of our assumptions, without any claim for innovation. We assume, for example, that one of the purposes of religious poetry is, typically, to reproduce effects characteristic of religious experience, or at least to display them. We also assume that religious poetry is sometimes quite successful in doing so.[2] Our main innovation in this respect is that we take this assumption more seriously than usual. We will try to identify some of the poetic means employed for that end. We do not presume to cover all the possibilities, merely to focus on some important techniques, to pinpoint some principles, wherever it is called for, and to exemplify these techniques and principles by pieces of religious poetry. We certainly will not try to avoid thematic discussions, since our concern is with the effects arising from an interaction between cognitive processes, varieties of stylistic devices and typologies, and the religious context—themes, practices, and ideas. We will not elaborate upon the meanings, ideas and symbols for their own sake, beyond the needs of the religious poetic discourse; though we will illustrate in what ways the cognitive argument can help us handle some problems of philosophical or religious interest (such as reconciling the biblical and Neoplatonic views of Creation in chapter 11).

The Religious Experience

As mentioned above, one of the main goals of the present study is to explore the techniques by which religious poetry may become a verbal imitation of religious

---

[1] This chapter was written in collaboration with Motti Benari.

[2] This last assumption is not so obvious as it might seem, and we will discuss it briefly later in this chapter.

experience. This will require at least a minimal clarification of the nature of the religious experience. For this purpose we will have to rely on some observations made by students of religion, concerning the essence of such experience.

First of all a distinction seems to be needed between a religious experience and a mystic one. Not every religious experience is mystic by nature. Beit-Hallahmi & Arggle (1997) made a thorough investigation, trying to reveal what they thought would be the core of religious experience, but were unbale to reach a definite straightforward conclusion. To any rule they found exceptions and every definition had its own problems. Ignoring a wide range of philosophical and theological issues, we might do with a very general definition like: A religious experience is an experience involving the apperception, recollection or reassurance that beyond the entire universe predominates a higher order, a pattern of some sort. Our concern is with the feelings and perceptions that accompany the contemplation of these issues, and therefore we might try to understand in what way certain feelings reported as typical to religious experience can be detected in a text. Greeley's experimental findings (1975) with US subjects may serve as a convenient illustration. He sampled 1,467 people reporting one or more religious experiences. Reports on the ingredients of religious experience included "an experience of great emotional intensity" (38%); "a sense of the unity of everything" (29%); "a sense of the ineffable nature of the experience" (26%); "a loss of concern about worldly problems" (19%) or even a sense of "being bathed in light" (14%), etc. We certainly do not claim that whenever a text displays one or more of these perceived effects we are confronted with religious poetry. Such effects are by no means necessary or sufficient conditions for "religious poetry"; however, we may expect much religious poetry to display some subset of these and similar qualities. The present study explores the stylistic conditions, the specific combinations of stylistic devices, that typically generate such qualities.

Mysticism is a religion in which God "ceases to be an object and becomes an experience", or in which "man lives in the presence of divinity", an existence in which the abyss between this world and the transcendental world is somehow bridged, overcome, blurred. Some of the features listed in the preceding paragraph apply in mysticism at a greater intensity than in "mere" religion. Such a definition of "mysticism" is very elusive and it seems that there is no one kind of mystic experience. As Horne (1978) has neatly shown, there are hardly any necessary or sufficient conditions for an experience to be demarcated as mystic. Rather, there are many different experiences assembled from a common "pool" of characteristics having a family resemblance. "Family resemblance" refers to relations among members of categories where two members might not resemble each other, while both resemble a third member, like a child who resembles both his parents whereas they don't necessarily resemble each other (Rosch & Mervis, 1975). Some features may occur in several mystic experiences, and not in others. There is no one feature that is obligatory to all of them. The categories "religious" and "mystic" are, then, what Wittgenstein called "open concepts"; that is, their members need not have any shared properties, merely a "family resemblance"; and there is no natural cut-off point between neighbouring concepts, as between "hills" and "mountains". For different purposes we may draw the boundary between them at different points. Thus, the boundary between mystic and nonmystic (even some kinds of secular) poetry becomes arbitrary.

Stace (1961: 131–132) distinguished two major categories among mystic experiences: introvertive and extrovertive. In this Jungian distinction the difference is, for present purposes, mainly in the sense of unity. In the extrovertive experience the subject experiences the multiplicity of the world as a unity: "the Unifying Vision— all things are one", while in introvertive experiences the Self is the essential object of the experience yielded: "the Unitary Consciousness; the One, the Void; pure consciousness". In the introvertive experience, everything (including time and space) fades or dissolves into a mystic oneness. In the extrovertive "all the things that are 'One' nevertheless retain their identity, while at the same time belonging to that one" (Horne, 1978: 15). "Oneness and separateness are maintained" (ibid.). Horne makes another important distinction concerning the two kinds of experience. The extrovertive experience according to Horne is always spontaneous, sensed as forced upon the mystics without any preliminary preparation. The introvertive is induced and is the result of a quest involving contemplation, concentration or other methods aimed at purifying the mind from distracting objects (usually known as meditative techniques). These distinctions are remarkably similar to certain aesthetic definitions. The romantics speak of poetry and imagination as "unity in variety"; James Smith says of the metaphysical conceit that its elements must be such that they may enter into a solid unity while preserving their warring identities. A central assumption in the ensuing study will be that there is some fundamental kinship between certain religious or mystic contents and the choice of certain style types.

The distinction between spontaneous and induced experiences is essential, and seems to be beyond dispute among scholars. The use of terms is still diversified. Huxley (1972) calls it simply "spontaneous" and "induced" experiences, while Horne (1978) integrates it with Stace's distinction between the introvertive and the extrovertive. Gimello (1978) quotes Smart (1958) on that issue, and they both follow Otto (1917 [1959]) in identifying all experiences that involve the immanent unity of all things as mystic and induced experiences. The spontaneous experiences are "numinous experiences" that involve a variety of contacts with a transcendent being.

extrovertive

1) [The numinous experience] is one of an encounter with a being wholly other than oneself and altogether different from anything else. Such an encounter is usually said to be gratuitous, in the sense that those subject to it are not themselves responsible for its occurrence, and it is typically described as both overwhelming and self-authenticating.

introvertive

2) The mystical experience, by contrast, is not so much an encounter with a 'sacred other' as it is the interior attainment of a certain supernal state of mind. Such an attainment is usually held, except by mystics in traditions strongly committed to the numinous, to be the result of the subject's own efforts in following a certain contemplative discipline or method (Gimello, 1978: 172).

The method through which one might bring oneself to experience mysticism might be meditation. Thus, some of the effects in spontaneous and induced experiences might be similar, but some might diverge as a consequence of different ways and degrees of self-involvement. Notwithstanding this conception, we tend to adopt Louis Martz's position, who distinguishes between meditation and mystical activity in terms of "the lower levels of the spiritual life" and "the operation of special grace" (see below).

It would appear that Otto (1917 [1959]), Smart (1958), Gimello (1978), Beit-Hallahmi & Arggle (1997) and some others regard all mystic experiences as basically introvertive, whereas extrovertive experiences are either considered numinous or not considered at all. The key to this jumble of terminology seems to be, again, "open concepts". The question of the "right" terminology is less significant for our needs. The distinction, however, might be very helpful for first approximations, and we will return to it time and again, in explaining the presence and importance of certain devices in a religious poetic text.

It may be worth noting that not every mystic experience is automatically considered religious. Beit-Hallahmi & Arggle (1997: 79) quote a table from Hay & Heald[3] based on a survey in Britain. This table indicates, for example, that only 55% of those who reported having experienced that all things are one, regarded this as religious, the rest did not interpret it religiously. Horne says that it is a mood-dependent distinction. Mystic experiences that are treated with seriousness get a religious nature and have long-term effects. Otherwise they become casual anecdotes (Horne, 1978: 21-23). This observation might become useful also for readers of religious poetry, since a degree of seriousness in the text (as perceived through emotional load, for instance) might affect the overall impression of certain devices. This will be discussed in later chapters at length.

Religious and Secular Mystic Poetry

It has been observed by several researchers of widely different persuasions that certain major characteristics of mystic-religious poetry and of the meditative poetry stemming from Jesuit meditation loom large in certain kinds of secular poetry. Let us mention only a few of those authors, who had the greatest influence on our work. Louis Martz, for instance, observed in the "Conclusion" to the revised edition of his book that some of the best romantic poems are secular versions of the meditative poem. "The genre of meditative poetry should be broad enough to include some of the Odes of Keats or the later poetry of Wallace Stevens, as well as the unorthodox, though still religious, poetry of a Yeats or a Wordsworth or an Emily Dickinson" (Martz, 1962: 324). Walt Whitman's poetry contains lengthy catalogues that have very little to do with God, or other notions of established religion. William James,

---

3   The exact reference according to Beit-Hallahmi & Arggle (ibid.) is: Hay D. & Heald G. (1987) Religion is Good for You, *New Society,* 17 April.

whose book *The Varieties Of Religious Experience* (1902) is subtitled "A Study in Human Nature", refers to Whitman's poetry several times in it, including in the chapter on "Mysticism" where, among other things, he begins a long footnote with the comment "Whitman in another place expresses in a quieter way what was probably with him a chronic mystical perception" (396).[4]

In a paper (which appears to have influenced the conception in this study more than any other work) called "Three Poems on Ecstasy", Leo Spitzer (1962) states its aim as follows: "I shall take up three poems dealing with approximately the same subject matter (the ecstatic union of a human ego with a non-ego), in order to study the magic transformation which actual words of the particular language have undergone at the hands of the poets who have succeeded in making their inner experience a poetic reality for the reader" (142). Only one of the three ecstatic poems refers to a religious experience proper, "En una noche oscura" by the sixteenth-century Spanish mystic St. John of the Cross. "This poem, written about 1577 by the Carmelite monk San Juan de la Cruz, is a perfect example of the manner in which the body can be made artistically tributary to the mystic experience. The Catholic saint treats no lesser a subject than the ecstatic union, not with a human being, but with the divine, in terms that constantly fuse soul and body" (153).[5] The other two texts are conspicuously secular. Their subject is the ecstatic union of human lovers: John Donne's "The Ecstasie", in which the lovers experience "mystic union of a Neo-Platonic order" (142); and the scene of Isolde's *Liebestod,* at the end of Richard Wagner's music-drama, *Tristan und Isolde.*

Spitzer's analysis of Isolde's *Liebestod* most powerfully anticipates our conception of oceanic dedifferentiation in poetry (see Chapter 9). In Isolde's words "we have the pantheistic idea of the melting into the universe of two souls who have consumed themselves in longing for each other [...] sinking, ever deeper, into the sea of nothingness" (Spitzer, 1962: 175). This sea of nothingness, however, "is not that void described by Jacopone and other mystics (including Juan de la Cruz): an emptiness created by the soul in order that it may be filled by God; it appears as a turbulent mass of waves, perfumes, breaths [...] ruled over not by a personal God, but by the violent forces of Nature" (ibid., 176).

The following excerpt from Spitzer raises two points of utmost interest, which we propose to pursue here at some length.

We are reminded of the progress in time of the mystic experience. Juan de la Cruz has been able to transcribe the unbroken line, the parabola of that ex-

---

4   Hanita Goodblatt (1990) has distinguished between illustrative and meditative catalogues in Whitman's poetry. Tsur has discussed in great detail the semantic differences between the two types of catalogue, in an attempt to account for the quality of "altered state of consciousness" in the latter type (Tsur, 1992a: 416–428).

5   Having recently re-read Spitzer's paper, we were surprised to discover that he had pointed out in San Juan's poem grammatical forms very similar to those we pointed out in chapter 4 in an anonymous Spanish sonnet, deployed for very similar effects.

perience in its evolution from energetic pursuit to self-annihilation, from human to divine action—and this is a short poem of eight stanzas (as though the poet would suggest that what happened with such intensity cannot be measured by man-devised clock-time) (Spitzer, 1962: 169).

Our first point concerns Spitzer's phrase "the progress in time of the mystic experience [...] from energetic pursuit to self-annihilation". Alternatively, the phrase "self-annihilation" may be replaced by "an emptiness created by the soul in order that it may be filled by God". This process is crucial. Tsur has elsewhere elaborated at great length on the "Obtrusive Rhythms & Emotive Crescendo", which sometimes yield what he has called "poetry of altered states of consciousness" (Tsur, 1992a: 431–454); he has also explored the emotive crescendo in a context of divergent rhythms (ibid., 455–470). Using Spitzer's terms, the emotive crescendo can be characterised as a verbal pattern that indicates an emotional progression from energetic pursuit to self-annihilation, culminating sometimes in an emptiness created by the soul in order that it may be filled by God, or some peak experience. Chapter 2 below will consider at great length the emotive crescendo in a sonnet by Donne. In chapter 3, excerpts 8–10 contain the closing couplets of three of Keats's most intense sonnets, in which the energetic pursuit leads to states denoted by such phrases as "in nothingness do sink", "swoon to death", and "Death is Life's high meed". These excerpts exemplify the points of climax of the same phenomenon. In chapter 7 the obtrusive rhythms in Blake's "The Tyger" will be considered at great length. To provide a comprehensive picture of the issue, it would be necessary to quote here entire chapters from Tsur's 1992 book, and also from some other books. Here we will confine ourselves to the reproduction of part of a brief discussion of Wordsworth's "Daffodils" (in which both the obtrusive rhythms and the emotive crescendo are conspicuous):

(1)   I wandered lonely as a cloud
        That floats on high o'er vales and hills,
        When all at once I saw a crowd,
        A host of golden daffodils;
        Beside the lake, beneath the trees,
        Fluttering and dancing in the breeze.

        Continuous as the stars that shine
        And twinkle on the milky way,
        They stretched in never-ending line
        Along the margin of a bay:
        Ten thousand saw I at a glance,
        Tossing their heads in sprightly dance.

        The waves beside them danced; but they
        Outdid the sparkling waves in glee:

> A poet could not be but gay
> In such a jocund company:
> I gazed—and gazed—but little thought
> What wealth the show to me had brought:
>
> For oft, when on my couch I lie
> In vacant or in pensive mood,
> They flesh upon that inward eye
> Which is the bliss of solitude;
> And then my heart with pleasure fills,
> And dances with the daffodils.

Many readers have detected an ecstatic quality in this poem. A few psychological distinctions concerning the nature of ecstasy will readily suggest why. On the one hand, according to some psychologists, emotional qualities involve a sudden deviation from normal energy level, and emotions related to joy and ecstasy involve an *increase* of energy to varying degrees (cf. Tsur, 1978; 1992: 56–61). On the other hand, Plutchik, in his work on emotion rooted in instinct, associates calmness, serenity, happiness, joy, and ecstasy (in this ascending order of judged intensity) on all levels of evolution with pulsatile or orgastic behaviour associated with the reproduction instinct. The term "reproduction"

> is used to represent the prototypic response associated with sexual behavior. Apparently at almost all animal levels, sexual behavior is associated with some form of pulsatile or orgastic behavior. Even the asexual reproduction of one-celled organisms has an intense pulsating quality as recorded by high speed photography. Pleasure is presumably associated with all forms of sexual behavior, and may be defined in terms of approach and maintenance-of-contact tendencies (Plutchik, 1968 [1962[1]]: 73–74).

In the dancing of the daffodils (reinforced by the exceptionally regular rhythms of the poem) readers may detect "some form of pulsatile or orgastic behaviour" characteristic of ecstasy too.[6]

This poem begins with a notion of "loneliness", and ends on a note of "solitude", developing as it were from "floating on high" to some "vacant or pensive mood", through a constant process of **intensification.** Consider the group of synonyms and otherwise closely related words

> sprightly→ glee→ gay→ jocund→ bliss.

---

6   As will be argued in Chapter 9, Newberg et al. relate mystic experiences, from the evolutional point of view, to neural circuitry initially evolved for reproduction.

First of all, these words have a cumulative impact, as far as the impression created by the poem goes. Secondly, when comparing the first and the last members of the group, there appears to be a considerable difference in intensity between them. The intervening members occur in a random order; they conform with the crescendo pattern only in a certain mental performance: when the pattern is "retro-related"[7] from the last member. Thus, for instance, the word *pleasure* may indicate a lower degree of pleasure than *bliss;* but it would still indicate the peak of the experience, by virtue of its place in the pattern. Harold Bloom has pointed out that there are here pairs of successive words in which the second member tends to be more "ample" (perhaps only by virtue of the crescendo pattern): *crowd→ host; fluttering→ dancing; shine→ twinkle* (add to this *sparkling*). Now, consider the contribution of the following two lines to this pattern: "The waves beside them danced; but they / Outdid the sparkling waves in glee". Here, *danced, sparkling* and *glee* are made *somehow* to participate in the same scale, suggesting degrees of emotional energy. The verb *outdid* acquires a crucial function in suggesting or generating the crescendo pattern. The expressions of movement and joy (reinforced by the expressions of shining) are drawn together in the metaphor of the last two lines:

> (2)   And then my heart with pleasure fills,
>   And dances with the daffodils.

Paradoxically enough, the height of intense movement occurs in a relaxed, "pensive mood", when the speaker is lying on his couch. "I gazed—and gazed—but little thought" connotes a kind of self-oblivion, while denoting 'I had no idea' (the speaker could not, at the moment of gazing, estimate how significant the 'show' was). Although there is here a break in the continuity of the experience, indicating, as it were, "emotions *recollected* in tranquillity", the last stanza takes up this connotation, and heightens it to "vacant" (denoting 'empty' or 'unoccupied with thought or reflection') and "pensive" (which suggests 'dreaminess or wistfulness', and may involve 'little or no thought to any purpose').

Maud Bodkin's comments on certain passages in Dante's "Paradiso" may throw some light on the issue. Our foregoing discussion implies that we need not be surprised that some elements in Wordsworth's presentation of bliss is more aptly characterised by some of Maud Bodkin's comments than the elements originally commented upon in Dante, as, for instance, it "can also be realized with imaginative sympathy, as constituting a cosmic dance in which the spirit of man may participate" (Bodkin, 1963: 145).[8]

---

7   That is, when a pattern is elaborated from its end point backward. Tsur has discussed in detail the cognitive mechanisms involved (Tsur, 1992a: 466–470).

8   We are certainly not suggesting that Dante's image is less apt than Wordsworth's, only that the applicability of Bodkin's comment is more conspicuous with reference to Wordsworth's image than to Dante's.

This poem can be taken, then, as a prototype of poems that progress from energetic movement to self-oblivion, "an emptiness created by the soul in order that it may be filled by God"—except that the vacant soul is filled here not by God, but by some intense, blissful experience. At this point one should become aware of a most disconcerting problem that haunted us throughout the present research. Some of the best examples for our conception of mystic or ecstatic poetry are secular, romantic or symbolistic, poems. It was not before writing the present introductory chapter (which happened to be the last one to be written) that we suddenly realised that the explanation was built into the theoretical system underlying our whole argument. This explanation will be suggested at the end of the next section of this chapter.

Recent advances in brain science and the biology of belief may reinforce our conception of the structure of this poem and the altered state of consciousness it suggests. Andrew Newberg, Eugene D'Aquili and Vince Rause (2001), in discussing the sympathetic and parasympathetic nervous systems as our arousal and quiescent systems, observe:

> There is evidence, however, of cases in which both systems function at the same time when pushed to maximal levels of activity and this has been associated with extraordinary alternative states of consciousness. The unusual, altered states can be triggered by various kinds of intense physical or mental activity, including dancing, running, or prolonged concentration (39).

Obviously, in this poem both systems are highly activated.

> The maximal stimulation of the arousal system can also cause a spillover effect, which causes quiescent responses to surge. The resulting trancelike state is experienced as an ecstatic rush of orgasmiclike energy. This state can be induced by intense and prolonged contemplation, during rapid ritualistic dancing, and sometimes, briefly, during sexual climax (42).

Further, in a footnote they comment: "Essentially any repetitive stimulation, whether it be physical, emotional, sensory, or cognitive, can potentially generate such states" (184). Tsur has repeatedly pointed out that in such poems as this one or "Kubla Khan" (Tsur, 1987b; 1992a: 445–452) the hypnotic-ecstatic effect is intimately associated with the more than usually regular rhythm on the prosodic level, and the dancing (daffodils or rocks) on the thematic level.

The contribution of the phrase "floats on high" to this effect will be illuminated by a comment by Maud Bodkin, speaking of "flight as it is known in dreams", with reference to a very different image in Dante's "Paradiso", characterising its effect as "the absence of any sensation of effort, the wonder at effortless attainment of a new sphere". To this we may add Michael A. Persinger's comment in his neuro-psychological study (1987), speaking of "God Experience involving temporal lobe instability" (26). "Few people appear to acknowledge the role of vestibular sensations in the God Experience. However, in light of the temporal lobe's role in the sensation of balance and movement, these experiences are expected. [...] Literature concerned with the God Experiences are full of metaphors describing essential vestibular inputs. Sensations of 'being lifted', 'feeling light', or even 'spinning, like being intoxicated', are common" (Persinger, 1987: 26). After quoting an account of such an experience, he observes: "Note the repeated references to vestibular sensations: 'floating,' 'lifted,' 'moving,' 'spinning'" (27). The phrase "as a cloud floating high" is introduced, as it were, merely as a simile for loneliness; by the same token, it suggests effortlessness as well as elements of the spiritual experience toward which it leads.

Our second point elaborating the above quote from Spitzer concerns the suggestion that "this is a short poem of eight stanzas (as though the poet would suggest that what happened with such intensity cannot be measured by man-devised clock-time)". This is the only point on which we tend to disagree with Spitzer's admirable paper. This kind of self-reference appears to me far-fetched in a mystic poem. Besides, the same problem arises in the secular version of mystic and meditative poetry ("Daffodils", for instance). Both Martz and we have independently noticed that most of the poems under discussion are all too short for an experiencer to build up the enormous psychological intensity suggested by them. Martz conjectures in the introduction to his anthology that these poems do not embody the meditative process itself, but may be merely a by-product of it.

> But what one should expect to find, more often, is some part of the whole meditative action, set down as particularly memorable, perhaps in accordance with the kind of self-examination advised by Dawson under the heading: "What is to be done after Meditation." One is urged here to scrutinize carefully the manner in which one has performed every part of the meditative process, from preparation through colloquy; to examine closely the distractions, consolations, or desolations that one may have experienced; and finally, to "note in some little booke those things which have passed in our Meditation, or some part of them, if we think them worth the paynes." Most of the poems in this volume, I believe, are the result of such retrospective examination of the practice of meditation: memorable moments of self-knowledge (Martz, 1963: xxii).

Even if we accept such an account of the poems' genesis (and we are not sure we should), we must approach this problem, I believe, from an aesthetic vantage point. Neither of the foregoing explanations can account for the brevity of "Daffodils", or Keats's and Wordsworth's sonnets. As I will argue in the next chapter, a poem, *as an aesthetic object,* is not meant *to arouse* a mystic or meditative (or any other emotional) experience in the reader. Rather, it should allow the reader *to perceive* a mystic or meditative (or some other emotional) quality in it, (just as in music one is capable of perceiving, say, some sad quality, without becoming sad). Such a perception may take place even in the absence of the duration so essential for entering into a mystic or meditative state. On the contrary, sometimes brevity may be even an advantage. Aristotle had some illuminating comments, *mutatis mutandis,* on this issue: "As [...] in the case of animate bodies and organisms a certain magnitude is necessary, and a magnitude which may be easily embraced in one view; so in the plot, a certain length is necessary, and a length which can be easily embraced by the memory" (Aristotle, 1951: 36). In other words, a mystic or meditative poem need not be long enough for undergoing the mystic or meditative experience, only for discerning the parts required for the perception of a mystic or meditative quality in it; at the same time, it must be short enough to be perceived as an integrated whole. Donne's Anniversaries or even "Good Friday, 1613. Riding Westward" cannot be experienced with the same intensity as some of his Holy Sonnets.

Semiotic Systems—Conversion and Adequacy

The issue at stake is the translation of perceived qualities from reality to some semiotic system, or from one semiotic system to another. In our case, this involves the representation of some of the salient features of religious experience in the verbal medium. The precision of translation depends on how fine-grained the sign-units of the system are. If the target system is sufficiently fine-grained and the nearest options of this target system are chosen to represent a source phenomenon, it may evoke a perception that the two are "equivalent". We will briefly illustrate the problem through a well-known linguistic-literary phenomenon: onomatopoeia. Onomatopoeia is the imitation of natural sounds by speech sounds. There is an open set of infinite noises in the world; any language contains a closed system of between twenty and one-hundred speech sounds. Nevertheless, we tend to accept many instances of onomatopoeia as quite adequate phonetic equivalents of the natural noises. How can language imitate, with such a limited number of speech sounds, an infinite number of natural noises? Take the bird called "cuckoo". Its name is said to have an onomatopoeic origin: it is said to imitate the sound the bird makes, and the bird is said to emit the sound [kukuk]. Now the bird emits neither the speech sound [k] nor [u]; it uses no speech sounds at all. It emits two continuous sounds with abrupt onsets, and a characteristic pitch interval between them, roughly a minor third. Each vowel has its characteristic "formant structure" (i.e., energy concentrations, at specified pitch ranges); as Tsur (2001) has shown, the formant structure of the cuckoo's continuous sound is nearest to that of the [u] in human speech. The [k] has no acoustic trace in the cuckoo's call. But stop consonants are phonetically abrupt, and being a voiceless stop, it is used to indicate its abrupt beginning; and being a back sound, it is co-articulated with [u], and thus preferred to, e.g., [p] or [t] in this sound imitation. Significantly enough, in a wide range of Chinese dialects too the same bird says "pu-ku" (with a falling-rising tone on the second syllable); that is, it contains two syllables consisting of an [u] sound each, preceded by a voiceless stop. In human language, European languages at least, pitch intervals are part of the intonation system, not of the lexicon. Consequently, the pitch interval characteristic of the cuckoo's call is not lexicalised in the bird's name. In this respect, the human phonological system is not sufficiently "fine-grained".

Now the cuckoo's call is sometimes translated to another semiotic system as well: the sound of a recorder, or some other wind instrument with a whistle mouthpiece—in Haydn's (or Leopold Mozart's?) "Toy Symphony", for instance. The overtone structure of the sound of these instruments is similar to the cuckoo's call (in Mahler's first symphony, where it is played by the traverse flute, the overtone structure sounds less similar). The onset of the sound played on these instruments can be abrupt too. The player may articulate it with the tip of the tongue touching the teethridge, producing "tu-tu" as it were. Unlike the lexicon of human language, this semiotic system does provide the option to produce the pitch interval of a minor third; but, on the other hand, it need not co-articulate the steady pitch sound with a velar consonant; so the player resorts to "tu" rather than "ku". Thus, the two semiotic systems are quite limited as to their means for reproducing the cuckoo's natural call; and they offer different sign vehicles for it. Neither of these systems offers the exact sounds for reproducing the cuckoo's call; in each one must choose the options that are nearest to the target sound. That is the best that semiotic systems can offer for the representation of qualities perceived in reality or in another semiotic system. A sound imitation is *perceived as* an equivalent of the imitated reality if the target semiotic system is sufficiently fine-grained in the relevant respects; as many salient features of the source phenomenon are represented as possible, and the most relevant options of the target semiotic system are chosen.

Sometimes it is the meaning that determines to which features of repeated units we attend. In Hebrew, *mətaktek* means "ticktocking"; we attend to the repeated voiceless plosives and perceive the word as onomatopoeic. *Mətaktak*, by contrast, means "sweetish". In Hebrew, the repetition of the last syllable is lexicalised, suggesting "somewhat (sweet)". The meaning directs our attention to this redoubling of the syllable, and we attend away from the phonetic features of the plosives.[9]

This excursus on semiotic systems may illuminate our handling of a central problem of the present book. Poetry is a complex of semiotic systems; it offers an indefinite (but by no means infinite) number of verbal strategies for capturing the felt qualities of such religious experiences as ecstasy, meditation or mystic experience. There is no one-to-one relationship between the various verbal strategies and the felt qualities suggested by them (in speech research, Al Liberman would call such a phenomenon "complex coding"). A divergent verbal structure may be "isomorphic" with mystic experiences, by virtue of the blurring of visual images and metric shapes; alternatively, it may undermine the psychological atmosphere of security and cognitive control, inspiring awe and anxiety, thus enhancing the felt qualities of an infernal landscape, for instance. Likewise, a convergent structure may generate such widely different felt qualities as simplified mastery of reality, rational predictability, or a hypnotic / ecstatic quality—by virtue of its various potentials which may be foregrounded at different times.[10] We accept a translation from one

---

[9]   This is what Wittgenstein would call "aspect-switching".
[10] In chapter 7 we will discuss divergent and convergent styles at length.

semiotic system to another as adequate (e.g., the representation of the felt quality of a mystic experience in the verbal medium), if the target system is sufficiently fine-grained; and if the options most similar to the source experience are chosen. When we print a picture, the higher the resolution (that is, the more fine-grained the system), the better is its resemblance to the original. And when we record music, the finer the metallic grains on the tape, the higher the fidelity of music achieved. We will expect the best quality afforded by our system, even if we are able to adapt ourselves to lower resolution pictures, or lower fidelity music. We may imagine hearing the bass sounds of a symphony on the speaker of a small portable radio; but the same sound quality would be unacceptable to us on a high quality stereo system. Some languages may be more fine-grained than others in some respects, and less fine-grained in other respects.

The notion "fine-grained" needs some elaboration. We have characterised poetry as "a complex of semiotic systems". From the interaction of the various semiotic systems very delicate constituent parts may come into existence. In the syllabo-tonic versification system an enormous complexity (consisting of extremely delicate units) may arise. We have, for instance, a conventional metric pattern consisting of regularly alternating weak and strong positions. We also have stress pattern, the irregularly alternating stressed and unstressed syllables; and patterns of alliteration. The prominent units of these three patterns may converge (suit each other consistently), or diverge in all sorts of odd combinations. Syntactic units (phrase, clause) may converge with prosodic units (e.g., line), or diverge from them. The presence of a rhyme pattern may enhance the verse lines as discrete perceptual units; at the same time, it may group them into a stanza. Their absence may generate an opposite effect. All this may interact in a variety of ways with clear-cut or blurred images, and with an infinite number of themes organised by linear convergent progress, or diverge into logical gaps, multiple options of understanding, figurative language, etc. Thus, for instance, the description of an infernal landscape and a heavenly choir may activate different potentials of the same stylistic configuration. The contrast here is not only between "infernal" and "heavenly", but also between "landscape" and "choir".

In syllabo-tonic verse, obtrusive rhythms may be generated by repeating highly prominent configurations four–five times in a line (strong position + stressed syllable + sound pattern) as, for instance, in **Týger**, **týger**, **búrning bríght** [11] Such
$$\underset{s\ \ \ w}{\text{Týger}},\ \underset{s\ \ \ w}{\text{týger}},\ \underset{s\ \ \ w}{\text{búrning}}\ \underset{s}{\text{bríght}}$$
fine-grained units are unavailable in some other systems, in French syllabic verse, for instance. In chapter 9, in the first stanza of Baudelaire's "Hymne" the obtrusive rhythm is less fine-grained; it consists of the repetition of prepositional phrases introduced by the preposition *à la*. This sequence of repeated phrase structures is segmented into octosyllabic verse lines with a compulsory caesura after the fourth syllable, clearly articulated and grouped by a rhyme pattern. The repeated phrase structure reinforces the repeated hemistiches, and has an impetuous forward sweep with a

---

[11] From Blake's "The Tyger"—this poem will be discussed in great detail in chapter 7.

convergent, incantatory effect. By the same token, a mild divergent effect is super-imposed: the main clause occurs only in the fourth line; the reader's attention must be split, so as to remember that an obtrusive syntactic prediction has not yet been fulfilled. A similar but less fine-grained structure is displayed, in the same chapter, by an old Hebrew mystic text from the so-called "mercaba" hymns. Here certain abstract magic formulae are reiterated. This text begins with four parallel verses, each one containing a prepositional phrase introduced by the preposition "from", predicting a verb, which occurs only in the fifth line. But here there are no independently established verse lines of equal length as in Baudelaire, no caesura, and no rhyme pattern. There is only the incantatory repetition of a phrase structure embodied in phrases of different length, mitigated by the need for splitting attention between the propelling repeated phrase structure and remembering that a crucial syntactic prediction has not yet been fulfilled. These poems are less fine-grained than those in the syllabo-tonic system. But they are prone to evoke the desired effect, as long as those options of the respective semiotic systems are chosen that are best suited to evoke a trance-inductive effect.[12]

We have introduced the issue of "fine-grainedness" and "equivalence" to explain in what sense a verbal structure may be perceived as an adequate imitation of a mystic experience. Long after having expounded this conception, we suddenly realized that it provides the obvious explanation for the disconcerting observation we have made above: that some of our best examples for our conception of mystic and meditative poetry are secular poems. We believe that the explanation is this: the poetic codes developed by romantic and symbolistic poetry are more fine-grained than any other poetic code developed by earlier styles, precisely in those respects that are advantageous in conveying a mystic experience, or displaying some mystic quality.[13] Thus, for instance, we will see that in chapter 4, excerpts 1–4, from Donne's Holy Sonnets (quoted by Martz as typical instances of the Composition of Place), there is barely any description of the scenery. In chapter 5, by contrast, we will see that the entire octet of Wordsworth's pantheistic Calais-Beach sonnet is devoted to a meticulous description of the evening landscape, in harmony with the poetics of romantic nature poetry. Many of the romantic and symbolistic poets were of a mystic disposition, but were adherents of some kind of secular humanism.

---

[12] There is a comparable device in "The Tyger", where there are six groups of four highly convergent lines with little or no syntactic prediction. The fifth stanza, however, begins with two parallel subordinate clauses, predicting a main clause in line 3: "When the stars threw down their spears, / And watered heaven with their tears".

[13] Regarding the perceived qualities of mystic poetry, to be analysed in the present study, at least.

Saying the Ineffable

Most scholars emphasise the ineffable nature of some religious experiences. One way to approach the problem is this. Just as someone may tell the events of a dream but fail to convey what is really significant about it, one may report the images, episodes and ideas related to some mystic or meditative event, but fail to convey its special character, the unique conscious quality of the experience, for instance. On the other hand, some religious poems are remarkably successful in conveying this conscious quality as well. Religious systems are conceptual systems. Language too is a conceptual system. Even such words as "ecstasy" or "mysticism" are supposed to be used as clear-cut concepts, or mere tags to identify some mental process. Yet, it seems that in good religious poetry the ineffable quality is somehow sensed through the language. Our objective is to explore how such a conceptual language can convey non-conceptual experiences such as meditation, ecstasy or mystic insights. We explore how the poet, by using words, can express the "ineffable".

Horne even points out a social element in the problem of recognising and expressing private experiences as such.

> Such experiences as pains, moods and dreams are had by only one person, so that I would think, offhand, that only the one who had the experience would be able to recognize his experience and decide whether a description of it was correct.
>
> However, after long and involved discussions which go back to John Stuart Mill, many philosophers have come to talk about private experience in quite another way. They argue that the person who is in the apparently privileged position of having the pain, dream, etc., is actually in no better position to know it than anyone else. Their reason for saying so is that if I ask how anyone knows that he has dreamed, or had a pain, I realize that his ability to identify the experience verbally (not have it, of course) arises out of social context. In his upbringing, he has learned from others to recognize and report such things (Horne, 1978: 42).

In his book on mysticism and philosophy, Stace examines this issue thoroughly.

> One of the best-known facts about mystics is that they feel that language is inadequate, or even wholly useless, as a means of communicating their experiences or their insights to others. They say that what they experience is unutterable or ineffable (Stace, 1961: 277).

Stace surveys the many theories that have been proposed to explain ineffability and shows that none of them is fully satisfactory. It could have been the intensive emotional load which is ineffable: "the deeper our emotions are, the more difficult they are to express" (ibid: 281). Yet Stace argues that the perceptive part and not just the emotional load is ineffable; that there is a logical difficulty as well.

Another explanation focuses on the gap between the teller who has experienced the mystic experience and the listener who has not. "Like the impossibility of communicating the nature of colour to a man born blind" (ibid: 283). Stace shows that this notion applies equally to every kind of experience, not just to mystical ones, making it useless to explain precisely the unique ineffability of the mystical experience.

The most common theory seeks to explain ineffability "as being due to an incapacity of the understanding or intellect to deal with mystical experience. [...] It can be directly experienced, thus goes the theory, but it cannot be abstracted into concepts [...]. Therefore mystical experiences being unconceptualizable are also unverbalizable" (ibid: 285). They are unconceptualisable because at least part of the experience is the oneness.

> Concepts depend on there being a multiplicity of distinguishable items. The mind notes resemblances and differences between them and arranges those which resemble each other in certain ways into the same class. The idea of the class is the concept. Hence where there is no multiplicity there can be no concept and therefore no words (ibid: 286).

In the introvertive experience oneness is an undifferentiated unity. In the extrovertive, oneness is experienced as "shining through from beyond or behind" the multiplicity. "Oneness" is an undifferentiated part and is therefore unconceptualisable.

Stace makes a distinction between the inability to describe the undifferentiated unity during the experience and remembering it afterwards. He argues that *"theorists have supposed that the impossibility of using concepts during the experience is also characteristic of the remembered experience"* (ibid, 298, italics in the original) and this supposition is mistaken (ibid). According to Stace, in retrospective look, most of the experience is not ineffable, and can be expressed through concepts (like the concept "undifferentiated unity" for example).

Our own solution, to be propounded in chapter 4, is a special version of this last point of Stace's. Some brain scientists and cognitive psychologists speak of relatively compact and linear processes (associated with the left hemisphere of the brain), as opposed to relatively diffuse and global mental processes (associated with the right hemisphere of the brain). The former characterise typically rational, conceptual, and logical processes; the latter—typically emotional, mystic, and other kinds of nonconceptual processes, including spatial orientation. Some brain scientists (e.g., Marcel Kinsbourne) assume that both kinds of processes consist of streams of information describable in terms of semantic features. It will be suggested in chapter 4 that the semantic features that constitute, e.g., some mystic experience *can* be paraphrased in conceptual language; what *cannot* be paraphrased is its diffuse structure, and the phenomenological quality of this diffuse structure. We can tell the events of a dream, but cannot convey its diffuse character that seems to determine its unique subjective nature. The same can be said of "oneness". Some brain scientists say that the right hemisphere of the brain processes information as a patterned whole. Words can paraphrase the information, but not the phenomenological quality of being processed as a patterned whole. The phrase "undifferentiated unity" mentioned in the preceding paragraph does not convey the experience; it merely serves as a tag for identification.

Thus, we argue that at least one other aspect of the religious experience, not mentioned by Stace, is ineffable. It is the way the meaning is organised. Again, as in a dream or in a figurative text, part of the uniqueness of the experience is the unique way in which the units of information are linked and clustered together. Such clusters are usually called "symbols". Stace mentions with approval the theory that religious experience is symbolic by nature, yet he sees no problem in conceptualizing it into literal language afterwards. To a large extent, information about mystic experiences is similar to information about figurative expressions: it cannot be paraphrased by literal language, only described to some extent, or partly imitated. Consider, for instance, our above discussion of Wordsworth's "Daffodils". The interaction between the theme of dancing daffodils and the poem's rhythmic structure may be regarded as such a partial imitation of what Newberg et al.. described as altered states of consciousness "triggered by various kinds of intense physical or mental activity, including dancing, running". Or, consider Wordsworth's "vacant or pensive mood" following the peak of the dancing movement, which may be referred to by such conceptual tags as "sweet thoughts recollected in tranquillity"; but may also be regarded as a verbal imitation of what Newberg et al. described as "the maximal stimulation of the arousal system [which] can also cause a spillover effect, which causes quiescent responses to surge".

Religious poetry uses a variety of techniques to generate its effects. Sometimes one religious element becomes a distinctive characteristic of a poem determining its genre, meditative poetry, for instance; but sometimes we ought to speak of mystic or meditative elements in a poem—even in a secular poem, where they do not necessarily determine its genre. Just as theological and philosophical elements may appear in genres other than "contemplative poetry", mystic elements may be found in other than mystic poetry as well. One of the main goals of the present study is to examine in what ways poetic devices of structure and organisation can be employed for conveying these qualities. How can stylistic features enable a reader to detect the presence of such qualities by way of "showing" rather than "telling"? This issue is discussed more thoroughly in the next chapter; in the subsequent chapters there is an attempt to unfold some of these poetic techniques, so essential for translating the religious subjective emotional experience into perceived qualities of a verbal artefact, such as a mystic quality, a sense of transcendence, the sublime, etc.

Poetic Techniques in Religious Poetry

Religious poetry uses many kinds of techniques to generate its effects. As mentioned above, one of the most important qualities perceived in religious poetry is a mystic quality, a sense of contact with other worlds. Such an effect is achieved by deviation from our ordinary consciousness. Thus, much of our discussion is focused on the techniques used to indicate deviation from ordinary consciousness.

Much of our concern is focused on poetic devices that undermine ordinary consciousness, which readers may experience to some extent, but tend to displace away from themselves, to the poem. Generally speaking, these devices operate by three basic methods:

1. Rendering our clear-cut categorisation less distinct—by blurring the borders between categories, softening the limits, and establishing a new uncategorised unity in our perception. A wide range of poetic devices discussed in this book functions in such a way, reinforcing thematic indeterminacies, which explicitly challenge the boundaries of known categories.
2. Undermining aggressively our sense of order by violating the stability of our ordinary consciousness, by emphasising paradoxes, creating unsettled situations and splitting our focus of attention by force.
3. Shifting our general focus toward less rational and less ordered processes, evoking holistic cognitive processes (as opposed to analytical ones), and stimulating emotional effects.

A wide variety of poetic means are available for these purposes, and we do not presume to give a comprehensive view of them. We discuss some of the techniques, and the effects they produce, while trying to make our humble contribution to establishing a more or less systematic relationship between poetic techniques and perceived qualities.

"Emotional" and "Aesthetic" Qualities

Finally, a word must be said about what we mean by such phrases as "mystic poem", or "ecstatic poem". We designate by these adjectives some aesthetic quality. Hepburn (1968) distinguished, with reference to aesthetic objects, between experiencing an emotion on the one hand, and detecting an emotion, or perceiving some emotional quality on the other. This does not mean interpreting a text as having an emotional topic; rather, certain verbal structures are recognised as similar, in some important respects, to the structure of emotional processes familiar to the readers from their own experience. In a recent paper (Tsur 2002) the point is re-stated as follows. Thought processes are relatively convergent streams of information that display specific directions, and whose elements are well-defined, compact, and tightly organised. Emotional processes are relatively divergent streams of information consisting of similar components, but more diffused in all respects, and less tightly organised. So, rather than specific directions, they display general tendencies. Ecstatic qualities, as in Wordsworth's "Daffodils", are based on regularly repeated convergent elements "heightened, to any degree heightened". Cognitive poetics assumes that poetic texts do not only have meanings or convey thoughts, but also display emotional qualities *perceived* by the reader. When one says "My sister is sad" or "That dervish is ecstatic", and "The music is sad" or "ecstatic", he uses the words "sad" or "ecstatic" in two different senses. In the first two sentences he refers to some mental process of a person. In the third sentence he does not refer to a mental process of the sound sequence, nor to a mental process it arouses. One may be perfectly consistent when saying: "That sad piece of music made me happy" or "That piece of ecstatic music induced in me a deep calm". He refers to a perceptual quality generated by the interaction of the particular melodic line, rhythm, harmony and timbre of the music. In other words, he reports that he has detected some structural resemblance between the sound patterns and emotions. When one says "This poem is sad", one uses the adjective in the second sense. In this sense "sad" becomes the *aesthetic quality* of the music or the poem. We will refer time and again to this distinction throughout the present study. As we said above, a mystic sonnet is not long enough to induce some mystic state of mind in the reader. But it may display a "mystic" quality, that is, display some structural resemblance to certain mystic experiences which, in turn, may be detected by the reader.

Chapter 2

Poem, Prayer and Meditation:
An Exercise in Literary Semantics

The Religious Poem—Aesthetic or Ritual Object?

Religious poems are most frequently discussed, as a matter of course, under the general heading of Poetry. It appears, however, that this approach is by no means to be taken for granted. For a great many religious poets, the aesthetic merit of their poem was only an accident, so to speak. They cultivated poetry for the truth of it.

The relationship between aesthetic and devotional value in Divine poems becomes particularly intriguing in English poetry in the seventeenth century and Hebrew poetry in the eleventh century. In these periods both religious and secular poetry flourished, and very frequently among the greatest representatives of the one we also find the greatest representatives of the other. The religious poetry of both periods draws liberally upon the poetic conventions of secular poetry; yet, at the same time, it aspires to a fair degree of autonomy.

One perplexing thing about devotional poems is the question whether one may legitimately treat them as *poems* at all. Authors of devotional poems, both Hebrew poets of the eleventh century and English poets of the sixteenth and seventeenth centuries, were inclined to make a sharp distinction between "poetry" and their devotional works.

> This division was clear in the Middle Ages. Secular poems were collected each in its author's particular *Diwan,* but Divine poems were collected according to their liturgical function. In the margin of Prayer Books, or concentrated in practical anthologies for particular festivals, *piyyutim* (liturgical poems) by various authors of various ages were presented together. The devotional poems of one single poet were never gathered together, for they were not considered as poems for 'poetry's sake'. . . . It is characteristic that Moses Ibn Ezra mentions his *piyyutim* only once in his poetics, casually, precisely as something outside the sphere of his treatise, that is, a study of the rules of poetry that follows Arab poems. He does not mention his own devotional poems, not even when he describes his 'metrical' poems; although he wrote quite a few of his *piyyutim* in the classical metre and style, he distinguished it from mere poetry (Pagis, 1970: 23).

Robert Southwell, writing in 1595 in his prefatory epistle to *Saint Peters Complaint,* suggests that the difference between devotional and secular poetry goes beyond the difference in topic. One of the main differences between the two kinds of poetry lies, according to him, in the truth values of the poems. Secular poetry tells lies, whereas devotional poetry should be written for truth's sake. Moses Ibn Ezra would have, presumably, agreed with this, but not with the consequences Southwell draws from this distinction. In Southwell's opinion, secular poetry is in the Devil's service, who "seeketh to have all the complements of Divine honour applyed to his service" (see Martz, 1962: 179). Ibn Ezra and his contemporaries sometimes felt the need to be apologetic about their secular poetry, but eventually they concluded that "The truest poetry is the Most Feigning" (Pagis. 1970: 46 ff.).

George Herbert thought that all one's poetic powers should be devoted to the writing of religious verse. As with everything else one does for the sake of God's name, one should try to make the most perfect verses one is able to. But the ultimate criterion for religious verse is not aesthetic. It is a matter of the devotion of the heart revealed by the words:

> Whereas if the heart is moved,
> Although the verse be somewhat scant,
> God doth supplie the want.
> ("A True Hymne")

(see also Summers' illuminating chapter: "The Proper Language" in his *George Herbert).*

The literary value of the devotional poems of Donne, Herbert and Hopkins seems to have deliberately some bearing on the heightened interest in them. They are indeed more intensively studied than other devotional poems, not because they are better prayers or meditations, but because they are better poems. These two kinds of value do not necessarily agree. What in a text typically "counts toward" a good aesthetic object, does not necessarily count toward a good ritual object. On the contrary:

> In ritual, form and content are strictly patterned, and repeated again and again with minimal deviation, on pain of losing the ritualistic efficacy. The ritualistic act is one of participation rather than creation: the response which the members of the group are required or expected to have is rigidly limited. As ritual becomes secularized, the priest gives way to the bard or poet. Conformity of reaction vanishes: interpretations are not rigidly confined to the institutional or doctrinal requirements, but proliferate in accord with the creative impulse of the individual artist. Poetry becomes ambiguous concomitantly with its emergence from ritual (Kris & Kaplan, p. 253).

A text which makes a good prayer as well as a good poem can be either at different times; their co-occurrence may be regarded as "a happy coincidence", so to speak. The ambiguities of the poem are to be suppressed in the prayer. Kris and Kaplan see, then, a major difference between poetry and ritual texts, one which subsists on the pragmatic level. Thus, to pursue a fruitful investigation, a few basic pragmatic distinctions may prove useful. First, as we have seen, one has to distinguish between poetry and devotion. Secondly, in devotion one may distinguish, in turn, between prayer and meditation; thirdly, in the latter there are two possible degrees: meditation proper, and mystical experience. Graphically we may present it thus:

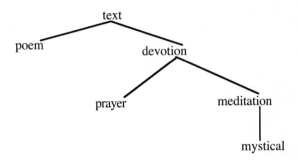

Gershom Scholem (1955: 7-10) distinguishes three stages of religion: I. The first is "the truly monistic universe of man's mythical age", when "the abyss between Man and God has not become a fact of inner consciousness". "In this first stage, Nature is the scene of man's relation to God". II. "In its classical form, religion signifies the creation of a vast abyss, conceived as absolute, between God, the infinite and transcendental being, and Man, the finite creature. . . Man becomes aware of a fundamental duality, of a vast gulf which can be crossed by nothing but the *voice;* the voice of God, directing and law-giving in his revelation, and the voice of man in prayer. The monotheistic religions live and unfold in the ever-present consciousness of this bipolarity, of the existence of an abyss which can never be bridged". III. "Mysticism does not deny or overlook the abyss; on the contrary, it begins by realizing its existence, but from there it proceeds to a quest for the secret that will close it in . . . to bring back the old unity which religion has destroyed, but on a new plane, where the world of mythology and that of revelation meet in the soul of man. Thus the soul becomes its scene and the soul's path through the abysmal multiplicity of things to the experience of the Divine Reality, now conceived as the primordial unity of all things, becomes its main preoccupation".

This appearance of mystical tendencies is also connected with another factor. "New religious impulses may and do arise which threaten to conflict with the scale of values established by historical religion."

> If and when such a situation arises, the longing for new religious values corresponding to the new religious experience finds its experience in a new interpretation of the old values. . . . In this way Creation, Revelation, Redemption, to mention some of the most important religious

> conceptions, are given new and different meanings, reflecting. . . the direct
> contact between the individual and God.
>
> Revelation, for instance, is to the mystic not only a definite historical
> occurrence . . . instead of the one act of Revelation, there is a *constant*
> repetition of this act.
>
> And thus, the substance of the canonical texts, like that of all other
> religious values, is melted down and given another form as it passes
> through the fiery stream of mystical consciousness.

At a first approximation one may sum up the relationship between prayer and
mystical experience as follows. Both attempt to reach across the abyss between the
human and the transcendental, the divine. However, (1) whereas in prayer it is the
words which one sends, so to speak, to reach Him, in mysticism the individual
internalises the contact with God, involving in it the entire intense activity of his
soul; "God becomes experience". Hence (2) whereas prayer can be the concern either
of the community or of the individual, the mystic experience is, primarily, a matter
of the individual living through intense and direct contact with God.

> With no thought of denying Revelation as a fact of history, the mystic still
> conceives of the source of religious knowledge and experience which bursts
> forth from his own heart as being of equal importance for the conception of
> religious truth (Scholem, 1955: 9).

This last statement, with a shift of emphasis, points to an important aspect of
the tradition of meditation. For the tradition of meditation proper, "Revelation as a
fact of history" is all-important. But in order to become "the source of religious
knowledge", this religious truth has to be experienced—though it is far from being
"of equal importance" with the original, unique Revelation.

Bearing this in mind, we may adopt the following distinction of Louis Martz as
the common ground of comparison:

> Meditation, then, cultivates the basic, the lower levels of the spiritual life;
> it is not, properly speaking, a mystical activity, but a part of the duties of
> every man in daily life. It is not performed under the operation of special
> grace, but is available to every man through the workings of ordinary grace
> (Martz, 1962: 16).

In the present chapter I shall follow up some implications of this relationship between prayer and meditation. I shall not, however, maintain a sharp distinction between meditation and mystical devotion. As Louis Martz has pointed out, meditation
may go "into something very close to a state of mystical contemplation." On the
other hand, even when we touch the state of mystical "recollection" in portions of

the work of Crashaw, Vaughan and Traherne, and even in portions of the work of Donne and Herbert

> it is not by any means valid to argue that the poetry is therefore the product of mystical experience. The meditative writers of the time are constantly using the threefold way of the mystics as a framework for purely ascetic and devotional exercises: mystical terms provide powerful metaphors frequently used in cultivating the realm of devotion (Martz, p. 20).

One way to handle the problem might be to accept Horne's distinction quoted in the preceding chapter, suggesting that meditation is basically the technique and not the effect itself.

The Pragmatic Switch

Sometimes the same piece of poetry may be read as a poem, a prayer, or a meditation. In such a case, the three relate to one another as three "deep structures", as potentials underlying one single "surface structure." Using Roman Jakobson's model of the fundamental factors in communication with the corresponding functions of language, I shall try to show how these three "deep structures" *can* be conveyed by the same words, as well as try to map out the points of similarity and of difference between these three. Jakobson (1960: 353) presents a model of the communication situation involving six factors:

Context

Addresser ...... Message ...... Addressee

Contact

Code

> Each of these six factors determines a different function of language. Although we distinguish six basic aspects of language, we could, however, hardly find verbal messages that would fulfill only one function. The diversity lies not in a monopoly of some one of these several functions but in a different hierarchical order of functions. The verbal structure of a message depends primarily on the predominant function (p. 353).

The diverse "deep structures" referred to may, then, consist of similar elements arranged in different hierarchical orders. The *functions* corresponding to the six factors are (p. 357):

Referential

Emotive . . . . . .   Poetic . . . . . .   Conative
(expressive)   (rhetorical)

Phatic

Metalingual

Let me illustrate these various functions by one sentence. The indicative sentence "It's getting dark" typically expresses a statement implying the speaker's beliefs about the extralinguistic context (referential function). It is usually intended to affect the addressee's beliefs about that context. If there is a corresponding fact in the context, the statement is true; if there is none, it is false. I may, of course, utter the sentence *without asserting* the statement, that is, without attempting to make the addressee believe that this is indeed the case. In this instance, it is neither true, nor false (As when I utter this sentence in broad daylight in a grammar class as an example for the use of the formal subject "it"; this may serve as an illustration of the metalingual function).

I may, further, utter the sentence and imply "Please, turn on the light." In this case, the dominant function is conative (addressee-oriented), to which the referential function is subordinated. Now, suppose the sentence is uttered in a play such as *Waiting for Godot*. Here it may serve the *phatic* function: it is said just in order to say something, to *maintain contact*. But notice that this "phatic" function is subordinated to the emotive function: the need for contact, the lack of anything better to say to each other, is expressive of the feelings and frame of mind of the two tramps. Now the utterance may have some conative implication too: "Let's go, then!" This, however, presupposes some referential validity in the play's context. But notice that such a "referential" function has little to do with extra-linguistic reality. One may read the play in full daylight, and still accept the utterance as expressing a "true statement". Some of the neighbouring sentences also seem to refer to evening, and it is this consistency of the linguistic context that suggests that the statement is "true", not its correspondence to some extra-linguistic fact. In this sense, the "statement" refers to the message itself and not to non-linguistic reality (its denotation is "internal")—it is the "message-oriented" *poetic function*. The utterance "The Hebrew sentence 'Maḥsïkh' means 'It's getting dark'" will be code-oriented; the function of our sentence will be *metalingual*.

I have said that a statement may be true or false in its context only if it is asserted, that is, if the speaker indicates in some way that he believes what he says and would have the addressee believe it, too. Suppose I utter the sentence "The earth is flat". If I assert the statement expressed, it will most probably be judged as false. But suppose I utter it in a history lesson, illustrating the medieval world picture. In this case I give no indication that I believe that this is indeed the situation, nor do I want my audience to believe it. Consequently, the statement is neither true nor false (I do assert, however, the statement "In the Middle Ages people believed that the earth was flat". I believe that this statement is true, and I would have my audience believe it too).

A similar problem arises when we consider the linguistic function oriented toward the addresser. When I utter an interjection, say, "ouch", or "alas", I may indicate that I have certain emotions or feelings. If I do have these emotions, that is, if there is a corresponding fact in the extra-linguistic context, the indicated emotions or feelings are *genuine*. If there are no corresponding extra-linguistic facts, the emotions and feelings are feigned. When we say that a person is saying his prayers with devotion (or, in Hebrew, with *kawwana),* we mean that (1) he asserts all its explicit and implicit statements, (2) that heightened mental activities are indicated, and (3) that these heightened activities are genuine.

Thus, different semantic contexts or altered pragmatic circumstances may activate a new modified hierarchy of functions. When we speak of three different "deep structures" of the same "surface structure" in respect of poem, prayer and meditation, we imply that the same message may have three different "predominant functions" at different times, conative (prayer), emotive (meditation), and poetic (poem).

Earlier it was suggested that the various functions are to be conceived in a hier-archical order. In the conative function language need not be exclusively focussed on the Addressee (God). When addressing a prayer to God, one usually wishes to affect His attitudes or actions. For this end, one usually makes some statement about one's own beliefs (referential function), or expresses one's feelings (emotive function).

At the same time when this article was first published, Mananzan distinguished metaphysical statements from religious statements. As opposed to metaphysical statements,

> Religious statements are not primarily concerned with making theoretical enquiries or answering them [...] a religious expression is not an enquiry but at most a rhetorical question, and more frequently an exclamation, a cry, an expression of despair, a reproach or a praise or an expression of wonderment (Mananzan, 1974: 91).

When we use a metaphysical statement for religious declaration it turns into a completely different speech-act: "it acquires explicitly illocutionary forces" (ibid.). The term "illocutionary act" is taken from Austin (1962). The illocutionary act is "the performance of an act *in saying* something as opposed to the performance of an act *of saying* something" (Mananzan, 1974: 53).

It should be further remarked that the use of words in prayer by no means stops there. Since God can presumably see the intent devotion in one's heart, words are, to all intents and purposes, unnecessary for addressing Him. In a sense, we use words in an address to God by way of analogy with human addressees. It is a need of the addresser rather than of the addressee. So that the phatic function, the wish for contact with God, is an important ingredient in prayer.

When meditating, the discourse is usually speaker-oriented (emotive); second to it is the referential function (focussed upon the object of meditation). One may, however, reasonably expect the conative function to be present too—third in the hierarchy. When meditation moves toward mysticism, the predominance of the emotive function becomes more and more obvious. Mysticism, says Dr. Mobley, is a religion in which God "ceases to be an object and becomes an experience". Although the discourse may thus be primarily oriented towards the speaker's experience, references to God-as-object and to God-as-addressee will still rank high in the hierarchy.

Regarding the two literary periods in question (that is, in Hebrew poetry of the 11th century and English poetry of the 17th century), an important observation seems pertinent. Whatever the differences, the great majority of prayers, meditations and poems have a remarkable common feature: they are in the public medium, yet they seem to have intimate ties with individual experience. "The religious poet", says Summers, "took upon himself the burden of voicing praise for those who could not write and sing" (p. 106). Sincerity of prayers in the seventeenth-century English Church did not imply—as certain post-Romantic conceptions would have it—the use of one's own inspired words, "the spontaneous overflow of powerful feeling". Sincerity at prayers implied rather *living up* to the words of the ready-made text. Here the ideal seemed to be—in the words of Yehuda Halevy, the 11th century Hebrew poet—that "the tongue should *agree* with the thoughts" (my italics). Spontaneous outpouring was not necessarily looked upon as desirable. George Herbert, according to his friend at Little Gidding, Nicolas Ferrar, had a rather low opinion of extemporaneous prayers: "'As for extemporaneous prayers,' he used to say, 'there needed little other confutation of them, than to take them in short-hand, & shew them sometime after to those very men, that had been so audacious to vent them. Ask,' saith he, 'their own judgment of them (for I think they will hardly know them again), & see if they do not blame them'" (quoted by Summers, p. 75).

For some research purposes it might be useful to separate theoretically the texts from their pragmatical use ("sentence meaning" from "utterer's meaning"), for other purposes it might not. The texts themselves may contain potentials that would tend to promote one function rather than another. The poetic-aesthetic function realises some potentials better than others. These potentialities and the way they are constructed, perceived, and construed are at the core of my interest.

One Text → Poem, Prayer and Meditation

Let us illustrate the foregoing distinctions by one "divine poem".

1	Batter my heart, three person'd God; for, you
2	As yet but knocke, breathe, shine, and seeke to mend;
3	That I may rise, and stand, o'erthrow mee,'and bend
4	Your force, to breake, blowe, burn and make me new.
5	I, like an usurpt towne, to'another due,
6	Labour to'admit you, but Oh, to no end,
7	Reason your viceroy in mee, mee should defend,
8	But is captiv'd, and proves weake or untrue.
9	Yet dearly'I love you,'and would be lovèd faine,
10	But am betroth'd unto your enemie:
11	Divorce mee,'untie, or breake that knot againe,
12	Take mee to you, imprison mee, for I
13	Except you'enthrall mee, never shall be free,
14	Nor ever chast, except you ravish me.

(Donne, Holy Sonnet 14)

From the grammatical point of view, one may observe in Donne's poem the predominance of the vocative in line 1, the imperatives in lines 1-4 and 11-12, and second personal pronouns throughout the poem. This suggests a possible dominance of the conative function. In lines 5-10, however, indicative sentences prevail which are typically referential. In addition, the poem has what may be termed an intense "emotional quality". In due course, I shall attempt to account for this, too, within the organisation of the "message".

To start with the context-oriented function, the sonnet is centered on some of the great commonplaces of Christianity. Man is kept captive by The Enemy. He will be free only if God enthrals him. That man is free only when enthralled by God is one of the great paradoxes of the monotheistic religions (exploited by Mediaeval Hebrew poets too).[1] Here we might mention also referential aspects, those of the precise allusions to the Trinity in lines 1–4, as pointed out by Louis Martz (to which I shall later refer in some detail). The possible conative function of this text (that is, as a prayer) consists not only in inducing God to general good will towards the speaker, but also in a specific plea: "Make me capable or worthy of freeing myself from the captivity of The Enemy; enthral me!".

The emotion pervading the poem is directly referred to in line 9 ("Yet dearly I love you, and would be loved faine"). As a prayer, such a statement may be rhetorically very effective, implying: "I love you so much, you can't possibly ignore my request" (the emotive function is apparent here; the speaker expresses his

---

[1]   Cf. the first stich of one of Yehuda Halevy's epigrams: "The slaves of Time are the slaves of slaves/The Slave of God alone is free."

love for God). In order for the emotions expressed in the prayer to be *genuine,* the person addressing God has to "live up" to the emotions indicated ("expressed").

Now if we conceive of the message as a piece of meditation, the emphasis is shifted from the addressee to the addresser. The direct address to God, the vocative and the imperatives serve to render the situation as vivid as possible. God, who is at the beginning the object of address, becomes at the end of the poem an experience in mystic communion with the addresser's self. The conative energy carried by the imperatives and the figurative language serves to affect the addresser as much as the addressee. Consequently, in order for the experience to be genuine, a much more intense mental activity is required for meditation than for prayer.

In one case the emotive function is subordinated to the conative function, in the other the conative is subordinated. In both cases the speaker must assert his statements and must have his emotions agree with his tongue. Otherwise his devotion is not sincere, is said without *kawwana* in the heart.[2]

If it is conceived as a mystic experience, devotion demands from the speaker even greater emotional intensity, culminating in a final abandonment of the self. This may possibly account for the fact that Donne's sonnet makes less of public impression than do some other devotional poems. The sonnet's imagery is most conventional; it is its heightened emotional demands from the believer that makes it less susceptible to public use.

If we conceive of the message as of a poem, the status of some of the aspects mentioned above greatly changes. Both the expressive and conative functions are then subordinated to the poetical one. In a prayer or a meditation, when the reader utters first personal pronouns (I, my), he necessarily means himself. He asserts his statements, and he experiences the emotions expressed by the words with the utmost intensity. Otherwise the devotion is false or insincere.[3] When the reader of the *poem*

---

2   The prevalent conception of prayer in Judaism (and in the majority of the Protestant sects) is that a prayer is to be *meant.* This is possibly indicated by "even though you make many prayers, I will not listen"*(Isaiah.* 1/15). Such a conception, at any rate, seems to have been accepted by some Rabbis of the Talmud: "When you pray, do not say your prayers as a routine duty, but in a pitiful and supplicant voice before the Existence-blessed-be-He" (Abhoth, II). "The praying person must direct [sheyyekhawwen] his heart towards Heaven" *(Bereshith Rabba,* XXXI). "The recitation of Shəmaᶜ requires devotion [kawwana]" (Yerushalmi. *Berakhoth.* V. 1). Yehuda Halevy, the eleventh-century Hebrew poet and Jewish thinker says: "And the tongue should agree with thought ...; every word should be loaded with thought and intent".

3   In liturgy, indicative sentences frequently serve a performative function. Saying so-and-so many psalms as against each sin implies the conception of language as performative. Language in its performative function does not depend on its truth-value or on the devotional intenity of the speaker. When the Pope utters the words "Absolvo-te," he makes no statement concerning the "absolution"; he *performs* it. When in the wedding ceremony the bridegroom utters the words "With this ring I thee wed", he conveys no information to the bride; he *performs* the wedding. The sentence can say nothing that is true or false. If uttered, it is a fact; if not, the fact does not

"Batter my heart" utters the first personal pronouns *I, my,* he does not mean himself as the speaker of the devotion would. He does not mean John Donne's empirical self, either. Just as in uttering the words of Donne's "The Apparition": "When by thy scorne, O murdresse, I am dead" the reader means by *I* neither himself nor John Donne, the words "Batter my heart" are to be attributed to a fictive "dramatic character".

The reader of the *poem* need not assert its statements. Furthermore, even if he does assert them, it is irrelevant to his appreciating it. Nor does the genuineness of the emotion in the poem depend on whether the reader experiences it or not. One can be perfectly consistent in asserting "I do not believe in a three-personed God; and I have never experienced any self-oblivion resulting from a mystic communion; but whenever I read this poem, it has a great aesthetic impact on me".

When reading the *poem* "Batter my heart," the reader contemplates a "dramatic" situation in which the speaker, a devout Christian, addresses God. Who is this speaker? His relationship to the reader is rather complex: (1) He exists in the reader's imagination only, and, as such, he is part of him. (2) The reader may not create the speaker in his own image; rather, he responds to certain symbols (words) which he interprets according to certain conventions of his culture. (3) On the one hand, the speaker is a "universal": MAN; on the other hand, the words he utters "individuate" him. They indicate what sort of a person he is. He is a MAN who addresses God and asks Him to batter his heart, etc. . . . He asserts such statements as "I labour to admit you", "dearly I love you", "except you enthrall me, I never shall be free", etc. He utters the words in a highly emotional state of mind.

As for the speaker's beliefs, their status is plain enough. He necessarily asserts all his statements unless he gives some indication to the contrary. Nor can the emotions indicated by his words be feigned. Since the speaker has no independent existence apart from his speech, since he is construed from what his speech indicates, there can be no discrepancy between the emotions indicated by his speech and his actual feelings. Similarly, there can be no disparity between the speaker's beliefs and what he says he believes: the very words that convey what he believes serve as signs which construe the speaker himself. Therefore, what the speaker *says* and what the speaker *is* necessarily agree. As for the reader himself, he does not assert the statements expressed by the poem any more than the history teacher when uttering the words "The earth is flat". If he asserts any statement, it is the statement "The Man who addresses God etc... and believes that he labours to admit God, etc. ... expresses his belief that he labours to admit God, etc. ...". Such an assertion cannot be false, and its truth seems to be rather trivial.[4]

---

exist. Furthermore, it does not depend on the "devotion of the heart", either. If the words are uttered by an "authorized" person in proper conditions, the wedding becomes a fact. One cannot undo the wedding by saying: "I did not assert what I said at the ceremony" (cf. Austin, 1962).

[4] Sir Philip Sidney seems to hold a very similar view in his "Apology":

That is why a Jew, a Moslem, or an atheist can appreciate Donne's poem without believing in a three-personed God. He only must believe that the speaker believes in a three-personed God; and the speaker necessarily believes in Him. The reader does not necessarily undergo the experience embodied in the poem with the intensity of a mystic or of a meditating believer. He contemplates a speaker who addresses God and undergoes the experience. In a most illuminating essay, R. W. Hepburn (1968) suggests that we do not necessarily *experience* the emotional qualities embodied in a work of art. We rather *recognise* them, although we may *partly* experience them too. The reader of Donne's poem does not necessarily experience the intense emotion that accompanies communion with God; but he follows the process, recognises the experience, and may emotionally respond to it.

Read as a poem, then, the issue at stake in this message is not whether the statements in it are true or false, nor whether the emotions in it are genuine or feigned, but whether there exist the perceptual conditions that typically count toward the emotional quality indicated (in other words, whether the "emotion" is there in the poem by way of "showing" or "telling"). The criteria for such a decision are not extra-linguistic, but structural; e.g., linguistic multivalence, the recurrence of certain semantic features, and this in a certain order rather than in some other, and so forth (with one exception, we shall not consider here phonological and metric features).

The poem has the shape of what I am inclined to call an *emotive crescendo* (which we have already encountered in Chapter 1). Its imagery presents the experience as highly unified and suggests some kind of gradually heightened intensity. At the very beginning, the poem strikes an intense note. "Batter" suggests vigorous, and possibly painful, action. The contradiction involved in the metaphor eliminates some of the physical implications of the action, such as "hammering", and points up such implications as vigorous and painful action, also suggesting, possibly, a pun with "better" (parallel to "seeke *to* mend"). The first signs of gradual intensification are found in lines 2 and 4. Louis Martz (1963: 90) remarks: "Note the precise allusion to the three persons of the Trinity: God, the Father *knocks,* but should *break;* the Holy Spirit *breathes,* but should *blow;* and the Son (sun) *shines,* but should *burn. Knocke* refers, in the first place, to *Batter.* "Spirit" in connection with *Breathe* (like "Son" in connection with *shine)* suggests a pun. Spiritus means, in Latin, *breathing* (likewise, Hebrew "ruaḥ" means both spirit and wind). *Knock, breathe, shine,* as compared with their counterparts in line 4, seem to suggest, then, some relatively *gentle* activity. The last two are also associated with some life-giving principle. "To breake, blowe, burn" amplify the previous three verbs. But the following should be noticed: whereas Louis Martz points up the logical relationship between the pairs of verbs and the various persons of God, Donne arranged them dif-

---

Now, for the Poet, he nothing affirmes, and therefore never lyeth. For, as I take it, to lye, is to affirme that to be true which is false . . . so think I none so simple would say that *Esope* lied in the tale of his beasts: for who thinks that *Esope* writ it for actually true, were well worthy to have his name cronicled among the beasts he writeth of (p. 216).

ferently. First, there are three verbs in succession, with no reference to the respective persons of God. Then there comes a second succession of verbs, also with no reference to the respective persons. Thus, attention is focussed upon the amplification from gentle to violent action. The cumulative impact of the verbs is foregrounded rhetorically by asyndeta (the omission of *and* in both sequences) and the alliteration in breathe, breake, blowe and burn, and prosodically by the conflict between the string of consecutive linguistic stresses and the alternating weak and strong positions in the iambic pattern,

> As yet but knóck, bréathe, shíne, and séek to ménd
> w s   w   s   w   s   w   s   w   s

and

> Your fórce to bréake, blówe, búrn and máke me néw
> w   s   w s   w   s   w   s   w   s

It should be noticed, however, that the three verbs introduced as the amplification of God's actions allude, together with *Batter,* to a "submerged" image that recurs time and again in the Old Testament: the work of the blacksmith or the silversmith, whose actions may be violent and painful but create something better, purer, from the old impure material; e.g., "For thou, O God, hast tested us; thou hast tried us as silver is tried" *(Ps.* 66, 10); "Behold, I will refine them and test them, for what else can I do?" *(Jer.* 9, 7). "Behold, I have refined you, but not like silver; I have tried you in the furnace of affliction" *(Isaiah,* 48, 10). Notice the paradox involved: in order to make me worthy of life, you must change your gentle, life-giving activities into violent and destructive ones. This paradox is reinforced by another, more apparent one: "That I may rise and stand, o'erthrow mee". The paradoxical quality is further amplified in the last two lines of the sonnet.

The next image is that of a besieged or captured town. The town cannot admit its lawful ruler. The viceroy should defend it, "but is captiv'd and proves weake or untrue". At the same time, the image refers to the Man–God relationship. "I labour to admit you, but Oh, to no end, Reason should defend me, but proves weak or untrue". There is thus little hope that the lawful ruler and the town would ever unite again. The speaker's efforts against the overwhelming power of Sin and Lust seem to be pointless. Yet, he is more active here than in the first quatrain. The image, however static, adds some force to the poem, by virtue of the martial connotations and the "metaphoric tension" inherent in the predicates referring to *Reason* and *Viceroy* at one and the same time.

Line 9 is significantly ambiguous, lending amplitude to the love so emphatically repeated in it. At first sight it seems to be a comment upon the preceding quatrain: "I . . . labour to admit you, but Oh, to no end.. .. Yet dearly I love you, and would be loved faine". The rest of the sestet, however, brings out the sexual implications of love. In the last two paradoxes (lines 13, 14), the two preceding images culminate, respectively: *captive* is related to "imprison me, for I / Except you enthral me, never shall be free". The love image culminates in "Nor ever chast, except you ravish me". Now *ravish* is another pun, most suited to serve as the culmination of an emotive *crescendo* in a "metaphysical poem". Etymologically it is related to both *rape* and *rapture*. In the context of love-imagery it is likely to mean *rape* here. But remembering that the poem is about some overwhelming spiritual experience, the other meaning of *ravish* becomes conspicuous: "to fill with intense emotion". The violent connotations of some of the verbs reinforce the intensity of the experience. Both *ravish* and *thrall* have strong connotations of ecstatic experience.

Comparing line 10 to line 14 may prove illuminating. For one thing, the speaker changes sides, from the Enemy to God. Secondly, whereas *betrothed* is a state, *ravish* implies violent action. Thirdly, whereas *betrothed* implies legitimate love, *ravish* connotes illicit love. In order to achieve the highest rapture, the mystic communion with God, not only one's habitual relationships, but one's very moral being must be shaken to the foundations. This "illicit love" feature should not strike us as utterly unlikely in a devotional poem. In addition to its connotations of extreme violence (strongly required here), it may become significant in the light of an observation I have earlier quoted from Gershom Scholem: in mystical tendencies "new religious impulses may and do arise which threaten to conflict with the scale of values established by historical religion".

In line 11, "Divorce mee" is linked with love-imagery; together with the subsequent verbs "untie, or breake that knot againe" it has a cumulative impact of gradation, similar to lines 2 and 4. "Breake" too, points back to line 4, and foreshadows the sexual violence of line 14. The final verbs, "enthral, ravish," seem to be amplifications—on the emotional and physical level—of the verbs throughout the sonnet.

This is thus a *poem* which has the shape of an "emotive crescendo" (with a beginning, a middle, and an end), with a high degree of vividness, multiple relationship of imagery (bestowing *unity*—upon *multiple* imagery), and mounting intensity. In this respect, it may be said to resemble meditation (or mystic experience). However, in the poem the reader *perceives* the process of mounting emotion, whereas in meditation or ecstasy he is supposed to *experience* it (one might add, nevertheless, that the sonnet would seem hardly long enough to allow the reader to work himself up to the "towering passion" implied by an ecstatic experience).

In an illuminating discussion of three ecstatic poems by Donne, St. John of the Cross, and Wagner, Leo Spitzer (1962) points out one element common to all three, "the ecstatic communion of a human ego with a non-ego." In all three poems love figures prominently. About Donne's "The Extasie" Spitzer makes the remark that "our poem, with its clear demarkation between body and soul, will remain a monument of intellectual clarity" (p. 151). To Donne's "Batter my heart," however, it would be more appropriate to apply some of those remarks of Spitzer which he makes about the Spanish mystics in general and San Juan de la Cruz in particular, as e.g., that religious mysticism "borrows from sex the raw material of psychophysical sensitivity with which to welcome, on a higher plane, *but still in one's body* as well as in one's soul, the invasion of the divine" (ibid. cf. Chapter 9).

The co-occurrence of rape imagery, the oxymora and the imperatives at the *fortissimo* of an "emotive crescendo" seem to be the perceptual conditions for a peculiar "tiptoe effect". The imagery of rape and thrall, as the summit of a verb-series of mounting intensity, brings connotations of immense force and urgency to the experience, as well as extreme passivity on the experiencer's part. Sexual rape ("in one's body as well as in one's soul") by an absolute force may result in rapturous self-oblivion, turning *passivity* into supreme *passion*.

The "tiptoe-effect" depends, to a considerable extent, upon the imperative verbal phrases "enthrall mee" and "ravish mee." As the summit of a series of mounting violence, these verbs carry an unusual degree of perceptual immediacy, so to speak. The semantic features common to a number of these words bestow a considerable degree of actuality upon them. On the other hand, being imperative verbs, they do not indicate the actuality of rape-rapture and thrall, but, at most, their urgency and imminence.

One obvious reason for the frequency of oxymora in mystical poetry is that the oxymoron is the device most suited "to express the ineffable". Furthermore, as William James and other authorities assure us, mystic experience involves elements that to the logical mind seem highly incompatible (what Kenneth Burke would call "the Mystic Oxymoron"). In later chapters I will also take up Steven Katz's suggestion that the conscious construction of paradoxes necessarily violate the laws of logic, forcing the hearers to consider who they are—to locate themselves vis-a-vis normal versus transcendental "reality".

In addition, an oxymoron typically heightens the *energy-level* of the message, amplifying its witty or emotional quality, whichever may be the case. In this sense the oxymoron, like so many poetic devices, is "double-edged": it may have opposite effects, depending on its relative conspicuousness in its context. Metaphysical poets as well as twentieth-century readers may be reluctant to accept Longinus' normative statement in chapter 17 of *Peri Hypsous:* "Wherefore a figure is at its best when the very fact that it is a figure escapes attention". However, the end of that chapter appears to provide a sound description of perceptual hierarchies:

> For just as all dim lights are extinguished in the blaze of the sun, so do the artifices of rhetoric fade from view when bathed in the pervading splendour of sublimity. . . . So also with the manifestations of passion and the sublime in literature. They lie nearer to our minds . . . and always strike our attention before the figures whose art they throw into the shade and as it were keep in concealment.

The converse seems to be equally true: when no "manifestations of passion and sublimity strike our attention before the artifices of rhetoric", the concomitant tension will tend to be perceived as *witty* rather than sublime or passionate (cf. Tsur, 1971).

The peculiar "tiptoe-effect" of the poem at its end appears to be related also to a balance that the last lines seem to strike between ecstatic rapture and "Metaphysical

Wit," a perceptual corollary of the oxymora that resist being "thrown into the shade" and refuse to "fade from view" into an overwhelming ecstatic experience. We have given a detailed account of the perceptual conditions of the intense emotional quality in this poem (or meditation), in the "pervading splendour" of which one might expect the oxymora to fade. However, "the fading from view of the artifices of rhetoric" is disturbed time and again through such devices as the *accumulation* of oxymora at the end, syntactic inversion in line 13, metrical disturbances, and so on. The last two paradoxical assertions, with their absolute "never . . . nor ever", have an atmosphere of finality, a quality of closure; at the same time, the imperatives leave the poem trembling on the verge of—without actually attaining—fulfilment.

Chapter 3

The Ultimate Limit—Transcendence and Appresentation

Man as Prisoner

As we will see throughout the present study, certain salient aspects of religious-mystic poetry loom large in the secular version of mystic poetry. Incidentally (or, as we suggested in chapter 1, not so incidentally), most of the issues discussed in this chapter are more conveniently introduced through such secular poems than through religious poems proper.

The present work is not concerned with religious and mystic ideas as such, but with the subtle qualifications they receive when they enter into a poetic context. Very roughly speaking, we are interested in two kinds of qualifications. First, how are religious and mystic ideas transformed into verbal imitations of religious and mystic experiences? Second, how do such poetic styles as romantic or metaphysical poetry affect the poetic structure and perceived qualities of those experiences? In the ensuing chapters we will discuss mainly verbal and cognitive strategies for differentiating between poetic styles. In chapter 11, for instance, we will compare instances of the same poetic images in two poems by Milton, and explore the subtle verbal and cognitive strategies which are the sources of different stylistic effects. In the present chapter, by contrast, we are going to explore the *condition humaine* underlying religious and mystic experience, and its influence upon poetic style. This *condition humaine* concerns the awareness of finitude, of Man being "hemmed in". Elsewhere (Tsur, 1992a: 257–274) I claimed that this *condition humaine* underlies not only religion and religious poetry, but is at the roots of most poetry. So, I borrowed from theology a model of the human condition for a systematic exploration of the "world stratum" of poetry in general. I showed how a wide range of poetic styles is generated, by the effective overstressing of various parts of this model. Here I am going to pay back cognitive poetics' debt to theology. I contend that the model proposed below does not merely present the human condition, in which religious and mystical experiences arise, but also may point up significant relationships between the ways in which remote literary styles typically cope with this condition. I am referring to such literary styles as Romantic and Metaphysical poetry both in their devotional and secular aspects, as well as some varieties of modernistic literature (e.g., Absurd drama, or Kafka, or Amikhai). In this chapter I will provide only a limited illustration of these theoretical claims, but many of the ensuing chapters will illuminate additional aspects. I will rely on the archetypal situation in which, according to Gordon D. Kaufman, people use "God-talk", that is, language in which such terms as *God,* or *the gods, angels, demons, the other world,* and so on, occur. "Such speech appears within the context of man's sense of limitation, finitude, guilt, and sin, on the one hand, and his question about the meaning or value or significance of himself, his life, and his world, on the other" (Kaufman, 1972: 46).

> In this respect the idea of God functions as a *limiting concept,* that is, a concept that does not primarily have content in its own right drawn directly out of a specific experience, but refers to that which we do *not* know but which is the ultimate limit of all our experiences. [...] It must be observed that we [...] are also involved in a certain duality here, between what is in fact concretely experienced, and the limit(s) of all experience and knowledge (ibid., 47–48).[1]

What literary movements as different as Metaphysical poetry, Romantic poetry and Absurd drama or literature of extreme situations (as, e.g., Kafka) have in common is a feeling of human limitedness, being confined to the "here and now"; but against this common background of shared feeling illuminating distinctions can be made. Kaufman's formulation may help us make two sets of distinctions. First, between Metaphysical and Romantic poetry on the one hand, and certain versions of modernistic literature (Absurd drama, for instance), on the other; and second, between the two poetic styles, Romantic and Metaphysical, themselves. One important feature of the *absurd,* for instance, is the sense of human limitation "heightened, to any degree heightened", in a world in which "God is dead".[2] Whereas for the Absurd drama any attempt to transcend this world is utterly futile, Romantic and Metaphysical poetry set themselves to *transcend* the limit. Most conspicuous and intriguing from the point of view of Cognitive Poetics is the observation that both Romantic and Metaphysical poetry are typically set in a concrete situation sharply defined *here and now.* Kaufman's conception of the nature of the ultimate and the immediate limit is illuminating here.

> For the awareness of finitude is not purely conceptual or hypothetical; it is an awareness of *my actual being* as here (in this time and place) rather than there, as restricted in this particular concrete way [...]. It is the awareness of

---

[1] Kaufman carefully emphasizes that his paper "is concerned with the question of the *meaning* rather than the *truth* of statements containing the word 'God'. No attempt will be made here to prove either that God does or does not exist, that is, that the word 'God' does or does not actually relate to a reality. Questions of that sort can be faced only if we already know what we mean when we use the word 'God'" (ibid, 44–45).

[2] Newberg et al. (2001: 128) quote the following graffito:

   God is dead
       ...Nietzsche
   Nietzsche is dead
       ... God

> *my being limited* that we are here dealing with and thus in some sense an
> actual "encounter" with that which *limits me* (ibid., 54).

It seems to be this *my being limited here and now* that mystics of all ages and
religions attempt to transcend. How do we experience the Ultimate Limit? Kaufman
makes the following suggestion (which is at variance with some of the existentialist
literature):

> All that we ever experience directly are particular events of suffering, death
> (of others), joy, peace, and so forth. It is only in *reflection upon these* and
> the attempts to *understand ourselves in the light of these happenings* that
> we become aware of our limitedness on all sides. Along with this
> awareness of our being hemmed in, powerful emotions of terror, despair,
> revulsion, anxiety, and the like, are often—perhaps always—generated, and
> this total intellectual-emotional complex may then be called the "experience
> of finitude" or awareness of the "boundary situation" or something of the
> sort. But it must be observed that this experience of radical contingency is
> not an *immediate* awareness of restriction, as when one butts one's head
> against a stone wall; it depends rather upon a generalization from such
> occasional immediate experience of limitation to the total situation of the
> self. [...] Thus, the so-called experience of finitude or contingency, however
> powerful the emotions that accompany and deepen and reinforce it, has an
> intellectual root, and it is possible only because man is a reflective being
> (ibid., 52–53).

We can use this description of "the so-called experience of finitude or contingency"
to explicate, within the framework of a situation sharply defined here and now, the
distinction between Romantic and Metaphysical poetry. I have said above that what
these two poetic styles have in common with the Theatre of the Absurd is a need to
express a feeling of human limitedness, of being confined to the "here and now".
However, unlike the Theatre of the Absurd, Romantic and Metaphysical poetry assume that there *is* some other world that enables one to transcend our limited world.

As for the distinction between Metaphysical and Romantic poetry, it is not
merely a difference between their respective presentations of "here" and "there", but
also, and more important for our purpose, a difference in the emphasis given to their
relative weight. Metaphysical poetry typically focuses attention upon the "total intellectual-emotional complex", the "powerful emotions [of terror, despair, revulsion,
anxiety, and the like]" and, at the same time, upon the "intellectual root" of the experience.[3] Metaphysical poetry typically focuses attention upon the afore-said emo-

---

3   That may be one of the things implied by Sir Herbert Grierson (1965: xxxiv) when he
    characterises Metaphysical poetry as "a strain of passionate paradoxical reasoning".
    The point appears to be that both passion and reasoning are separately amplified up
    to a point when they are not in harmony with one another any more.

tional and intellectual processes, while also giving some indication of the attempt to transcend the ultimate limit. Romantic poetry, on the other hand, typically *attends away from* these processes *to* the attempt to actually transcend the ultimate limit. At the same time, much of Romanticism's culture-pessimism draws upon this "awareness of our being hemmed in". Furthermore, just as the "generalization from such occasional immediate experience of limitation to the total situation of the self" may account for the structure of typical Metaphysical reasoning, it may also account for the structure of typical Romantic nature imagery, which consists of a description of nature that is at once a real situation and the vehicle of a metaphor pointing to some more general idea, or some supersensory reality.[4] The two styles differ in the extent of the presence and explicitness of their inferences. While in Metaphysical poetry the reader is aware of complex inferences during the transition from the image upon which his awareness is focused, in Romantic poetry the transition occurs with the immediateness of perception.

Of considerable literary interest is the following distinction, also due to Kaufman:

> The self's awareness of being restricted on all sides, rendering problematic the very meaning of existence, gives rise to the question: *What* is it that in this way hems us in? How is this *ultimate* Limit, of which we are aware in the "experience of finitude", to be conceived? There appear to be four fundamental types of limiting experience, and these supply models with the aid of which the ultimate Limit can be conceived. The first two are relatively simple: (a) selves experience external *physical* limitation and restriction upon the activities through the resistance of material objects over and against them; (b) they experience from within the *organic* limitation of their own powers, especially in illness, weakness, failure, and exhaustion. The other two are somewhat more complex: (c) they experience the external *personal* limitation of other selves engaged in activities and programs running counter to their own—the clash of wills, decisions, and purposes—but precisely because matters of volition and intention are subjective, this experience is neither simply internal, nor external, but is interpersonal and social; (d) they experience the *normative* constraints and restrictions upon them, expressed in such distinctions as true–false, real–illusory, good–bad, right–wrong, beautiful–ugly, which distinctions, though felt subjectively and from within, appear to the self not to be its own spontaneous creations but to impinge upon it with categorical demands and claims (ibid., 56).

---

4   In this case, and in contrast to Metaphysical poetry, there are efforts to keep the situation, the generalisation, and the passion abstracted in harmony with one another. This is one way to indicate the nature of the "integrated focus" discussed in chapter 11.

Limited by all four types of experience, human beings may be looking for ways to overcome their sense of being "hemmed in". The attempt to break out, to cross the ultimate boundary and reach beyond, is only natural under the conditions. The present study investigates a regional perceptual quality in religious and mystic poetry that reflects the mental state characteristic of such "transcendence".

This chapter will elaborate on three different conceptions in poetry, each of which handles the world beyond the ultimate limit in a different way. According to one conception the other world consists of the same kinds of objects and human relationships as this world, perceived in the same ways, only everything is more perfect. According to a second conception the world beyond is presented to us by way of the dissolution of gestalts and can be accessed only through intuitive knowledge, altered modes of perception, and altered states of consciousness. The present study will focus mainly on this second conception. According to the third conception there is nothing beyond the ultimate limit. This conception may be presented in a romantic style, but is intimately associated with an "absurd" style. Both possibilities will be considered.

Appresentation

How can mystic poetry arouse an immediate perception regarding something that is beyond the ultimate boundary, not by *telling,* but by *showing?* It should be realised that when a detailed description of the other world is given, it very likely stops being otherworldly. The "vision" obtained may be "fanciful", "unusual", even "mythological"; but it is most likely to be experienced as if it happened on this side of the ultimate limit. This seems to be true of both poetry and the visual arts. Obviously, some additional means of presentation are involved. I contend that the "otherwordly" quality results from some interference with the smooth functioning of certain cognitive and/or psychodynamic processes.[5] I will suggest three different techniques resulting in such interference:

1. Oceanic dedifferentiation.
2. The implicit suggestion that beyond some inaccessible or impenetrable barrier there exists an unseen reality.
3. The grotesque.

This chapter will be devoted mainly to the second possibility, though occasionally I will refer to oceanic dedifferentiation as well (to which later a whole chapter will be devoted). The grotesque in the visual arts will be discussed in Chapter 10.

In his paper on metaphors, transcendence and indirect communication, Hubert Knoblauch adopts Alfred Schutz's phenomenological theory of symbols and signs based on the notion of "appresentation". "While perceiving an object, we almost au-

---

5 Characteristically, Ehrenzweig, in discussing oceanic dedifferentiation, uses both cognitive-gestaltistic and psychoanalytic terminology. The same may be noticed in Chapter 10, in my discussion of the grotesque.

tomatically 'appresent' that the object has an unseen background. By appresentation we refer to the connection between the object or event directly experienced and the object or event which is not immediately present to experience but constituted by our consciousness" (Knoblauch, 1999: 79). We must complement this conception with a distinction between conceptual and perceptual categorisation. Both organise the same kind of information. But there are certain additional restrictions on perceptual categorisation of which two are relevant to our concern: the stimulus material must be present at the time of categorisation; and the perceiver must not be aware of complex inferences.

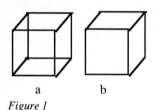

a   b

Figure 1

Consider the two cubes in figure 1. We see both designs as three-dimensional; but *a* seems to have a fuller existence as a cube than *b*. The lines present in *a* but not in *b* indicate the unseen side of the cube, as we *know* it, not as we *see* it. Notwithstanding this knowledge, we *perceive* it as a cube, not merely *know* it is a cube—because it is immediately present, and we are not aware of complex inferences. Why should we perceive these designs as three-dimensional in the first place? The gestalt-laws of perception may suggest an answer. "The psychological organisation of every stimulus pattern will always be as good as the prevailing conditions permit". The fewer the structural features, the better is the organisation. If we view the design as two-dimensional, we will see a wide range of structural features: rectangles, sharp angles and obtuse angles, as well as longer and shorter lines. If we view it as three-dimensional, all the angles will be right angles; all the lines will be of equal length, and all the planes will be of equal shape and size. Three-dimensionality becomes, therefore, the solution of a perceptual problem. The additional lines do not merely convey information about the unseen side of cube *a:* they increase the number of constraints on the solution to the perceptual problem. The phrase "the prevailing conditions permit" implies that though a sphere would have a better shape than a cube (it has fewer structural features), we do not perceive these designs as spheres, because the various angles, for instance, do not "permit" it. It took impressionist painting to eliminate from the paintings what we *know;* but in earlier paintings we are not aware that we are presented with more than what we see. This difference has to do with what psychologists call "cognitive stability".

Now suppose we *see* a door; we also *apprehend* some open or closed space to which it leads. We realise that we have such an apprehension only when something goes wrong; when, for instance, we open the door and bump straightaway into a brick wall. In this case, it is not our *inference* concerning some further space that is refuted, but some subliminal immediate knowledge. Poets frequently exploit this cognitive disposition in their attempts to suggest transcendence of the ultimate boundary. Consider the following apostrophe to nature from "Nocturno", a poem by the great Hebrew romantic poet, Saul Tchernichovsky:

1.   Ye Mighty Brothers in the whole Universe,
       Explosion-fragments and splinters of Chaos!
       Eternity has shut its gates before you...

The infinite "beyond" is indicated in this excerpt by two different notions: Chaos and Eternity. Both are inaccessible, and beyond the Ultimate limit. The sublime entities of the created Universe, such as the celestial bodies, the forest and the huge mountains (mentioned in the preceding two lines), have an intermediate position: on the one hand, they are (or were) in direct contact with the inaccessible reality beyond the Ultimate limit, but now they are "shut out"; at the same time, *they* are accessible to humans. Eternity, which is infinite *duration,* is translated into spatial terms: it is in space, beyond the Ultimate limit. The closed gates of Eternity "appresent" their other side; in this way, the reader may have an "immediate" perception of its inaccessible side.

The poetic effect of this "other side" is, however, much stronger than what can be accounted for by mere "appresentation". Some readers have a feeling that "Eternity" in this excerpt evokes some intense supersensuous presence. I submit that this metaphor elicits a radical change in the cognitive processing of this abstraction. Eternity is a compact concept; the metaphor transforms it into some diffuse, supersensuous mass that fills all space. As we will argue in chapter 4, it is space perception involving orientation rather than shape perception that activates mental processes whose output is diffuse and constitutes a "patterned whole"; as such, they resemble mental processes underlying "altered states of consciousness". Now translating the durational concept into a spatial concept is trivial in itself, perhaps a dead metaphor. Two aspects of the text turn the spatial concept into the perception of a spatial presence. The implied phrase "gates of Eternity" turns the spatial concept into "concrete" space in a very special sense. It is defined "here and now", but *in* Eternity there are no concrete objects and stable shapes; so that the perceiver is deprived of imaginable self-specifying information in the optic array, needed for locating himself in the environment.

The other aspect concerns what Aristotle in his *Rhetoric* called *energeia,* usually translated into English as "vividness". Inferring from Aristotle's examples from Homer, vividness results from a predication that attributes an improper kind of energy to a noun. The higher the energy, not merely in degree but also in kind, the more vividly is the noun's referent perceived. Thus, vividness results when physical motion is attributed to a stable object, or a mental process to a moving object, or a process (physical or mental) to a physical state. For evoking the intuition of an intense, supersensuous presence, poets of all ages have had recourse to an extreme instance of this device, involving a static abstraction or mental state in a spatial context, to which some physical process or physical action, or mental process is attributed. Consider the following lines from Andreas Gryphius' sonnet (discussed below in Chapter 5): "Verlassen Feld und Werk; wo Tier' und Vögel waren, / Traut itzt die Einsamkeit" (leave field and work; where animals and birds were, solitude now mourns). Consider the last clause: "Traut itzt[6] die Einsamkeit". "Traut" in these lines does not mean what it would mean in modern German (trusts, or gets married), but seems to be an intransitive verb related to the noun "trauer" (sorrow). This intransitive verb suggests sorrow as a mental process rather than a static quality. Had the poet used the noun phrase "die traurige Einsamkeit" (sad solitude), it would have suggested a compact concept (personified perhaps), in which the epithet foregrounds a permanent feature. The use of a predicate instead of an epithet attributes a mental process to the abstraction, turning it into an intense, supersensuous, elusive presence filling the entire "field". An even more extreme effect can be achieved when the subject phrase denotes not merely an abstraction, but an abstraction that suggests *absence,* such as "silence, darkness", or "night". In this respect, "infinity" too is a negative concept, suggesting no positive traits, only the absence of limits. Consequently, the line "Eternity has shut its gates before you" does not suggest merely some impenetrable ultimate limit and an infinite space beyond it. The "gates" turn "Eternity" into a concrete situation perceived as a diffuse, all-engulfing supersensuous mass, enhanced by the energy attributed to it by the action predicate "shut".

Chaos, by contrast, extends in infinite space, but is removed beyond the ultimate limit in time — beyond a well-specified ultimate limit: the creation of the universe. Now notice that those "Mighty Brothers in the whole Universe" were scattered across creation by some enormous explosion, crossing the ultimate limit from *there* to *here* (a metaphor which has nothing to do with George Gamow's "big bang" hypothesis of the creation of the universe). Thus, they are not only in a metonymic relationship with the Chaos that existed before the creation of the universe; the phrase "Explosion-fragments" also connotes enormous energy. This phrase is a clumsy English translation of the ambiguous Hebrew word נִפְצֵי *(nifṣey),* which may mean either "explosion" or "fragments scattered by explosion". Thus, the word suggests at the same time stable objects with stable shapes, and the enormous energy that created them.

In the romantic view, man's energies are suppressed, and cannot be properly realised. Romanticism struggled to liberate those energies and achieve a fuller existence. According to this view, culture and civilisation result from subduing the forces of nature; liberation can be achieved by going out from civilisation to nature. Nature, in turn, came into existence when Creation harnessed the infinite forces of Chaos. Tchernichovsky's poem proceeds in the opposite direction, from the domain of restrained to the domain of unrestrained energies. The "I" of the poem leaves the city

6   The adverb "now" serves as a deictic device, directing attention to some immediate situation.

and goes out to the mountain, to the "forest of the night". Through contact with the "explosion-fragments and splinters of the Chaos" he intuitively grasps something of the enormous energy that flung these huge masses into their present places.

The Present Conception and What It is Not

The most illuminating way to clarify what my objective is would be to point out what it is not. Let us have a look at lines 9–40 of Sir Walter Ralegh's "The Passionate Man's Pilgrimage" (supposedly written by someone at the point of death).

> 2.   Whilst my soul, [...]
>   Travels to the land of heaven;
>   Over the silver mountains,
>   Where spring the nectar fountains;
>   And there I'll kiss
>   The bowl of bliss,
>   And drink my eternal fill
>   On every milken hill.
>   My soul will be a-dry before,
>   But after it will ne'er thirst more;
>   And by the happy blissful way
>   More peaceful pilgrims I shall see,
>   That have shook off their gowns of clay,
>   And go apparelled fresh like me.
>   I'll bring them first
>   To slake their thirst,
>   And then to taste those nectar suckets,
>   At the clear wells
>   Where sweetness dwells,
>   Drawn up by saints in crystal buckets.
>   And when our bottles and all we
>   Are fill'd with immortality,
>   Then the holy paths we'll travel,
>   Strew'd with rubies thick as gravel,
>   Ceilings of diamonds, sapphire floors,
>   High walls of coral, and pearl bowers.
>   From thence to heaven's bribeless hall
>   Where no corrupted voices brawl,
>   No conscience molten into gold,
>   Nor forg'd accusers bought and sold,
>   No cause deferr'd, nor vain-spent journey,
>   For there Christ is the king's attorney...

I have claimed above that when a detailed description of the other world is given, it is very likely to stop being otherworldly. The "vision" obtained may be "fanciful", "unusual", even "mythological"; but it is most likely to be experienced as if it happened on this side of the ultimate limit. In excerpt 2, the speaker leaps quite easily over the "silver mountains", so they are by no means perceived as insurmountable obstructions, and what the speaker will find on their other side is not unlike what is familiar from this side of the mountains, only more perfect. It is more like moving from second class to first class than crossing the ultimate boundary. This is very different from the way the other side is perceived in excerpt 3.[7] Let us then briefly compare the improved version of this world as presented in excerpt 2 to the kind of perceptions to be explored in the present study, as presented in the following excerpt from Coleridge's "Biographia Literaria" (235). Through this passage, by the same token, I wish to illustrate the difference between "appresentation" and philosophical inference:

3.   The first range of hills, that encircles the scanty vale of human life, is the horizon for the majority of its inhabitants. On *its* ridges the common sun is born and departs. From *them* the stars rise, and touching *them* they vanish. By the many, even this range, the natural limit and bulwark of the vale, is but imperfectly known. Its higher ascents are too often hidden by mists and clouds from uncultivated swamps, which few have courage or curiosity to penetrate. To the multitude below these vapors appear, now as the dark haunts of terrific agents, on which none may intrude with impunity; and now all *a-glow,* with colors not their own, they are gazed at as the splendid palaces of happiness and power.

Coleridge presents human life as "hemmed in" in a "scanty" (that is, limited, narrow) vale.[8] The genitive link artificially splits, to use Christine Brooke-Rose's terminology, one notion into two: "scanty vale = human life". The rest of the passage elaborates, at great length, on the "scanty vale" member of the equation. Owing to this elaboration, it assumes a real existence in our consciousness; but still, its boundaries are apprehended, at the same time, as the boundaries of human life. Beyond this "ultimate boundary" there is the unknown; very much like the theological notion we are discussing. A remarkable thing about Coleridge's passage is that it suggests, in fact, three alternative ways of becoming aware of these boundaries and what is beyond them. First, "On *its* ridges the common sun is born and departs. From *them* the stars rise, and touching *them* they vanish". People in the valley can

---

[7]   I am not implying that this is a wrong way to present the other world; merely that I am interested in this study in a different kind of perception.

[8]   Gryphius' German sonnet (in chapter 5), too, refers to human life as "the vale of darkness". Perhaps all these metaphors go back to Psalms (23.4): "Even though I walk through the valley of the shadow of death, I fear no evil"

see the "first range of hills" and their "higher ascents", but not what is beyond them; they do, however, perceive the sun and the stars disappear behind them and rise from behind them, and so have some immediate intuition of the unseen background.[9] Likewise, "its higher ascents are too often hidden by mists and clouds" suggests what is directly seen, as well as an inaccessible crest that is unseen but intensely present. For the second way, excerpt 3 continues: "But in all ages there have been a few, who measuring and sounding the rivers of the vale at the feet of their furthest inaccessible falls have learned, that the sources must be far higher and far inward; a few, who even in the level streams have detected elements, which neither the vale itself or the surrounding mountains contained or could supply". Here the knowledge about the "beyond" is obtained while being aware of complex inferences. The first and second ways of knowing the "beyond" are paradigms of perceptual and conceptual categorisation, respectively. The former offers a direct immediate perception of the "beyond"; the latter—philosophical knowledge.[10] Later, Coleridge remarks that "it is the essential mark of the true philosopher to rest satisfied with no imperfect light, as long as the impossibility of attaining a fuller knowledge has not been demonstrated" (237). On the other hand, the sun and stars setting in some inaccessible space may thus evoke in the reader the sense of a direct perception of the unseen, which is not unlike mystic insight. In Wordsworth's Immortality Ode, for instance, we read: "The soul that rises with us, our life's star / Hath had elsewhere its setting". The third way is "the multitude below" to whom "vapors appear, now as the dark haunts of terrific agents, on which none may intrude with impunity; and now all *a-glow,* with colors not their own, they are gazed at as the splendid palaces of happiness and power". These are thing-free, illusory appearances to the senses, upon which the multitude's fears or hopes-and-desires can be projected. This way of knowing suggests mythological thinking.

"Ordinary consciousness" aims at maximum cognitive economy, by organising the overwhelming stream of sensory information into stable objects and rigid concepts or schemata. "The over-automatization of an object permits the greatest economy of perceptive effort" (Shklovsky, 1965: 12). We know things about the unseen side of the cube or the door, because we have acquired the appropriate schemata, which contain information about the entire object. In this way, however, reality may

9   This can be connected to what is known as one of our basic cognitive competencies: object stability. Human babies gain such competence around 6–9 months old: a child becomes able to know that his/her mother is there, even when s/he doesn't see her, or to know that if you cover a ball by a blanket—the ball is still there. This cognitive ability is the ground for such immediate perception: if the object (sun) is still there—there is a place that can be called "there", and as a viewer I can partly experience its existence.

10 Notice that in the first way of knowing, too, complex inferences are involved, but we are *less aware* of them. On the other hand, in the second way of knowing, too, apart from the awareness of complex inferences, there still may be a strange feeling of being in contact with "elements" that belong to the other, inaccessible reality.

wither away. "The purpose of art is to impart the sensation of things as they are perceived and not as they are known. The technique of art is to make the object 'unfamiliar', to make forms difficult, to increase the difficulty and length of perception because the process of perception is an aesthetic end in itself and must be prolonged" (Shklovsky, ibid). In religious poetry it might become not just an aesthetic goal but a thematic objective as well—to momentarily shake our firm conceptions concerning the impenetrable limits between the worlds, or to blur these limits for touching the beyond. The purpose of such "defamiliarisation" is to liberate the cognitive system from the tyranny of rigid schemata and concepts, and its perceived effect is quite frequently (but not always) witty rather than intuitive-emotional. According to the conception propounded throughout this book, one of the main characteristics of such altered states of consciousness as intuition, and religious or mystic experiences as well, is that they liberate the cognitive system from the tyranny of rigid concepts: they enable us to experience the stream of elusive, pre-categorial sensory information. Long after having written the present chapter I ran into a similar conception with reference to "Meditation and Deautomatization" in Arthur J. Deikman's essay "A Functional Approach to Mysticism", using almost exactly the same words as Shklovsky and myself. It occurred to him, the author says, that the perceptual changes reported in an experiment that consisted in concentrating on a blue vase

> represented a reversal of the normal developmental process whereby infants and children learn to perceive, grasp and categorize objects. This learning progresses and as it does it becomes automatic; they no longer have to pay such close attention to the nature of objects. Instead, more and more attention is freed and put in the service of thought, of abstractions. The meditation activity that my subjects performed was the reverse of the developmental process: the percept (the vase) was invested with attention while thought was inhibited. As a consequence, sensuousness, merging of boundaries and sensory modalities became prominent. A deautomatization had occurred, permitting a different experience of the vase than would ordinarily be the case (Deikman, 2000: 77).

The appresentation of "the other side of the gates", however, clearly involves a cognitive schema of doors and gates. The solution to this paradox appears to be as follows. Appresentation does not always yield an immediate perception of the unseen side of objects and situations, only in very special circumstances. Cognitive schemata may *replace* perception, or *assist* it. A single feature of an object, may activate them, helping us ignore all the rest; but in certain circumstances they may assist the fast integration of rich, diffuse, precategorial information. Our analysis of the "gates of eternity" may indicate how such diffuse and elusive precategorial information is generated in conceptual language. Or, consider the sun and stars setting on the ridges of the hills, as well as their "higher ascents [...] hidden by mists and clouds" in the Coleridge passage. In that case we have a situation that is well-defined in space, suggesting an image as it is *seen,* not as is *known.* There is an elusive mental shift from thought processes to perceptual processes.

To understand this we must first distinguish between what we *know* and what we *see:* we *know* that the setting sun and stars have nothing to do with the ridge of hills; but we *see* them touching their ridges when disappearing. Second, we have absolutely no information about the space into which they disappear. Third but not least, we must distinguish between two ways of completing the available information: by what we know, and by a process governed by what the gestaltists call the "Law of Good Continuation". This process is nearer to the perceptual than conceptual pole of mental processes:

> A shape or pattern will, other things being equal, tend to be continued in its initial mode of operation. Thus, "to the factor of good continuation in purely spatial organization there corresponds the factor of the smooth curve of motion and continuous velocity in spatio-temporal organization". [...] Actually, of course, a line or motion does not perpetuate itself. It is only a series of lifeless stimuli. What happens is that the perception of a line or motion initiates a mental process, and it is this mental process which, following the mental line of least resistance, tends to be perpetuated and continued (Meyer, 1956: 92).

In the foregoing examples, completion by good continuation replaces the completion by knowledge. In the case of the setting sun and stars there is, indeed, a "smooth curve of motion", the perception of which "initiates a mental process" that "tends to be perpetuated and continued". Consequently, there is a vague apprehension of the continuous progression on the unseen side. The same happens, mutatis mutandis, with the "higher ascents [...] hidden by mists and clouds". "Mists and clouds", though seen, are vague, fuzzy. As for the hills and mountains, they have a seen and an unseen part. Again, our apprehension of the unseen part need not rely on our explicit and conscious rational assumption, but on the "good continuation" of the curved lines.

Ralegh, Ronsard and Ibn Gabirol

We have been discussing the conception underlying this study, and what it is not. Our discussion has been focused on a poetic passage by Sir Walter Ralegh. We compared at some length its conception of the "beyond" to that in a prose passage by Coleridge. In this section, I will briefly compare two details in Ralegh's account to two excerpts by Pierre de Ronsard and Shlomo Ibn Gabirol, locating Ralegh between two poetic conceptions explored in the present study. Consider Ralegh's verse lines "More peaceful pilgrims I shall see, / That have shook off their gowns of clay, / And go apparelled fresh like me." The image "shook off their gowns of clay" was a cliché in the sixteenth and seventeenth centuries. Ronsard too uses it in his sonnet beginning "Il faut laisser maisons", but with a difference:

4.   Heureux qui ne fut onc! plus heureux qui retourne
       En rien, comme il était; plus heureux qui séjourne,
       D'homme fait nouvel ange, auprès de Jésus-Christ,

       Laissant pourrir çà-bas sa dépouille de boue,
       Dont le sort, la fortune et le destin se joue,
       Franc des liens du corps pour n'être qu'un esprit.

Happy is he who never was, happier he who returns to the nothingness which he was, happier (still) he who dwells, transformed from man into a new angel, at the side of Jesus Christ,
    Leaving to rot down here his body of clay, with which fate and fortune and destiny sport, free from the bonds of flesh to be nothing but a spirit.

Both texts make use of the same figurative cliché. Both substitute a genitive phrase as periphrasis for "body, corpse", suggesting that the body is made of clay or mud, and that at death it is shaken off as a garment, or cast off as slough. But there is a substantial difference between the outcomes. In Ralegh, the souls now "go apparelled fresh", that is, in a different kind of "gown". While in this context the blessed souls change shapes, at best, "nothingness" in Ronsard is the prototypical gestalt-free and thing-free entity. What is more, Ronsard carefully emphasises that rather than a place as in Keats's sonnet (see below, excerpt 8), "nothingness" suggests here a state of existence. Two degrees of nonexistence are suggested: having never been, and returning to nothingness. In the latter, one passes from a state of focused gestalt to a gestalt-free existence. It is the dissolution of an ego in a gestalt-free and thing-free non-ego. By the same token, the absence becomes intensely present. This fusion carries overtones of the mystic communion, and is different in kind from all existence in the "body of clay", while in Ralegh the blessed souls merely exchange one apparel for a more perfect one.
    The other comparison concerns Ralegh's lines "At the clear wells / Where sweetness dwells, / Drawn up by saints in crystal buckets. / And when our bottles and all we / Are fill'd with immortality...". The configuration "wells" and "Drawn up [...] in crystal buckets" calls for a comparison to an image by the eleventh-century Hebrew poet Ibn Gabirol, giving an account of the creation of the world out of light (discussed at greater length below, in Chapters 11–12):

5.   And it draweth from the Fountain of Light *without a bucket,*

which contains similar elements. Ralegh's phrase *"crystal* buckets" is an additional instance of his consistent poetic strategy of upgrading from second to first class. The buckets are the same as the ones on this side of the ultimate limit, only made of a purer substance. Ibn Gabirol, by contrast, generates a powerful metaphysical conceit. The metaphorical contradiction is inherent in the phrase "the Fountain of Light"; the italicised prepositional phrase appears to be redundant. However, it seems to have here a twofold purpose. First, it prevents "fountain" from becoming a dead metaphor—by forcing the reader to accept "fountain" literally and then delete those features that are incompatible with "light". Second, it merely pretends to eliminate the bucket from the context; in fact, it does the exact opposite: it introduces the bucket where it was not required at all, domesticating the sublime act of creation.

To be sure, Ralegh too has recourse to some of the poetic devices we typically find in our other texts. In the lines "At the clear wells / Where sweetness dwells" he uses a construction which we have already encountered and are going to encounter time and again. The abstraction "sweetness" is a nominalised attribute of "wells" ("sweet wells")—manipulated into the referring position, and amplified in consciousness by two predicates of action ("dwells" and "Drawn up"). In the present context, however, it serves to increase the preciousness of a familiar object rather than induce a perception that is different in kind. The image "And when our bottles and all we/ Are fill'd with immortality" follows the pattern (INFINITE) ABSTRACTION in (LIMITED) SPACE, frequently endorsed by a romantic vision of supersensuous presence. But its effect is local, and cannot change the anthropomorphic character of the description as a whole.

Transcendence and the Meaning of Life

In this section we will consider issues related to the final limit and transcendence as embodied in an ideological controversy between a Hebrew prophet and a pagan philosopher in the biblical verse drama *Tyre and Jerusalem* by the Hebrew poet Matityahu Shoham. They appear to be making statements about the nature of the universe, Man's destiny and his relation to the universe, rather than suggesting the subjective experience of coping with them. As we will soon discover, however, even here the abstract arguments cannot escape the effects of the verbal subtleties in which they are actualised. As a result, it suggests not only what the protagonists *think* of the nature of the universe, but also how they *feel* it. In the second act, Shoham contrives an encounter between the Prophet Elijah and Akhikar, a wise man from Tyre, on the edge of the wilderness. In their dialogue, the prophet and the philosopher expound their contrasting world views, precisely on the ultimate limit. These views conform with our foregoing discussion of Man as hemmed in by the ultimate boundary. Let us have a look at the following section from their exchange of ideas (my translation):

6.   Akhikar: It's good, indeed, to sit
       Face to face—not worrying about the light
       Of future.
       Elijah: Cursed be he who gropes in his darkness

And is content.
Akhikar: Cursed be he who ravages Man's
Lair, wherever he found repose—
What will you give him in return?
Elijah (after brief silence): A chariot of fire,
Old man.
Akhikar: Why should he want
Your horses of fire, and is there a place to fly to?
Listen to me, Prophet: leave him, and his darkness,
And his dung alone—only so will you do him good.
[...]
Akhikar: There is no deliverance!... There is human suffering, a swaying
            shadow
Shedding the leaves of its days without relief
To the abyss of eternity that closes in upon one's bountifulness.
                    With bitter irony
I have just come, loitered for a minute here
And there—and I am already harvesting eighty years,
And my shadow already stole over all the roads...
And where is your miracle, Prophet, where is your deliverance?
        Elijah (staring at the clouds of the sun at the border of the wilderness,
                    as if speaking to himself):
Yet, there is... someone who drives
Every day an iron harness from the stable of the East [...]
Tell me, old man:
What will be left to you from the Universe, at the final resolution,
When the time of accounting comes, if you deny
The wonder of Man?
Akhikar (bitterly): His nothingness, his hardship... One miserable
            account
In Tyre and Jerusalem.

Shoham's *dramatis personae* are engaged here directly in the issue: what is and is not beyond the ultimate boundary. The prophet proposes a chariot of fire, in a figurative sense, for transcending the ultimate boundary. He has great expectations for man. Therefore he curses anyone "who gropes in his darkness and is content". The wise man of Tyre, Akhikar, believes, by contrast, that there is no place to emigrate to from this world. Beyond the ultimate boundary there is nothing but the "abyss of eternity", and therefore Man has no use for the prophet's "horses of fire". Thus, he advises the prophet to reverse his attitude. It is the answer to this question that gives meaning to the suffering and destiny of Man.[11] What is or is not beyond the ultimate boundary determines the destiny of Man and the meaning of his suffering. If there is no place to fly to by the chariot of fire, the most one may aspire to is a comfortable lair for man, "wherever he found repose".

Nothingness and the Mystic Oxymoron

To conclude this discussion of *Tyre and Jerusalem,* it must be pointed out that Akhikar presents, very much like Beckett, e.g., a world view that conceives of Man as hemmed in on all sides by the ultimate limit, beyond which there is nothing—it cannot be transcended. But unlike Beckett, he does not resort to a style that is characteristic of the absurd, or literature of extreme situations. Like his antagonist in the play, the prophet Elijah, he uses figurative language in a way that is basically characteristic of romantic poetry, even though it contains here and there elements that are characteristical of metaphysical poetry. In view of this observation, it might be illuminating to consider at some length his image: "Shedding the leaves of its days without relief/ To the abyss of eternity". Akhikar's eternal abyss can be compared to the abyss in varieties of mysticism or baroque and romantic poetry. All of them suggest that beyond the ultimate limit there is an eternal abyss, or nothingness, or the like. However, when Akhikar says "abyss" he means absolute void, nothingness. In mysticism or baroque and romantic poetry, by contrast, the abyss, or nothingness, or infinitude mean something very different. Consider Milton's account of what appears to be the creation of the universe out of nothing:

> 7.   Boundless the deep, because I am who fill
>   Infinitude, nor vacuous the space.
>   *(Paradise Lost* VII: 168–169)

This is, according to Scholem, the mystics' position too:

> The mystics, too, speak of creation out of nothing; in fact, it is one of their favourite formulae. [...] This *Nothing* from which everything has sprung is by no means a mere negation; only to us does it present no attributes because it is beyond reach of intellectual knowledge. [...] In a word, it signi-

---

[11] "Shedding the leaves of its days" involves an interesting ambiguity in Hebrew. The Hebrew word *ṭarfey* may mean here either "leaves of a tree", or the "detachable daily leaves of a calendar". Days (a metonymy for time) are perceived as leaves shed one by one into nothingness, that disappear in the abyss; the fleeting-time aspect of the image is reinforced by the detachable leaves of the calendar. Human time is meaningless: it leads to nothingness.

fies the Divine itself, in its most impenetrable guise (Scholem, 1955: 25).[12]

In view of such a conception of nothingness, we should not be surprised if in mystic or baroque or romantic poetry nothingness functioned differently from Akhikar's musings on the eternal abyss that renders any attempt to transcend the ultimate limit futile. Let us compare, then, Akhikar's image to a fairly similar one in a sonnet by Keats:

8.   ...then on the shore
            Of the wide world I stand alone and think
            Till Love and Fame to nothingness do sink.
                              (Keats, "When I have fears")

In Akhikar's image, the leaves=days are shed into the abyss, where they disappear for ever. The same happens, apparently, in Keats's sonnet to "Love and Fame" which sink and dissolve into nothingness. In these lines, the ultimate limit is not perceived as some impenetrable obstacle, but as "the shore of the wide world". The speaker stands face to face with the infinite abyss beyond the shore which, far from being inaccessible, threatens to suck up and dissolve his defenseless self. One of the underlying principles of the present work (to be discussed at length in the subsequent chapters) is that the imaginative activation of spatial orientation mechanisms in poetry (as well as in meditation) may activate certain diffuse mental processes that underlie altered states of consciousness. The image of the poet standing on the shore of the wide world vis-a-vis the abyss beyond the ultimate limit may be conducive to such "mystic" mental processes. But while Akhikar's abyss suggests the complete cessation of existence, the abolishment of all mental activity, Keats's image suggests a process that leads to a highly-activated mental state that involves

---

[12] One of the great commonplaces of theology is that certain things about God can be said only by negation. God is nothing we know: He is wise without wisdom, good without goodness etc. We will encounter Rudolf Otto's handling of this issue. Derrida and some associated theoreticians (see Budick and Iser 1989) are very much interested in "the presence of the absence"; but they are more interested in what it means than how words can convey what it feels like (we will explore this issue in chapter 5, in relation to Andreas Gryphius' and Wordsworth's sonnets; see also our discussion of excerpts 8, 9 and 10 here). Derrida formulated this commonplace as follows:

> [Negative theology] is always occupied with letting a superessential reality go beyond the finite categories of essence and existence, that is, of presence, and always hastens to remind us that, if we deny the predicate of existence to God, it is in order to recognize him as a superior, inconceivable, and ineffable mode of being (Derrida, 1973: 134–135)

self-abandonment, and self-oblivion, what some mystics call "peak experience". Ronsard, as we have seen, perceives the fulfilment of life in one's "return to the nothingness which he was". William James quotes an illuminating description of such a state from a letter by Tennyson: "all at once, as it were out of the intensity of the consciousness of individuality, individuality itself seemed to dissolve and fade away into boundless being [...] where death was an almost laughable impossibility—the loss of personality (if so it were) seeming no extinction, but the only true life" (James, 1902: 384n).

Thus, the much more intensely sensed poetic quality of "transcendence" in Keats' lines is not just the outcome of a different theological attitude to the essence of nothingness. In the preceding chapters we have mentioned the emotional pattern "emotive crescendo", where tension and energy gradually build up, leading to some peak experience. In some of Keats's sonnets death or nothingness occurs precisely at the peak of such a pattern, in the final couplet: ecstasy is achieved by using death-imagery in a context of intense passion. The "emotive crescendo" enhances the sensed quality of transcendence. Suppose someone tells us "I have just entered a mystic state of self-oblivion". He will not sound very credible. As long as he can tell he is in a state of self-oblivion, it is no real self-oblivion. Death or nothingness, by contrast, are states in which the actively organising mind is suspended, objects that have stable characteristic shapes disappear. When a poem presents death or nothingness at the peak of some gradually mounting intense emotional experience— this is the nearest a poetic code can come to presenting an intense state of self-oblivion by way of "showing" rather than "telling".

Thus, we can add to the three techniques mentioned at the beginning of this chapter some specific means that enhance the total affect. If appresentation and negativity are the elements that form what I called "the [implicit] suggestion that beyond some inaccessible or impenetrable barrier there exists an unseen reality", then "emotive crescendo" is a poetic pattern that amplifies the sensed quality of transcendence.

Let us consider the endings of some additional sonnets in which Keats achieves his "many havens of intensity".

> 9.   Still, still to hear her tender-taken breath,
>   And so live ever—or else swoon to death.
>   (Keats, "Bright Star")

> 10.   Love, Fame and Beauty are intense indeed,
>   But death intenser; Death is Life's high meed.
>   (Keats, "Why did I laugh?")

This reconciliation of opposites is what Kenneth Burke calls "the mystic oxymoron". "Identification in itself is a kind of transcendence. [...] So identification attains its ultimate expression in mysticism, the identification of the infinitesimally frail with the infinitely powerful. Modes of identification with the 'sublime' in nature would then be analyzable as large 'fragments' of the mystical motive" (Burke,

1962: 850). Thus, the individual becomes "infinitely powerful" and *"lost* in the in-finitely powerful" at one and the same time. In chapter 9 we will discuss such states under the heading of the Freudian term "oceanic dedifferentiation". In the foregoing instances, it threatens with the suspension of boundaries between self and not-self. It is an experience that points toward what may be characterised in Ehrenzweig's words as "Oceanic dedifferentiation [that] is felt and feared as death itself". But having over-come that fear, the individual may experience what is very much like a mental trans-port from the contemplation of divine things.

The combination of nothingness or death with exceptionally high mental energy yields, then, an oxymoron, whether explicitly stated or implied. The "alchemy" of this figure is remarkable; it serves to evoke a quality that seems to be inaccessible to our rational faculties: that of ecstasy. In one respect, death and ecstasy are irrecon-cilable opposites. Death is a state in which vital force is totally absent, whereas ec-stasy is a state in which all the forces of the psyche are mobilised to an extreme de-gree; hence the apparent contradiction. In another respect, however, the two states are similar: in both, the everyday rational faculties disappear: in death, through the dis-appearance of all functions; in ecstasy, because our rational faculties are absorbed in the overwhelming experience of the *whole* self. The use of the word *ecstasy* itself or any of its synonyms may tend to classify this state conceptually under one fixed cat-egory, whereas the use of this most irrational of figures tends to keep categories fluid. The energy built up in the course of a poem, ending in a *fortissimo,* fulfils a double function in this scheme. On the one hand, it constitutes one of the incompat-ible terms of the figure. On the other hand, incompatible terms may generate a witty quality. As we will see in chapter 8, one of the features that may turn bold, potentially witty, figures into the exponents of a sweeping emotional experience is an extreme change in the level of psychic energy. Furthermore, since the contradiction between the death-imagery and the level of high energy usually remains implicit, the element of sharp contradiction is "mitigated", as "Longinus" would have put it—even where both incompatible terms come explicitly to the fore, as in the emotive *fortissimo* of Keats's "Bright Star" (excerpt 9). Here, the disjunction *or* mitigates the contradiction, smoothing over the opposition on the surface. Even though the opposition "live" ~ "death" is reinforced by the opposition "ever" ~ "swoon", with its element of *sudden change* of mental state, the rational mind is appeased so as to accept these incompatible terms; however, in the domain of poetry, whenever one says "this *or* that", the depth-mind perceives "this *and* that".

On the basis of the above, it seems possible to identify the following typical fea-tures of ecstasy as a peak experience of transcendence in poetry: emotional intensity (or, rather, intensified emotions), the experiencing of union sometimes involving dissolution of the self, and insight into some inaccessible reality. It is hard to tell which of the three is to be regarded as the causal antecedent of the other two. Perhaps the process varies from case to case; maybe the ecstatic experience occurs only when the three are present simultaneously.

The Teleological and the Interpersonal Models of Transcendence

I have discussed Kaufman's (1972) conception of the ultimate boundary and the mystic effort to reach beyond it; I have also explored some aspects of mystic and Romantic poetry devoted to such an effort. In explaining the nature of the *"ultimate limit"*, Kaufman points out four fundamental types of limiting experience in everyday life which supply models with the aid of which the ultimate Limit can be conceived. In the following chapter of his book, he makes a further distinction, between two models of transcendence (and of God) based, again, on everyday life experiences: the *interpersonal* and the *teleological* model. The former assumes that "insofar as our knowledge of another self emerges within the process of communication, we are here encountering a reality which is, strictly speaking, beyond the reach and observation of our senses, which, therefore, must be understood in contrast to objects of ordinary sensory perception" (ibid., 74). The latter proceeds from the assumption that "a self is able to formulate objectives, to set them as goals to be realized, and then to organize his life in such a way as to move toward and often to realize them" (ibid., 75). These two models of transcendence lead to quite different theological conceptions. The interpersonal model leads to personalistic notions of ultimate reality, whereas

> If one makes teleological transcendence the model, one is led toward a theology of *being*. The ultimate reality will be understood as the good "which moves [all other things but is] itself unmoved". All finite reality will be viewed as necessarily grounded in this ultimate reality, and as, in turn, striving toward it (ibid., 77).

Mystic attempts to achieve a higher mode of existence by reaching beyond the ultimate limit, by getting a glimpse of the reality beyond it, or dissolving in this reality would be instances of such teleological transcendence. But this "theology of *being*" applies to the very emergence of matter itself as well. One can briefly illustrate this distinction *via* the following verse line by the eleventh-century Hebrew poet, Ibn Gabirol, in which both conceptions are manifest in a peculiar way:

וְהוּא נִכְסָף לְשׁוּמוֹ יֵשׁ כְּמוֹ יֵשׁ / כְּמוֹ חוֹשֵׁק אֲשֶׁר נִכְסָף לְדוֹדוֹ

11. And it is yearning to turn into existence from quasi-existence
    like a lover who is yearning for his belovèd [13]

---

[13] This verse is highly enigmatic in Hebrew, and scholars disagree about its meaning. In my translation I have adopted the majority interpretion. Hebrew has only masculine and feminine third personal pronouns. Consequently, the pronoun here can be translated as "and it" or "and He", referring to God the creator. According to the latter

This line is the sixth in a short philosophical poem ("I love thee with the love of a man to his only one"), the Arabic gloss to which says: "And he had, further, an answer to someone who asked him about the nature of existence". One of the putative meanings of the first hemistich in this line is: "Matter is aspiring to pass from an imperfect mode of existence to a perfect mode of existence". The first hemistich conveys, then, the "teleological model", the "theology of *being"*, whereas the second hemistich conveys a model based on interpersonal love. The two models are stitched together in this verse by the verb *yearning,* a verb with two salient meaning components: [+PURPOSEFUL] and [+INTENSE EMOTION]. According to Kaufman's analysis, moving or striving toward some objective is of the essence of the "teleological model"; the component [+INTENSE EMOTION] is less relevant to this model. The simile in the second hemistich, by contrast, serves to accentuate precisely this component. Thus, the verse focuses attention on the *stitch* between the two theological models of ultimate reality (paraphrasing Dr. Johnson, it yokes together the two models with violence). Hence the sense of *splitting the focus of attention* (cf. below, chapter 11), of *metaphysical wit.*

Much (but not all) devotional poetry is based on interpersonal models of transcendence (and of God). Much of mystic poetry, and much of Romanticism's craving for the infinite, is based on the kind of teleological transcendence suggested by Kaufman. Some of the relevant issues will be touched upon in later chapters.

This distinction receives an interesting twist when we look at the metaphorical "chariot of fire" from Shoham's dialogue. Elijah's "chariot of fire" metaphor antici-pates the literal "chariot of fire and horses of fire", which were to take him "by a whirlwind into heaven" (2 Kings 2, 11–12). But from literal to figurative meaning the image underwent an interesting transformation, unfolding the two models of transcendence. In the Biblical story, the interpersonal model of transcendence is dom-inant. In the drama, too, such verse lines as "Yet, there is... someone who drives/ Every day iron harness from the stable of East" evoke the interpersonal model. But "chariot of fire" as a metaphor for transcendence makes a sudden shift to a teleologi-cal model, and becomes a powerful metaphor for *striving toward* the ultimate reality. At the same time, the reader or spectator familiar with the Biblical text may perceive here an intense dramatic irony.

These two models result in two ways of transcendentally identifying with reality. Keats's lines in excerpt 6 may well suggest transcendence of the *teleological* kind. In Goethe's *Faust,* too, identification is usually *teleological.* One of the most conspicuous instances of a revelation of the *interpersonal* kind is Faust's encounter with the Earth Spirit conjured up in his study. There is a reddish flame to heighten the numinous awe when the Earth Spirit appears. The dialogue suggests an

interpretation (suggested by Vajda, 1957), both hemistichs suggest the interpersonal model.

interpersonal encounter; such exclamations of Faust as "Terrible to see!" suggest numinous awe. Faust sums up this experience as follows:

> 12. When that ecstatic moment held me,
>   I felt myself so small, so great ...
>   (626–627)

The scene consists of the perception of a personal representation of some ultimate reality, usually inaccessible to ordinary senses; it also involves tremendous energy, and "the mystic oxymoron".

Another illuminating case of combining the two kinds of transcendence is found in excerpt 4 above. The first tercet explores how death may lead to a higher mode of existence by reaching beyond the ultimate limit, both in the teleological and the interpersonal mode. What is more, the former is perceived as leading to the latter. The ascending modes of existence are suggested both by the threefold exclamative predicates: "Heureux ... plus heureux ... plus heureux ...", and their subject clauses. In the first two units there is a deep-seated paradox. In the first of the three sentences the predicate "hereux" refers to a "non-subject", so to speak, "qui ne fut onc!". It should be noticed that it does not say "who has not been born" (that is, someone who does exist but whose turn to be born has not yet come); it says "who never was" (that is, who never existed), generating the paradox. In the second one, "nothingness" is equated with "being: "En *rien,* comme il *était*". These things being analogous, one may perceive a course of development. There is a grammatical gradation in the three sentences, foregrounded by their gradually growing length. There is also a positive statement in terms of interpersonal transcendence ("plus heureux qui séjourne, / D'homme fait nouvel ange, auprès de Jésus-Christ") gradually emerging from a sequence of paradoxical statements concerning being, or rather non-being: first as a paradoxical happy non-subject, then happy nothingness resulting from the dissolution of a former ego. This, in turn, is finally individuated in an anthropomorphic state of blessedness, as a new angel dwelling at the side of Jesus Christ, as the highest state of existence.

The second tercet literally enacts transcendence through the separation of the soul from the body, capturing, as it were, the moment when one mode of existence is changed into another. The identification of the human body with earth goes back to the creation of man in the Book of Genesis. The returning of "ashes to ashes, earth to earth" at death, and the conception of death as the separation of the body of *clay* from the soul has a venerable ancestry in the poetry of the Judeo-Christian tradition. To foreground the special characteristic of Ronsard's poem, let us compare its ending to a similar idea expressed by the eleventh-century Hebrew poet Shlomo Ibn Gairol, who ends one of his poems of wisdom with the following two verses:

> יְמֵי חַיֵּי אֱנוֹשׁ יִשָּׂא עֲמָלִים / וְיִשָּׂא אַחֲרִיתוֹ גוּשׁ וְרִמָּה
> וְתָשֹׁב הָאֲדָמָה לָאֲדָמָה / וְתַעַל הַנְּשָׁמָה לַנְּשָׁמָה

13. All his life man bears sufferings /
        and at his end he bears clod and worm
     And the earth will return to the earth /
        and the soul will ascend to the Soul

Here the ultimate fortunes of the body and the soul after death are expressed by parallel co-ordinate sentences, symmetrically. The sharpening of the opposition between body and soul, the opposite definite directions of the (finite) verbs of motion ("return" and "ascend"), and the symmetrical structure bestow upon this verse a sense of equilibrium and finality. A lasting stable order is achieved.

Ronsard's poem, as I said, captures the same process *in medias res,* at an unsettled, mutable stage. For this end, he deviates from the ordinary use of verbal structures. While in Ibn Gabirol's poem the body and the soul are the syntactic agents and the actions attributed to them are expressed by finite verbs of motion, in Ronsard's poem the same development is expressed in a succession of states rather than actions: syntactically, it consists of a long series of adverbials of state. Consider the last clause of the poem: "qui séjourne, / D'homme fait nouvel ange, auprès de Jésus-Christ, / Laissant pourrir çà-bas sa dépouille de boue, / [...] Franc des liens du corps pour n'être qu'un esprit". All this constitutes a single clause, which serves as the subject of an exclamatory sentence ("hereux"). This longish sequence contains only one finite verb, "séjourne" (i.e., sojourn, stay for a while), suggesting a state rather than movement or change. The completion of the threefold gradation, the static verb suggesting lack of progress, and the apparent coincidence of the sentence ending with the first tercet's ending, arouse a sense of a complete, closed unit.

The sequel, however, reopens this closed unit by a long series of adverbials of state governed by the preceding verb, generating a sense of fluidity. Then it ends, significantly, with an adverbial of purpose ("pour n'être qu'un esprit"), *in medias res,* so to speak. Thus, the whole "story" is told through a sequence of states rather than a sequence of more conclusive finite verbs, using such nonfinite verbs as a present participle ("Laissant"), infinitives ("pourrir", "n'être qu'un"), or an adjective ("Franc"), or an appositive phrase containing a past participle as well ("D'homme fait nouvel ange"). The main predicate of the exclamatory sentence "heureux", too, denotes a state of mind ("happy"). This long subject clause is interrupted by an adjective clause, in which "his body of clay" is the patient, not the agent of the finite verb "se joue" (play); "fate and fortune and destiny" are the agents. A special tiptoe effect is achieved by the concluding negative prepositional phrase "pour n'être qu'un esprit". It suggests a purpose, that is, an intended, desired result, not yet reached. In contrast to Ibn Gabirol's poem, this poem achieves no stability; it ends at a transitory, intermediate point of a process—both the process and the poem are felt to remain incomplete, in the very *process of* "striving toward" the ultimate reality. Notwithstanding this, the all-exclusive double negation ("nothing but" for "only") introduces an overtone of conclusiveness into this volatile state of affairs.

Creature-Feeling: Man as Earthworm

Man's sense of finitude and limitedness is sometimes expressed by presenting him as infinitely small, or insignificant, or of limited faculties. Akhikar's phrase "leave him, and his darkness,/ And his dung alone" suggests the image of an earthworm. In this section I will compare this image to two additional literary earthworms. The first one is by the great eleventh-century Hebrew poet Ibn Gabirol, in one of his devotional poems:

לְפָנֶיךָ אֲנִי נֶחְשָׁב בְּעֵינַי / כְּתוֹלַעַת קְטַנָּה בַּאֲדָמָה

> 14.   In your presence I am considered in my own eyes /
>   as a small worm in the soil.

The first element Rudolf Otto points out in the numinous is what he calls "creature-feeling" or "feeling of dependence": Otto illustrates it by the episode when Abraham ventures to plead with God for the men of Sodom, saying (*Gen.* 18, 27): "'Behold now, I have taken upon me to speak unto the Lord, which am but dust and ashes'. [...] It is the emotion of a creature, submerged and overwhelmed by its own nothingness in contrast to that which is supreme above all creatures" (Otto, 1959: 23-24). In Ibn Gabirol's verse line, the worm serves as a strikingly exemplary representation of the speaker's feeling of nothingness, his "creature-feeling" as analysed nine centuries later by Rudolf Otto. Other potentials of the image are not exploited. In the other two excerpts this, and much more, is suggested.

In Goethe's *Faust,* the protagonist uses the earthworm image to enforce a contrast between himself and his small-minded famulus, Wagner.

> 15.   mit gier'ger Hand nach Schätzen gräbt,
>   und froh ist, wenn er Regenwürmer findet!
>
>   which digs with hand for buried ore,
>   and, when it finds an angleworm, rejoices.

This description could be literally true. Nevertheless, it is perceived as figurative language, owing to three of its aspects. First, it is out of keeping with the literal situation. Second, two different potentials of digging are exploited: looking for buried treasures, and looking for angleworms. Thus, finding one instead of the other realises two different potentials of one image. Third, the things sought or found become strikingly exemplary illustrations of something hard-to-access and valuable, and something easily-accessible and worthless, respectively; and in combination, of a mind marked by pettiness, narrowness, or meanness. Rather than suggesting some identity between the angleworm and Wagner, or Wagner's spirit, the angleworm is only a metonymy: it is suggested that Wagner's spirit *is content with digging out* an angleworm.

In Shoham's play, too, the small-minded and the "Faustian" man are contrasted. Here they are not represented by two persons—there are two conflicting interpretations of the essence of Man. Elijah's "chariot of fire" becomes a metaphor for Man who has an "aspiring mind" (to use Marlowe's phrase in *Tamburlaine),* who aspires to transcend all the boundaries, even the ultimate one. But what is more significant is the worm's relationship to the perceiving consciousness. In Goethe the angleworm is an external entity, merely the object of perception, the petty cause that is sufficient to satisfy Wagner's spirit. In Shoham, by contrast, the earthworm is identified with the perceiving consciousness. The external world for it is not merely an external object for perception. It is the space in which it locates itself and from which it receives self-specifying information. In Goethe there is a distinct boundary between self (Wagner) and not self (angleworm); Akhikar's metaphor is a typical example of blurred, or even suspended, boundaries between Man and worm, worm and dung. Dung and darkness suggest something repulsive on the one hand, and restricted perspectives on the other—the earthworm feels comfortable in what is repulsive, and in its restricted perspectives. Thus for Wagner, as described by Faust, the angleworm suggests a way of *judging* the value of things. For Akhikar it suggests a way of *feeling* the world. The only sense the earthworm has is tactile, making it capable of such immediate sensations as warmth; it has no senses for remote perception, such as seeing, hearing, or smelling. It is capable of sensing the pleasurable warmth of the dung, but not its repulsiveness, nor of perceiving what, we know, is beyond the dunghill. As to Man, Akhikar believes there is nothing beyond the huge dunghill in which he lives.

God's Telephone Number

I have discussed above at considerable length the archetypal situation in which, according to Kaufman, people use "God-talk". "Such speech appears", says Kaufman, "within the context of man's sense of limitation, finitude, guilt, and sin, on the one hand, and his question about the meaning or value or significance of himself, his life, and his world, on the other". In this respect, he says, the idea of God functions as a *limiting concept,* that is, a concept that refers to that which we do *not* know but which is the ultimate limit of all our experiences. I suggested that romantic and metaphysical poetry set themselves to *transcend* the limit; I have shown this regarding romantic poetry, and will demonstrate it with respect to metaphysical poetry as well, in chapter 6. We have seen that for Akhikar, the wise man of Tyre in Shoham's play, any attempt to transcend this world is utterly futile; this is also the case with some more modernistic kinds of literature, as with the drama of the absurd, which acknowledges only man's sense of limitation, but nothing beyond the ultimate limit—"God is dead".

One of the basic assumptions of the present work is that in poetry adaptation mechanisms are put to aesthetic use. Emotion and wit are just such adaptation mechanisms, devised for coping with rapidly changing realities. Accordingly, in Western literature there are two major poetic traditions, that of "high-seriousness", and the "line of wit". Romanticism and most kinds of mysticism typically exploit "high-serious" emotions; the various kinds of mannerism, that is, *précieux* and metaphysical poetry, absurd drama, and some kinds of modernism, exploit various degrees of wit. While *précieux* poetry uses wit playfully, most of the other kinds of mannerism have recourse to wit as a device for coping with the complexities of a world run wild, where sudden and fast readjustments are required. The particular effect of such literature arises from the witty treatment of extremely grave issues. In such instances, rather than treating those grave issues lightly, wit assumes their gravity.

Neo-classic theoreticians spent much effort on distinguishing between true and false wit. One of the most fruitful distinctions is due to Joseph Addison: true wit consists in the similarity of ideas, false wit in the similarity of words. This distinction is very intriguing and useful as long as we ignore the value judgments, suggested by terms like "true" and "false". For our purpose, this principle can be extended as "true" wit consists in the similarity of signifieds, "false wit" in the similarity of signifiers. In some varieties of mannerism we find precisely this kind of "false wit" exploited for coping with "the terrible seriousness of life".

Wit in this kind of literature is frequently perceived as the drastic amplification of an attitude more properly termed "irony". "What an ironic observer typically feels in the presence of an ironic situation may be summed up in three words: superiority, freedom, amusement" (Muecke, 1970: 36–37). From this point of view, "the pure or archetypal ironist is God—'He that sitteth in the heavens shall laugh: the Lord shall have them in derision'. He is the ironist par excellence because he is omniscient, omnipotent, transcendent, absolute, infinite, and free. [...] The archetypal victim of irony is man, seen, per contra, as trapped and submerged in time and matter, blind, contingent, limited, and unfree—and confidently unaware that this is his predicament" (Muecke, 1970: 37–38). As we have seen, Akhikar, in Shoham's play, resorts to an essentially romantic imagery in expressing his attitude that "God is dead". He treats man as the archetypal victim of irony, as trapped and submerged in time and matter, blind, contingent, limited, and unfree.

In what follows, we will consider a poem by the great Hebrew poet Yehuda Amikhai (16), that resorts to absurd and witty strategies to indicate that there is no ultimate reality that might render our life, death, and experience meaningful. Here the implied author becomes "the pure or archetypal ironist"; God is perhaps nonexistent or, at best, himself the victim of irony; those who habitually use "God-talk" are blind, and contingent—and confidently unaware that this is their predicament.

אַחֲרֵי אוֹשְׁוִיץ אֵין תֵּאוֹלוֹגְיָה:
מֵאֲרֻבּוֹת הַוַּתִּיקָן עוֹלֶה עָשָׁן לָבָן,
סִימָן שֶׁהַקַּרְדִּינָלִים בָּחֲרוּ לָהֶם אַפִּיפְיוֹר.
מִמִּשְׂרְפוֹת אוֹשְׁוִיץ עוֹלֶה עָשָׁן שָׁחוֹר
סִימָן שֶׁהָאֱלֹהִים טֶרֶם הֶחְלִיטוּ עַל בְּחִירַת
הָעָם הַנִּבְחָר.
אַחֲרֵי אוֹשְׁוִיץ אֵין תֵּאוֹלוֹגְיָה:
הַמִּסְפָּרִים עַל אַמּוֹת אֲסִירֵי הַהַשְׁמָדָה
הֵם מִסְפְּרֵי הַטֶּלֶפוֹן שֶׁל הָאֱלֹהִים
מִסְפָּרִים שֶׁאֵין מֵהֶם תְּשׁוּבָה
וְעַכְשָׁו הֵם מְנֻתָּקִים אֶחָד, אֶחָד.

אַחֲרֵי אוֹשְׁוִיץ יֵשׁ תֵּאוֹלוֹגְיָה חֲדָשָׁה:
הַיְּהוּדִים שֶׁמֵּתוּ בַּשּׁוֹאָה
נַעֲשׂוּ עַכְשָׁו דּוֹמִים לֵאלֹהֵיהֶם
שֶׁאֵין לוֹ דְּמוּת הַגּוּף וְאֵין לוֹ גּוּף.
שֶׁאֵין לָהֶם דְּמוּת הַגּוּף וְאֵין לָהֶם גּוּף.

16.   After Auschwitz there is no theology:
       From the chimneys of the Vatican white smoke rises,
       It is a sign that the cardinals have chosen their Pope.
       From the crematories of Auschwitz black smoke rises
       It is a sign that the Gods have not yet decided upon to choose
       The chosen people.
       After Auschwitz there is no theology:
       The numbers on the extermination prisoners' forearms
       Are God's telephone numbers
       Numbers that do not respond
       And now are disconnected one by one.

       After Auschwitz there is a new theology:
       The Jews who died in the Holocaust
       Came to resemble now their God
       Who has no body image and no body.
       Who have no body image and no body.

The line "After Auschwitz there is no theology" is a straightforward, apparently nonfigurative statement. It is the basis of a repetitive scheme that constitutes the poem's structural skeleton. It occurs at the beginning and middle of this poem; then a third, altered version occurs: "After Auschwitz there is a new theology". Ballad and drama critics call such a threefold repetition *significant variation*. This is "a type of structure in which the effect is secured by an alteration in a pattern of action which has become familiar by repetition" (Brooks and Heilman, 1966, Glossary: 51). Here it imposes unity on the apparently unrelated images; obstinately reiterates a certain claim; and, eventually, as we shall see, affects the meaning in at least two interesting ways.

This baffling poem is infused with a perception that the universe is irrational and meaningless and that the search for order brings the individual into conflict with the universe. Theology is the study of God, His attributes and His relations to the world. The straightforward, unqualified statement "After Auschwitz there is no theology" is conspicuously dispassionate but also conspicuously false. On second thought, however, "there is no theology" may be construed as "we know there is no God to study", or "theology must lay down its arms: anything it may have to say is inadequate, or irrelevant". Kenneth Burke wrote somewhere that theologians must always cheat when they want to explain the existence of evil in a world created by an omnipotent and wholly good God; and there is no evil like Auschwitz.

Lines 2–3 refer to the procedure for electing the Pope. On first sight, this may be construed as "having to do with theology"— although it is not quite clear in what sense. But it may also have to do with Auschwitz: Pope Pius XII was sharply criticised for his silence in the face of the Auschwitz atrocities. One of the strongest and most thoroughly-documented pieces of criticism was Rolf Hochhuth's play *Der Stellvertreter* (The Deputy), a German masterpiece translated into Hebrew by Amikhai. Both God and His deputy were silent when the Holocaust took place. Lines 2–6 offer a brilliant piece of "false wit". They juxtapose two similar signifiers, the signifieds of which seem to have nothing in common: the white smoke of the Vatican and the black smoke of Auschwitz. The reader may compare these two images, but at his own risk: the speaker pretends to make no suggestion that he should do so. Apparently, the two kinds of smoke are signs of the same sort: white smoke is a sign that a decision has been made; black smoke—that no decision has yet been made. In this way, white and black smoke become quite straightforwardly opposite signs. But this construal is misleading at best. Smoke as a sign of decision or indecision is an artificial sign. The smoke from the crematories, however, is a different, more natural kind of sign. We have quoted Knoblauch above on appresentation: "While perceiving an object, we almost automatically 'appresent' that the object has an unseen background. By appresentation we refer to the connection between the object or event directly experienced and the object or event which is not immediately present to experience but constituted by our consciousness". The inmates of Auschwitz directly saw and smelled the black smoke, and became aware of its natural source: that inside the buildings living human beings were being mass-murdered in gas chambers and then cremated in crematories. Hebrew has one verb for electing and choosing. Thus, again, two similar words rather than similar ideas are juxtaposed: electing a pope, and choosing the chosen people. Thus, a very loose connection is established between electing a pope and choosing the chosen people; between the pope and Auschwitz; between being the chosen people and being relentlessly mass-murdered; between mass-murder, the pope, and the study of God, His attributes and His relations to the world. The implied author makes no such explicit statement as "All this is absurd or appalling". There is considerable uncertainty as to whether one ought to, or may not, make these connections; but the absurdity of the situation emerges from those juxtapositions.

The sequel of these juxtapositions includes two masterstrokes of "false wit". The first one relies on the word "numbers":

> 17.   The numbers on the extermination prisoners' forearms
>   Are God's telephone numbers
>   Numbers that do not respond
>   And now are disconnected one by one.

The word "numbers" is the same in the different contexts; and it refers to similar digits. What its two tokens stand for, however, have nothing to do with one another: one serves to dehumanise human beings; the other one is a telecommunication device. What Amikhai did was to elaborated his image in a way that suggests an intense network of "Resemblance of Ideas" between the two "numbers", generating unity in variety (cf. my discussion of Herbert's "Anagram" in chapter 8). The phrase "Numbers that do not respond" becomes meaningful in a variety of ways: in the context of telephone dialling, it means that nobody picks up the handset at the other end of the line; in the Auschwitz context, it suggests that human beings who were reduced to numbers and then exterminated, could not respond any more; with respect to God, it suggests indifference, lack of sensitivity or regard for others' needs or troubles. Finally, the phrase "now are disconnected one by one" expresses extermination (of human beings) by literally developing the metaphor "God's telephone numbers". The other piece of "false wit" occurs at the end of the poem:

> 18.   The Jews who died in the Holocaust
>   Came to resemble now their God
>   Who has no body image and no body.
>   Who have no body image and no body.

The last two lines show striking verbal similarities, even stale, monotonous repetition. The verb "resemble", however, only points up the enormous, ironic difference: God has no body image and no body because He is "the wholly other", the purely spiritual; the Jews who died in the Holocaust, by contrast, have no body image and no body, because they were cremated and went up in smoke. Now this piece of "false wit" assumes a quality of inevitability owing to overdetermination by two additional patterns. First, we are told in the Bible that God created Man in his own image. Later Jewish theologians (Maimonides, for instance) felt uneasy about such an anthropomorphic view; for them, whenever God's body parts are mentioned in the Bible, it should be understood metaphorically. Now, at long last, the Jews who died in the Holocaust come to resemble their God not in having faces and hands as the Biblical God, but in having no body image and no body, as suggested by later theology. Second, in an important sense, the two versions of the statement "After Auschwitz there is no theology" are synonymous: both suggest that after Auschwitz the traditional tenets of theology are irrelevant or invalid. The *significant variation* based on the line affects the meaning of the poem in at least two interesting ways. On the one hand, such a significant variation may arouse a feeling that the whole point of this poem was to lead up to this insight. On the other hand, the false wit of the comparison reverses the positive statement into a denial: everything we thought we knew about God, His attributes and His relations to the world is false or irrelevant.

No superlative can do justice to our response to the atrocities of Auschwitz. Irony offers an alternative way of handling it: it has an element of detachment. "We can choose from among a number of terms: detachment, distance, disengagement, freedom, serenity, objectivity, dispassion, 'lightness', 'play', urbanity" (Muecke, 1970: 35). All the statements of Amikhai's poem are characterised by this psychological atmosphere of detachment, distance, or disengagement. The poet works by juxtaposing dispassionate, disengaged, statements based on false analogies, and pretending that those analogies are significant. The verbal resemblance of the last two lines suggests a new harmony between God and his creatures. But this harmonious appearance only points up a reality in which there is a discrepancy between a wholly spiritual almighty God, and the terrible things that happen in His world. These are the new insights of the "new theology".

There are two additional, quite conspicuous techniques by which the ironic effect is generated, or at least reinforced. First, the unmarked way of poetic expression is the use of concrete predicates from which certain significant abstractions are abstracted. "After Auschwitz there is no theology" is, by contrast, an unqualified, apparently nonfigurative, statement in which the predicate is an abstract, learned word, suggesting certain less abstract, nonspecific implications. Such a "marked" construction may have an ironic effect. Second, for reasons beyond our present inquiry, sublime effects or high-serious emotions are typically suggested by natural objects; the introduction of technical inventions or man-made instruments (such as "telephone") may serve to "domesticate" God, and generate an ironic effect.[14]

Thus, the implied author rather than God becomes the supreme or archetypal ironist. As Winner and Gardner suggested,

> The primary function of irony is not to describe something in the world, but to show something about the speaker. Irony functions to show the speaker's attitude toward something, and that attitude is almost always critical [...]. A literal remark [...] is rarely if ever equivalent to an ironic one, because the choice of irony carries with it particular social effects. The ironist is perceived as being a certain kind of person—wittier, less confrontational, and more in control, than the utterer of a literal expression of dis-

---

[14] Cf. my discussion of Ibn Gabirol's "To draw from the source of light without a bucket" above, and in chapter 11.

pleasure [...]. The achievement of these side effects may be one of the primary determinants for a choice of irony over literal discourse (Winner and Gardner, 1993: 429).

Another side effect may be this: where literal discourse merely imparts knowledge, the false wit and irony of a text allow the reader to have an *insight* into the reality behind the false appearance, exposing their real nature.

According to Kaufman, then, God-talk typically "appears within the context of man's sense of limitation, finitude, guilt, and sin, on the one hand, and his question about the meaning or value or significance of himself, his life, and his world, on the other". After Auschwitz there is only a sense of God's limitation, finitude, guilt and sin or, perhaps even more horrifying, man's certainty that there is nothing beyond the ultimate limit, denying man all meaning or value or significance of himself, his life, and his world. The implied author of Amikhai's poem becomes the archetypal ironist.

To Conclude

Mysticism and romanticism may yield an insight into the "ultimate reality" beyond the ultimate limit; false wit and irony may yield insight into the true reality behind the false appearance. This needs some qualification. In extra-literary discourse, the phrase "insight into the ultimate reality" presupposes the existence of an "ultimate reality"; in a poem it requires only some detectable correlates of experiencing such an insight. The constraints of translating from one semiotic system to another (as discussed in chapter 1) should be relevant here. Likewise, the phrase "true reality behind the false appearance" need not (though in some instances it certainly would) affect the reader's extra-literary convictions about, e.g., the existence of God; it may merely evoke the experiencing of a shift from one kind of perception to another. In some kinds of mannerism, false wit has merely a playful quality. But in much metaphysical and modernist poetry it may reveal some deep existential truth of which many people are *confidently unaware*—as in Amikhai's poem (in this case, concerning God, His attributes and His relations to the world). In most mystic and romantic poetry, the striving to transcend the ultimate boundary, or, at least, to have a direct perception of the ultimate reality, becomes a metaphor for the suspension of boundary between self and not-self: the identification of the infinitesimally frail and the infinitely powerful. Thus, transcendence of the ultimate boundary becomes transcendence of the boundaries of self, a kind of "mystic union". Amikhai, by contrast, uses God-talk to ironise the traditional notions of religion, suggesting the opposite of identification: *alienation*.

Chapter 4

Composition of Place, Experiential Set, and the Meditative Poem

Figure 1. Georges de la Tour of Lorraine "La Madeleine au Miroir"

Preliminary—On Jesuit Meditation[1]

Meditation is an "altered state of consciousness". *Altered states of consciousness* are mental states in which adults relinquish to some extent their acquired control of "ordinary consciousness". The first author has elsewhere explored at length the cognitive structure of the poetry of altered states of consciousness (Tsur, 1987a; 1992a: 411–470; 1992b: 111–135; 1998; Glicksohn et al.: 1991).

What kind of "altered state of consciousness" is meditation? To elucidate this, we must first understand how "ordinary consciousness" handles God. For this, one should read perhaps Chapter 1 of Rudolf Otto's admirable book in its entirety; we shall confine ourselves to only one short passage:

> It is essential to every theistic conception of God, and most of all to the Christian, that it designates and precisely characterizes deity by the attributes spirit, reason, purpose, good-will, supreme power, unity, selfhood. The nature of God is thus thought of by analogy with our human nature of reason and personality; only, whereas in ourselves we are aware of this as qualified by restriction and limitation, as applied to God the attributes we use are "completed", i.e. thought as absolute and unqualified. Now all these attributes constitute clear and definite concepts: they can be grasped by the intellect; they can be analyzed by thought; they even admit of definition. An object that can thus be thought conceptually may be termed rational (Otto, 1959: 15).

Meditation attempts to capture something of the non-conceptual, irrational nature of God. Very much like mystic experience, meditation is a mental process in which God is grasped not merely conceptually or analytically, but becomes *experience*. It seems that meditative poetry has the ability to reproduce this experience in part; not necessarily to evoke such a state of mind, but to display some perceptible "meditative quality". We explore the problem with reference to Louis Martz's work on meditative poetry and other meditative art (Martz, 1962). For instance, let us have a look at the frontispiece, Georges de la Tour's painting, and Martz's description of it:

> I do not mean simply the photographic realism of the composition, but rather the way in which every detail of the work is controlled by a human figure in profound meditation. This person's thoughts are not abstract: the left hand, with its sensitive, tapered fingers, probes the eyesocket of a skull; the arm, so delicately clothed, conveys a rude sensation to the brain. Meanwhile the eye is focused on a mirror, where we are accustomed to pursue the work of preparing "a face to meet the faces" that we meet: yet here the inquiring eye meets "the skull beneath the skin," a skull that seems to devour the book on which it rests. Sight and touch, then, meet to form

---

[1] This chapter was written in collaboration with Motti Benari.

these thoughts, meditative, piercing, looking through the mirror, probing whatever lies beyond. [...] (Martz, 1962: 1).

Such meditation is the subject of Martz's study: an intense, imaginative condition that brings together the senses, the emotions, and the intellectual faculties of man; brings them together in a moment of dramatic, creative experience. Martz's mind-expanding description of this painting is representative of the merits and limitations of his book. He gives a thorough description of the mental faculties involved in meditation. Intuitively, they are most relevant to the particular effect of meditation; but he says nothing about the source of this particular effect.

What is it that brings this particular effect about? By what techniques can a text generate what is perceived as the "meditative quality"? We hope to supply part of the answer below. For this, we need to look slightly deeper into the nature of the meditative experience (in its western version). The Jesuit Luis de la Puente gives a most illuminating account of the meditative mental process. It is "a single viewe of the eternall veritye, without variety of discourses penetrating it with the light of heaven, with great affections of admiration, and love; unto which ordinarily no man arriveth, but by much exercize of meditation, and discourse" (Martz 1962: 16). Translating his words into our cognitive terms, we can say that meditation is a holistic, not an analytic or a conceptual, grasp of God ("eternal veritye" in Puente's words); it is charged with great emotional energy ("with great affections of admiration, and love"), leaving no room in the mind for any other thought ("without variety of discourses"). This state can be achieved only through much discipline and exercise, and the whole process has an extraordinary nature.

Ignatius Loyola (1491–1556) was the founder of the Jesuit order, and laid the foundations of a special, spiritual way of prayer and meditation. His "spiritual exercises" are among the most influential meditative texts in western tradition. The first important part of Loyola's method of spiritual meditation requires that the Scriptural text be used as a stimulus for "seeing the places", like a story that the readers become involved in, and imagine themselves being a part of.[2] This method was described in St. Ignatius' book *Spiritual Exercises* and was known later as "the composition of place".[3] Like Ignatian meditative exercises, both metaphysical and romantic lyric poetry typically begin with some well-defined situation. Is this mere coincidence?

---

[2]   The website of the Ignatian Spirituality Centre in Glasgow, Scotland, is the source of this definition: http://www.22auchincruive.ic24.net/home.htm.

[3]   *The Spiritual Exercises of St. Ignatius of Loyola*, Translated into English from Spanish Autograph of St. Ignatius by Father Elder Mullan, S.J. New York: P.J. Kennedy and Sons, 1914. All citations of the exercises in this paper were taken from an Internet site dedicated to The Spiritual Exercises of St. Ignatius of Loyola, and based on Mullan's translation.
URL: http://ccel.org/i/ignatius/exercises/exercises1.0.html

One purpose of cognitive poetics is to relate the structure of texts systematically to their perceived effects, by having recourse to cognitive or neurological hypotheses. In the present chapter we will apply this methodology to relate the practice of "seeing the place" to its reported "meditative" effectiveness. We will make use of terms like *control, orientation* and *diffuseness* to clarify its perceived effect: the non-conceptual meditative quality. This, in turn, may illuminate some questions concerning literary techniques, too.

A crucial distinction must be made between *meditation* proper and the *poetry of meditation*. In Chapters 1 and 2 we argued that reading a meditative poem does not mean that the reader actually *experiences* the meditative process; s/he only *perceives* a "meditative quality" in the poem. The reader does not enter an altered state of consciousness, only detects one in the poem. In a wide range of studies, the first author has applied cognitive research to the emotional qualities of poetry; now we shall apply this methodology, both to *meditation* and to the *poetry of meditation*.

We argue that three main properties of the text are responsible for the meditative quality identified in them. These are:

1. The text's ability to evoke the orientation process.
2. The text's ability to support diffuse perception and encourage divergent ways of processing.
3. The text's ability to integrate with the mental set required for this experience, to wit the absence of purpose, and to supply the conditions that enable such a mental set to exist over time.

"The composition of place", we argue, is an efficient means for generating these effects. The concrete situation evoked is typically detached from daily life, and thus very helpful in establishing the first and third principles, and does not necessarily damage the second one.

Martz emphasizes the importance of "the composition of place": "Among all the varied ways of using the senses and physical life in meditation, the most important, most effective and most famous is the prelude known as the 'composition of place'" (Martz, 1963: XIX). We find this complex procedure to be crucial, and will explore it from the cognitive point of view.

Poetry of Meditation

In the concluding chapter of his book Martz claims that meditative poetry is a genre that satisfies "a natural, fundamental tendency of the human mind to work from a particular situation". It could be written not only in baroque or metaphysical style, but in any poetic style, romantic and modernistic for instance, and should be defined in a way that would include some poems by Wordsworth, Keats, Emily Dickinson and Wallace Stevens. He reviews meditative poetry in a wider historical perspective, explaining the difficulty of defining the genre. Eventually, he points to three major aspects:

But this much, at least, may be said: a meditative poem is a work that creates an interior drama of the mind; this dramatic action is usually (though not always) created by some form of self-address, in which the mind grasps firmly a problem or situation deliberately evoked by the memory, brings it forward toward the full light of consciousness, and concludes with a moment of illumination, where the speaker's self has, for a time, found an answer to his conflicts (Martz, 1962: 330).

Thus, the three aspects are: 1. A self-address that puts in the center of one's conscious attention something that is regularly in the background; 2. Grasping some problem; 3. The emergence of an illumination, which results from this. This third stage frequently takes the form of a "colloquy", that is, "some affectionate speach" or colloquy with God or the saints, in which "wee may talke with God as a servant with his Maister, as a sonne with his Father, as one friend with another, as a spouse with her beloved bridgrome, or as a guilty prisoner with his Judge, or in any other manner which the holy Ghost shall teach us" (Martz, 1963: xviii).

The Composition of Place

In the Ignatian method, the first phase is typically supported by imagining a concrete situation that is detached from daily life. The "composition of place" is described by Ignatius as the necessary first step of meditation; it is the first prelude of all exercises in the first week and, with some variation, of all other exercises as well.[4] The exerciser is not supposed to move on before performing it properly (Ninth Annotation).

Martz characterizes it as "this brilliant Ignatian invention, to which the Jesuit *Exercises* owe a large part of their power" (1963: xix). What is so brilliant about this invention? Why is it so effective? Martz supplies no answer. Instead, he quotes some of the instructions given by the Jesuits themselves:

"We must see", says the English Jesuit Dawson,

the places where the thinges we meditate on were wrought, by imagining our selves to be really present at those places; ... to have noted well the

---

[4]   In Ignatius' words as quoted from the first prelude of the first exercise:
"A composition, seeing the place:
    Here it is to be noted that, in a visible contemplation or meditation—as, for instance, when one contemplates Christ our Lord, Who is visible—the composition will be to see with the sight of the imagination the corporeal place where the thing is found which I want to contemplate. I say the corporeal place, as for instance, a Temple or Mountain where Jesus Christ or Our Lady is found, according to what I want to contemplate... "

> distance from one place to another, the height of the hills, and the situation
> of the townes and villages... (§ 2, ¶ 10) (Martz, 1962: 27)

How can this practice, said to be so brilliant and effective, help the relinquishing of "ordinary consciousness"? Knoblauch (1999: 83), following Schutz, suggests a definition of "ordinary consciousness" that includes the phrase "an attitude of full attention to life". We may add that it requires an "actively organizing mind". By contrast, one of the four *necessary* factors William JamesWilliam discerns in all mystic experience is *Passivity,* when "the mystic feels as if his own will were in abeyance" (James 1902: 381). "Ordinary consciousness" is our way to organize reality; to create, in Meyer's phrase, "a psychological atmosphere of certainty, security, and patent purpose, in which the [perceiver] feels a sense of control and power as well as a sense of specific tendency and definite direction" (Meyer, 1956: 160). "Ordinary consciousness" is one of Man's most impressive achievements. But once achieved, it is hard to relinquish it *voluntarily*. It cannot be done by a mere "switch"; that is why the Jesuits had to have recourse to "spiritual *exercises*". It would appear that the "composition of place" involves something that facilitates this "switch". We argue that this has to do with two main processes induced by the "composition of place":

1. The orientation process and its consequences.
2. The ability to supply an alternative order and an illusion of control in the absence of rational, utilitarian purposiveness.

Orientation

The orientation process has a complex effect on the sense of control. Ascertaining your true position in an unfamiliar environment or atmosphere can definitely help to achieve a sense of control. The self-specifying information of orientation is a way to gain a sense of coordination and some hold on reality. At the same time, orientation processes in the absence of a focus typically result in a holistic mode of processing with a diffuse output that does not provide the means for rational control, and weakens the ability to construct a clear picture of the data, that is so essential for the sense of full control.

As Orenstein (1975) argued most convincingly, meditation, like the emotions, is a typically right-hemisphere brain activity. To understand the overwhelming importance of the "composition of place" for meditation, one should understand the typical way the right hemisphere functions, and how it differs from the left hemisphere.

> If the left hemisphere is specialized for analysis, the right hemisphere [...] seems specialized for holistic mentation. Its language ability is quite limited. This hemisphere is primarily responsible for our orientation in space, artistic endeavour, crafts, body image, recognition of faces. It processes information more diffusely than does the left hemisphere, and its responsibili-

ties demand a ready integration of many inputs at once. If the left hemisphere can be termed analytic and sequential in its operation, then the right hemisphere is more holistic and relational, and more simultaneous in its mode of operation (Orenstein, 1975: 68).

Orenstein's description suggests, then, that the "switch" from "ordinary consciousness" to "meditative consciousness" involves replacing the analytic and sequential information-processing mode with a holistic, relational, and more simultaneous one. Structurally, there is a drastic increase in the diffuseness of the brain's output. This passage may illuminate several aspects of the meditative process as described by Martz and Dawson. First, the right hemisphere's capability for the "ready integration of many inputs at once" may account for the bringing together of "the senses, the emotions, and the intellectual faculties of man in a moment of dramatic, creative experience". The orientation process does not mean just getting a grip on the environment, the atmosphere or the surroundings. Orientation is above all the subject's ability to situate himself in these surroundings, and to ascertain his relation to them. It is never detached from the subject as an objective survey of the world. Indeed, that is the precise procedure aimed at by the Ignatian spiritual exercises.

Second, the claim that "this hemisphere is primarily responsible for our orientation in space" can account for what Dawson describes as "imagining our selves to be really present at those places", and "to have noted well the distance from one place to another, the height of the hills, and the situation of the townes and villages".[5] A heightened awareness of our body image is required for imagining our selves to be really present.

Furthermore, there are good reasons to suppose that the various functions related to the right hemisphere interact with and enhance each other. Deric Bownds (1999: Chapter 7) commented in his book: "Listening to Mozart results in better performance on spatial tasks, and 3-year-old children given weekly piano lessons register 80 percent higher scores in spatial and temporal reasoning than average". Orenstein brings some convincing experimental evidence that when a memory image concerning spatial orientation is called up, the right hemisphere may be activated, even though one is engaged in verbal activity at the time (1975: 77). We suggest that this interaction may gain great importance with reference to the respective operating styles of the two hemispheres.

Orientation processes occur whenever one is located in some unfamiliar environment: an unfamiliar space, time, or atmosphere. When you enter a room with unknown people under unknown circumstances, frequently you resort to what may be called "fast orientation": you collect information with all your senses and faculties, integrating it with an intuitive speed. You perceive the overall atmosphere rather

---

5   Notice, for instance, the portrayal of the fifth exercise, first prelude, which includes the following instruction: "to see with the sight of the imagination the length, breadth and depth of Hell".

than ascertain the stable objects, facts, and logic of the situation. Speed is achieved at the expense of precision. The same happens with orientation in space. This kind of orientation is typically a right-hemisphere activity like emotions or meditation (Orenstein, 1975).

There is no evidence in Orenstein's discussion for our conjecture concerning this effect of the orientation mechanism on meditation and poetic language. But after this article had already been accepted for publication by *Pragmatics and Cognition* we encountered some brain research that may support this conception. Andrew Newberg, Eugene D'Aquili and Vince Rause (2001) conducted a SPECT camera brain-imaging study (the acronym stands for Single Photon Emission Computed Tomography) of Tibetan meditators and Franciscan nuns at prayer. To our pleasant surprise, these researchers claim that what they call the "orientation association area" (OAA) is "extremely important in the brain's sense of mystical and religious experiences, which often involve altered perceptions of space and time, self and ego" (29). This would massively support our speculations above based on the structure of literary texts, introspection, and earlier brain research. Their study attempted to obtain experimental evidence for their claim. They point out that there are two orientation areas, situated at the posterior section of the parietal lobe, one in each hemisphere of the brain:

> The left orientation area is responsible for creating the mental sensation of a limited, physically defined body, while the right orientation area is associated with generating the sense of spatial coordinates that provides the matrix in which the body can be oriented. In simpler terms, the left orientation area creates the brain's spatial sense of self, while the right side creates the physical space in which that self can exist (Newberg, D'Aquili & Rause, 2001: 28).

These researchers found a sharp reduction in the activity levels of the left orientation association area. A SPECT image of the brain's activity during meditation indicates that the activity of "the left orientation area... is markedly decreased compared to the right side" (ibid., 4). They assume that both orientation areas were working as hard as ever, but in the left area the incoming flow of sensory information had somehow been blocked (6).

In a later chapter they highlight the right hemisphere orientation activity during what they call "the active approach" to meditation:

> Active types of meditation begin not with the intention to clear the mind of thoughts, but instead, to focus it intensely upon some thought or object of attention. A Buddhist might chant a mantra, or focus upon a glowing candle or a small bowl of water, for example, while a Christian might pray with the mind trained upon God, or a saint, or the symbol of a cross. For the sake of discussion, let's imagine that the focus of attention is the mental image of Christ. [...] In this case, since the intention is to focus more

intensely upon some specific object or thought, the attention facilitates rather than inhibits, neural flow. In our model, this increased neural flow causes the right orientation area, in conjunction with the visual association area, to fix the object of focus, real or imagined, in the mind (ibid., p. 120).

We consider these findings extremely valuable for interpreting the meditative experience. If the boundaries between self and not self are to be suspended in meditation, that is, if the self is to dissolve in infinite space, the boundaries of the self must be de-emphasized, and the perception of the surrounding space overemphasized. The process must begin, therefore, with activities having opposing effects in the two orientation areas: in the right area "the sense of spatial coordinates that provides the matrix in which the body can be oriented" must be reinforced; in the left area "the mental sensation of a limited, physically defined body" must be reduced. What is more, the diffuse information-processing mode originating in the right hemisphere may help to blur, as an initial step, the mental sensation of a well-defined physical boundary of the body—whatever the later stages of the cognitive and neurological processes. In imaginative processes, objects that have stable characteristic visual shapes enhance the feeling of their separateness and our separateness from them; abstractions as well as gestalt-free and thing-free qualities enhance a feeling of the suspended boundaries.

This might account for certain verbal structures that are quite common in our corpus: these structures draw attention to the surrounding space, but focus on thing-free and gestalt-free entities (such as abstractions) rather than on stable characteristic visual shapes. Consider, for instance, the following phrase from the passage by Dawson quoted above: "to have noted well the distance from one place to another, the height of the hills, and the situation of the townes and villages", or Ignatius' "the length, breadth and depth of Hell" in note 4. Here the focus of attention is shifted from spatio-temporally continuous objects to certain abstract relations: *distance ... height ... situation,* or *length, breadth* and *depth,* manipulated into the referring position (cf. Strawson, 1967). According to our interpretation, such abstractions and gestalt-free qualities are perceived differently by the two orientation association areas. In the left area they enhance a feeling of the blurring of boundaries; in the right area they are perceived as unstable, fluid information, comparable to the fast-integrated output of right-hemisphere orientation processes, that cannot settle as solid objects.

These findings suggest that the switch from "ordinary consciousness" to "meditative consciousness" involves the substitution of a holistic mode of operation for the analytic and sequential information-processing mode. Structurally, there is a drastic increase in the diffuseness of the brain's output.

Indeed, both Orenstein and Puente, using each his respective terms, while discussing meditation, account for holistic perception, and for the integration of many inputs at once.[6] Furthermore, a heightened awareness of our "body image" is required for what Dawson describes as "imagining our selves to be really present at those places". Right-hemisphere orientation is associated with the subject's ability to locate *himself* in the surroundings, and to ascertain his relation to them. It is never detached from the subject as an objective survey of the world. Indeed, that is the precise procedure aimed at, by the *Spiritual Exercises.*

Hence, the "composition of place" is intended to evoke a right-hemisphere orientation process. The right-hemisphere process is responsible for the "diffusion" of compact inputs. The activation of the orientation mechanism arouses an information-processing mode that is diffuse, holistic, and simultaneous. This mode of functioning characterises the meditative process, and typically involves diffuse and intuitive impressions.

The skeptical reader may object that what we are up against is not actual orientation in space, only *imagined* orientation. This is not a real problem for the present conception. Recent neurological experiments reveal that the same brain centers are involved in imagining an action and in the performance of that action. According to Bownds, imagining a movement and performing such a movement will activate the same premotor cortex (Bownds, 1999). Activated cognitive features are processed exactly like an external input (Kahneman, 1973: 69). Even in terms of vitality and intensity, mental imagery is experienced as an actual sensory input (Verbrugge, 1980: 93).[7] The only difference in this sense is that mental imagery is a reconstruction, and as such, does not have to be as detailed as visual perception. It builds what Johnson (Johnson, 1987: 23-28) calls "image schemata": For economical reasons (using less processing resources) the reader can usually do with the least detailed images, unless the text or other circumstances expressly require more. Since right-hemisphere orientation is mostly about abstract relations and proportions, such schematic perception may be even useful.

When a meditator or a reader is required to place him/herself inside an imagined situation, right-hemisphere orientation is clearly part of it. Recent neurological experiments show that even the mere presence of a concrete stimulus calls for an orientation process of some sort. Mapping the brain activity during the processing of concrete nouns showed that such cognitive activity involves intense activation of some centers in the right hemisphere, known to be responsible for the construction of spatial schemata (Jessen et al., 2000).

"The composition of place" calls for a right-hemisphere orientation process, which facilitates meditation by encouraging holistic perception, and by diffusing the streams of information. However, too detailed descriptions might damage the holis-

---

6   And see Dixon which typifies the right hemisphere mode as "more holistic, irrational and dreamlike" (Dixon, 1981: 210).

7   "Mental Imagery" is defined as" *the mental invention or recreation of an experience that in at least some respects resembles the experience of actually perceiving an object or an event, either in conjunction with or in the absence of, direct sensory stimulation"* (original italics) (Finke, 1989: 2).

tic perception, and allow the construction of stable visual shapes. Holistic perception is a key element in preventing rational control. As Wilson says, as long as the stimulus is not anatomized and analyzed, the rational mechanism of thinking is unable to get control (Wilson, 1972: 225).

Stable visual shapes attract the reader's attention to precise elements and clear-cut borderlines. The relations and orders become more explicit and conscious, and elicit the rational mechanism. Strong gestalts encourage the involvement of the rational faculties (Meyer, 1956: 160; Arnheim, 1957: 324-325; Tsur 1978; 1987b; 1988; 1992a), and hence a higher degree of control. Detailed descriptions will always promote the sense of control, and we might be able to explain their absence or presence in meditative texts by differing needs for control in these texts. We argue that "the composition of place" arouses right-hemisphere orientation, and at the same time builds a physical setting that provides readers with a sense of order and control, an alternative to the "ordinary consciousness", which is abandoned through the meditative process.

"The composition of place" as an alternative sense of order

In poetry of any kind there is always a balance between elements that undermine the reader's sense of control and certainty, and those that increase them. If a writer uses an element that disturbs the reader's sense of control (like delaying comprehension in some ways), s/he will have to balance it by supporting the reader's sense of control by other means (like rhythmic order), or get a different point of balance. What interests us mostly is the effects such a choice has on the reader. Since meditation is an "altered state of consciousness", it presupposes separation from the daily course of life, relinquishing of "ordinary consciousness", and voluntary surrender of control. The subject of meditation (in meditative poems, or spiritual exercises) is always detached from daily life. A certain willingness of readers to be cut off from their everyday life is implied by the very act of meditating or reading such poetry. The degree of this readiness might vary, a point we will discuss in later stages of the chapter.[8]

The "composition of place" can be seen as a factor that helps to establish this readiness, while at the same time reinforcing an alternative sense of control. It calls for abandoning reality for an imaginary world. To do so, the reader must believe that this imaginary world has validity, not in the sense of actual existence, but a belief in its values, its spiritual importance and its gist of truth. This belief is by itself not enough. Applying oneself to the composition of place begins with separation from

---

[8]   We will try to demonstrate in what ways the variance within meditative texts can be related, among other things, to the absence or the presence of some elements that provide the reader with a stronger sense of control, a variation that results in a different balance point of control.

everyday life, which enables readers to loosen their defenses against relinquishing the already acquired control of "ordinary consciousness".

"Ordinary Consciousness" is, then, a state of mind in which the experiencer "feels a sense of control and power", involving a "psychological atmosphere of certainty, security, and patent purpose" (see above). The abandonment of the "sense of control and power" and the "psychological atmosphere of certainty and security" involved in ordinary consciousness may arouse great anxiety, and so be hard to tolerate for some people.[9] Meditation presupposes such abandonment, that is, a state of mind which Keats called "Negative capability", namely "the capability of being in Uncertainties, Mysteries, Doubts, without any irritable reaching after fact and reason".

Separating oneself from everyday life along with the readiness to be driven elsewhere might make a decreased need for control possible. The "composition of place" not only results in such separation, but also, at the same time, provides an alternative. The Ignatian "composition of place" offers the practitioner of meditation a technique for avoiding the anxiety that can arise from self-abandonment, especially among "beginners".

Thus, the composition of place helps to regain the sense of control, and by the same token it promotes through right hemisphere orientation a diffuse mode of information processing. That is why that "Ignatian invention" is so brilliant and effective.

Physical and Human Setting

Still, a significant distinction can be noticed between *two* possible "compositions". In Ignatius' original text, as in the Dawson quote above, the *physical scene* is emphasized at considerable length; but the Jesuit Puente puts the *human action* in the core of the meditating imagery. Dawson dwells at great length on the physical scene, while the human action is *implied* at best. Puente, by contrast, expounds in some detail the human action to be imagined, while the physical scene is back-grounded. We must attempt, he says,

> to procure with the imagination to forme within our selves some figure, or image of the things wee intende to meditate with the greatest vivacity, and propriety that wee are able. If I am to think upon hell, I will imagine some place like an obscure, straight, and horrible dungeon full of fier, and the soules therin burning in the middest of those flames. And if I am to meditate [on] the birth of Christ, I will forme the figure of some open place

---

9   The abandonment of strong perceptual shapes and of ordinary consciousness differs, of course, in the degree of anxiety they arouse. While there are persons intolerant of ambiguity whose perception becomes less accurate when contemplating poor gestalts, the abandonment of ordinary consciousness seems utterly intolerable to many people.

without shelter, and a childe wrapped in swadling cloutes, layed in a manger: and so in the rest (Martz, 1962: 28).

Thus, there is a significant difference of emphasis between those forms of "composition". In the following examples quoted by Martz from Donne's Holy Sonnets as typical instances of "composition of place", barely any "place" can be detected. Most instances begin with some powerful human situation, in which sometimes no place at all is mentioned, sometimes it is merely hinted at, and only rarely presented in any detail.

We have explored the advantages of "the composition of place", but as suggested above, there is also a risk in such a procedure. The detailed description of the physical setting carries the risk of over-visualisation: the formation of stable visual shapes or strong gestalts, and rational take-over. Dawson solves this problem on the verbal level, as we have seen, by manipulating the abstract attributes of concrete nouns into the referring position. An alternative solution would be to shift attention to a "human setting". A glance at these examples will reveal a remarkable gap between Donne's meditative poetry and the Ignatian requirement as presented by Dawson and approved by Martz.

1. Oh my blacke Soule! now thou art summoned
   By sicknesse, deaths herald, and champion;
   Thou art like a pilgrim, which abroad hath done
   Treason, and durst not turne to whence hee is fled,
   Or like a thiefe . . . .

2. This is my playes last scene, here heavens appoint
   My pilgrimages last mile; and my race
   Idly, yet quickly runne, hath this last pace,
   My spans last inch, my minutes latest point . . . .

3. Spit in my face you Jewes, and pierce my side,
   Buffet, and scoffe, scourge, and crucifie mee . . .

4. What if this present were the worlds last night!

5. At the round earths imagin'd corners, blow
   Your trumpets, Angells . . .

These are the openings of some of Donne's Holy Sonnets. Let us look for instance at excerpt 3. Typically enough, the speaker identifies with Christ's suffering and humiliation, or reenacts the situation, specifying his own self with reference to it. No indication of place is required for that.

The use of a human setting in Donne's Holy Sonnets arouses the question how can the authors of meditative poetry (like Donne) afford partly to ignore the need for an alternative supporting sense of control? We submit that if every text aims to achieve some balance between elements that increase the sense of control and those that weaken it, then, in comparison to other texts, meditative texts (of any kind) can typically "afford" to diminish the elements of certainty or control. The reason for that should be quite clear by now. Meditation and poetry reading are both freely chosen processes, which indicate the readiness of the reader/meditator to give up such control voluntarily. Both require a mental state that enables the reader/meditator to invest resources of time and processing energy without any immediate benefit or utility for everyday life; to experience the reading in the absence of purpose.

Mental readiness, motivation or meditative experience may counterbalance the urgency for an alternative order, and the "physical setting" is then less needed. Surprisingly, we can find some support for this conception in the exercises themselves. In the first week, all first preludes contain the instruction for "the composition of place" in its detailed physical version, but from the second week on, and even more so in the third week, this "composition of place" takes the form of various "human settings". Let us consider the First Prelude of the first day of the third week in Ignatius' own words:

> The first Prelude is to bring to memory the narrative; which is here how Christ our Lord sent two Disciples from Bethany to Jerusalem to prepare the Supper, and then He Himself went there with the other Disciples; and how, after having eaten the Paschal Lamb, and having supped, He washed their feet and gave His most Holy Body and Precious Blood to His Disciples, and made them a discourse, after Judas went to sell his Lord.

This kind of instruction is even more human-oriented than Puente's quoted above, let alone Dawson's. It seems that "the composition of place" in its strict physical form is so brilliant mainly for the beginner who does it for the first few times; as you become more experienced, the detailed "physical setting" is not so important even in Ignatius' text.

Moreover, we have suggested that in reading poetry the reader does not *experience* an altered state of consciousness, only *perceives* it. Therefore, unlike meditation, the sense of self-abandonment while reading meditative poetry is weaker. The advantage of the "physical setting" is that a stronger alternative order is less required.

Notice that visualisation does not vanish, but is done by other means. Adding details, or describing the concrete natural surroundings of an object, are probably the two most basic and widespread techniques to visualise (or sensualise through other senses) an image in our perception. These techniques are at the core of "the composition of place". Still, they are not the only ones. In Benari's dissertation, (Benari, 2000) other techniques are presented and exemplified. One of these is the addition of a dynamic force. In order to imagine the motion of a concrete object, many relations and environmental details that were not mentioned are needed. The amount of data activated to fill the gap from a human setting is larger than from a physical setting that is more detailed from the start. Transforming a static image into a dynamic one, by adding verbs or other elements of motion, will call for a restoration of more proportions and more features. Therefore, motion (when related to some concrete object) becomes an element that elicits more comprehensive visualisation, even though it can maintain many parts of the visualised scenery as schematic (that is precisely why dynamic computer games, for instance, take up so much more memory than static graphics).

It seems that the human setting can serve as a sort of substitute for a detailed physical setting. Such a substitution should not damage the need for orientation.

Diffuseness and the Ineffable

The foregoing analysis can help us solve an additional problem. As we mentioned in Chapter 1, Rudolf Otto, William James, and many other writers insist that the "holy", the "numinous experience", is *ineffable:*

> All language, in so far as it consists of words, purports to convey ideas or concepts—that is what language means—and the more clearly and unequi-vocally it does so, the better the language.[10] And hence expositions of reli-gious truth in language inevitably tend to stress the "rational" attributes of God (Otto, 1959: 16).

Now the "holy", the "numinous", says Otto, consists precisely in what exceeds the "rational attributes of God"; and is, therefore, ineffable.

This should by no means surprise us. As Orenstein stated, the right hemisphere's "language ability is quite limited"; and meditation is a typical right-hemisphere ac-tivity. During the past fifty years or so linguists have propounded a semantic-feature conception of meaning. Cognitive psychologists and brain scientists too speak of cognitive "features". Marcel Kinsbourne refutes the naive belief that the right hemi-sphere's output is featureless: "A holistic approach, leaving features and their rela-tions unspecified, is as alien to right-hemisphere function as it is inimical to ratio-nality in general" (Kinsbourne, 1982: 417). We claim that the right hemisphere's output is "ineffable" not because no semantic features are involved, but because those features are *diffuse* and *simultaneous.* It is not the information that is unpara-phrasable, but its integration and diffuseness. Diffuseness and integration are not semantic information *added,* but the *structure* of information *as it appears in*

---

[10] Otto's formulation concerning the conceptual nature of language bears a weird resemblance to the first author's position concerning the problems involved in the response to figurative language in general, and devotional poetry in particular (Tsur, 1987: 4; 1992: 360; 1998). He may have been unwittingly influenced by Otto, since he read this book as an undegraduate.

consciousness. Whereas semantic information can be paraphrased, the impression that arises from its structure can only be *described*.

As the first author has suggested in various places (Tsur, 1987b: 4; 1992a: 360; 1998), since language is compact and linear by nature, the phrases "emotional poetry" or "mystical poetry" ought to be, but are not, contradictions in terms. Now the phrases are not contradictions in terms, precisely because poets found exactly the same solution as Ignatius found. In romantic nature poetry, for instance, the insights into supersensuous reality are intimately associated with detailed nature descriptions, a "composition of place", as it were. The orientation mechanism involved imposes diffuseness on language. Indeed, Martz argues in the concluding chapter of the revised edition of his book (1962) that romantic nature poetry is a secular version of meditative poetry.

Emotion and Meditative Texts

Emotional states are an important part of meditative activity. In Ignatian exercises, emotion is an indication for the success of the meditative act. After praying, every individual should discuss his emotions with another. On the one hand, an emotional state is evidence, to some extent, of the abandonment of control, and, on the other, it proves an individual involvement, the relevance of the process to the meditator. This last issue will later be discussed at greater length.

Emotion is very often connected with diffuse or non-linear elements; and we have elsewhere discussed this issue at length (Tsur, 1978; Benari, 2000). Poor gestalts or an undifferentiated mass generated by diffuse elements are known to have emotional effects (Meyer, 1956: 160; Tsur, 1987: 149–150; 1992a: 113–115). Wilson argues that diffuse elements (like those found in the painting discussed above), stimulate certain areas in the hypothalamus, which activate sympathetic and parasympathetic activities, related to states of affect, emotions and moods (Wilson, 1972: 222).

Rational activity is by nature convergent, one-directional, and has a goal, clear rules and active control (Guilford, 1970). Increasing the diffuse nature of processing might decrease rational control and hence could be perceived as an emotional quality. As mentioned above, right-hemisphere orientation is one factor that might increase diffuseness. The presence of divergent, non-linear elements in the text might be another one.

But not only diffuse elements can be identified as the source of an emotional quality. Non-linear elements (like those discussed later in Donne's poem, for instance) prevent the rational modus operandi from taking over completely, and reduce the reader's sense of control.[11] Changes in the individual's sense of stability and control were identified as elements that constitute high attentiveness for emotional stimula-

---

[11] The ability to avoid strong gestalts and to maintain non-linear dominance, without breaking the proper linear character of language, is not an easy task. It requires a delicate balancing act that prevents the rejection of the text altogether.

tion (Frijda, 1994: 200; Ellsworth, 1994: 193). This might explain the source of the relatively high emotional awareness typical to the reading of meditative poetry.

Creativity and Emotion

We have argued that the main importance of the physical setting as built by "the composition of place" is that in addition to generating an orientation process it makes it easier for the inexperienced reader to cope with the abandonment of "ordinary consciousness". A detailed physical setting, however, may harm the diffuseness of perception. When it is possible, therefore, it might become beneficial to avoid the detailed physical setting, because that would make it possible to maintain the orientation process without the risk of impairing its diffuseness.

In poetic texts it is advantageous for another reason to avoid the formation of stable visual shapes—that is, strong gestalts—and the rational take-over: it arouses the reader's creativity more intensely. Every word is a stimulus that activates an enormous amount of information (definitions, encyclopedic knowledge, connotations, private associations, etc.). The less specified, stable and detailed the poem's words are, the greater the diversity of activation among readers. This diversity is not arbitrary—the activation process is partially selective and flexible. Each reader tends to activate various private, subjective features. These features could help interpret the whole utterance in the most relevant way—relevant not just to the topic of discussion, but to the reader's own life and experience (Sperber & Wilson, 1986). Some of these features carry an emotional load with them that is to some extent experienced again and again (Gibbs, 1997). Even when these cognitive features do not become conscious, or do not participate in the production of the final meaning, they still might have an affective impact (Dixon, 1981).

We argue that human setting (and diffuse information) arouse greater creativity and a greater individual emotional load. Furthermore, for readers this high degree of processing involvement results in accepting the final product of the creative reading as at least partly their own. Greater processing involvement results in a more personal touch. Readers embrace the final product with a sense of originality and intimacy (Benari, 2000). Intuitive comprehension, typically associated with the right-hemisphere mode of operation, is another factor that increases the tendency to adopt the final output as one's own. Intuitive comprehension is characterised by the lack of awareness of the processes of meaning construction. The process remains blurred and gives the reader a sense of emergence originating in private mysterious ways.

All these factors turn diffuseness and the avoidance of rational control into a key element in enhancing the emotional potential.

Experiential and Instrumental Sets—the Absence of Purpose

In the first section of this article we argued that there are three major characteristics responsible for generating the meditative quality perceived in a poem:

1. The text's ability to evoke an orientation process.
2. The text's ability to arouse diffuse perception.
3. A special mental set in the reader's mind: the absence of purpose.

This last characteristic is largely based on pragmatic conditions. A text might encourage it by avoiding the mention of any specific purposes, and by generating an atmosphere cut off from daily purposeful life; but these are not sufficient, only necessary, conditions.

In Chapter 2 above, a distinction was made between poem, prayer, and meditation, in terms of Roman Jakobson's model of language functions (Jakobson, 1960). In *poem* the poetic function is dominant,[12] in *prayer* it is the "conative" function, and in *meditation* the "expressive" function. That chapter argues that these differences of dominance entail further logical, semantic and structural differences. It also demonstrates that the same Holy Sonnet by Donne can be read as a poem, a prayer or a meditation at different times, following up the changing implications of the changing dominant functions. For our present purpose, the main point is that the *prayer* has a "patent purpose": it purports to affect God's attitudes or actions toward the speaker. When meditating, by contrast, the discourse is usually speaker-oriented (emotive). A secondary yet important function in a verbal imitation of meditation might be the phatic one. The phatic function brings into the focus of attention the communication channel, the mere existence of contact between addresser and addressee. The meditation is aimed to establish such a link, and to get an emotional thrill from its presence as an experiential instant. Its main characteristic is the speaker's attempt to intensify as far as possible the emotive experience. Even when the speaker addresses his/her words to God, this is subordinated to the emotive function: its function is to enhance his/her own meditative experience.

This distinction has been further refined in Idith Eynath-Nov's doctoral dissertation on the Mediaeval Hebrew liturgical genre called *rəšut* (literally: "asking for permission"). There is a general consensus that a substantial proportion of the masterpieces of Mediaeval Hebrew liturgical poetry belongs to this genre. She contrasted this genre to other liturgical genres as well as to the "personal" Psalms in

---

[12] Dominance of a function can never be discussed as an objective isolated quality. Some of the criticism of Jakobson's view was based on the fact that he did not give enough weight to pragmatics (Pratt, 1977). Therefore, when we talk about the dominance of a function, we talk about a potential of dominance. Sentences with exclamation marks, for instance, have a good potential to be dominated by the conative function, although in certain circumstances they can be used to illustrate a grammatical principle (meta-linguistic function), or to express pain or anger (emotive function) etc.

the Bible. In all these genres as well as in the Psalms the praise of God is, naturally, central. But the personal *rašut* differs from the rest in one essential feature. In the other genres as well as in the personal Psalms there is, typically, a "patent purpose", conspicuously absent from the personal *rašut*. In the other genres a "give-and-take" is suggested, so to speak. You rescued me in my distress, or delivered me from my enemies, so I am singing your praise; or, I am singing your praise in order to affect your attitude toward me. In the genre called *səliḥa* (forgiveness), the patent purpose consists in asking for forgiveness; in the genre called *tokheḥa* (admonition), the patent purpose consists in a warning to the soul that time is flying by, and it (the soul) will have no time left to make amends. The only genre that is typically devoid of patent purpose in this sense is the personal *rašut*. No give-and-take, no benefit, no warning is suggested. The speaker sings the praise of God merely because he feels like doing so, or because he knows that God likes songs of praise. No patent purpose is indicated; it is, so to speak, "purposiveness without purpose".

This distinction between two types of prayer interestingly corresponds to the dichotomy of *experiential set* and *instrumental set,* propounded by Tellegen (1981: 222):

> By experiential set is meant a state of receptivity or openness to undergo whatever experiential events, sensory or imaginal, that may occur, with tendency to dwell on, rather than go beyond, the experiences themselves and the objects they represent. In this set, experiences have a quality of effort-lessness, as if they happened by themselves, and in that sense, of involuntariness.
>
> Instrumental set, on the other hand, is defined as a state of readiness to engage in active, realistic, voluntary, and relatively effortful planning, decision making, and goal-directed behavior. Input from receptors is not used to enhance experiencing but to make the discrimination needed for guiding instrumental acts and evaluating achievements against standards.

Tellegen propounded this dichotomy in his effort to isolate the personality variable "absorption", devised to predict a person's hypnotisability. Absorption may be defined as the propensity to adopt an experiential set. Such altered states of consciousness as hypnosis and meditation strongly presuppose an experiential set.

Now the great paradox of Jesuit meditation is that their "Spiritual Exercises" require intensive mental effort to achieve a state of mind of "receptivity", in which experiences have "a quality of effortlessness, as if they happened by themselves, and in that sense, of involuntariness". This alteration of mental state is identified by James:

> Although the oncoming of mystical states may be facilitated by preliminary voluntary operations, as by fixing the attention, or going through certain

bodily performances, or in other ways which manuals of mysticism pre-
scribe; yet when the characteristic sort of consciousness once has set in, the
mystic feels as if his own will were in abeyance, and indeed sometimes as if
he were grasped and held by a superior power (James 1902: 381).

The "composition of place" and the use of the "image-making" faculty as discussed above is the trigger that sets off this "quality of effortlessness" and "involuntariness", that effects the "switch" from the instrumental to the experiential set. In
the experiential set, then, input from receptors is used to enhance experiencing, to
dwell on, rather than go beyond, the experiences themselves.

We have seen above a quotation from the Jesuit Puente, one of Martz's illuminating examples of the insistence upon "seeing the place". By the same token, this is
an exquisite illustration of the experiential set. One could *go beyond* the image of
hell and warn oneself of the tortures in that "horrible dungeon full of fier". But
Puente's instruction is only to dwell on the picture, "forme within our selves some
figure, or image of the things wee intende to meditate with the greatest vivacity";
there is no warning here, only an extreme heightening of the experience. Ultimately
this can, of course, serve as a warning; but the meditation per se concerns only some
intense experiencing. The same holds true, mutatis mutandis, of meditating on the
birth of Christ in the same passage. The same attitude is explicitly recommended in
the fifth annotation to the spiritual exercises: "to enter into them with great courage
and generosity towards his Creator and Lord, offering Him all his will and liberty".
Here too, the emphasis is on what you are supposed to feel, not on what you might
benefit from it.

Literary Examples: Two Masterpieces
Holy Sonnet 7

Now let us consider at some length two literary examples. We have chosen them not
as prototypical, but as *outstanding* examples of their genre. The first excerpt is the
beginning of *Holy Sonnet 7* by Donne (excerpt 5):

>   At the round earths imagin'd corners, blow
>   Your trumpets, Angells . . .

This vigorous opening presents a most striking visual and auditory image which,
in turn, presents a visual paradox, involving the prototypical geometric impossibility: a round object having four corners. This impossibility is mitigated, though, by
"imagined". A paradox typically arouses a witty effect. A witty effect, in turn, calls
for some rational mechanism, and is opposed to the diffuse and emotional nature expected. Donne's sonnet alludes to the Biblical world picture, as suggested in *Revelation* 7:1: "And after these things, I saw four angels standing on the four corners of

the earth, holding the four winds of the earth". Donne "yokes together by violence" this picture with the Ptolemaic and Copernican views of the earth as round. This geometrical impossiblity does not only represent the conflicting conceptions of the cosmos; it allows the imagination to comprehend or encompass the conflict in one single intuition. Thus, to paraphrase Kant, the paradoxical picture evokes wit and bafflement, and at the same time offers a space for orientation, and this the imagination can encompass in a single intuition. The conflicting world pictures cause the perceiving consciousness to lose its bearings; but instead of an abstract presentation, it is displayed in an immediately-sensed situation.[13] To borrow Martz's phrase, such a picture satisfies "a natural, fundamental tendency of the human mind to work from a particular situation"—in this case the particular situation contains the conflicting world pictures blended in the great monotheistic religions.[14]

There is a backgrounded metaphysical pun too in this quote which, when noticed, may enhance this sense of disorientation and bafflement. The phrase "four winds of the earth" in the biblical passage means "the four cardinal points of the compass". The verb "blow" at the line ending suggests "wind" in the sense of "natural movement of the air". After the enjambment, however, this expectation is refuted when the meaning "sounding a wind instrument" emerges. Thus, two incompatible meanings of "wind" and of "blow" are activated, establishing two powerful metaphysical puns. However, in the typical pun the first or expected meaning is negated by the second one. The two meanings cannot exist simultaneously. This is not the case when the meaning "sounding a wind instrument" emerges. Two separate meanings of "wind" and of "blow" might be activated, not necessarily in an incompatible way. The blowing of a trumpet does not exclude the option of the expected blowing wind. In this sense the expectation was ignored, not negated. The effect is a loose end that can contribute to the sense of undirected energy—not a strong gestalt of negation, that would be perceived as compact and witty.

[13] In the seventeenth century there may have been exceptional sensitivity to conflicting world views. People in that century had to cope with conflicting world pictures: the traditional Ptolemaic Cosmology, and a Copernican one. Though according to both cosmologies the earth was round, there was fierce controversy whether the earth turned around the sun or vice versa. As Milton's and Donne's poetry witness, this conflict was still not resolved in the seventeenth century, and was actually very much alive.

[14] Tsur has pointed out in several articles another problem of conflicting perceptions arising from conflicting world pictures: that the attempts to fuse the Biblical conception of a personal Creator and the Neo-Platonic conception of light emanation entangled such poets as Milton, the eleventh century Hebrew poet Ibn Gabirol, and the thirteenth century Armenian poet Kostandin of Erznka, in the need to reconcile not only conflicting ideas but also conflicting perceptions of stable visual shapes and gestalt-free qualities. Milton attempted to blur these conflicting perceptions in a soft focus, whereas Ibn Gabirol preferred the metaphysical path of sharpening the conflict as much as possible (see Chapters 11-12 below).

The imperative verb "blow" suffuses the image with enormous energy. Such an import of energy, with no specification of direction, has an immediate affective impact. In addition there is another support to the non-rational aspect, related to orientation. In his stimulating book *God the Problem,* Gordon Kaufman (1972: 46) claims that we use "God-language" in dealing "with experiences that are beyond the *absolute limit* of our experience, construed by analogy with the relative limits of our every-day life". This kind of analogy was already emphasised, as we have seen, by Rudolf Otto half a century earlier. Donne's sonnet, by placing the action inside apocalyptic scenery, purports to offer a direct glimpse of the absolute limit itself. In other words, the corners of the earth both indicate the absolute limit and serve as points of orientation for the perceiving self.

The physical and human settings have varying relative weights in this poem. Only the first line refers to the physical setting; the "round earths imagin'd corners" establish a physical setting, and orientation (or disorientation) arise. The sequel, from "blow" on, refers already to the *action* that takes place in this setting. To do justice to this action, we have to consider in some detail the whole octet of the sonnet. The accumulation of imperative verbs "blow [...] arise, arise [...] goe" constitute a very effective deictic device, powerfully directing attention to the immediate situation. An imperative is, typically, addressed to someone immediately present. The sonnet provides a very detailed account of the human setting; but, instead of the indicative mode, it uses a series of imperatives, indicating the speaker's involvement in the scene. This use of grammar contributes to the perceived effect of "imagining our selves to be really present at those places"—in Dawson's phrase.

The last trumpet that awakens the dead, transcends the ultimate limit of time. But, again, the self-specifying information available in the immediate surrounding is destroyed. The dead bodies, which have been so far part of inanimate nature, suddenly become literally *animate* and the whole human setting is on the move. The person who contemplates the scene finds himself in a pandemonium. In this tumult all firm points of stability vanish, resulting in a state of mind of loss of control.

6.   *Holy Sonnet 7*
    At the round earth's imagin'd corners, blow
    Your trumpets, Angells, and arise, arise
    From death, you numberlesse infinities
    Of souls, and to your scattred bodies goe,
    All whom the flood did, and fire shall o'erthrow,
    All whom warre, dearth, age, agues, tyrannies,
    Despaire, law, chance, hath slaine, and you whose eyes,
    Shall behold God, and never tast deaths woe.
    But let them sleepe, Lord, and me mourne a space,
    For if above all these, my sinnes abound,
    'Tis late to aske abundance of thy grace
    When wee are there; here on this lowly ground,

> Teach mee how to repent; for that's as good
> As if thou'hadst seal'd my pardon, with thy blood.

"To your *scattred* bodies goe" makes a decisive contribution to the diffuseness of the scene evoked. Indeed, the ambiguity of the phrase evokes diffuseness at two different levels: each soul must find its body wherever it is; and each body is scattered all over the world, wherefrom the souls must collect and assume them.

Here a few more comments of "close reading" might be appropriate. Lines 5–8 enumerate the "numberlesse infinities of souls". These have an enormous cumulative effect, foregrounded by the anaphora of the all-inclusive "all whom", and the asyndeton in lines 6–7. The list of violent deaths packed up in so small a space amplifies the intensity of the experience expressed.

The psychological atmosphere of impetuous movement and unstable reality in which there is no firm point for orientation is reinforced by the poem's sophisticated prosodic structure. It has to do with enjambment and requiredness, consistently generating a sense of stability and consistently subverting it. "Requiredness" is the demand which one part of the perceptual field may have on another part. Tsur (1972) shows that the nearer a syntactic break is to the line ending, the stronger is the requiredness of the remaining part, that is, the greater is the tension as well as the satisfaction it generates. At the end of line 1 a single syllable is strongly required; the verb "blow" effectively completes the iambic pentameter line. At the same time, the emerging meaning remains outrageously incomplete: one cannot even know whether the verb refers to a swift and forceful movement of the air, or to sounding a wind instrument (in this cosmic scene, the first meaning is more available). This ambiguity generates an impetuous forward-driving "perceptual force". The uncertainty of meaning upsets, so to speak, the perceptual stability already achieved. The next line, too, ends with the reiterated imperative "arise, arise". According to the default grammatical rule, if a verb occurs without an explicit subject, it is to be attributed to the last-mentioned subject (that is, "Angells"). In such a construal, the line-ending and the sentence-ending would coincide. This closed unit is reopened when another syntactic subject is specified by the vocative in the next line. Thus, syntactic indeterminacy reopens the line closed from the prosodic point of view. "Arise, arise" is a longer (and therefore less required) perceptual unit than "blow"; but here the impetuous movement is reinforced by the reiteration of the imperative verb of motion. At the end of line 3 there is an interesting variant of this process, with a very different effect. I will not discuss the eye-rhyme, which does and does not confirm the rhyme pattern. "Infinities" is a polysyllable, which does complete the number of syllables required, but places an unstressed syllable in the last, crucial strong position of the verse line. "Numberless infinities" can be understood as a *simple replacement* for "souls", to use Christine Brooke-Rose's term; and as such, the meaning is perceived as satisfactory and complete. But the genitive phrase "numberless infinities of souls" reopens the syntactic unit already perceived as closed, generating an enjambment. Here the effect of the reopening of the closed line is not so much an increase of the impetuous movement. Rather, by weakening the closure of the third line of the quatrain, it confers an increased sense of requiredness and closural force on the fourth. In additional respects, too, the end of the first quatrain displays a remarkable closural quality. There is a feeling that the first quatrain is firmly closed. First, the a-b-b-a rhyme pattern is completed. Second, a kind of equilibrium is reached between souls and bodies: the arisen souls go to their scattered bodies. Third, this is the first place where the sentence can be said to be complete and to have an end coinciding with the line ending. Fourth, two of the imperative verbs at line-endings (blow, arise) enhance fluidity by running on to the next line. In the fourth line, by contrast, there is a syntactic inversion: the adverbial of place precedes the imperative verb, manipulating it into the last position of the line. This generates a psychological atmosphere of completeness and finality. When, however, this feast of stability is achieved, there follows a series of exceptionally elaborate appositions to "numberlesse infinities of souls": "All whom [...] All whom [...] and you whose eyes", reopening the closed quatrain and frustrating the sense of stability already achieved.

This sonnet, like so many meditative poems, comprises two parts that correspond to two essential stages of meditation: the "composition of place", and "colloquy", completing the meditative pattern outlined by Martz. As we have seen, the octet of this sonnet is characterised by "disorientation" which, with reference to Donne's tumult, here suggests the sudden loss of self-specifying information in the optic array. "Disorientation", emotional or physical, arouses the need for reorientation and readjustment, effected by the "colloquy" in the sestet. Indeed, the transition to the sestet restructures the whole sonnet, generating a sudden sense of insight. "Let them sleepe" of the sestet switches from an attitude of total movement to its opposite. Here the reorientation coincides with one of the most important conventions of the sonnet form: "the sestet must throw some transforming light upon the octave" (cf., e.g., Schneider, 1975: 249–250). The impetuous resurrection of the dead has an effect that might be described, perhaps, as "fascinating". In the sestet, the speaker grasps a problem; the resurrection of the dead may turn out to be a grievous thing for him: he has not yet learnt how to repent. There is also a drastic change in certain verbal elements: the speech act indicated by the imperative mode of the verbs, and the semantic structure of the verb "mourne". The scene conveyed in the octet is not presented in the indicative, but in the imperative mode. Here, the imperatives act as commands, inciting to action from an authoritative attitude, as it were. In the sestet, a different tone emerges. At first it is unclear whether it is a "request", or involves some humbler attitude. Later it becomes more like an imploring, a piteous supplication. There is also a significant semantic change in the verb "mourne" in line 9. In the context of the octet, it suggests mourning for the dead, before they resurrect. "Repent" in line 13 foregrounds the component of "sorrow" shared by both verbs; "mourne" thus assumes the meaning of feeling sorry or self-reproachful for some past action or attitude, as preparation for repentance. All these shifts enhance the sense of sudden insight reached in the colloquy.

The absence of purposiveness in this poem is also quite apparent. There is a clear separation from daily life. It is true that Donne mentions some purposes ("let them sleepe" "teach mee"), but these can and should be treated more as ways to reveal the speaker's mental state, or emotional position, than as an actual request. The poem is exposing inner fears, trust and love, not demanding or soliciting remission. The absence of purposiveness is even more unmistakable in the next poem.

To Christ Crucified

At this stage we propose to have a close look at a Spanish sonnet, probably from the sixteenth century, by an anonymous poet.

7.   *A Cristo Crucificado*

> No me mueve, mi Dios, para quererte,
> el cielo que me tienes prometido,
> ni me mueve el infierno tan temido
> para dejar por eso de ofenderte.
>
> Tú me mueves, Señor; muéveme el verte
> clavado en esa cruz, y escarnecido;
> muéveme el ver tu cuerpo tan herido,
> muévenme tus afrentas, y tu muerte.
>
> Muéveme, al fin, tu amor, y en tal manera,
> que aunque no hubiera cielo, yo te amara,
> y aunque no hubiera infierno te temiera.
>
> No me tienes que dar porque te quiera;
> pues aunque lo que espero no esperara,
> lo mismo que te quiero te quisiera.

To Christ Crucified

It is not the heaven that You have promised me, my God, that moves me to love You, nor is it the hell I so fear that moves me to cease sinning against You.

You move me, Lord; it moves me to see You nailed to that cross and despised; it moves me to see Your body so wounded; the insults You suffered and Your death move me.

Finally, Your love moves me, and so much that even if there were no heaven, I should love You; and even if there were no hell, I should fear You.

You have not to give me anything to make me love You; for even if I did not hope for what I do hope for, I should love You just as I do. (Cohen, 1960: 163)

The editor and translator of *The Penguin Book of Spanish Verse,* J.M. Cohen, makes the following comment: "This magnificent sonnet has been attributed to many, including Ignatius Loyola, but without adequate foundation" (xii). In our intuitive judgment, too, this is a masterpiece. Close scrutiny of this sonnet reveals that there is no novel figurative language in it. There are only two hackneyed, dead metaphors: "move" in the sense "to cause" or "to stir the emotions, feelings, or passions"; and "seeing" (with the "mind's eye"). Thus, rich figurative language cannot be the cause of such magnificence. The extraordinary power of this sonnet can be felt even in Cohen's plain prose translation; so, it is not necessarily due to its prosody either, though it can be reinforced by it. As we will see, not even the central paradox by itself can account for its unique quality. One might, rather, look for the reason in the powerful means by which the sonnet evokes the experiential set. We shall point to four techniques that help to liberate the dominant attitude from the control of the instrumental set: straightforward negation of goals; dwelling on an emotionally-loaded imaginary situation; employing "linguistic devices that shift the speaker to a non-volitional role" (cf. Balaban, 1999: 259); and violation of the conversational maxim of quantity: "unnecessary" repetition of assertions. In our critical discourse we can point them out analytically, one by one. But then we must add a meta-statement. All these devices have similar effects; from them there *emerges* what the gestaltists call a regional quality, that is, a quality that characterises a whole, but not its parts; in this case, a nonconceptual quality of the experiential set.

To paraphrase Rudolf Otto yet again, in this sonnet the reader is "guided and led on by consideration and discussion of the matter through the ways of his own mind, until he reaches the point at which the 'experiential set' in him perforce begins to stir". The crucial phrase for us here is "guided and led on [...] through the ways of his own mind". "The ways of his own mind" are here of two kinds. On the one hand, it is the contents that may lead us to other regions of the mind; on the other hand, as with the orientation mechanism, it may arouse some different way of responding. Consider the first quatrain. Here we have an unusually sophisticated version of "This X of ours is not precisely *this* experience, but akin to this one and the opposite of that other". In this phrase Otto suggests that religious experiences can be understood only by analogy with some non-religious everyday experience, e.g., numinous fear by analogy with everyday fear. The first quatrain of this sonnet leads the reader further on, to some indescribable religious experience, this time by analogy with some more orthodox religious experience (which, in turn, is understood by analogy with some everyday experience). Statements like "the heaven that You have promised me, my God, moves me to love You; the hell I so fear moves me to cease sinning against You" would express some conspicuously goal-directed attitudes. My attitude is such and such, because I want to go to heaven, or because I want to avoid hell.[15]

---

[15] Of course, it does not have to be so straightforward. An individual purposeful intention is sometimes camouflaged by other "less beneficial" intentions, without giving up the conative declaration. In the Hebrew liturgical poem "Avinu Malkenu" used for a request of forgiveness, some lines call God to help the people, if not for their own individual sake, then for other reasons, like for His name and glory, or as a sort of revenge.

The naive believer's attitude to Hell and Paradise is admirably presented in the "Ballade made by Villon at his mother's request, for praying to Our Lady":

8.   Femme je suis povrette et ancïenne,
     Qui riens ne sçay; oncques lettre ne lus.
     Au moustier voy dont suis paroissienne
     Paradis paint, ou sont harpes et lus,
     Et ung enfer ou dampnez sont boullus:
     L'ung me fait paour, l'autre joye et liesse
     La joye avoir me fay, haulte Deesse,
     A qui pecheurs doivent tous recourir,
     Comblez de foy, sans fainte ne paresse :
     En ceste foy je vueil vivre et mourir.

I am a poor and old little woman, / who knows nothing, neither to write nor to read. / In the church where I am parishioner I saw / Paradise painted where there are harps and lutes, / and Hell where the damned are tortured: / one frightens me, the other gives me joy and delight — / Let me have joy, high Goddess, / to whom sinners must run back, / full of faith, without failure, or laziness: / In this faith I want to live and die.

Unlike the speaker in the sonnet *"A Cristo Crucificado"*, the speaker in this ballade is moved to run untiringly toward "our Lady" by fear of Hell and hope for Paradise.

The negation in the sonnet arouses expectations for some *different* goal-directed attitudes (if not heaven and not hell, then what?). There is here, in fact, a double negation: first, the usual orthodox goals are negated as irrelevant; and then, the very goal-directed response is negated *("You* move me, Lord"). There is here an extreme switch of emotional attitudes, from an "instrumental set" to an "experiential set". The effect of this double switch is *bafflement,* getting the reader emotionally involved to an unusual degree. The abandonment of purpose is relatively strange and agitating. Whereas the information conveyed by the sentences may be conceptual, the bafflement is a nonconceptual experience. This bafflement is smoother, not so disorienting as the one in Donne's sonnet.

The first quatrain has a symmetrical structure, not only in its rhyme pattern, but also in its rhetorical structure: love, heaven and promise, as opposed to sin, hell and fear. In psychological terms, "emotion is a tendency towards an object judged suitable, or away from an object judged unsuitable" (Arnold and Gasson, 1968: 203). Love and fear in the first quatrain are such opposite emotions (tendencies *toward* and *away)*. According to Aristotle, the characteristic emotional effect of tragedy depends on the arousal of pity and fear. The opposite emotions in strict parallelism impose on this sonnet a psychological atmosphere of totality. This psychological atmosphere is enhanced by the involvement of God, heaven and hell in the process.

The emotions conveyed by the sonnet are directly named and reiterated. The verb *mueve* (move) recurs seven times in the first three stanzas, with various suffixes. We wish to point out three conspicuous components in this verb: it is derived from the perceptual vocabulary (kinaesthetic sense); its figurative meanings include "to cause" and "to stir the emotions, feelings, or passions"; and it is a linguistic device that shifts the speaker to a non-volitional role. Victor Balaban (1999: 259) speaks of "non-visual metaphors for knowledge, as a way to emphasize the passive relation-ship to the divine". In our sonnet there are two obsessively-repeated perceptual metaphors for mental processes, "see" and "move". The former, the visual metaphor, occurs twice; the latter, the non-visual metaphor, is reiterated no less than seven times. In Balaban's experiment with stories recounted by pilgrims to a Maria appari-tion site and by members of the APPARITION LIST on the internet, "of the visual metaphors used, only approximately half are active visual metaphors of 'looking' and 'seeing', and they tend to be used to describe the pilgrims' earlier, pre-conversion selves". The "seeing" metaphor in our sonnet may serve a similar rhetorical end: it is related to the more active stage of "seeing the place", embedded in a psychological atmosphere of "receptivity or openness to undergo whatever experiential events, sen-sory or imaginal", generated by the reiterated non-visual metaphor "move".

Repetition is a common means of meditation, mentioned in the Ignatian exercises as well. The purpose of repetition is to improve the ability to concentrate, to facili-tate the separation from daily life by reducing cognitive effort. This mode of opera-tion is partially valid in this Spanish poem as well, where it is overdetermined by a variety of effects. The intensive repetition in a relatively orderly manner creates sim-plicity, and reduces the cognitive effort required. At the same time, it can be per-ceived as an indication of some impediment in the speaker's ability to express him-self, owing to some persistent preoccupation (Benari, 1993). Like a child fully con-centrated on his one world, the speaker repeats the same expressions over and over. His voluntarily limited world might account for his inability to express himself more elaborately. Israel Levin (1986: 48) gives an illuminating account of this kind of repetition in an essay on a rigidly formulaic genre in Ibn Gabirol's mystic poetry: the multitude of repetitions that say the same thing in different ways testify, as it were, to the failure of conceptual language to express something elusive, something that it attempts to capture in vain, struggling to say it with its tortuous rhythm. The obsessive yet more flexible repetition in the Spanish sonnet arouses a more credible impression: the intense emotional quality does have some more positive contents.

Newberg et al. (2001: 87) point out an intriguing resemblance between the effects of such repetition and the effects of the "composition of place" on suspending the boundaries of the self in meditation, as propounded above. We have quoted them suggesting that when the orientation area is forced to operate on little or no neural input, the likely result is a softer, less precise definition of the boundaries of the self. Now they claim that the same neurobiological mechanism can also be set in motion, "in a slightly different manner, by the intense, sustained practice of slow ritual activity such as chanting or contemplative prayer. These slow rhythmic behaviors stimulate the quiescent [parasympathetic] system, which, when pushed to very high levels, directly activates the inhibitory effects of the hippocampus", eventually depriving the orientation area of information "and, ultimately, blurring the edges of the brain's sense of self".

In his brilliant article, Victor Balaban (1999) mentions a wide range of religious discourses in which the speakers feel motivated to use "linguistic constructions that reduce their agency" (257). Among other instances, he quotes Linda Coleman who "found that 'born-again' Evangelical Christians systematically avoided using transitive sentences with first-person subjects as a way to avoid portraying themselves as volitional agents". This is conspicuously the case in the first nine lines of our sonnet. The subjects of all the verbs in these lines are external, whereas the first person occurs only as a direct object, as a passive object of action: "(not) heaven moves me to love You [...], You have promised me [...], (not) hell moves me to cease sinning". Perhaps the most notable instance is a nominal construction that would be hardly acceptable in English: "el infierno tan temido", that is, "Hell so feared by me". In the second quatrain the root "see" occurs twice; this mental process is attributed to "I". However, it occurs in an exceptionally complex syntactic construction, the conspicuous purpose of which is to "depersonalise" seeing, turning the agent into a passive object: "seeing You nailed to that cross and despised moves me". The phrase "seeing You nailed to that cross and despised" contains no overt subject or finite verb, but is itself the subject of the finite verb "moves me". Thus even "seeing" is not a volitional act; it just "happens" to the speaker.

The second quatrain of this sonnet proposes, in Puente's words, to "procure with the imagination to forme within our selves some figure, or image with the greatest vivacity", dwelling on the details of an imaginary scene, rather than go beyond it: the crucifixion of Christ, nailed to the cross, his body wounded. In the section "Physical and Human Setting" we claimed that "the more detailed our visualization, the less diffuse it might become. Spatial orientation elicits a diffuse mode of processing, but stable visual shapes may evoke rational domination. The detailed description of physical setting, so useful for the 'composition of place', bears the risk of [...] the formation of stable visual shapes, namely strong gestalts, and rational take-over". In the section "Visualisation and Emotion" we argued that "human setting and diffuse information give us less organised data, and therefore create larger gaps", and that "the amount of data activated to fill the gap from a human setting is larger than from a physical setting, that is more detailed from the start". The situation in this quatrain is emotionally loaded. But the prominent emotion is not so much Christ's physical injuries as his humiliation. The indignity inflicted on him is repeated in the phrases "despised" and "the insults You suffered", involving the reader in a strong emotional response.

This last item is also a good example of "unnecessary" repetition of assertions. There is, however, a more conspicuous instance of such "unnecessary" repetition. There is a positive and a negative goal in this poem (heaven and hell), negated in strict parallelism. The negation of patent goals is three times asserted in this sonnet: first in the first quatrain, then in the first tercet, "even if there were no heaven, I should love You; and even if there were no hell, I should fear You"; and then, two parallel tokens of only the positive goal in the second tercet: "You have not to give me anything to make me love You; for even if I did not hope for what I do hope for, I should love You just as I do". This unnecessary repetition displays a psychological atmosphere of lack of progress, a lack of onward movement toward a goal.

This lack of progress is perceived as evidence for a more permanent inner spiritual state. The repetition weakens the option to interpret the assertion as a short-lived moment of spiritual elevation. This is not a transient instant. At the same time the most important impact of such a repetition is indeed the speaker's willingness to dwell upon his expressive state, to give it all the time needed, not to move forward, not to rush things; after all, it is not that he is waiting for something to happen. He is not going anywhere—he has abandoned all utilitarian purposes.

We have seen the sophisticated turns of the powerful paradoxical phrasings in the first quatrain of this sonnet. But even these paradoxes appear to have been a commonplace in the seventeenth century and before. Rabia, a Sufi mystic, for instance, prayed dramatically for relief from self-centred aims:

9.   Oh Lord:
     If I worship you from fear of hell, cast me into hell,
     If I worship you from desire for paradise, deny me Paradise
                                            (Quoted by Deikman 2000: 86).[16]

To be sure, Rabia's paradoxes too have an exceptionally powerful effect. Nevertheless, the present suggestion is that if this sonnet is judged a unique masterpiece, it is due to the interaction of the powerful paradoxes with the effects generated by the stylistic manipulations discussed above.

Conclusion

This chapter began with issues related to Jesuit meditation, and then proceeded to the poetry of meditation. But actually we worked in a very different order. Our starting point was how poetic language—which is, like all language, conceptual and linear—is able to convey experiences that are non-conceptual and non-linear. We also noted that romantic poetry typically presents such experiences by way of presenting some detailed landscape description. Likewise, both metaphysicalpoetry and romantic poetry typically begin with some well-defined situation. To account for these and additional problems in poetry we had recourse to the findings of cognitive and brain sciences. Only later did we apply the tools developed by cognitive poetics to meditation proper.

---

[16]   There is also a forthcoming book by M. Cyria Huff with the suggestive title *Sonnet— No Me Mueve, Mi Dios—Its Theme in Spanish Tradition* (AMS Press).

Religious systems are conceptual systems. Language too is a conceptual system. Even such words as "ecstasy" or "mysticism" are supposed to be used as clear-cut concepts. Our objective was to explore how such a conceptual language can convey non-conceptual experiences such as meditation, ecstasy or mystic insights. Briefly, we explored how the poet, by using words, can express the "ineffable".

In cognitive poetics, the danger of reductionism lurks at every turn. Very little is gained by describing the same literary phenomenon three times: in critical language, in cognitive language and in brain language. As Tsur (1987b: 289–308; 1997) has pointed out, there is no excuse for departing from critical language, unless this solves some otherwise unsolvable problem. In the present instance, reliance on the orientation mechanism and lateralisation (that is, division of the brain into left and right hemispheres) helped us to confer a positive meaning on the negative term "ineffable" and to relate landscape descriptions and emotional effects in poetry in a principled manner.

Our research did not try to explore religious ideas for their own sake, but how religious ideas are turned into verbal imitations of religious experience by poetic structure.

We considered some cognitive mechanisms underlying the "composition of place" in Jesuit meditation and used them to systematically relate this practice to its perceived effect: a kind of altered state of consciousness in meditation, and the representation of some of its salient features in the verbal medium. We have dwelt upon three characteristics of meditative texts: their power to arouse the orientation mechanism, their diffuseness, and their absence of purpose, and analysed them in relation to the alternative visual settings, physical and human. These characteristics were discussed, in turn, as the source of two major effects on the reader: governing the relative emotional potential, and the relative sense of control. This method yielded some illuminating insights into the process of meditation and the perception of meditative poetry. Finally, we applied our distinctions to actual texts.

In Donne's Holy Sonnet, for instance, we scrutinized a complex poetic effect. The first two lines present a paradoxical visual image that suggests conflicting world pictures in a form that the imagination can encompass in a single intuition. Consequently, it evokes an exceptionally strong sense of wit and bafflement; but, at the same time, it also offers a space for orientation. As a result it becomes, in Sir Herbert Grierson's (1965: xxxiv) words, the onset of "a strain of passionate, paradoxical reasoning".

In the Spanish sonnet "No me mueve" ("A Cristo Crucificado") we have followed the verbal techniques by which it switches from the instrumental to the experiential set that emerges as the intense perceptual quality of the text. Our analytic approach pointed out one by one a wide variety of poetic devices that indicated absence of goals and linguistic constructions that reduced the speaker's agency.

Finally, the following should be noticed. The critic's language can point to these elements only in a *sequence* of statements. The sentences of the poem likewise occur in a sequence. But when elements from different levels indicate similar qualities, they are integrated into a compound effect in the reader's mind. Sometimes (in the second quatrain of "A Cristo Crucificado", for instance), the same string of words is the exponent of the various elements that contribute to the same effect: the syntactic structure, the semantic structure of the verbs, the structure of perceptual metaphors, and the nature of the scene imagined. Thus, the sequential and analytical critical statements may evoke a perceptual quality that is a regional quality of an integrated patterned whole.

Chapter 5

Mystic Poetry—Metaphysical, Baroque and Romantic

Mysticism and Poetic Style

An important assumption of the present study is that devotional, meditative, mystic poetry is first of all poetry, shaped and constrained by possibilities and constraints inherent in the various poetic styles. Our main interest is in how language and poetic style can convey experiences which notoriously escape expression in words. The analysis of devotional, meditative, mystic poetry must therefore be similar to the analysis of any poetry. In this respect, meditative and mystic qualities are treated just as any other "poetic qualities". At the same time, there is a significant interaction between poetic style and, e.g., mystic experience. When we say "mystic experience", we refer to a wide variety of extremely complex mental processes, some of which apparently have conflicting aspects. I argue that there may be some overlap between certain aspects of mystic experience and certain aspects of the various poetic styles. A given poetic style may foreground certain aspects of mystic experience and background others. And conversely, some mystics may exploit the potentials of one poetic style or other to communicate those aspects of mystic experience which are of great importance to them. In order to pursue these processes fruitfully, I shall appeal to certain distinctions relevant to poetry in general, which cut across a wide range of poetic styles. In this chapter I am going to organise my argument around two dichotomies. John Crowe Ransom (1951) distinguishes between three "ontological" models: Physical, Platonic and Metaphysical poetry, of which I am going to make use of the last two only. Elsewhere (1992a: 347–384) I make a distinction between "poetry of orientation" and "poetry of disorientation". In order to demonstrate all the afore-said qualities and interactions, we will have to perform exceptionally close readings, to dwell on very minute details of the texts to be discussed.

Consider Ransom's triad. It suggests that in different poetic styles visual imagery functions differently. In this chapter I will explore types of relationships between the visual and some abstract elements in the use of imagery, in the service of religious poetry. I will discuss Platonic and Metaphysical poetry at some length, and compare the two. All three types of poetry make liberal use of visual imagery, but in different ways. Physical poetry, says Ransom, uses sequences of physical images that indicate no abstractions. I am not sure that this is possible at all, unless deliberate measures are taken to prevent abstraction. It would appear that our abstraction mechanisms are set into motion as soon as we encounter poetic imagery. Platonic poetry uses physical images as "good examples" to represent, or illustrate, abstract notions. In classicist and romantic poetry, "typical representatives" of the abstract category are usually used; alternatively, in classicist and romantic poetry, abstractions are derived from the most salient features of the objects described. Sometimes notions are abstracted from a variety of objects. In this way, Platonic poetry smoothly directs attention away from the physical image to the abstract notion. In certain circumstances such a smooth shift of attention may be experienced as the intuitive perception of a supersensuous reality.

Platonic poetry may present a wide variety of very dissimilar objects; it is the common idea which they represent that unifies them. Metaphysical poetry, by contrast, forces the reader to attend back to one physical image. In metaphysical poetry, an image may represent, just as in Platonic poetry, some abstraction. But then, the poet develops precisely those physical aspects of the image which are irrelevant to that abstraction, by making each such aspect represent a different abstraction. In Platonic poetry only that feature of each image is emphasised which suggests the common idea; the other, irrelevant features, are de-emphasised. In metaphysical poetry every physical object is conceived of as of a bundle of features. The features are elaborated, one by one, as relevant to some abstraction; at the same time each feature forms an irrelevant texture to all the others. Thus, the two kinds of poetry display different types of unity. If in Platonic poetry the common abstraction bestows unity upon a variety of images, in metaphysical poetry, on the contrary, the one image bestows unity upon a variety of abstractions.

Romantic and classicist poetry are similar, then, to each other in being typically "Platonic", in contrast to metaphysical poetry. On the other hand, the structure of their imagery typically differs, among other features, in a most important respect: in romantic nature imagery, the objects that are striking representatives of "Platonic" ideas are not only parallel to one another, but are also subsumed in a coherent landscape. W.K. Wimsatt explored "The Structure of Romantic Nature Imagery" (1954): he shows how a metaphor organises a romantic nature poem, how, e.g., the river landscape in Coleridge's sonnet "To the River Otter" is "both the occasion of reminiscence and the source of the metaphors by which reminiscence is described", how romantic poems blur the distinction between the literal and the figurative because the poet wants to read a meaning into the landscape, but also wants to find it there. As we will see, this characterisation is appropriate to Wordsworth's Romantic-Pantheistic sonnet "Composed upon the Beach Near Calais" as well as to Andreas Gryphius' Baroque-Christian sonnet "Abend".

This last point brings us to the distinction of "poetry of orientation" versus "poetry of disorientation". The landscape unifies the analogous "Platonic" representative objects in a coherent entity, exploiting those features of the objects that are irrelevant to the "Platonic" idea. This unity is not unlike that of the metaphysical image, but there are some crucial differences. As Wimsatt (1954: 109) pointed out, "If this romantic wit differs from that of the metaphysicals, it differs for one thing in making less use of the central overt statement of similitude which is so important in all rhetoric stemming from Aristotle and the Renaissance. The metaphor in fact is scarcely noticed by the main statement of the poem". I wish to point out another difference. The typical metaphysical image is outside the perceiver, and is separated from him and from other images by clear-cut boundaries. In Romantic (and some

Baroque) poetry, by contrast, the perceiver is placed *within* the landscape; and rather than separating himself, he uses his orientation mechanisms to *relate* himself to the surrounding scenery. As we have suggested in chapter 4, the application of orientation mechanisms to clear-cut concepts may render them as diffuse, supersensuous, emotionally-loaded qualities perceived in a landscape.[1]

After reviewing a wide range of attempts to define the nature of romanticism, René Wellek comments: "they all see the implication of imagination, symbol, myth, and organic nature, and see it as part of the great endeavor to overcome the split between subject and object, the self and the world, the conscious and the unconscious" (Wellek, 1963: 220). The same "great endeavor to overcome the split between subject and object" is central to most mysticisms around the world. I argue that the abstractions handled in concrete poetic landscapes become not unlike the fluid, diffuse information utilised in orientation in an attempt to obtain self-specifying information from one's environment, and locate oneself in it with reference to time, space and people. Thus, the poetry of orientation, in extreme instances at least, may offer a verbal imitation of the intuitive perception of, and relating to, elusive information in one's environment.

The poetry of disorientation, by contrast, works by wit or shock. Consider, for instance, the paradox. It is frequently used for witty play with words. But in some poetry it is used to express the inextricable complexity of human existence. In the use of the mystics, however, it may have a much more far-reaching effect, as Steven T. Katz (1992: 7–8) indicates:

> Such linguistic ploys exist in many places throughout the world, usually connected with the conscious construction of paradoxes whose necessary violation of the laws of logic are intended to shock, even shatter, the standard epistemic security of "disciples," thereby allowing them to move to new and higher forms of insight/ knowledge. That is, mystics in certain circumstances know that they are uttering nonsensical propositions, but in so doing they intend, among other things, to force the hearers of such propositions to consider who they are—to locate themselves vis-a-vis normal versus transcendental "reality". The object of such exercises is existential rather than propositional (though this practice involves propositional claims that are inherent in the respective metaphysical systems of which such linguistic practices are a part).

---

[1] "If the left hemisphere is specialized for analysis, the right hemisphere [...] seems specialized for holistic mentation. Its language ability is quite limited. This hemisphere is primarily responsible for our orientation in space, artistic endeavour, crafts, body image, recognition of faces. It processes information more diffusely than does the left hemisphere, and its responsibilities demand a ready integration of many inputs at once. If the left hemisphere can be termed analytic and sequential in its operation, then the right hemisphere is more holistic and relational, and more simultaneous in its mode of operation" (Ornstein, 1975: 68).

I maintain that most stylistic devices typically used by metaphysical poetry may be used for such a disorienting purpose. In chapter 8 I extend this principle to George Herbert's experiments with visual ingenuities.

Potentials of Visual Objects

In the next section we are going to observe how Francis Quarles exploits the potentials of the visual object "rib" in the manner of metaphysical poetry, as opposed to Platonic poetry.

In the book of Genesis we get the following account: "So the LORD God caused a deep sleep to fall upon the man, and while he slept took one of his ribs and closed up its place with flesh; and the rib which the LORD God had taken from the man he made into a woman" (Genesis 2: 21–22). This is part of a much wider concrete story of how all things in the world were created. But from this concrete story some abstract principle may be abstracted. The text itself indicates the nature of this abstraction: "Therefore a man leaves his father and his mother and cleaves to his wife, and they become one flesh" (Genesis 2: 24). This comment suggests, then, the abstract principles "fast bonds, firm commitment". "One flesh" may also suggest "carnal bonds". Thus, by virtue of a metonymic relationship (derived from the Genesis story), "rib" becomes a strikingly representative example of an abstract idea. In our days, the title *Spare Rib* for a feminist journal may imply that this story degrades women to an inferior status. This may be unfair to the biblical text, which emphasises only a husband's duty toward his wife, not vice versa. But, as we will see, the inferior-status conception was not alien to sixteenth and seventeenth century religious poetry.

Thus, based on this biblical story, we might expect "rib", and "one flesh" to suggest in Platonic poetry "firm commitment, carnal bonds" between man and wife. The fact that the ribs form an enclosure is irrelevant to this abstraction; and so are some other properties of ribs: that they may break, and that they cannot move as freely as the limbs, but are slightly flexible still. As I have suggested, Platonic poetry directs attention away from the physical image to the abstract notion. The more the reader dwells on features of the object that are irrelevant to the abstraction, the more he attends back to the physical image. Let us consider for a moment the following poem by Francis Quarles:

> 1. Since of a Rib first framed was a Wife,
>   Let Ribs be Hi'rogliphicks of their life:
>   Ribs coast the heart, and guard it round about,
>   And like a trusty Watch keepe danger out;
>   So tender Wiues should loyally impart
>   Their watchfull care to fence their Spouses' heart:
>   All members else from out their places roue

> But Ribs are firmely fixt, and seldom moue:
> Women (like Ribs) must keepe their wonted home,
> And not (like Dinah that was rauish't) rome:
> If Ribs be ouer-bent, or handled rough,
> They breake; If let alone, they bend enough:
> Women must (vnconstrain'd) be plyent still,
> And gently bending to their Husband's will.

Contrary to the biblical text, this poem confers all the duties on the wife rather than on her husband. The fact that "of a Rib first framed was a Wife" emphasises that man and woman are "one flesh", but places the burden of firm loyalty not on the husband, but on the wife: she is a part of him, and that must determine all her conduct. From the structural point of view, the poem's imagery makes great "use of the central overt statement of similitude", to use Wimsatt's phrase. The sequel enumerates a series of properties of the ribs which are irrelevant to the "one-flesh" notion and forces the reader to "attend back" to the physical, visual image. Each of these concrete details, irrelevant to the original abstraction, is exploited for a "Platonic" illustration of some additional abstraction. Thus, each "Platonic" image is embedded in a network of irrelevant concrete detail yielding a concrete texture. This is how *Précieux* and Metaphysical poetry work. There is a multiplicity of abstractions related to one coherent image. Obviously, only a few of these abstractions relate to salient features of the physical object. Concomitantly with the increase in the number of features exploited, their relative salience must decrease. That is one reason for these poetic images to be perceived as witty, ingenious. While "Ribs coast the heart" is a relatively salient feature of ribs, their flexibility, suggested in the last two couplets, is of very low salience, and therefore strained.

Joseph Summers quotes this poem in a chapter called "The Poem as Hieroglyph", pointing out that the word "Hi'rogliphicks" itself occurs in it. But his definition of this notion is not sufficiently illuminating: "A hieroglyph is 'a figure, device, or sign having some hidden meaning; a secret or enigmatical symbol; an emblem'. [...] 'Hieroglyphic, the older form of the noun, was derived from the Greek for 'sacred carving,' and the root usually retained something of its original religious connotation" (1954: 123). This definition is not very helpful, if we want to know to what extent and in what respects it is the same as, or differs from, such devices as "metaphor, allegory, symbol, emblem, or metaphysical conceit". Some of the paradigmatic cases which Summers adduces for "hieroglyph" and Rosemary Freeman for "emblem" (1979) are the same, and there are good reasons to suppose that these two scholars refer to roughly the same thing by their respective terms. And the anatomy of the hieroglyphic significance of the rib discussed above has exactly the same structure as Donne's compass image, usually mentioned as a prototypical instance of the metaphysical conceit. Rickey (1979: 314) suggests a more workable definition: "a hieroglyphic poem [i]s one the physical shape of which reinforces its actual meaning". In view of Summers' and Freeman's examples, this seems to include visual elements both in the semantic and the typographic treatment of poems. The typographic elements in George Herbert's poetry will be discussed at considerable length in chapter 8. Here we may conjecture that in the semantic respect, Rickey intended the visualisation of the concrete image as in "Francis Quarles's anatomy of the hieroglyphic significance of the rib" (Summers, ibid.). Rickey's definition must be complemented by Rosemary Freeman's insights into the nature of emblems. The following two excerpts lend some support to my conception mentioned above: "The details, however, never illuminate the image: they merely extend it. The more curious and unusual the comparison the better the 'wit'. Thus Bunyan, in his Emblem Book, *A Book for Boys and Girls* (1686), chooses an egg and finds no less than fourteen points of resemblance between the state of man and that unpromising symbol" (Freeman, 1979: 219). Choosing the egg doesn't even have the metonymic justification underlying the choice of the rib in the foregoing example.

Writing on George Herbert's "The Church Floore" Freeman refines the foregoing conception: "His method is always to evolve meaning by creating likenesses; the likenesses are rarely inherent or to be seen from the outset". We will see an extreme instance of "creating likenesses" in chapter 8 in his "Anagram", in which he creates likeness between "Mary" and "Army". "Each of the epithets in 'The Church Floore' adds simultaneously to the image and to the generality behind it, creating the picture in the moral and the moral in the picture, and at the same time maintaining the sharp outlines of both" (Freeman, 1979: 224). Thus, according to Freeman, the emblem (or hieroglyph) is focused on a multiple relationship between a visual image and an abstraction, generating odd resemblances between them. Unlike Platonic poetry, this structure enhances the vividness of both the visual and the abstract element, "creating the picture in the moral and the moral in the picture, and at the same time maintaining the sharp outlines of both". That is an instance of what I have called "split" or "sharp focus" in poetry.

Two Adaptive Devices: Wit and Emotion

Cognitive poetics assumes that in the response to poetry adaptive devices are turned to aesthetic ends. In Western literature there is a poetic tradition that aims to achieve emotional effects; and another tradition that aims to achieve mainly witty effects. The poems in the latter tradition are often playful, but in some instances they become momentous. Now both emotions and wit are effective adaptive devices. Emotions keep a stream of fluctuating information in an active state, without pre-empting everything else. Such a stream of information frequently serves as an effective device of fast-orientation in rapidly changing circumstances. Wit is the phenomenological quality (that is, as it appears to the mind), of the shift of "mental sets". "Mental set" is the readiness to respond in a certain way. "Shift of mental sets" is the shift of one's readiness to respond in a certain way. Both are powerful adaptation devices. The former is necessary for handling a situation consistently; the latter for meeting sudden changes in a situation. The foregoing anatomy of the hieroglyphic significance of the rib relies on both attitudes: there is a succession of shifting mental sets from aspects of the concrete image to aspects of human relationship; at the same time, from shift to shift there is a sustained attitude toward the wife's status of caring subordination to her husband.

The message of the above rib-poem consists of rather shallow sermonising; it does not attempt to face the great existential problems of religious poetry. In such a context, its witty shifts of mental sets generate a psychological atmosphere of playfulness. However, wit being the phenomenological quality of a powerful adaptation device, in certain circumstances it may have a serious side as well. When one chooses an egg just in order to find no less than fourteen points of resemblance between it and the state of man, or the rib just in order to enumerate one by one the attitudes a wife is expected to display toward her husband, it is its sheer ingenuity that is foregrounded—ingenuity for wit's sake. But when it is applied to the complexities of human existence or is used to stagger the reader forcing him to seek to regain his balance by locating himself with reference to his environment—in brief, when the adaptation potential of the device is revived—it becomes momentous.

In the present work we assume two polar prototypes of mystic poetry, with an indefinite number of intervening types. Both prototypes are intimately related to orientation. In chapter 4 we explored at considerable length the importance of orientation mechanisms for voluntarily inducing such altered states of consciousness as meditation or varieties of mystic experience, in which volition is typically suspended. These mental processes are typically related to the right hemisphere of the brain, and consist of a diffuse stream of information in a highly active state. They frequently result in intuiting some imperceptible presence, or in an insight into the reality beyond the ultimate limit, or in a dissolution of the ego in infinity. Such mental processes are at their best when the very fact that they are mental processes escapes attention—to adapt an expression from "Longinus". This prototype tends to focus attention on the resulting altered state of consciousness.

The other prototype is typically related to varieties of metaphysical poetry. It is based on shock strategy, that can by no means "escape attention". In its contents it may violently shake a person's moral being; in its formulation it may be "connected with the conscious construction of paradoxes whose necessary violation of the laws of logic are intended to shock, even shatter, the standard epistemic security" of the reader, or with the disruption of the smoothly functioning cognitive system, as in the typographic patterning of the graphemic signifier in the poem (see chapter 8). In chapter 2 I discussed at length Donne's Holy Sonnet "Batter my Heart". This sonnet ends with a shock based both on the shaking of one's moral being by violence and sexual rape, and on the shattering of one's epistemic security by paradox: "for I / Except you'enthrall mee, never shall be free, / Nor ever chast, except you ravish me". In this type of mystic (or meditative) poetry readers face a two-stage adjustment process. First they meet staggering shock; second, they must regain their balance and orientation. This forces them "to consider who they are—to locate themselves vis-a-vis normal versus transcendental 'reality'". This prototype tends to focus attention mainly on the moment of the baffling shock. The metaphysical conceit at its boldest is one of the means intended to shatter "epistemic security"; but in its milder versions it may be accommodated in both prototypes of poetry.

Gryphius: "Abend"

The octet of the sonnet which is our next example is a striking instance of Platonic poetry by the German poet Andreas Gryphius (1616-1664):

> 2. *Abend*
> Der schnelle Tag ist hin, die Nacht schwingt ihre Fahn'
> Und führt die Sternen auf. Der Menschen müde Scharen
> Verlassen Feld und Werk; wo Tier' und Vögel waren,
> Traut itzt die Einsamkeit. Wie ist die Zeit vertan!
> Der Port naht mehr und mehr sich zu der Glieder Kahn.
> Gleich wie dies Licht verfiel, so wird in wenig Jahren
> Ich, du, und was man hat, und was man sieht, hinfahren.
> Dies Leben kömmt mir vor als eine Rennebahn:
> Laß, höchster Gott, mich doch nicht auf dem Laufplatz gleiten,
> Laß mich nicht Ach, nicht Pracht, nicht Lust, nicht Angst verleiten,
> Dein ewig heller Glanz sei vor und neben mir,
> Lass, wenn der müde Leib entschläft, die Seele wachen,
> Und wenn der letzte Tag wird mit mir Abend machen,
> So reiß mich aus dem Tal der Finsternis zu dir!

> Evening
> The swift day is over, night brandishes her banner and leads on the stars. The weary companies of men leave field and work; where animals and birds were, solitude now mourns. How time has been wasted! The harbour approaches closer and closer to the boat of the limbs. Just as this light vanished, so I and you and all that people have and see, will pass away in a few years. This life seems to resemble a race-course; O highest God, let me not slip on the track, let neither lament nor splendour nor pleasure nor fear lead me astray, let Thy eternally bright glory be always before me and beside me. Let, when the weary body falls asleep, let the soul remain awake and, when the last day brings my evening on, then snatch me out of the vale of darkness to Thee!

This is an exquisite piece of Baroque poetry. It begins with a description that gives no indication whatever that this may be a meditative, or any other kind of devotional, poem. In the first five lines there is a description of a certain scene at a certain time, generating an emotional quality by means that are more typical of romantic nature poetry than of metaphysical poetry. The beginning of this sonnet, like so many poems in the Western literary tradition, describes "evening", an actual evening, generating an intense emotional atmosphere. In considering the poetic techniques displayed in this poem, one must examine this description at three levels, which we will present here in bottom-up order. First, Lessing's comment on Homer is true of this description as well: "I find that Homer paints nothing but actions in progress, and all bodies, all separate objects he paints as they take part in these actions...." (quoted by Lukács 1962: 87). In Gryphius' sonnet, at this specific evening all bodies, all separate objects, are presented as they take part in some action. This technique appears to have here a very clear purpose: what Aristotle called in his *Rhetoric* "energeia": presenting the objects most vividly. Secondly, many of these actions illustrate the same "idea": the weary companies of men go home where they will have a rest; animals and birds have withdrawn from the fields in order to have a rest; the boat approaches closer and closer to the harbour, where it will come to a standstill. In this respect, Gryphius' description is Platonic poetry at its best. The only part of the evening that suggests the onset of activity rather than "calming down" is the night and the stars. But they, too, will have an important function in generating the emotional quality, in the perspective of the third level of description.

Thirdly, these separate objects are not merely parallel in that they suggest the same abstraction; they also display a certain measure of coherence. Apart from representing the same abstraction (calming down), they all belong to the same time (evening), implying some relatively limited space. The description is not what in classical rhetoric would be called "topographia" (description of place), but "chronographia" (description of time). It is a set of circumstances related to one another and to some person who grasps them at a certain time. The perceiving consciousness cannot encompass all the objects at once from its vantage point; but they nevertheless constitute a simultaneous whole. That is why this coherence is looser than that of a straightforward landscape description. In this context, the image "die Nacht schwingt ihre Fahn'/ Und führt die Sternen auf" deserves special attention. It is introduced to indicate a certain time. But it also refers to the only part of the scenery which can be seen wherever the speaker may be situated. The night sky can be seen when observing the "weary companies of men" returning home, or the empty fields, or the port "approaching" the boat. Thus it imposes a certain spatial coherence upon the "chronographia", suggesting some temporal and spatial relationships of the observer, that may be the source of self-specifying perceptual cues. In chapter 4 we pointed out the intimate relationship between the orientation mechanism on the one hand, and emotional processes and altered states of consciousness on the other. What we said there of spatial orientation applies here, too. Accordingly, the orientation mechanism activated by the spatial coherence of the "chronographia" *does* something to the abstractions derived from the parallel objects: it transfers their processing to the right hemisphere of the brain, giving them an intense, thick emotional quality that suffuses the evening scenery. Thus, the "Platonic" abstractions generated from the parallel entities at the second level are turned into a lowly-differentiated, diffuse and intense quality perceived by the reader and experienced by the speaker in the sonnet. All this suggests a tranquil mood suffusing the surroundings.

Aristotle's notion of "energeia" ("vividness" in English) suggests: strong, distinct or clearly perceptible; forming distinct and striking mental images. A moving object is more readily perceptible than an immobile one. That may be the reason why Gryphius (and Homer) prefer to paint all separate objects as they take part in actions rather than describe merely what they look like. The image "die Nacht schwingt ihre Fahn'/ Und führt die Sternen auf" (the night brandishes her banner and leads on the stars) contains what Christine Brooke-Rose calls "sensuous metaphors". They serve here to vividly present to the imagination the appearance of the night, rather than to illustrate some abstract idea. The most salient visual feature of a banner is a piece of cloth waving in the air. When darkness is presented as the banner of the night, something more dense than mere air is suggested; and since the metaphor cancels the material aspects of the banner, it is perceived as less tangible than a piece of cloth. Thus, some "dense", immaterial presence is vividly suggested to the mind. Motion is introduced into the description by saying "night brandishes her banner" instead "the darkness of night became apparent". Likewise, instead of saying "the stars became visible", "The stars were paraded" suggests motion.[2]

In this instance, the means by which "energeia" is achieved are quite palpable. But even in the other, more evasive instances, some significant deviation from normal expression is involved. Consider "The harbour approaches closer and closer to the boat of the limbs". This description reflects a poetic conception that is more salient in nineteenth-century symbolism, and twentieth-century Russian formalism, than in seventeenth century poetics: that the task of poetry is to present things not as we know them, but as we perceive them. We *know* that the boat is moving, while the port is standing still; but from the point of view of a person on the boat, it is the port that is *perceived* as moving toward the boat.

To appreciate two further instances of energeia in the first quatrain, we need to distinguish, semantically, between three kinds of predicate: *predicate of state, predicate of process,* and *predicate of action.* Such sentences as *John is tall. This coat is dry. Peter is weak. This house smells.*, contain **predicates of state.** Such sentences as *John became tall. The grass grew. The coat dried. Churchill died.*, contain *predicates of process.* Such sentences as *She laughed. The children became aggressive. The animals scattered.*, contain *predicates of action.* A *predicate of state* indicates that an associated noun is in a certain state. A *predicate of process* indicates some process, that is, a *change of state.* A *predicate of action* indicates a process that is self-arising, subject to voluntary control, and may be purposeful (cf. Fowler, 1974: 80–82). *Predicates of action* are predicated only of *voluntary agents.* Aristotle's examples of energeia in Homer can be characterised as using predicates of greater or higher energy than what the extra-linguistic referents would justify. "Thus, to say that a good man is 'four-square' is certainly a metaphor; both the good man and the square are perfect; but the metaphor does not suggest activity. On the other

---

2   It seems to me that "parade" is a more adequate translation for "führt auf", even though "lead" by itself is an exact translation of "führt" by itself. Thus, the exhibitory aspect rather than some patent purpose and definite direction is foregrounded in the act. Both "parade" and "banner" are taken from the military semantic field, and are perhaps a realisation of the biblical phrase "the host of heavens" (Nehemia 9,6; Zephania 1,5).

hand, in the expression 'with his vigour in full bloom' there is a notion of activity". Static objects and states of affairs are presented as moving or displaying some process; and moving objects as performing some human action, e.g., "Downward anon to the valley rebounded the boulder remorseless". "Remorseless" means here something like 'endlessly', 'showing no abatement' + a human attitude; the spear is not just flying, it is *eagerly* flying. As we have seen, in Gryphius' sonnet the darkness of night and the stars are not merely there, they are brandished and paraded, respectively. And night (as separate from the darkness of night) performs only human **actions**, though no characteristic human shape is indicated. In Baroque and romantic poetry, this principle is extended to instances which would have puzzled Aristotle: when the text attributes to abstractions properties or processes that only voluntary agents may have, it generates a feeling of some intense shape-free or thing-free presence.

Consider now "The weary companies of men leave field and work". The motion verb "leave" ("verlassen") is perfectly appropriate here. But there are some significant manipulations in the noun phrase. First of all, there is the genitive "companies of men". It removes "men" from the referring position and manipulates a collective noun into its place. Secondly, in line with traditional "poetic diction", there is a transferred epithet here: in the world of referents, it is not the "companies", but the "men", who are "weary". As a result, "companies" attract attention as an intense, unified, gestalt-free *quality* instead of a group of separate individuals that have a stable characteristic visual shape. The epithet "weary" enhances the perceived presence of this gestalt-free entity.

The case of "weary companies of men" is little more than trivial, but it corroborates a significant stylistic tendency in this poem. Consider: "wo Tier' und Vögel waren,/ Traut itzt die Einsamkeit" ("where animals and birds were, solitude now mourns"). "Traut" in these lines does not mean what it would mean in modern German (trusts, or gets married), but seems to be an intransitive verb related to the noun "trauer" (sorrow). This intransitive verb suggests sorrow as a mental process rather than a static quality. Hence the translation "mourns". Now consider this: a person may be lonely, and therefore sad. We could therefore just as well have used the phrase "a sad and lonely person". In our poem men, beasts and birds have withdrawn from the fields, and only loneliness remains there, as a thing-free quality; there is no person to be perceived as sad and lonely. Now let us compare two possible descriptions of this state of affairs: "sad loneliness is present", and "loneliness saddens" (or "mourns"—English lacks the appropriate verb). The latter sentence says roughly what the former does, but with a difference. It is clear that a lonely person may be sad. But here, it is the abstraction "loneliness" that is "sad". Most likely, the phrase is not meant here to contrast "sad loneliness" to, say, "cheerful loneliness"; "sad" is conceived here as a more or less permanent feature inherent in "loneliness". The predicate "saddens" (or "mourns"), by contrast, conveys here both the feature "sad", and the predicative component "is present", "occurs". In addition, it suggests not a more or less permanent feature, but an ongoing, active, mental process. As a result, "loneliness" is perceived as an intense, supersensuous, emotionally-loaded, active presence.

The foregoing distinction may be illuminated by Riffaterre's brilliant analysis of epithets. "We find", he says, "that certain epithets feel poetic no matter what noun they modify. Such is the French *agile,* 'agile,' 'nimble,' for instance" (Riffaterre, 1978: 28). But, more important, the *structure* of the phrase may be decisive for this effect:

> Thus poeticity disappears when the adjective is modified or qualified or enters into a predicative relationship—in short, when it ceases to be an epithet. We must therefore conclude that the agent of poeticity is a specific relationship between epithet and noun, which designates a quality of the noun referent, or a seme of that signifier, as characteristic or basic. So that the poetic is born where an adjective's meaning, normally contingent, accessory, in any case context-determined, is represented *a priori* as a permanent feature (Riffaterre, 1978: 28).

I am using Riffaterre's terminology, to point out an opposite quality. There are two crucial differences in our use. First, all the head nouns qualified by "agile" in Riffaterre's examples are concrete nouns, whereas in Gryphius I have meticulously pointed out the means by which he directed the focus of attention away from concrete nouns, to abstractions. Second, though I have acknowledged the far-reaching difference between the use of an epithet and a predicate, I have not characterised it as "poeticity" versus "nonpoeticity". When we use an epithet, in certain circumstances the adjective's meaning is represented *a priori* as a permanent feature of the noun modified by it. This characteristic disappears when the adjective is modified or qualified or enters into a predicative relationship. When the same properties are attributed to the head noun as a predicate rather than an epithet, especially when it denotes some abstraction or thing-free quality, and especially when this quality is presented as filling some coherent landscape or time-description, the "permanence" feature of the adjective disappears, and an elusive quality is generated or intensified.

The nearest phrase to Riffaterre's examples in Gryphius' sonnet is contained in its first sentence: "Der schnelle Tag ist hin" ("The swift day is over"). The adjective "schnelle" happens to be the German equivalent of "agile" extensively discussed by Riffaterre. It is "exemplary, strikingly representative" (Riffaterre, 1978: 28) of the lack of permanence. It should be noticed that in contrast to what happens in such verbal constructions as "Traut itzt die Einsamkeit", the abstract noun "Tag" in the epithet-construction "schnelle Tag" does not become a diffuse emotionally-loaded perceptual quality, but remains a compact conceptual entity. Thus, the two abstract nouns achieve two very different kinds of vividness.

In the first five lines of Gryphius' sonnet, then, the "Platonic" representation of such ideas as "calming down" is part of a wider poetic strategy of manipulating attention away from the solid objects of the landscape to gestalt-free and thing-free qualities. At the same time, the orientation mechanism activated by the landscape

turns these abstractions ino a supersensuous presence, or, an intense emotional quality, intuitively perceived in the scenery. The various stylistic devices of "energeia"
further enhance these effects. As we will see, the use of such stylistic devices is
sometimes "heightened, to any degree heightened", in romantic poetry.

The sonnet begins with the description of a special point of time in an ordinary
evening of an ordinary working day. Even the first sentence, "The swift day is over",
seems to indicate only that special point in time, rather than the transience of life.
However, Wimsatt's characterisation of the structure of romantic nature imagery
seems to apply to this baroque poem as well. To paraphrase Wimsatt, the description of this particular evening is both the occasion of reflection and the source of the
metaphors by which the reflection is described. The disappearance of daylight is the
most salient, perhaps the defining, feature of evening; so it is required for the realistic fullness of description. The realistic plenitude of this description is supplied by
the simile "Just as this light vanished, so I and you and all that people have and see,
will pass away in a few years". (In the last but one line of the sonnet, though the
structure of imagery is changed in the sestet, death is still described as "when the last
day brings my evening on", and this world as "the vale of *darkness"*). In the exclamation "Wie ist die Zeit vertan!" (How time has been wasted!—line 4), the referent
of "Zeit" (time) is too vague: it is not clear whether it refers to the past five minutes, the past day, the past year or a lifetime. So, the exclamation may serve as an
effective summing up of the day that has passed, or it may mark the beginning of an
understanding of the meaning of life. In the course of reading, the former possibility
seems very likely; the image in lines 6–7 reinforces, in retrospect, the latter possibility, by turning the "innocent" description of evening into a "Platonic" image of
the transience of life, a suggestion of the traditional theme *memento mori*. There is
still no indication that the description in the octet might be the "composition of
place" for the meditative process; this turns out to be the case only in retrospect,
again, when the sestet turns out to be a "Colloquy" with God. The issue of the
meaning of life (in line 4) assumes great importance when the reader realises that he
is reading a meditative poem.

When one realises the transience of life, it may lead one to adopt the wisdom of
Ecclesiastes (1, 2–5): "Vanity of vanities, says the Preacher, vanity of vanities! All
is vanity. What does man gain by all the toil at which he toils under the sun? A
generation goes, and a generation comes, but the earth remains for ever. The sun
rises and the sun goes down and hastens to the place where it rises". This in turn,
may lead us to adopt the *Carpe Diem* (pluck the day) position as, e.g., in Marvell's
"Now therefore, while the youthful hew / Sits on thy skin like morning glew, / [...]
Now let us sport us while we may". Alternatively, since "I and you and all that
people have and see, will pass away in a few years", one may adopt Sir Philip
Sidney's commendation: "Grow rich in that which never taketh rust"; or, in
Talmudic terms, "Prepare thyself in the corridor, so as to enter the salon". It is only
in the sestet that the reader is forced to decide in favour of the second possibility.

The octet is exceptionally well-articulated, by effective closures at the end of each
quatrain: the conclusive tone of the exclamation "Wie ist die Zeit vertan!" (How

time has been wasted!) at the end of the first quatrain; and the sudden deviation at the end of the second quatrain. A text or a section of it may arouse a sense of ending when there is a sudden deviation from a principle established earlier. The first seven lines present a continuous description of evening; the eighth line suddenly introduces an entirely different image: "Dies Leben kömmt mir vor als eine Rennebahn" (This life seems to resemble a race-course), suggesting the fairly traditional metaphor LIFE IS A RACE "derived" from the Lakoffian conceptual metaphor LIFE IS A JOURNEY. But there are two additional deviations in this line, in the description strategy on the one hand, and in the structure of imagery on the other. We have pointed out that in the first seven lines Gryphius, like Homer, paints all bodies, all separate objects, as they take part in actions. In the eighth line we find the opposite poetic strategy, based on what Kenneth Burke called scene-act ratio. The text substitutes the static path for the dynamic race, suggesting "the principle whereby the scene is a fit 'container' for the act, expressing in fixed properties the same quality that the action expresses in terms of development" (Burke, 1962: 3). As to the structure of imagery, the first seven lines (just as in romantic nature descriptions) offer the description of an actual evening in space and time, the objects of which serve, at the same time, as metaphors for some unmentioned abstractions. In the eighth line, the abstraction (life) is explicitly mentioned; what is more, it is in the referring position and it is the spatial object (the racecourse) that is conceived in a figurative sense.

Thus, the description of the particular evening becomes, in retrospect from line 8, part of a poem whose message is *memento mori* and possibly *carpe diem*. This, in turn, becomes in retrospect from the sestet part of a meditative poem. Louis Martz characterises meditation as the "practice of the presence of God", including "the deliberate, orderly operation of the 'three powers of the soul' — memory, understanding, will" (Martz, 1963: xviii). What in the course of reading was understood as a realistic description of an actual evening with its disappearing daylight, in retrospect, from the second quatrain and the sestet, becomes an object of meditation, a symbol (or emblem, or hieroglyph) of transience: "Gleich wie dies Licht verfiel, so wird in wenig Jahren / Ich, du, und was man hat, und was man sieht, hinfahren" (Just as this light vanished, so I and you and all that people have and see, will pass away in a few years). Thus, eventually, the description of the evening becomes part of a poetic structure regularly attributed to the "meditative poem": it consists of a composition of place followed by a colloquy with God; at the same time, the composition of place arouses insights into man's transience and "creature-feeling".

Earlier we have described how an intense, supersensuous, emotionally-loaded, active presence is perceived in the description of an actual evening. In the meditative perspective, such a supersensuous active presence may suggest the mental state required for meditation, or the "practice of the presence of God".

The metaphor of life-as-a-racecourse is peculiarly situated in this sonnet. By the end of the octet it seems to have three functions. First, by deviating from the previously established description, it serves as a powerful closure to the octet. Secondly, it enhances the sudden understanding that the preceding section may be no mere description of an actual evening, but may also suggest a sudden understanding about the meaning of life. Third, it suggests that whatever is symbolised by the movement in space, it will be over with the greatest speed. In this sense, the metaphor closes, rounds out, the octet, culminating in a sudden insight into the meaning of life. From this point on, the sestet is expected to shift to some new direction. This expectation is confirmed and refuted at the same time. There is, indeed, a shift from a descriptive tone to a "colloquy" addressing God; but, at the same time, this is done in terms of the life-as-a-racecourse metaphor, culminating in a return to "evening": death as the last evening. In this sense, the last day and the last evening have a double relationship to life. On the one hand, "day" is analogous to "life", and the end of the day analogous to the end of life. On the other hand, the last day completes life, and the last evening completes the last day before death.

According to Wilie Sypher, metaphysical imagery is transformed in Baroque poetry, losing its witty character—its disturbed balance, unresolved tensions, richness in directions and discontinuities (Sypher, 1955: 100–179)—through a number of "resolutions", one of them being resolution in space (ibid, 212–219). Our analysis has pointed out that this is what happens in Gryphius' poem too. "Light" is treated in this poem as a typical metaphysical conceit. Light and its absence suggest day and night. In lines 6–7 other potentials of the vanishing light image are exploited, and in line 11 still another one. This treatment is characteristic of the metaphysical conceit. The light image in line 11 "Dein ewig heller Glanz sei vor und neben mir" conforms with the Lakoffean notion of LIGHT IS SEEING and SEEING IS KNOWING. The fact that in the first quartet it occurs literally and in lines 6–7 it suggests transience is a counter-example. At the same time, it is a good example of the view propounded in chapter 12, that images are bundles of meaning potentials; the poet may move freely from one potential to another, and bring to life hitherto unrealised dormant potentials. These lines evoke in the reader a kind of openness to experience; only then does the traditional metaphor LIFE IS A RACE appear, compatible with Lakoff's LIFE IS A JOURNEY metaphor. Here a "colloquy" between the speaker and God takes place; and the purposelessness of *memento mori* is transformed into the vision of a purposeful life. In the last two lines, again, some very traditional but unexpected potentials of evening are exploited. "The evening of life" is a traditional proportional metaphor; this poem preserves the literal meaning of "evening", but still suggests end of life in "letzte Tag wird mit mir Abend machen". The phrase "Tal der Finsternis" exploits the darkness typically associated with evening, implying a suggestion concerning our *condition humaine*.

Romanticism, Pantheism and Meditation: Wordsworth

In this section I am going to consider in some detail a sonnet by Wordsworth. Before that I would like to remind ourselves of two suggestions by Louis Martz: he characterises meditation as the "practice of the presence of God"; and he suggests that some of the outstanding pieces of romantic nature poetry belong to the genre of meditation.

> 3. It is a beauteous evening, calm and free:
>   The holy time is quiet as a Nun
>   Breathless with adoration; the broad sun
>   Is sinking down in its tranquillity;
>   The gentleness of heaven broods o'er the Sea.
>   Listen! the mighty Being is awake,
>   And doth with his eternal motion make
>   A sound like thunder—everlastingly.
>   Dear Child! dear Girl! that walkest with me here,
>   If thou appear untouched by solemn thought,
>   Thy nature is not therefore less divine:
>   Thou liest in Abraham's bosom all the year;
>   And worship'st at the Temple's inner shrine,
>   God being with thee when we know it not.
>   Wordsworth, "Composed upon the Beach Near Calais"

I am going to state my position toward this poem through reference to two classical discussions by two great "New critics", F. R. Leavis and Cleanth Brooks. In his influential article "Imagery and Movement", Leavis (1945–46) claims that the abstractness of this sonnet renders it one of the prototypical bad poems. Cleanth Brooks, by contrast, argues in his *The Well-Wrought Urn* that this poem is paradoxical, and by virtue of the paradox he regards it as one of his prototypical good poems, in spite of its abstractmess. I argue that precisely by virtue of its handling the abstractions, this sonnet is a masterpiece of mystic-pantheistic poetry. The poetic techniques we have encountered in Gryphius' evening sonnet are enhanced and amplified in Wordsworth's evening sonnet.

In order to demonstrate how bad this poem is, Leavis compares it to Wordsworth's own Westminster-Bridge sonnet, which he considers somewhat less bad.

> The structure analysed [in the Westminster-Bridge sonnet] is not a complex one, and perhaps may be thought too obvious to have been worth the analysis. The point to be made, however, is that Calais Beach hasn't even this measure of complexity; it has no structure, but is just a simple one-way flow of standard sentiment. Consider the key words "beauteous" "calm", "Holy," "quiet", "Nun", "adoration", "tranquillity", "gentleness", "broods", "mighty Being", "eternal", "everlastingly", "solemn", "divine", "wor-

shipp'st", "Temple", "shrine", "God"—there is nothing to counter the insistent repetitious suggestion; nothing to qualify the sweet effusion of solemn sentiment. In fact, the cloying sameness aggravated by an element not yet noted: instead of the kind of complexity introduced by "smokeless", we get the sestet, which, with its "Dear Child! dear Girl!" and "Abraham's bosom", adds saccharine to syrup and makes the sonnet positively distasteful (Leavis, 1968: 243).

In order to demonstrate the paradoxical quality of this supposedly single-minded sonnet, Brooks (1968: 6) too asks us to consider a list of words, and makes extremely fine discriminations in the analysis of its first quatrain:

> ... consider the adjectives in the first lines of Wordsworth's evening sonnet: *beauteous, calm, free, holy, quiet, breathless*. The juxtapositions are hardly startling; and yet notice this: the evening is like a nun breathless with adoration. The adjective "breathless" suggests tremendous excitement; and yet the evening is not only quiet but *calm*. There is no final contradiction, to be sure: it is *that* kind of calm and *that* kind of excitement, and the two states may well occur together. But the poet has no one term [...] He must work by contradiction and qualification.

This passage offers quite convincing evidence against the claim that there is in this description "nothing to qualify the sweet effusion of solemn sentiment". The various adjectives qualify each other in a quite complex way. This complex emotional state of mind interacts in a peculiar way with the landscape. The nun could be visible, but actually is not present; she is only a simile. The "holy time" is invisible, and shows no visible sign of excitement. In the present context of abstract qualities, the excitement is devoid of physical activity, and all its immense energy is fused with the other abstract qualities: *calm, holiness, tranquillity, solemnity* in order to intensify them. As in Gryphius' sonnet, the intense but imperceptible emotional processes suffuse the abstractions with "energeia".

"The holy time" (like "beauteous evening") is, obviously, an abstraction from certain natural objects *at a given time*. It occurs in a fairly particularised situation. It is not sequential time, but a particular *now* in a particular *here*. The immediate subtlety of the minute is reinforced by the particular "tiptoe effect" of "calm excitement", which, as suggested by Brooks, is dependent on the particular combination of apparently incompatible elements. The abstractness of *time* is reinforced, as we have seen, by the surrounding abstract nouns, even by the adjective *holy*. On the other hand, *time* serves here to shift attention away from the perceived objects of the scene to its felt quality. In the physical reality represented, it is not *time* that is quiet, but the natural objects of the landscape seem quiet *at this time*. Thus, "the holy time" oscillates, as it were, between an abstract existence and its function as metonymy for a concrete situation: it is more concrete than a mere abstraction, but, still, less than a physical—visible, audible, tangible—entity. It is perceived as a thing-free quality hovering in a concrete landscape. The nun may be "breathless with adoration", but this meaning does not come into full focus. *Breathless* may apply to a landscape as well, in the sense of "there is not the slightest current of air". This is corroborated, in retrospect, by one of the meanings of *calm*—"not windy". Similarly to the invisible presence of *breathless* air and the *mighty being*—thing-free qualities as holiness, adoration, tranquillity, solemnity are intensely present. The nominal style of the quatrain is remarkable. There are only three finite verbs in four lines: only one that denotes spatial motion *(is sinking down)*, and the verb *is* twice, once as a copula, and once denoting existence. Time is not associated with vigorous actions (as in so many of Shakespeare's sonnets), but with states and gestalt-free qualities. Owing to this nominal style, the argument has no beginning, middle or end, and allows the reader to contemplate the parallel phrases, and abstract common qualities from them.

Although the atmosphere of the sonnet has been subsumed under a well-defined scene, this has been indicated only in the title in some editions ("Composed upon the Beach near Calais"), and by two concrete nouns: *sun, sea*. The rest is done by the deixis "It is" and the deictic ingredient in the imperative verb "Listen!", directing attention to an immediate situation. What is important here is not the landscape but the atmosphere, the impressive solemnity hovering over it. Instead of talking about natural objects in the landscape—as usual with Wordsworth—he talks about the spirit that informs them, by turning some attributes and circumstances of the possible landscape into abstract nouns, which have a strong cumulative impact of thing-free qualities, together with some other abstract nouns: *evening* (with *time* as its synonym), *the gentleness of heaven, adoration, tranquillity*. In this context, line 5 of the sonnet deserves special attention:

> 4. The gentleness of heaven broods o'er the Sea.

The phrase *gentleness of heaven* is noteworthy in this respect, especially if one compares it to two possible alternative phrasings:

> 5. The gentle heaven broods o'er the Sea.

> 6. The gentleness of heaven *rests* o'er the Sea.

In excerpt 4 Wordsworth resorts to a poetic device which I have elsewhere called "transferred attribute", or "nominalised predicate", or simply the-ABSTRACT-of-the-CONCRETE metaphor. This is a conspicuous device to direct attention *away from* the objects and concepts *to* their felt qualities.

What is the source of the unique quality in excerpt 4? Strawson (1967) explores what is the most natural assignment of nouns to the subject and the predicate in a statement. The most natural order is when the more concrete noun occurs in the referring position, and the less concrete one in the predicative position as, for instance, when *a spatio-temporally continuous particular* occurs in the referring position, whereas a *property* of a spatio-temporally continuous particular is assigned to the predicative position. The difference between the two formulations in excerpts 4 and 5 is that in excerpt 5 a *spatio-temporally continuous particular* ("heaven") is in the referring position, whereas in excerpt 4 an *abstract property* of a spatio-temporally continuous particular ("gentleness") is manipulated into the referring position. Such a construction is not uncommon in our texts. It occurs with similar effect in chapter 9, in the phrase "the *presence of* Presence" in an ancient Hebrew *Mercabah* hymn, or in Cawley's verse line "To drowne the *wantonnesse of* this wilde thirst", or in Baudelaire's "Hymne", in the lines "Et dans mon âme inassouvie / Verse le *goût de* l'éternel". I have elsewhere shown (Tsur, 1992a: 416–428) that Whitman's "meditative" catalogue differs from his "illustrative" catalogue, among other things, in using liberally this "the-ABSTRACT-of-the-CONCRETE" construction. Likewise, in Gryphius' poem above, in the clause "Traut itzt die Einsamkeit" (solitude now mourns), the abstract noun "Einsamkeit" is abstracted away from "solitary things (or beings)", and then manipulated into the referring position. A similar—though less radical—process can be discerned in the phrase "Der Menschen müde Scharen" (the weary companies of men). In all of these instances, the relationship of the attribute to the compact "thing" or "concept" has been loosened by this transformation. In some of them, the "thing" from which the properties were abstracted (heaven, thirst, presence, l'éternel) themselves lack stable, characteristic visual shape.

Wordsworth's thematised predicate has the following significant characteristics. First, the spatio-temporally continuous particular is a thing-free and gestalt-free entity. Second, both the spatio-temporally continuous particular and its abstract property are *simultaneously present*. Third, the spatio-temporally continuous particular exceeds the capacity of the imagination to comprehend or encompass its whole representation in a single intuition. Fourth, the phrase occurs in the description of a set of circumstances related to one another and to some person who grasps them, that is, of a landscape immediately defined "here and now". As a result, *gentleness* is perceived as a diffuse but intense quality infusing the whole perceptual field. This diffuseness is reinforced by "o'er the Sea" which, again, adds an important detail to the visual scene and designates a shape-free particular perceived as boundless.

Now let us corrupt for a moment the predicate of this line, as in excerpt 6. In this corrupt line, I suggest, the affect under discussion is much weakened. What is the source of this difference? Some people would say that whereas *rests* is plain nonfigurative language, *broods* personifies *gentleness*. Suppose that we accept this account: then we will have called the phenomenon by a name, but explained nothing. "The gentleness of heaven" will be positioned "o'er the Sea" in the same way, with both predicates. A much more illuminating way would be to rely on the semantic distinction proposed above between three kinds of predicate: *predicate of state, predicate of process,* and *predicate of action.* It will be noticed that the three kinds of predicate are arranged in an ascending order of energy. It will also be noticed that when a "higher" kind of predicate is applied instead of a lower one (that is, a predicate of process instead of a predicate of state, or a predicate of action instead of a predicate of process or state), the "extra" energy conveyed by the predicate is perceived as an amplification of the *vividness* of the description. If we return now to

Wordsworth's line and its corrupted version, we may notice that *rests* and *broods* suggest *the same state.* The difference between them is that whereas the former designates a *physical state,* the latter designates a mental process *(action),* infusing the diffuse thing-free quality *gentleness* with a high level of energy, increasing its impact upon perception.

I wish to make three further comments on lines 6–8. First, *Listen!* shifts the mood of the poem from description to the imperative; this is a vigorous deictic device to place the perceiving consciousness right in the midst of the situation, activating its "emotional" mechanism of locating itself in its environment with reference to time and space. Second, some important aspects of the object of *listen* are inaudible. *The mighty being* may be an abstract periphrasis for "God", imperceptible to the senses. *Is awake* denotes a mental state, and is similarly imperceptible in itself, but still active. Thus, again, a more refined sensation of the supersensuous is evoked, possibly intimating, by the same token, a pantheistic deity. *A sound like thunder* is introduced only two lines after *listen.* Third, the thing-free sound-perception of line 6, then, gets belatedly a "thingy" (though gestalt-free) motivation in lines 7–8. It should be noticed, however, that *And doth with his eternal motion make / A sound like thunder—everlastingly* is to be attributed to the sea more suitably than to an abstraction. One could suggest, therefore, that lines 7–8 as well comprise intense, thing-free sound-perceptions, a supersensuous atmosphere which has, nonetheless, a dislocated motivation in line 5 *(sea).* This dislocation is, of course, "mitigated" by an animistic pantheistic view, informing this and some other poems by Wordsworth.

Let us turn now to that section of the sonnet which "adds saccharine to syrup and makes the sonnet positively distasteful"—the sestet. Cleanth Brooks offers precisely this section as a crucial example of the sonnet's paradoxical sophistication:

> The poet is filled with worship, but the girl who walks beside him is not worshipping. The implication is that she should respond to the holy time, and become like the evening itself, nunlike; but she seems less worshipful than inanimate nature itself. [...] The underlying paradox (of which the enthusiastic reader may well be unconscious) is nevertheless thoroughly necessary, even for that reader. Why does the innocent girl worship more deeply than the self-conscious poet who walks beside her? Because she is filled with an unconscious sympathy for all of nature, not merely the grandiose and solemn. [...] Her unconscious sympathy is the unconscious worship. She is in communion with nature "all the year", and her devotion is continual whereas that of the poet is sporadic and momentary (Brooks, 1968: 1–2).

I embrace this interpretation. I would like to point out that the octet is devoted to the description of an evening landscape; the sestet shifts to a direct address. According to my conception of this sonnet as a meditative poem, the octet constitutes a "composition of place" as discussed at length in the preceding chapter, that effectively arouses an intuition of perceiving some supersensuous presence. This leads to a "colloquy" that yields an insight of great religious importance as Martz describes it:

"The understanding then proceeds to analyze ('discourse' upon) the meaning of the topic, in relation to the individual self, until gradually the will takes fire and the personal affections arise. It is clear too from Dawson's account that these affections of the will inevitably lead into the colloquy, where the speaker utters his fears and hopes, his sorrows and joys, in 'affectionate speach' before God" (Martz, 1963: xxii). Wordsworth's colloquy is not addressed to God, but this is not a necessary condition, as Martz himself explains:

> St. François de Sales, as usual, sums up beautifully the whole range of possibilities in colloquy, when he advises that "Amidst these affections and resolutions" which follow from meditation "it is good to use colloquies, or familiar talke, as it were somtime with God our Lord, somtime with our blessed Ladie, with the Angels, and persons represented in the mysterie which we meditate, with the Saints of heaven, with our selves, with our own hart, with sinners, yea and with insensible creatures" (Martz, 1962: 37).

To sum up

This chapter adopts from John Crowe Ransom (1951) a distinction between three "ontological" models: Physical, Platonic and Metaphysical poetry, of which I am using the last two only. In Platonic poetry, a variety of images illustrate one idea; in metaphysical poetry, the various aspects of one image may each suggest a different idea. Both neoclassical and romantic poetry are "Platonic"; but the former focuses on the ideas as represented by highly general images, whereas the latter typically subsumes the concrete images in a particular, coherent landscape. The orientation mechanism evoked by the landscape renders the compact abstractions diffuse, so that they may be perceived as an intense, supersensuous presence. This chapter discusses the handling of a metaphysical image in a very minor seventeenth century poem by Quarles, and two exquisite pieces of "Platonic" poetry by the German baroque poet Andreas Gryphius, and the English romantic William Wordsworth. In both sonnets, the octet offers an evening landscape description in which the abstractions are perceived as a supersensuous presence; the sestet offers a "colloquy" that leads to an insight into the human significance of the preceding landscape description.

Chapter 6

The Sublime and the Absolute Limit

The Ultimate Limit and the Ineffable

One of the major concerns of the present study is the absolute limit and the variety of strategies adopted by poets in facing it. One of the recurring motives is that experiences related to this absolute limit are notoriously inaccessible to conceptual thinking and conceptual language. Thus, religious poetry in general, and mystic poetry in particular, must face the essential paradox of speaking the unspeakable.[1] There is no categorical solution to this paradox. In chapter 1 we discussed some constraints on translating natural and psychological processes to such semiotic systems as language, music, or poetic style. I argued there that the "fine-grainedness" of the target system constrains the accuracy of translation, and that the most one can expect in such translations is that the nearest options offered by the target system be chosen. This solution can be extended to the paradox of the unspeakable as well. The present chapter will begin with a brief consideration of this "ineffability" and then proceed, in greater detail, to the age-old solution of expressing the divine *via* the sublime. Finally, I will consider a magnificent move by which Donne sabotages the absolute limit and the sublime; he does not reach the conclusions of sceptic philosophy or absurd drama, but rather shifts the locus of religious experience from the beyond to the inner self.

In chapter 3 I propounded Gordon Kaufman's conception of God as a limiting concept, according to which God is the unknown beyond the ultimate limit. There we saw a confrontation between the Hebrew prophet and the wise man of Tyre in Shoham's play: according to both, man is hemmed in within the confines of the ultimate boundaries; but the former offers man a chariot of fire to transcend the absolute limit, whereas the latter insists that there is no place to fly to. We also saw Amikhai's vision of man's predicament in the world after Auschwitz, in which God becomes a mere manner of speaking, and there is no room for theology. One important feature of the *absurd* is the sense of human limitation "heightened, to any degree heightened", in a world in which "God is dead". Whereas for the absurd any

---

[1] A recent collection of essays, *Metaphor and God-talk* (Boeve and Fayaerts eds., 1999), applies pragmatics, semiotics and cognitive linguistics in a discussion of this problem. The conception presented here heavily draws upon Rudolf Otto's phenomenological analysis of the "holy" (originally published in 1917) and Gordon D. Kaufman's analysis (1972) of the *meaning* of "God-talk", irrespective of the *truth value* of the sentences that contain those expressions. In my experience these two books are more conducive to significant literary insights than many other works that sometimes express very similar views.

attempt to go beyond this world is utterly futile, romanticpoetry and metaphysical poetry set themselves to *transcend* the limit. "Along with this awareness of our being hemmed in, powerful emotions of terror, despair, revulsion, anxiety, and the like, are often—perhaps always—generated, and this total intellectual-emotional complex may then be called the 'experience of finitude' or awareness of the 'boundary situation' or something of the sort". Metaphysical poetry typically focuses attention upon this "total intellectual-emotional complex", while also giving some indication of the attempt to transcend the ultimate limit. Romantic poetry, by contrast, typically *attends away from* this "total intellectual-emotional complex" *to* the attempt to transcend the ultimate limit. In chapter 4 we suggested a psychological relationship between the application of the orientation mechanism and the meditative process and other "altered states of consciousness". In chapter 5 we saw how the orientation mechanism helps to generate an "unseen presence" in some examples of baroque and romantic poetry. At the end of the present chapter I am going to discuss a piece of metaphysical poetry in which the processes of orientation and of transcendence are blatantly sabotaged.

According to Rudolf Otto, such notions as the "holy" do comprise certain rational elements, such as morality, or duty; but there is, in addition, an irrational element which notoriously escapes conceptual thinking and, therefore, also language, which is conceptual in its very nature. He calls this additional element the "numinous" (coined from "numen", as "ominous" is coined from "omen"). The original meaning of the words for "holy" in ancient languages, as Hebrew *qadoš,* Greek *hagios,* Latin *sanctus* and *sacer* referred precisely to this "numinous", irrational element. Otto claims that "There is only one way to help another to an understanding of it. He must be guided and led on by consideration and discussion of the matter through the ways of his own mind, until he reach the point at which 'the numinous' in him perforce begins to stir, to start into life and into consciousness" (Otto, 1959: 21). In this chapter I will extend Otto's notion of guiding and leading to a point at which "the numinous" begins to stir, so as to cover a most important poetic problem. I will explore some ways in which poetic language guides the reader to those "ways of his own mind" in an attempt not only to make him understand those notions, but also to perceive their experiential quality.

Kaufman (1972) carefully emphasises that his paper "is concerned with the question of the *meaning* rather than the *truth* of statements containing the word 'God'. No attempt will be made here to prove either that God does or does not exist, that is, that the word 'God' does or does not actually relate to a reality. Questions of that sort can be faced only if we already know what we mean when we use the word 'God'" (ibid, 44–45). In Rudolf Otto's discussion, too, the ontological status of the phenomena is "bracketed"; he is interested in "the holy", or "the numinous", as it appears in experience. Otto's work can thus be most inspiring for the present work, the business of which is to explore how theological thoughts are turned in poetry into experience.

The Sublime

In the present section I shall briefly focus attention on the *sublime*. "We call that *sublime* which is *absolutely great*" (Kant, 1951: 86), *"what is great beyond all comparison"* (ibid.). We still need some definition that may attach a descriptive content to these critical terms. *Absolutely great* may be regarded as a positive description of the negative notion *boundlessness* or *infinity*. Kant suggests that the sublime be defined in psychological terms. "As this, however, is great beyond all standards of sense, it makes us judge as *sublime,* not so much the object, as our own state of mind in the estimation of it" (ibid., 94). Edmund Burke provides an illuminating description of this state of mind:

> ... astonishment is that state of the soul, in which all its motions are suspended, with some degree of horror. In this case the mind is so entirely filled with its object that it cannot entertain any other ... Astonishment is the effect of the sublime in its highest degree; the inferior effects are admiration, reverence and respect *(A Philosophical Enquiry into the Origin of Our Ideas of the Sublime and Beautiful.* London 1858, Part Two, section I, p. 57).

Similarly, the eighteenth-century Hungarian Hebrew poet Shəlomo Levisohn devotes about half of his treatise on poetics, *Yəšurun's Poetry,* to discussions of the sublime in Biblical and post-Biblical Hebrew poetry. He characterises the sublime state of mind as follows: "The sublime is that which by the thunders of its activities overpowers the mind, leaving no thoroughfare in it for any other thought". The English reader will readily recognise in this a state of mind that is the opposite of the state of mind described by Keats as "to let the mind to be a thoroughfare for all thoughts", which we have already mentioned in chapter 4. We have here, perhaps, opposite varieties of religious experience; but in some instances it is precisely the sublime variety that leads to a variant of the Keatsean experience "heightened, to any degree heightened" characterised by Leo Spitzer (1962: 169) as "an emptiness created by the soul in order that it may be filled by God" (an interesting instance of such an emotional pattern we will encounter below in the passage from 1Kings 19, 11–14).

Let us proceed now with some of Kant's conceptual distinctions, as summarised by Beardsley:

> When we estimate magnitudes through numbers, that is, conceptually, the imagination selects a unit, which it can then repeat indefinitely. But there is a second kind of estimation of magnitudes, which Kant calls "aesthetic estimation", in which the imagination tries to comprehend or encompass the whole representation in one single intuition. There is an upper bound to its capacity. An object whose apparent or conceived size strains this capac-

ity to the limit—threatens to exceed the imagination's power to take it all in at once—has, subjectively speaking, an absolute magnitude: it reaches the felt limit, and appears as if infinite. [...] imagination reaches its maximum capacity, shows its failure and inadequacy when compared to the demands of Reason, and makes us aware, by contrast, of the magnificence of Reason itself. The resulting feeling is the feeling of the sublime (Beardsley, 1966: 218–219).

This absolute greatness arouses in the perceiver a feeling of threat and awe and causes him to feel immeasurably small. When he manages to gain some "psychic distance" from this threat, he may experience it as fascinating, as irresistibly attractive, but with an ingredient of the awesome. Experiencing the sublime crucially depends on the *unknown*. When I look down from the top of a high mountain, I may experience the abyss as threatening and sublime. To an army general who looks down from the same mountain knowing behind which bushes the canons are concealed, and behind which the tanks, the landscape may appear less than sublime.

Now these elements of the sublime, namely, feeling immeasurably small, experiencing awe and fascination, and being baffled by the unknown, are precisely those experiences in our familiar world that come nearest to what is experienced in the numinous. What is more, there appears to be a striking affinity between Kaufman's conception of God as a limiting concept, and Kant's conception of "absolute magnitude"—they both threaten to exceed the imagination's power "to take it all in at once": reach the felt limit, and appear as if infinite.

At the beginning of my inquiry I thought that I could take credit for this insight into the psychological similarity between the sublime and the numinous —until I had to realise that eighteenth-century theorists of the sublime as well as Rudolf Otto long preceded me in this discovery. In any case, this definition of the sublime in psychological terms is nearly identical with Otto's phenomenological definition of the numinous. Thus, things described as sublime may serve as symbols to arouse in spectators or readers an experience that accords substantially with the experiencing of the numinous, as analysed by Otto. Let us consider at some length one such symbol: heaven. The word literally means: "the expanse of space that seems to be over the earth like a dome". In religious symbolism it suggests "the dwelling place of the Deity and the joyful abode of the blessed dead". There is no need for humans to *learn* that heaven is sublime: if they merely look at it, they *experience* it as such. Thus, the conventional symbol reflects a spontaneous experience. It should not, therefore, surprise us that the dwelling place of the Deity in many religions and unrelated cultures is in heaven or on the top of a high mountain, not only on the Olympus. Hebrew "El Shaddai" which is in the Bible usually associated with the most numinous aspects of God is derived from the Cana'anite "Ilu Shaddi Rabbi"— the God of the Big Mountain.[2] In Kant's phrasing, both the vertical and the horizon-

---

2   The sublime aspects of altitude may be reinforced by other elements: "Since the temporal lobe is very sensitive to changes in hypoxia (lack of oxygen), blood sugar

tal dimensions of heaven exceed the imagination's capacity to comprehend or encompass the whole representation in one single intuition: it is "absolutely great".

The Sublime in Biblical Poetry

Eighteenth-century theorists—English and Hebrew alike—do not discuss the sublime merely as an aesthetic variable. They do not merely point out the presence of certain elements of the sublime in order to account for certain effects of the text. They also offer aesthetic generalisations for preferring, in a principled way, one text to another, containing similar elements. The key to the sublime in literature is, according to all these theorists, a peculiar combination of great ideas with brevity of expression. The verse "And God said, 'Let there be light'; and there was light" (Genesis 1, 3) is given as the standard example for this principle by some eighteenth-century theorists (Lowth, Levisohn), following "Longinus".[3] The eighteenth-century Hungarian Hebrew poet Shəlomo Levisohn, however, interprets this principle in his treatise on poetics *Yəšurun's Poetry* in an additional sense, too. According to this interpretation, the Prophet Isaiah was the greatest poet among the biblical prophets. He illustrates this contention through comparisons that are not at all "brief", as between the following passages:

> 1. With weeping they shall come,
>   and with consolations I will lead them back,
>   I will make them walk by brooks of water,
>   in a straight path in which they shall not stumble;
>   for I am a father to Israel,
>   and Ephraim is my first-born.
>
>   Jeremiah 31, 9

(hypoglycemia), and blood flow, situations that produce these symptoms are most correlated with the God Experiences. The most common source of hypoxia (outside of frank suffocation) is high altitudes. At the heights of tall mountains or high plateaus, the oxygen tension of the air begins to approach the bare requirements for normal function. [...] Many ancient religious figures were known to climb to the tops of mountains. Upon these heights, religious experiences took place. God spoke to the listener and gave special messages" (Persinger, 1987: 31).

3   Consider "Longinus'" remark: "A similar effect was achieved by the lawgiver of the Jews—no mean genius, for he both understood and gave expression to the power of the divinity as it deserved—when he wrote at the very beginning of his laws—I quote his words—"God said"—what?—'Let there be light.' And there was. 'Let there be earth.' And there was."

2.   Every valley shall be lifted up,
      and every mountain and hill be made low;
      the uneven ground shall become level,
      and the rough places a plain.

                                                                Isaiah 40, 4

3.   I will open rivers on the bare heights,
      and fountains in the midst of the valleys;
      I will make the wilderness a pool of water,
      and the dry land springs of water.
      I will put in the wilderness the cedar,
      the acacia, the myrtle, and the olive;
      I will set in the desert the cypress,
      the plane and the pine together;

                                                            Isaiah 41, 18–19

Obviously, these quotations from Isaiah are not instances of that impressive and sublime *brevity* praised in the verse from Genesis. Levisohn, however, construes "brevity" differently with reference to these passages. He points out that Isaiah's passages convey the same kind of information as Jeremiah's passage. But Isaiah's images are exploited to convey some additional information at the same time.

In all these passages, God promises the prophets that He will lead the children of Israel back to their country, and will provide them with water, shade, and a comfortable path through the desert. Levisohn argues that in the Isaiah passages additional pieces of information are conveyed at the same time, manifesting the Lord's supernatural and wonderful forces. Isaiah, who is "more sublime" than Jeremiah, "depicts the delivered people's travels through arid deserts where there is no waterspring nor straight track or even path". Nonetheless, they will not suffer from these conditions, not merely because the Lord will find the more comfortable routes, but because He will command those natural obstacles to change their nature.

In the last quotation, Levisohn traces back the sublime effect of wonder to a poetic structure in which, e.g., the same trees participate in several cycles of wonder, "miracle on miracle": they render the desert more comfortable to the wanderer; in addition, it is a great miracle that in the desert such trees should grow; it is an additional miracle that these trees are brought here together from a wide range of natural habitats. Tova Cohen in her academic edition of Levisohn's treatise comments that his last point is entirely derived from English theorists of the sublime:

> This is admirable painting, and displays a most happy boldness of invention: The trees of different kinds transplanted from their native soils to grow together in the desert; the fir-tree and the pine, which are indigenous to Lebanon, to which snow and rain and an immense quantity of moisture, seem almost essential; the olive which is the native of Jerusalem; the Egyptian thorn—indigenous to Arabia—both of them requiring a dry soil;

and the myrtle, which flourishes most on the sea shore" (Lowth, *Lectures,* p.69 fn.).

In twentieth century aesthetics such a use of poetic images would be called multivalence, multiple relationship, overdetermination, or the exploitation of potentials.

Even when the Lord deigns to appear on this side of the ultimate boundary, the great dynamic forces of the sublime are contrived in the Bible to serve as the circumstances of his revelation. "In the scripture, whenever God is represented as appearing and speaking, everything terrible in nature is called up to heighten the awe and solemnity of the divine presence. The psalms, and the prophetical books are crowded with instances of this kind..." (Burke, 1858: 69). I will illustrate this through passages from other books of the Bible, as "Then the LORD answered Job out of the whirlwind" (Job 38, 1); or, to take a more elaborate instance, "On the morning of the third day there were thunders and lightnings, and a thick cloud upon the mountain, and a very loud trumpet blast, so that all the people who were in the camp trembled. Then Moses brought the people out of the camp to meet God; and they took their stand at the foot of the mountain. And Mount Sinai was wrapped in smoke, because the LORD descended upon it in fire; and the smoke of it went up like the smoke of a kiln, and the whole mountain quaked greatly" (Exodus 19, 16–18). Such passages illustrate a widespread biblical technique for rendering anything sublime or numinous: they place the Lord in the midst of the dynamic sublime forces of nature, thereby conferring upon him an immediately-apprehended sublimity. We don't merely *know* that the Lord is numinous; we directly *perceive* Him as numinous.

Let us attempt another descriptive comparison that may have far-reaching normative implications. Among Levisohn's introductory examples for the sublime in biblical poetry we find the following two passages side by side:

4.   Thy grace, O LORD, is in the heavens,
thy faithfulness—to the sky.
Thy righteousness is like the mountains of God,
thy judgments are the great deep [the great abyss][4]

(Psalms 36: 5–6)

5.   Can you find out the deep things of God?
Can you find out the limit of the Almighty?
It is higher than heaven—what can you do?
Deeper than Sheol—what can you know?
Its measure is longer than the earth,
and broader than the sea.

(Job 11: 7–9)

[4]   I have made some corrections in the translation of this passage.

I will explore the sublime effect of the Job passage in two stages. First I will compare the standard translation to a possible near-literal translation; and then I will compare the excerpt to the Psalms passage. A readable but accurate translation of this passage appears impossible.[5] A near- literal translation would be:

The search of God can you find out?[6]
The limit [purpose] of Shaddai can you find out?
The heights of heaven how can you do [act]?
Deeper than Sheol how can you know?
Its measure is longer than the earth,
and broader than the sea.

The authorised version may serve as an alternative formulation to which the Hebrew original may be compared, so as to point up its stylistic subtleties. Though all its words are easily understood, this Hebrew passage is rather obscure — and quite systematically so. The King James translation, by contrast, quite systematically clarifies the obscurities, rendering the text much easier. In the Hebrew original, in some of the object phrases the referring noun is replaced by a roundabout phrase that makes it difficult to look for the referent. In the first line, for instance, it is left unclear precisely what attributes of God are to be found out. In the authorised version, "things" in "deep things of God" suggests some entity that cannot be specified; but, at least, the noun appears to refer to something. The Hebrew uses a verbal noun: חֵקֶר [ḥeqɛr], that refers to an action ("search"), with the possible objects of the search left unspecified. The simple sentences of lines 3–4 are broken up in the authorised version into two independent sentences each. In line 3, the non-predicative phrase "The heights of heaven" of the Hebrew original is turned into a predication: "It is higher than heaven". In this version, the first sentence has a formal subject "it", which indicates a fairly focussed (though unspecified) referent, to which a spatial relationship expressed by an adjective is attributed by the predicate ("higher than"); the second sentence makes a vague suggestion that anything Job would do about it would be futile. Thus, the verse line is clearly articulated into two loosely-related predications. In the Hebrew original, by contrast, the two ideas are packed into one simple sentence. In line 3, the spatial relationship "high" is

---

5   הַחֵקֶר אֱלוֹהַ תִּמְצָא?

אִם עַד תַּכְלִית שַׁדַּי תִּמְצָא?

גׇּבְהֵי שָׁמַיִם – מַה תִּפְעָל?

עֲמֻקָּה מִשְּׁאוֹל – מַה תֵּדָע?

אֲרֻכָּה מֵאֶרֶץ מִדָּה

וּרְחָבָה מִנִּי יָם.

6   A quite accurate but clumsy paraphrase of this rhetorical question could be "Your attempt to find out the searchables of the unsearchable God is doomed to failure".

expressed by the abstract noun "heights", manipulated into the referring position of a genitive phrase, which, in turn, serves as the object of the predicate of the sentence. The plural form of "heights" further amplifies but blurs the notion. Thus, the highly abstract, unspecified action of the verb is exerted not on a focussed object, but an elusive spatial relationship (heights); that is, the addressee is supposed to act not upon "heaven", but upon its "heights". The same can be said, mutatis mutandis, about line 4. In the authorised version "deeper" appears to be a predicate parallel to "higher", whereas in the Hebrew original it is the referring expression of an object phrase subordinated to the predicate "know". In the authorised version, again, the utterance is broken up into two independent sentences, the second sentence making, again, the vague suggestion that anything Job would do would be futile. Thus, the Hebrew original is suffused by a psychological atmosphere of vagueness which in the authorised version is mitigated to a considerable extent by well-articulated syntactic units.

When we now compare the Job passage to the Psalms passage, we find the following elements: first, in both passages the greatest extensions observable in nature are used to indicate the sublimity of the things described. Second, while "mountains of God" refer to stable objects, the "extension" phrases in Job refer to *spatial dimensions;* in one instance, "heights of heaven", the spatial dimension is expressed by an abstract word and manipulated into the referring position, indicating an absence that is intensely present. Third, in the excerpt from Psalms, magnitudes are *delimited,* not *exceeded,* whereas in the excerpt from Job some of the dimensions are "deeper than . . . longer than . . . broader than". Fourth, in the excerpt from Psalms well-defined attributes of God are likened to (or identified with) those extensions, or placed in those remote places (moreover, in Otto's terms, "grace, faithfulness, righteousness", and "judgments" belong to the more rational part of the Holy); in the excerpt from Job it is left unclear what attributes precisely are meant. Fifth, in the excerpt from Psalms all the predications are predicates of state (see chapter 5), whereas in the excerpt from Job the predications are predicates of actions ("Can you find out", "how can you do", "how can you know"), and thus more dynamic (in Aristotle's term, have greater "energeia"; see chapter 5). Sixth, both excerpts imply the infinite smallness of Man relative to nature's grandeur; but the Job excerpt also suggests a sense of helplessness and ignorance. As a result, the sublime in the Job excerpt is perceived as much more effective. It might be suggested that in the Psalms passage the sublime dimensions of nature are used in a fairly conventional manner, whereas in the Job passage they are used to arouse an intense but vague feeling of the unknowable numinous.

Overload and Absence

"But in neither the sublime nor the magical, effective as they are, has art more than an indirect means of representing the numinous. Of directer methods our Western art has only two, and they are in a noteworthy way negative, viz. darkness and silence"

(Otto, 83). There is an apparent discrepancy here between Otto and Levisohn. The latter regards silence and darkness as two of the most effective aspects of the sublime, whereas the former sees them as more direct and more effective means of representing the numinous than the sublime. This is not a real problem. The issue at stake, in Wittgenstein's terms, is where you draw the boundary of the open concept "sublime". In Rosch and Mervis' terms, they are less prototypical instances of the sublime than "infinite things": they have a similar psychological effect, but not a similar spatial expansion. Otto further comments: "Besides silence and darkness Oriental art knows a third direct means for producing a strongly numinous impression, to wit, emptiness and empty distances" (84). The adjective transformed into an abstract noun and manipulated into the referring position in "The heights of heaven" (instead of "The high heavens") may suggest precisely such "empty distances".

There seem to be good psychological reasons for attributing such effectiveness to darkness and silence. In the psychological laboratory, "two major ASC [Altered States of Consciousness]-induction procedures have been found, those of perceptual overload [...] and perceptual deprivation" (Glicksohn, 1989: 12). Clearly, darkness and silence constitute such "perceptual deprivation". Let us consider the effect of perceptual deprivation as an intensifying device in the following biblical passage:

> 6.   And behold, the LORD passed by, and a great and strong wind rent the mountains, and broke in pieces the rocks before the LORD, but the LORD was not in the wind; and after the wind an earthquake, but the LORD was not in the earthquake; and after the earthquake a fire, but the LORD was not in the fire; and after the fire a still small voice. And when Eli'jah heard it, he wrapped his face in his mantle and went out and stood at the entrance of the cave. And behold, there came a voice to him, and said, "What are you doing here, Eli'jah?" He said, "I have been very jealous for the LORD, the God of hosts" (1Kings 19, 11–14).

Thus the revised King James version. Though I am usually satisfied with this version, this time a few comments on the translation are needed. This is most convenient from the methodological point of view: the King James version may serve me, again, as an alternative formulation to which the original formulation can be fruitfully compared, so as to point up certain subtleties of the original which do, indeed, generate the sublime or numinous effect. First, in Hebrew, רַעַשׁ is ambiguous: it means "disorderly sound" (anything between "noise" and "tumult"), as well as "earthquake". In the first sense it suggests perceptual load, as well as a thing-free presence, avoiding such stable objects as "mountains" or "earth", on which "ordinary consciousness" can be focused. Second, the Hebrew Bible says "קוֹל דְּמָמָה דַקָּה" , that is, "the voice of thin [or fine] silence". In the King James version "voice" is in the focus of the phrase; "still" mutes but doesn't necessarily cancel the auditory component in it. This is a logical phrase referring to a percept to which ordinary consciousness may safely cling. *"Small* voice" means "lacking in strength", but audible, however faint. The original Hebrew, by contrast, contains an oxymoron: the voice of fine silence. Such an oxymoron may baffle the reader while it also cancels the auditory component in "voice" — suggesting, perhaps, a message conveyed by perceptual deprivation. The Hebrew adjective for "thin, fine" *may* mean "measuring little in cross section" or, when qualifying "voice", "somewhat feeble, shrill, and lacking in resonance". But, as a qualifier of "silence", it is most likely to suggest "not coarse, having a subtle texture". Thus, the elusive nature of the negative entity "silence" is reinforced by two of the most irrational figures of speech, oxymoron and synaesthetic metaphor (in this case, speaking of the more differentiated sense, the aural sense, in terms of the least differentiated one, the tactile sense): "the voice of thin [or "fine"] silence". The undifferentiated quality of tactile sensations foregrounds the possible undifferentiated aspects of "silence". Thus, silence is perceived as an unseen and unheard presence, that has, nevertheless, some intensely felt, fine but dense texture.

To better appreciate the enormous impact of this passage, let us compare it to some other biblical passages quoted earlier, the LORD answering Job from the whirlwind, or descending upon Mount Sinai in fire. In the passage from 1Kings, the wind differs in two important respects from, e.g., the Job verse. First, it produces a more vivid impression on the senses and suggests greater force, by specifying its effects: "rent the mountains, and broke in pieces the rocks"; and second, it refutes expectation for the biblical formula, baffling the reader: "but the LORD was not in the wind".

Here again I must insist on certain subtleties of the original, as compared to the English translation. While the predicates of the English version are in the past tense, in the Hebrew original, the sequence following the interjection "behold" is entirely in the present tense. And the conjunction "but", occurring three times in the translation, is only implied, never explicitly mentioned, in the original:

וְהִנֵּה יְהוָה עֹבֵר וְרוּחַ גְּדוֹלָה וְחָזָק מְפָרֵק הָרִים וּמְשַׁבֵּר סְלָעִים לִפְנֵי יְהוָה; לֹא בָרוּחַ

יְהוָה; וְאַחַר הָרוּחַ – רַעַשׁ; לֹא בָרַעַשׁ יְהוָה; וְאַחַר הָרַעַשׁ – אֵשׁ; לֹא בָאֵשׁ יְהוָה;

וְאַחַר הָאֵשׁ קוֹל דְּמָמָה דַקָּה.

> (And behold, the LORD passes by, and a great and strong wind rends the
> mountains, and breaks in pieces the rocks before the LORD; not in the
> wind [is] the LORD; and after the wind a tumult (earthquake), not in the
> tumult [is] the LORD; and after the tumult a fire, not in the fire [is] the
> LORD; and after the fire the voice of fine silence).

The interjection "behold" directs attention to emerging events, and suggests wonder and surprise; the present tense of the sequence suggests a minute-to-minute emergence and wonder, in "real time", as it were. As to "but", it is a conjunction used to connect contrary but co-ordinate elements, sharpening the opposition into a logical, clear-cut gestalt. The negation baffles the reader by thwarting his expectation (based on such biblical passages as the ones quoted above from Job and Exodus) that the Lord would be in the wind, the tumult, the fire. "But", three times occurring in the translation, suggests a logical opposition, pointing up the impression that in the Hebrew original, where it is absent, the succession is vaguer, less predictable, more baffling. Moreover, the rigid opposition suggested by "but" may interfere with the superimposition of a more complex pattern on the sequence, to be discussed later.

Furthermore, in the English text, the "theme" and the "rheme" have changed places. Compare "but the LORD was not in the wind" to "not in the wind [is] the LORD". M.A.K Halliday speaks of "the association of theme with 'given', rheme with 'new'" (1970: 162). "We may think of this as governed by a 'good reason' principle: many linguistic systems are based on this principle, whereby one option [the 'unmarked option'—RT] will always be selected unless there is good reason for selecting otherwise" (ibid., 159). The king James version follows the unmarked option: subject + copula + adverbial phrase (adverbial predicate). The Hebrew text, by contrast, suggests that there is good reason for manipulating the adverbial phrase into the theme and the subject phrase into the rheme. "The theme is the point of departure for the message" (ibid., 162). The forces of the dynamic sublime (wind, earthquake [tumult], fire) are "given" in the preceding sentences. More significantly, it is they that are available to immediate perception; the presence of the Lord is only inferred. So, it should be hardly surprising that it is they that are in the focus of negation in the text ("not in x, but in y"—as it were). In this formula, however, "in y" is much less explicit, less unambiguous, than one might expect.

I wish to point out two additional patterns in the poetic structure of this passage: "significant variation", and "emotive crescendo". There is, in our passage, a remarkable repetitive scheme, whose formula is "And behold x; not in x [is] God; and after x, y; not in y [is] God"—and so forth. In chapter 3 we mentioned *significant variation,* a repetitive scheme frequently discerned in ballads and drama. This is "a type of structure in which the effect is secured by an alteration in a pattern of action which has become familiar by repetition" (Brooks and Heilman, 1966, Glossary: 51). Here this structure is more than usually sophisticated. The reader might expect something like the following description: "And behold, [there was] a great and strong wind, rending the mountains, and breaking the rocks in pieces; and the LORD answered Eli'jah out of the wind". Such an expectation is thwarted by "not in the wind [is] the LORD". This negation is repeated two more times. The effect is secured by an alteration in this pattern: "and after the fire the voice of fine silence". There follows neither negation nor confirmation. The deviation from the established pattern suggests that God *may* be in the voice of fine silence, but there remains considerable uncertainty. The repeated negative statements generate an increasingly baffling uncertainty. The faint "fine silence" appears to offer a resolution to this uncertainty. But it is "sabotaged" by another uncertainty: the absence of negation or confirmation. Thus, the sensory deprivation of "silence" is reinforced by the lack of definite information.

In earlier chapters we mentioned several times the emotive crescendo, which is a poetic device for dealing with experiences that are inaccessible to conceptual language and are of unusually great intensity. Our passage conveys such an experience. Words that suggest an extreme or unsurpassed level of emotive force are quickly worn out. If the poet attempts to express (or "show") such an experience by using superlatives or words of great emotional intensity, his effort will be regarded as reflecting an empty pose rather than a credible experience. In poetry, something can be perceived as intense only when it is *compared to something else*. The items in the sequence "wind rending the mountains", "tumult [earthquake]", "fire" bear no index that would indicate their relative strength; but every new item in the sequence of negations increases the resulting suspense and generates mounting tension. The passage under discussion can be construed as "the presence of the LORD has a much stronger impact than a wind rending the mountains", "the presence of the LORD has a much stronger impact [even] than an earthquake", "the presence of the LORD has a much stronger impact [even] than fire". In such a reading, the last item, "the voice of fine silence" may be seen in two contrasting ways at the same time: on the one hand, it is perceived as the opposite of the enormous dynamic forces of nature; on the other, it may be perceived as the peak of this mounting sequence of intensity. The perception arising from sensory deprivation is presented as much stronger than the one arising from sensory overload. Such a conception of this passage is reinforced by the instances of emotive crescendo mentioned in earlier chapters: quite a few of them culminate with such terms of absence or cessation as "vacant", "death", or "nothingness". Silence suggests absence of sound; the occurrence of silence after the mounting sequence of sensory overload amplifies enormously the sense of deprivation.

This mode of presentation has an additional cognitive aspect, related to "rapid" and "delayed closure". In a formulation like "Then the LORD answered Job out of the whirlwind", the position of the LORD relative to the great forces of nature is immediately given. In our passage, the resolution is repeatedly postponed, by negating the expected assertion. The "resolution" eventually comes not as a straightforward confirmation, but merely as the absence of a negation.[7] As a result, the presence of the LORD is perceived as an absence of an enormously great magnitude.

Finally, two details in Elijah's response reinforce the numinous character of the episode, both related to the "wrath of Yahweh". First, Elijah "wrapped his face in his

---

[7] Cf. "The neurophysiological mechanisms underlying selective attention are complex, but some progress has been made in analyzing them. For example, if a person is asked to count the number of faint clicks embedded infrequently in a regular, one-per-second train of louder clicks, [...] a person who is attending shows a large positive [brain] wave between 300 and 600 milliseconds after the target (the faint click) occurs. The occurrence and magnitude of this process seem to depend on the resolution of uncertainty, not on the physical properties of the stimulus" (Miller and Johnson-Laird, 1976: 26).

mantle"; and second, he said, "I have been very jealous for the LORD, the God of hosts" (in fact, he said this twice, before and after the LORD's appearance). The former response suggests the most numinous aspect of God, described by Otto (ibid., 32) as follows: "it is patent from many passages of the Old Testament that this 'wrath' has no concern whatever with moral qualities. There is something very baffling in the way in which it 'is kindled' and manifested. It is, as has been well said, 'like a hidden force of nature', like stored-up electricity, discharging itself upon anyone who comes too near" (as when the Lord says to Moses "you cannot see my face, for man shall not see me and live"; Exodus 33, 20).

The latter response, too, may be illuminated by Otto's discussion of "the 'wrath' or 'anger' of Yahweh". "Beside the 'wrath' or 'anger' of Yahweh stands the related expression 'jealousy of Yahweh'. The state of mind denoted by the phrase 'being jealous for Yahweh' is also a numinous state of mind, in which features of the *tremendum* pass over into the man who has experience of it" (Otto, 33). The Hebrew translation, which appears to follow a more complete version of Otto's book, mentions here (p. 24) the verse "for zeal for thy house has consumed me" (Psalms 69, 9). According to this reading, the "zeal for thy house" is a thing-free, autonomous force, discharging itself involuntarily, consuming the person who serves as shelter for it.

The Absolute Limit and Self-Specifying Information

When I look at the heaven and perceive it as "the expanse of space that seems to be over the earth like a dome" and know nothing about what is beyond it, I don't experience it only as sublime, but also as "the absolute limit", which I cannot even approach, let alone pass. Furthermore, this domelike space perceptible above us has an additional psychological function. It provides us with "self-specifying information". Ecological psychologists devoted much attention to the processes by which we pick up self-specifying information from the optical array around us. The availability of this kind of optical structure means that one can see one's own position and one's own movements, as well as the layout of the environment. "Such perception is not indirect or inferential; information about oneself is as directly available and as fully specific as information about anything else" (Neisser, 1976: 115).

One may better understand the nature of this self-specifying information if one considers instances in which this information is destroyed or impeded. Let me try to illuminate the issue of the sudden disintegration of self-specifying information with two concrete examples taken from our everyday physical reality. When you are sitting in a stationary train and the train nearby pulls out, you may feel it as if your own train were moving in the opposite direction, even though you don't experience the typical rocking movement of your body. Similarly, many drivers experience panic, when the parked car they are about to pass suddenly pulls out. The reason is that the self-specifying information in the optic array is being destroyed. Or, consider the following experiment:

A one-year-old child standing on the floor of the room will fall down if the walls are silently and suddenly moved forward a few inches, although nothing touches him. This is, because the optical pattern produced by the moving walls would normally specify that the observer was plunging backward. The child compensates by shifting forward, overbalances and falls. Even an adult who knows about the experimental arrangement can be 'knocked down' in this way if he is balancing on a narrow beam (Neisser, 1976: 116).

Thus, the perceptible heaven, the domelike space above us, contributes to the optic array, so essential for our ability to locate ourselves with reference to time and space; to ascertain our true position in novel situations. At the same time, it arouses a sense of the sublime which is experienced in a way that is not unlike the experiencing of the numinous. By the same token, it arouses the direct perception of an impenetrable limit that arouses in us an "awareness of finitude", and suggests "a *limiting concept"*, that "refers to that which we do *not* know but which is the ultimate limit of all our experiences".

Religious poetry, as well as its secular-mystic counterpart frequently has recourse to these natural potentials of "heaven", in an attempt to bring the perceiving consciousness in what is perceived as direct contact with a reality "beyond". I will illustrate this by two short excerpts from two sonnets, one from the English Renaissance, the other from English Romanticism. In chapter 12 below I will quote some lines from a religious sonnet by Sir Philip Sidney, and analyse the ways in which it exploits a wide variety of potentials in the light image. Here I will reproduce a part of that discussion. The speaker is addressing his soul in the following lines:

> 7.   Draw in thy beams, and humble all thy might
>   To that sweet yoke where lasting freedoms be;
>   Which breaks the clouds and opens forth the light,
>   That doth both shine and give us sight to see.
>   O take fast hold; let that light be thy guide
>   In this small course which birth draws out to death,

I will discuss only two aspects of this argument: First, "Which breaks the clouds and opens forth the light" exploits a very conspicuous potential of light: light can put us in contact with worlds inaccessible to us; it can travel to our place from far beyond our reach. We do not *infer* this; we *perceive* it directly. In this case, it reaches us from some place that is not only inaccessible to our body; we cannot even see its source, it is both far away and hidden by the clouds. With reference to Gordon Kaufman's conception, light in this case puts us in contact "with some reality that is beyond the *absolute limit* of our experience".

Secondly, the line "Which breaks the clouds and opens forth the light" evokes an unlimited landscape, with a perceiving consciousness locating itself with reference to the clouds and the light. This is reinforced by the "LIFE AS A JOURNEY" metaphor: "let that light be thy guide / In this small course which birth draws out to death". The "small course", though used metaphorically, has an additional function here: it suggests a situation defined "here and now" evoking a consistent landscape. The light breaking through the clouds indicates some reality beyond one's reach; the thing-free and Gestalt-free nature of "clouds" and "light" enhances the non-conceptual nature of the experience indicated; the orientation-mechanism evoked by the situation amplifies the diffuseness of these perceptions; this diffusing effect is mitigated, but not cancelled, by the persuasive argument pervading the poem, displaying a psychological atmosphere of definite direction and of patent purpose.

My next example is from a sonnet by Keats, "When I Have Fears". This is a secular poem; but it has some conspicuous elements of mystic nature. As Louis Martz observed in the "Conclusion" to the revised edition of his book, some of the best romantic poems are secular versions of the meditative poem. "The genre of meditative poetry should be broad enough to include some of the Odes of Keats or the later poetry of Wallace Stevens, as well as the unorthodox, though still religious, poetry of a Yeats or a Wordsworth or an Emily Dickinson" (Martz, 1962: 324). I will consider here only one quatrain from it (we have discussed its final couplet in chapter 3).

> 8.   When I behold, upon the night's starred face
>   Huge cloudy symbols of a high romance,
>   And think that I may never live to trace
>   Their shadows, with the magic hand of chance...

I shall refrain from discussing all the semantic and prosodic subtleties of this quatrain, even some of those relevant to our discussion. In this stanza we find one of the most exquisite attempts of the Romantic poets to achieve direct experiencing of a supersensuous and superrational reality, beyond physical access, and also inaccessible to the logical, analytic mind. In the best tradition of Romantic nature poetry, the stanza suggests a natural landscape which, at the same time, serves as a metaphor for that inaccessible reality. One conspicuous feature of this landscape is that it exceeds the capacity of humans to comprehend it in one act of perception, and thus it suggests the existence of realities far beyond the scope of human perception. The same is suggested (in the vertical direction) by the trite sensuous metaphor "the night's starr'd face" which suggests precisely what *can* be seen by the perceiving consciousness, namely the outward appearance turned toward the perceiver; on the other hand, it may suggest *surface,* too. This would indicate a functional metaphor at the same time: the starry surface of the night *hides*, as it were, some unfathomable depths. But the most conspicuous feature of the description is that it is dominated by such amorphous thing-free entities as night, clouds and shadows. Without going into the semantic subtleties of "Huge cloudy symbols of a high romance", the line manifests an interesting ambiguity. One may conceive of the clouds as symbols of a higher reality; in this case, we have in *cloudy symbols* a transferred epithet, meaning "clouds that are symbols of…". On the other hand, *cloudy* may be more than a transferred epithet—a direct modifier of *symbols:* "obscure, indistinct symbols", hard to distinguish, and even harder to "decipher" or interpret. The choice of *huge,* in preference to its many synonyms, seems significant, too. According to *The Random House College Dictionary,* "when used of concrete objects [it] usually adds the idea of massiveness, bulkiness or even shapelessness" to its designation, i.e., "extraordinarily large".

Shadows may be interpreted here in a very real sense: the clouds may cast their shadows on the earth; while the clouds themselves are out of our reach, their shadows at least (so similar to them) may be within our reach. Shadow may serve as *the* thing-free quality *par excellence:* although it may have the *shape* of the original object (perhaps distorted to some degree), it is less real; it has got neither *weight* nor *volume*—it is *intangible.* That is why *shadows* are considered in Platonic philosophy to have a lesser reality than physical objects (which, in turn, are said to have a lesser reality than their Ideas); and that is why the shadow became the central symbol of how we can perceive an inaccessible reality in Plato's parable of the cave.

"To trace [...] with the magic hand of chance" may mean, in this context, two things: either "to trace with the help of (personified) Chance", or merely "to have the opportunity of (that is, the chance of) tracing". Thus, *hand* may mean both "my hand" and "Chance's hand" at one and the same time. *Chance* itself becomes ambiguous: on the one hand, it may mean "the absence of any known reason why an event should turn out one way rather than another"; on the other hand, "it is spoken of as if it were a real agency" *(The Random House College Dictionary),* and so it leaves ground for the semi-mythological personification of a hidden *power.* The connotation of a hidden power is supported by *"magic* hand".

"To trace / Their shadows with the magic hand of chance" is a synaesthetic metaphor, a touch→sight, or upward, transfer. Treating a more differentiated sense in terms of a less differentiated one keeps perception further away from reason and consciousness. A shadow is a highly elusive, transient thing; tracing shadows with one's hands implies the lowly-differentiated perception of infinitesimally delicate sensations. At the other end, one could extend this "great chain of differentiations" by pointing out that the lowly-differentiated clouds, perceived through sight, seem to reflect a more differentiated, "more real" reality.

Donne and Sabotaging the Sublime

Let us now turn to a poem by Donne, where he makes use of some of the elements mentioned above but, as we might expect of him, with several unexpected twists. I have emphasised the function of the orientation mechanism in evoking the non-rational processes required for such religious and mystic experiences as transcendence of the ultimate boundary, or suspension of the boundaries between self and not self, leading to dissolution in nothingness, or the perception of a supersensuous presence, in mystic poetry of the Baroque and Romantic style. Now I am going to consider at some length a poem of disorientation, in the metaphysical style, Donne's "Holy Sonnet 5":

> 9.   I am a little world made cunningly
>   Of Elements and Angelike spright,
>   But black sinne hath betraid to endlesse night
>   My world's both parts, and (oh) both parts must die.
>   You which beyond that heaven which was most high
>   Have found new sphears, and of new lands can write,
>   Powre new seas in mine eyes, that so I might
>   Drowne my world with my weeping earnestly,
>   Or wash it if it must be drown'd no more:
>   But oh it must be burnt! alas the fire
>   Of lust and envie have burnt it heretofore,
>   And made it fouler; Let their flames retire,
>   And burn me ô Lord, with a fiery zeale
>   Of thee and thy house, which doth in eating heale.

I will discuss this sonnet from a variety of angles: the structure of mannerist poetry; the structure of the metaphysical conceit; the clash between the "Elizabethan World Picture" and the world picture shaped by Copernicus and the great geographical discoveries; the numinous. It has been frequently suggested that "manneristic" or "metaphysical" styles and related phenomena tend to occur in periods of great social, political and ideological upheaval, when more than one scale of values prevail, in societies and eras marked by strife, radical change or disorientation (Sypher, 1955; Isaacs, 1951; Thomson, 1972: 11; Tsur, 2001). I will argue that Donne's sonnet reflects such a crisis but that, nonetheless, it yields an insight through it into the religious significance of human life.

What Tillyard called the "Elizabethan World Picture", did not greatly differ from the Greek or the Mediaeval world pictures. It was based on the "great chain of being", the correspondence of microcosm and macrocosm, and Ptolemaic cosmology. Though Copernicus died in 1543, his revolution began to undermine the dominant world picture only in the seventeenth century. English poets in that century gave expression to their sense of disorientation resulting from this clash. Milton presented in one passage (in *Paradise Lost* VIII) a Ptolemaic and a Copernican account of the universe, insisting that only the Great Architect knows the truth, who "his fabrick of the Heavens/ Hath left to their disputes, perhaps to move/ His laughter". Another forceful presentation of this perplexity we find in Donne's sonnet.

The first quatrain of the sonnet presents a well-ordered traditional world, in which the "little world", the microcosm, is in its proper place in the hierarchy, and parallels the macrocosm at a higher level of the same hierarchy. The speaker's "chemistry" (referring by "I" perhaps to himself, perhaps to Everyman) is well-balanced, too. He is made up of (four) elements which, in turn, are balanced by an "Angelike spright". This harmony is disturbed by original sin, the Fall ("for the day you eat of it, *you shall die*"); but the cosmic order is preserved. The sonnet begins quite conventionally: "I am a little world ", that is, a microcosm. The traditional meaning of this statement is: "my parts are put together in accordance with Divine Order at its best, and they act in full harmony, similarly to the macrocosm" (So, when speaking of "world picture", I include conceptions of Man's nature). The Divine Order as understood in the Middle Ages and the Renaissance is reinforced by line 2, stating that this little world is made of "elements and Angelike spright". This implies that Man's nature and place in the Great Chain of Being is defined to be between the Angels and lifeless elements (three at least of the four elements, earth, water and fire are further developed in the course of the sonnet). The adverb "cunningly" connotes a large degree of technical or mental subtlety, nicety, or meticulousness — incompatible with the Maker's or Nature's grandeur, "domesticating" the metaphor ("cunning" here denotes great skill in construction rather than guileful or devious).

The invocation "You which beyond that heaven which was most high / Have found new sphears" is quite sophisticated. It alludes to the great astronomical and geographical discoveries of the age, but this whole story is squeezed down to an elaborate "vocative phrase". By the same token it has a double effect: on the one hand, it suggests the violation of this well-ordered, stable, intellectually-conceived world picture; on the other hand, the past tense of the copula "was" does something to the picture. The actual height of heaven does not change; what may change is its subjective height, as it is immediately *perceived*. The past tense contrasts the sublimity of the sky before and after the discoveries, from the *perceptual* point of view. When I first wrote about this poem, about thirty-five years ago, I realised only that the discovery of new spheres beyond the heaven caused it to become less high, and thus less sublime (reinforced by the knowledge gained which, too, tends to violate the sense of the sublime). In line with my foregoing analysis of "heaven" as a religious symbol, we may now add two further aspects. If Kaufman is right that God-language refers to everything that is beyond the ultimate limit, the dome perceived above us ceases to be the final boundary: what is beyond it is not God, but further spheres, perhaps into infinity. Robert Neville (1999: 16) claims (with some exaggeration, perhaps):

> The principal hypothesis about the differentiation of religious symbols from others is that they are symbols whose primary referents are finite/ infinite contrasts. [...] A finite/infinite contrast is some finite thing that can be referred to that is taken to be a boundary-line or world-founding element in the culture, community, or person bearing the referring symbol. Peter Berger has argued persuasively that religions in general articulate what he calls "sacred canopies" or conceptual and mythic systems that define the existence and meaning of the world for a culture.

The domelike space above us can be seen as such a "sacred canopy"; the discovery of "new spheres" beyond it interferes with the "neat way of summing up the universe as bounded" (ibid, 24), so essential for effective religious symbolism. The violation of finite/infinite contrasts is bound to lead to a sense of total disorientation:

> In general, finite/infinite contrasts shape cultures' apprehension of the physical world, the place of people within that world, the grounds for value and meaning, and for world-significant identity, and the elements of religious purpose (ibid, 17).

But, by choosing the visible "canopy" above us as the boundary to be abolished, the self-specifying reference points in the visual array are destroyed. Thus, an immediate sense of disorientation is generated.[8]

Donne was very much preoccupied with the disorienting effect of the world that was falling to pieces, in which he lived. In "An Anatomie of the World", for instance, he wrote:

> 10. And new Philosophy calls all in doubt,
>   The Element of fire is quite put out;
>   The Sun is lost, and th'earth, and no mans wit
>   Can well direct him where to looke for it.
>   And freely men confesse that this world's spent,
>   When in the Planets, and the Firmament
>   They seeke so many new; they see that this
>   Is crumbled out againe to his Atomis.
>   'Tis all in peeces, all cohaerence gone

This passage presents the same disintegration of the world picture as the one presented by the Holy Sonnet we have been discussing. But its focus is very different. While this passage emphasises the all-pervasive nature of the disintegration process, in loosely-related images, the phrase "that heaven which was most high" subordinates the whole passage to a well-defined situation, in which the perception of the boundaries has suddenly changed, entailing a change of self-perception as well (as if the walls had been silently and suddenly moved forward a few inches). Donne's invocation "You which beyond that heaven which *was* most high / Have found new sphears", with its past-tense copula, effectively sabotages, then, three aspects of the

---

8   In East Asian cultures, this whole conception may differ very much: "In cultures such as in East Asia that do not have a neat way of summing up the universe as bounded, symbols of the creation of the world as if by a maker cannot refer to the world's finite/infinite contingency. Those cultures rather make something like that reference by symbols of the relation between non-being *(wu-ji)* and fecund great being *(tai-ji);* that relation appears in every part of the world, and requires no conception of a summing up of the world" (Neville, 1999: 24).

situation that are so essential for religious symbolism: the experiencing of the sublime; the experiencing of the ultimate boundary with the "finite/infinite contrasts"; and the orientation process in one's physical environment. The discovery that the ultimate boundary is not ultimate after all, however, does not lead Donne to Akhikar's or Amikhai's scepticism encountered in chapter 3. In the final couplet he moves the locus of the religious experience to the inside, shifting to a different kind of religious symbolism: "And burn me ô Lord, with a fiery zeale/ Of thee and thy house, which doth in eating heale". In the concluding "Colloquy", the boundary experience (so effectively sabotaged) is replaced by what Otto characterised above as "a numinous state of mind", related to the "wrath of Yahweh", or "jealousy of Yahweh"— through an allusion to *Psalms* 69: 9, discussed above.

Such a shift may be in harmony with, for instance, Louis Martz's following paragraph from his discussion of the "Composition of Place":

> It is clear from the various practices mentioned by these writers that there were three different ways of performing this imaginary "composition". The first is to imagine oneself present in the very spot where the event occurred [...] The second is to imagine the events as occurring before your eyes [...] And the third is performed when persons "imagin that everie one of these thinges whereupon they meditate passeth within their owne harte"—a method strongly recommended by Fray Luis, although St. François de Sales warns that this method is "to subtil and hard for young beginners" (Martz, 1962: 30).

Metaphysical Structure

In chapter 5 we distinguished, following John Crowe Ransom, between "Platonic" and "metaphysical" poetry. Platonic poetry may present a wide variety of very dissimilar objects; it is the common idea which they represent that unifies them. Metaphysical poetry, by contrast, forces the reader to attend back to one physical image. In metaphysical poetry, an image may represent, just as in Platonic poetry, an abstraction. But then the poet develops precisely those physical aspects of the image which are irrelevant to that abstraction, by making each of them represent a different abstraction. In metaphysical poetry physical objects are conceived of as bundles of features. The features are elaborated, one by one, as relevant to some abstraction; at the same time each constitutes irrelevant texture with respect to all the other features. In chapter 5 we exemplified this structure of metaphysical poetry with a very minor poem, exploiting the various potentials of a "rib". Here we may observe the same metaphysical techniques embodied in one of the masterpieces of its kind.

Donne's sonnet explicitly deals with the destruction of the world—it is less explicitly stated whether this concerns the little or the great world. Similarly, it reflects distortion, although it is not quite clear whether the world or the world-picture has been distorted. The poem slips in sudden shifts from one "plane of reality" to the other. There is a growing tension between the two planes of reality; microcosm and macrocosm do not correspond in a well-balanced hierarchy—they are rather equated, so that one of them is always shown in distorted proportions, as in "powre new seas in my eyes [...] by weeping earnestly". As Sypher (1955: 118) said, in mannerist art and thought "the harmony between microcosm and macrocosm was untuned". The joining of "new seas" with weeping is no mere hyperbole: "new seas" are placed in a context of geographical and astronomical discoveries, which are irrelevant to the "argument" of weeping, and deliberately belong to the macrocosm. These tensions may be, and *are,* resolved on the verbal level only; words like "world, fire, wash, seas, new" figure in more than one sense, and refer in one and the same poem to different things on different planes of reality, combining them at the verbal level at least. This may happen in a romantic poem, too (as we have seen in a line like "huge cloudy symbols of a high romance"), but the reader is less aware of this. One *may* (although *need not),* read the poem so that one makes up one's mind as to the literal and metaphorical sense of the words, and sticks consistently to them. There is in such a romantic poem at least an even surface; the point of view changes, if at all, smoothly and gradually—scarcely perceived by the reader. In Donne's poem there are two perspectives, inconsistent with one another, clashing now and again. Microcosm and macrocosm appear similar in magnitude; the reader *knows* that when seen from one consistent perspective, the latter should be perceived as enormously large as compared with the former; or, if one closely inspected the microcosm, so that it appeared disproportionately large—the macrocosm should have been left far away in the background. Such a "revolving view" is, according to Sypher (1955: 156), quite typical to mannerism: "the mannerist artist is always experimenting with points of view and approaches". Thus, for instance, "the mannerist flamelike statue cannot be satisfactorily seen from any one point of view" (1955: 157).

Joseph Addison's distinction between the various kinds of wit may fruitfully contrast this technique of Donne's to the Neo-Classic and romantic uses of resemblance: "As *true Wit* consists in the Resemblance of Ideas, and *false Wit* in the Resemblance of Words, according to the foregoing Instances; there is another kind of Wit which consists Partly in the resemblance of Ideas, and partly in the Resemblance of Words; which for Distinction Sake I shall call *mixt Wit"*. The "mixt Wit" underlying Donne's sonnet consists of a double point of view. On the one hand there is the "Resemblance of Ideas"—of microcosm and macrocosm. But these two, inconsistent and clashing with one another, are "reconciled" by "Resemblance of Words": change the words (in lines 3–4, for instance, to "black sin has betrayed to Everlasting Hell both my parts"), and the sonnet will fall apart.[9] This is another way of saying that

---

9   In the context of the first quatrain, "my worlds both parts" refers to the elements and the Angelike spright. "Endless night" is a periphrasis for eternal death. In perspective of the new cosmology, "endless night" assumes what Ransom would call a "miraculous" quality: in the Copernican universe, in one part of the world it is day, while on the opposite side it is night. This natural balance has been miraculously upset.

the poem most consistently exploits the potentials of words and images—even when inconsistent with one another.

Water and fire are conceived here as bundles of features. "Sea" refers to the salt waters that cover the greater parts of the earth's surface. In the context of "new spheres" and "new lands", "new seas" suggests "newly discovered parts of the world", beyond what used to be thought of as the absolute limit; the fact that they contain water is quite irrelevant. Even when we think of "seas" as salt water, we don't think of them as of potential tears. On the other hand, shedding tears suggests painful emotions; the fact that tears consist of salt water is, again, quite irrelevant. The next image "Powre new seas in mine eyes" foregrounds precisely this salt-water potential of tears adding the idea of "enormous quantity", and combining these with the notion of "painful emotions". The phrase "Drowne my world", too, emphasises the salt-water aspect of weeping; the fact that it serves to express painful emotions becomes irrelevant. Nor is it unambiguously clear whether the "little world" or the macrocosm is to be destroyed by water. The next line, "Or wash it if it must be drown'd no more" alludes to God's promise that "never again shall there be a flood to destroy the earth" (Genesis, 9: 11). At the same time, it suggests an alternative way of destroying the physical world by water: washing it away, eroding it by the flow of water. At the same time, the verb "wash" in the sense of cleanse, purify, contains the seeds of moral renewal, anticipating similar elements in "fire" in the last two lines. The sequel foregrounds an additional aspect of water: that it is the opposite of fire. Donne thus handles his metaphysical conceit of water very similarly to Quarles' rib conceit (in chapter 5). But while Quarles exploits his image rather playfully in the service of shallow sermonising, Donne deploys it in facing man's momentous moral and existential tangle in a universe run wild. This is not a mere freak of Donne's mind. I have elsewhere discussed at great length the nature of mannerist devices such as the metaphysical conceit, and suggested that mannerist styles tend to recur in "periods of great social, political and ideological upheaval, when more than one scale of values prevail". I have claimed that the metaphysical conceit is a cognitive device turned to aesthetic ends, originally developed for adaptive purposes (Tsur, 1992a: 367–384).

Fire, as the opposite of water, further develops this elaborate conceit: "But oh it must be burnt!" that is, at the Day of Judgment. This transition from water to fire proceeds through an allusion to 2 Peter 3:5–7: "by the word of God heavens existed long ago, and an earth formed out of water and by means of water, through which the world that then existed was deluged with water and perished. But by the same word the heavens and earth that now exist have been stored up for fire, being kept until the day of judgment and destruction of ungodly men". The ensuing lines, however, exploit other potentials of fire that have little to do with the destruction of the world. In our cultural heritage, the identification of intense passions with fire goes back at least to the Old Testament: the Song of Songs, and the Book of Psalms. Love, jealousy, religious zeal are all like fire. Consider: "For zeal of thine house hath eaten me up" (Psalms 69: 9), and "For love is strong as death, jealousy is cruel as grave. Its flashes are flashes of fire, a most vehement flame. Many waters cannot quench love" (Song of Songs 8: 6-7). "Metaphysical" poets at least from Ibn

Gabirol on took up this partial identification of passions (mainly love) with fire and turned it into a total identification: those passions may literally burn the body. Love could be quenched with many waters, Ibn Gabirol suggests at variance with the verse in Solomon's Song, the trouble is that God has already sworn that Noah's waters will not be exceeded. Donne uses in this sonnet the same conceit about drowning his world in a flood of tears, appealing to the same promise not to destroy again the earth by flood ("Or wash it if it must be drown'd no more").

Thus, Donne here makes use of an additional elaborate metaphysical conceit and a (concealed) metaphysical pun that lead to an oxymoron. The result is a split focus, a strain of passionate paradoxical reasoning. Passions involve great internal heat, great energy, and may be painful and destructive. Other potentials of fire, such as its ability to destroy huge sections of the physical world, or to smelt and refine ore into pure metals, are irrelevant to the identification of passions with fire. But these are, precisely, the meanings attributed to fire in Donne's poem: the fire of lust and envy will destroy Donne's "little world", unless the "fiery zeal" smelts and purifies — purges — it. Donne uses the verse quoted above from Psalms and inserts it into his poem almost verbatim. The verb "consume" of the Revised version is ambiguous, meaning "to destroy as by burning", or "to eat or drink up". Donne seems to rely on a version that has "hath eaten me up", and uses straightforward "eating" as in the original Hebrew Bible. The oxymoron "which doth in eating heal" suggests the painful process of purification, and keeps the focus split. I have said that Donne creates here a concealed metaphysical pun, too. The Hebrew Bible uses the same noun קִנְאָה [kinʾa] for "jealousy" in the above verse from Solomon's Song ("envy" in the Sonnet), and for "zeal" in the verse from the Psalms. Thus, the Hebrew word denotes a negative and a positive passion at one and the same time. Both passions are partially identified with fire, according to the conventional uses of the metaphor. But Donne also exploits those features of fire that are irrelevant to passions; again, a negative and a positive action, respectively. Thus, the sonnet ends with a physical and mental process of enormous intensity that has great destructive as well as purifying power, and leads to a "Colloquy" culminating in a "numinous state of mind". In fact, if Rudolf Otto is right, that "fiery zeale" is not exactly a "positive passion"; it is, rather, "like a hidden force of nature, like stored-up electricity, discharging itself upon anyone who comes too near".

To Sum Up

This chapter further elaborates on the absolute limit and the numinous. These are said to be associated with unspeakable experiences, confronting the poets with the paradox of speaking the unspeakable. Rudolf Otto suggests that "there is only one way to help another to an understanding of it. He must be guided and led on [...] through the ways of his own mind, until he reach the point at which 'the numinous' in him perforce begins to stir, to start [...] into consciousness". In this chapter we have explored how the sublime may serve this end. We have considered three aspects of the sublime in biblical poetry: unlimited space, the destructive forces of nature, and great silence. In this respect, we have distinguished, in biblical poetry, between the straightforward uses of sublime imagery with rather conventional effects, and uses that deviate from conventional expectations, so as to induce experiences resembling in some respect the numinous. We have considered "heaven" as a symbol of the absolute limit, and observed how renaissance and romantic poetry may suggest the transcendence of this limit. Finally, we have followed John Donne, who had to cope with the great seventeenth-century crisis resulting from conflicting world pictures, the untuning of the harmony between microcosm and macrocosm, and the discovery that the ultimate boundary is not ultimate after all. Donne, however, does not reach the conclusion of sceptic philosophy or absurd drama, but shifts the locus of religious experience from the beyond to the inner self. The boundary experience (effectively sabotaged in the sonnet) gives way to what Otto characterised as "a numinous state of mind", related to the "wrath of Yahweh", or "jealousy of Yahweh". The sonnet accomplishes this shift through an exemplary use of the metaphysical conceit based on the images of water and fire.

Chapter 7

Rhythmic Structure and Religious Poetry
The Numinous, the Infernal, and *Agnus Dei*

This chapter attempts to establish reasoned, systematic relationships between poetic structures on the one hand, and, on the other, poetic qualities of religious interest, regularly attributed to them by generations of poets, readers and critics. It will offer a theoretical framework which may account for perceived qualities of poems by relying on an interaction between rhythm and stanza structure, and semantic, syntactic and thematic elements. Let us begin our discussion with two fairly informal statements by a great poet and a great literary theorist, concerning two qualities perceived in poems: the infernal and the ecstatic, respectively. In a stimulating book on the language of *In Memoriam,* Alan Sinfield (1971: 72) quotes Tennyson as saying: "Milton's vague hell is much more awful than Dante's hell marked off into divisions". I argue that Tennyson's aphorism should be taken with a grain of salt. It does not perform the speech act it seems to. Rather than making an assertion (as the indicative mode would indicate), it makes a crucial recommendation in an epigrammatic form—to paraphrase Morris Weitz. It draws attention to an important aspect of Milton's poetic technique, which will be spelled out in the course of this chapter. This, however, implies nothing about Dante, who achieves *his* awful effects, as we shall see, by different techniques (see Chapter 10).

In his discussion of Blake's "The Tyger", E.D. Hirsch pointed out a relationship between that poem's "rhythmic pulses" and its ecstatic quality, in a rather impressionistic vein: "As the rhythmic pulses of the Songs of Experience verse fall like hammer blows, the speaker looks alternatively at the maker and the thing made, in an ecstasy of admiration and empty horror" (1962: 249–250). I will propose a theoretical framework within which one may account, systematically, for the different effects of the same metric structure in this poem, and, e.g., "The Lamb".

I will not try to account for the mystic or ecstatic effect of, e.g., Blake's "The Tyger" by invoking the source of his ideas in such mystics as Boehme or Swedenborg, or by relying on the meaning of the same images in his other poems. I will mention these only to point out how they interact with other formal elements, irrespective of their sources; or only to suggest that they cannot illuminate the perceived effects discussed. I am not interested in theological or mystic ideas for their own sake, but for indicating how they are turned into the verbal imitation of, e.g., an ecstatic experience. Our key terms will be "stability", "security", or their absence; or, in gestaltistic terms, strong and weak shapes.

We live in a world in which external reality floods our system with an overwhelming stream of fluid information. As Heraclitus insisted, everything is in a flux, and you cannot put your leg twice into the same river. One of his disciples corrected him: you cannot put your leg into the same river even once, because the river is constantly changing. Nevertheless, we can delineate the river on the map and do things with reference to it with considerable consistency. Individuals achieve their "ordinary consciousness" by constructing from the flux of information a more-or-less stable world, in which they can go twice to the same place; repeatedly recognise the same person as the same person, even from different angles, and in different illuminations; or recognise vastly different sound streams emitted by different persons, males and females, foreigners and native speakers, as the same word. The stream of percepts in the physical world is organised into objects that have stable visual shapes with clear-cut boundaries between them; their mental representations are organised into stable categories with, again, clear-cut boundaries between them: the world is "marked off into divisions". Scenes and situations can be expected to have a certain degree of consistency: near a table in a room we would expect to see chairs and a sofa more frequently than a steam boat and a human-size ice cream cone. Recent experiments in cognition indicate that it is easier to process a situation with internal consistency than a concoction of random objects.[1] Such a stable universe enables us to make more or less reliable predictions, go beyond the information given, or experience some permanence in change. This state of affairs allows us to exercise control over the world, and even adjust sections of it to our needs and purposes. It inspires humans with a sense of intelligibility, control, comfort and security.

Double-Edgedness

There are domains in which anything you do is a mixed blessing. By achieving cognitive stability, you irrecoverably lose evasive, undifferentiated precategorial information, which is no less crucial for adequate adjustment to a world-in-flux. When you consider the geographic situation of a river, you have to ignore the drops of running water. And conversely, by abandoning cognitive stability, evasive precategorial information essential for adequate adaptation becomes accessible; but the sense of control and security is weakened or lost. Thus, both poetic strategies that evoke a stable world, and those that indicate a vague, unstable world are double-edged.

The present work is a study of the poetic strategies and devices that may indicate some regression from this achievement of ordinary consciousness. The evasive precategorial information may become accessible to intuition or "Oceanic dedifferentiation" (to be discussed in chapter 9), restoring a feeling of mental flexibility. In real

---

[1] As we will see in Chapter 10, it is this consistency of size and grouping of objects on the one hand, and the boundaries between categories on the other, that are most blatantly violated in Hieronymus Bosch's representation of Hell. Dante too, as we will see, achieves his infernal effects by abolishing the clear boundaries between categories.

life, the difficulty with these modes of access is that they are not available to conscious effort. At the same time, Tennyson's assertion suggests that hell can be rendered awful not only by the threat of painful punishment, but also by suspending the sense of intelligibility, control, comfort and security afforded by ordinary consciousness, that is, by suspending the clear-cut boundaries of objects and thought categories, and blurring the divisions into which the world is marked off. This, in the final resort, may evoke a much stronger response of "exasperated helplessness".

The foregoing discussion may hold the clue to the solution of a serious problem in the consistency of my argument. We could begin many chapters of this book with the same discussion of achieving ordinary consciousness and regression from it. The verbal strategies that generate vagueness in Milton's Hell would be used in generating a variety of altered states of consciousness that involve "Oceanic dedifferentiation", such as mystic experience, varieties of ecstasy and meditation. When William James's informants speak of their mystic experiences, they speak of release from individual existence and fusion with infinity or nothingness. The same verbal strategies used in poetry to generate these mystic qualities also render Milton's Hell vague. What is more, as I have pointed out in several of my writings, the same verbal strategies are used to generate emotional qualities in poetry that is not necessarily of a religious nature.

The clue to this riddle is that certain poetic strategies are "double-edged"; that is, in different contexts they give rise to different perceptual qualities. As a first step to understanding this double-edgedness one should point out that double-edged devices have a variety of features, each of which may generate a perceptual quality that is not necessarily compatible with others. Consider, for instance, a succession of states and images each of which announces the one which follows and contains that which precedes it; none of which, in reality, begins or ends, but all extend into each other (Bergson). The structure of such a succession of states and images may be similar to the structure of such mental processes as "metaphysical intuition" or mystic experience. Alternatively, such a succession may undermine the sense of control and security yielded by "ordinary consciousness" and cognitive stability, and inspire the reader with awe and anxiety. Consequently, such a verbal strategy may cause certain descriptions to display the felt qualities of a mystic experience; but in a description of hell it may inspire the reader with awe and anxiety. These differing potentials may be realised in different contexts by, for instance, the different contents and different figurative language of the texts.

The same holds true, *mutatis mutandis,* of prosodic structures. J.C. Ransom has suggested that a fairly predictable meter may dispel anxiety in the presence of ambiguity — give "false security to the Platonic censor in us" (quoted by Chatman 1965: 212) — so that the reader may feel free to attend to ambiguities in the other layers of the poem. When stressed syllables converge with metrical strong positions and unstressed syllables with weak positions, metre is entirely regular and predictable. Another important aspect of this prosodic structure is that the contrast between prominent and non-prominent events is maximal. Now consider the opposite case, in which the stress pattern diverges from the metric pattern. The sequence of metric events is less predictable, and the clear-cut contrasts between prominent and non-prominent events become blurred. This may, correspondingly, evoke two different kinds of "perceived qualities": on the one hand, it may arouse awe, apprehension and anxiety, owing to the undermining of the Platonic censor's security; on the other hand, the sequence of blurred shapes and contrasts may be perceived as isomorphic with emotional processes (see also the comments on the *terza rima* in Dante's *Inferno* and *Paradiso* in Chapter 10).

The divergent and convergent effects may be reinforced by a variety of additional variables. Thus, for instance, alliteration patterns may reinforce convergence when they occur in stressed syllables and strong metrical positions, with an intervening unstressed syllable in a weak position. When stress patterns, metric patterns and alliteration patterns diverge, the metric shapes and contrasts become increasingly blurred, and amplify one of the two "perceived qualities" mentioned above. In addition, they may arouse an impression of musicality, the smooth, harmonious blending of speech sounds. Likewise, syntactic units (phrases, clauses) may converge with metrical units (hemistichs, lines), or diverge from them. Stanza form too may contribute its share to the total effect. The stanza may have a simple, predictable, or symmetrical rhyme pattern; or, alternatively, a complex, or unpredictable, or asymmetric rhyme pattern. The former will reinforce convergence, the latter divergence.

"Convergent" style is marked by clear-cut shapes, both in content and structure; it is inclined toward definite directions, clear contrasts (prosodic or semantic)—toward an atmosphere of certainty, a quality of intellectual control. "Divergent" style is marked by blurred shapes, both in content and structure; it exhibits general tendencies (rather than definite directions), blurred contrasts, an atmosphere of uncertainty, an emotional quality. Convergence appeals to the actively organizing mind, divergence to a more receptive attitude. The two are not solid categories; the differences are of degree and shadings are gradual, along a spectrum. In one style the various linguistic aspects *tend* to act in convergence, in the other in divergence. When the boundaries of metric and phonetic units, visual designs and those between self and not-self are blurred, the interaction of their precategorial elements is increased. This may amplify the musicality and the nonconceptual perceptions in the text.[2]

Turning now to convergent, regular rhythms, we may point out at least three features relevant to our purpose: they are relatively simple; they are predictable; but, first and foremost, they consist of a sequence of recurring events that mobilise as well as organise mental energies. Consequently, they, too, have at least three kinds of potential effects. They may impose a simplifying structure on reality (as in nursery rhymes); or, being predictable, they may arouse a feeling of rational control (as in Neo-Classic, witty poetry). But regular, predictable metre may also have a very different effect: an ecstatic effect, or what Snyder called "hypnotic", or "trance-inductive", or "spell-weaving" poetry (as in Blake's "The Tyger", Wordsworth's "The Daf-

---

[2]   I have elsewhere adduced some empirical evidence for this possibility (Tsur, 1992a: 466–470; cf. Ehrenzweig, 1970: 170–171).

fodils", Coleridge's "Kubla Khan", or Poe's "Ulalume"). The neuropsychological foundations of such effects have been explored during the past few decades:

> Research reveals that repetitive rhythmic stimulation [...] can drive the limbic and autonomic systems, which may eventually alter some very fundamental aspects of the way the brain thinks, feels, and interprets reality. These rhythms can dramatically affect the brain's neurological ability to define the limits of the self (Newberg et al., 2001: 79).

> Other investigators (Walter and Walter 1949) have also shown that repetitive auditory and visual stimuli drive cortical rhythms and can produce intensely pleasurable, ineffable experiences in human beings (Newberg et al., 2001: 193).

I have elsewhere discussed this kind of poetry at great length (Tsur, 1987c; 1992: 431–454; Glicksohn et al., 1991). Here I only wish to point out a few principles and techniques underlying "hypnotic", "trance-inductive" poetry. Above I quoted John Crowe Ransom as saying that regular, predictable metre gives "false security to the Platonic censor in us". A crucial distinction in this formulation concerns the word "false". In nursery rhymes and witty poetry regular metre gives genuine certainty: it reinforces other elements in other strata of the poetic structure that arouse a sense of certainty. In "hypnotic", "trance-inductive" poetry, by contrast, it joins irrational or irregular elements that the Platonic censor in us finds hard to take. In much poetry there is a rivalry between the irrational contents and regular metre—they vie for dominance. Very much depends on the relative strength of these elements. Up to a certain point, the irrational elements are subordinated to the control of the predictable, convergent prosodic structure. Then, having gathered momentum, the irrational element breaks through the barriers of the "rational" metre, and the poem abruptly becomes "hypnotic", "trance-inductive". In such cases regular recurrence gains an opposite effect. The convergence amplifies the weight of the irrational elements and increases their "enthralling" effect. The obtrusive rhythm then becomes the primitive "drum-beat" underlying "spell-weaving" ecstatic experiences. Frequently, the irrational contents need some kind of reinforcement for overcoming the restraining effect of convergent metre. This can be done in one of two ways: either by foregrounding the energising potential of the convergent prosodic structures, or by weakening their restraining power. On the one hand, the dance of Wordsworth's daffodils, the dancing rocks of "Kubla Khan", or the enormous emotional energies of "The Tyger",[3] foreground the energising potential of regular rhythms. On the other hand, irregular or asymmetric rhyme patterns, irregular line lengths, irregularly interspersed alliterative patterns, or prolonged syntactic anticipations spread over several lines, may weaken the restraining power of convergent prosodic structures.

---

[3] Most critics have a few words to spare on the enormous energies of "The Tyger". .

This analysis foregrounds a central problem of the present book. Poetry is a complex of semiotic systems; it offers an indefinite (but by no means unconstrained) number of verbal strategies for capturing the perceived qualities of such religious experiences as ecstasy, meditation or mystic experience. There is no one-to-one relationship between the various verbal strategies and the felt qualities suggested by them (in speech research, Al Liberman would call such a phenomenon "complex coding"). A divergent verbal structure may be "isomorphic" with mystic experiences, by virtue of the blurring of visual images and metric shapes; alternatively, it may undermine the psychological atmosphere of security and cognitive control, inspiring awe and anxiety, thus enhancing the felt qualities of an infernal landscape, for instance. Likewise, a convergent structure may generate such widely different perceived qualities as simplified mastery of reality, rational predictability, or a hypnotic / ecstatic quality—by virtue of its various potentials which may be foregrounded at different times, and under different thematic designs.

Tennyson's Nightmare and Milton's Vage Hell

Above I quoted Alan Sinfield, who begins a discussion of Tennyson's nightmare description with Tennyson's own dictum: "Milton's vague hell is much more awful than Dante's hell marked off into divisions." This remark draws attention to certain relationships between poetic structures and felt qualities: the emotional qualities associated with weak shapes, and the non-emotional qualities associated with strong shapes, as discussed above. Sinfield demonstrates the relationship between "the vague and the poetical" in *In Memoriam*. Among other passages, he quotes the following "sequence of nightmare images":

1. Cloud-towers by ghostly masons wrought,
    A gulf that ever shuts and gapes,
    A hand that points, and palled shapes
    In shadowy thoroughfares of thought;

    And crowds that stream from yawning doors,
    And shoals of pucker'd faces drive;
    Dark bulks that tumble half alive,
    And lazy lengths on boundless shores.

Sinfield's illuminating method of demonstrating how ambiguity (in the sense of vagueness) contributes to the total impact of the passage involves comparing the passage's first line to an earlier version, which read:

2. *A fort* by ghostly masons wrought,

Having thus set poetic effects against a firm background of "other things being equal," Sinfield is able to remark: "With the vaguer replacement we are left wondering whether the poet saw clouds or towers" (p. 72). But even here one cannot take "other things being equal" for granted. The exchange of phrases changes the text in two additional relevant respects, rhythmic and grammatical. Not only the image has been made ambiguous by this replacement; the metric shape has, too. In the first (weak) position, an unstressed indefinite article, with a reduced vowel, has been replaced by a stressed noun with an (irreducible) long diphthong, thus blurring the perception of a clear iambic pattern, in a poem in which irregularities are scarce:

3.   Clóud-tówers by ghóstly másons wróught.
       w   ⌊s⌋   w   s   w   s   w   s

There is an additional significant contrast between the two versions: [±PLURAL]. In a paper on Racine, Leo Spitzer (1969: 127-128) argued at great length that the plural has a muting, contour-blurring effect. One should notice the great abundance of plural phrases in this passage.

Sinfield rightly insists that the vagueness of imagery makes a major contribution toward the nightmarish quality of this passage. It is, however, not necessarily *vagueness*. There is here a broader strategy of generating a psychological atmosphere of uncertainty and loss of control by a variety of means, of which vagueness of imagery is only one. Consider "A hand that points". This is anything but vague: it has a stable characteristic visual shape, and displays a gesture of definite direction and patent purpose. Nonetheless, it does contribute toward the nightmarish quality. As I said above, scenes and situations can be expected to have a certain degree of consistency: "A hand that points" is more frequently encountered as an extension of a human body than detached from a body and grouped with "towers". This grouping even suggests a comparable size of "hand" and "towers". Moreover, in spite of its lack of attachment to a body, the hand displays great vitality. In these respects, the hand is akin to the pair of ears in Hieronymus Bosch's Hell (see Chapter 10). Faces detached from the body or even from the head, fused in some undifferentiated mass, are presented in "shoals of pucker'd faces". On the whole, Tennyson attempts to concoct his nightmare description of images as unrelated as possible.

Lack of light impedes the control of reality. In these two stanzas we encounter three words that suggest lack of light: "cloud, shadowy, dark". Clouds and shadows also suggest visible but insubstantial entities. Disintegration of "ordinary consciousness" is blatantly indicated by "Dark bulks", that condenses a wide range of effects mentioned above: it is characterised by darkness; it is in the "contour-blurring" plural; and it blurs the iambic pattern by a stressed syllable in a weak position. Semantically, it denotes not a physical object, but qualities abstracted from physical objects: magnitude in three dimensions. Further, it suggests weight, and often a recognisable, though perhaps unwieldy, shape. In Ehrenzweig's terms, it suggests thing-destruction and thing-free qualities. A less complex thing-free quality is suggested by "lazy lengths" (here, both the plural and the combination of noun and adjective are anomalous!). "Tumble" suggests loss of control in two different senses: falling suddenly and helplessly, and issuing forth hurriedly and confusedly. Control requires energy. Reduced energy is suggested by such words as "palled, half alive, lazy", and also perhaps "puckered". The phrase "crowds that stream" suggests an unstable physical environment. The boundaries between animate and inanimate things are blurred too, in such expressions as "A gulf that ever shuts and gapes" and "yawning doors"—very much in the grotesque manner (see Chapter 10). The lack of boundary (rather than the sublime potential) seems to justify the inclusion of "boundless shores" in this description.

The phrase "shadowy thoroughfares of thought" points up a basic assumption of the present work: that even loss of control can be double-edged. Compare this phrase to Keats's "to let the mind be a thoroughfare for all thoughts". In both phrases suspension of control is suggested. But whereas in Tennyson's description it suggests desperate helplessness, Keats's phrase concerning "Negative Capability" suggests the release of creativity from the tyrannous control of ordinary consciousness. True, Keats implies that this process is a difficult achievement, and some, perhaps many, people are unable to overcome the anxiety it arouses.[4] Another basic assumption of the present study will be pointed up if we compare the effect of the phrase "ghostly masons" to the rest of the passage as discussed above. To me, at least, its effectiveness is impaired in a curious way. This is the only expression in the passage which directly refers to the demonic. That is precisely what vitiates its effectiveness. "Ghostly" suggests a visible disembodied spirit, or something that haunts or perturbs the mind. A visible disembodied spirit is, of course, a cognitive and practical anomaly that could, according to the foregoing discussion, enhance the psychological atmosphere of lost control, insecurity, helplessness; haunting or perturbing the mind too could enhance it. However, the fact that there are well-established categories in our thought with such labels in our language as "ghostly" and "demonic", strongly vitiates the exasperated helplessness provoked by them. A basic assumption of the present study is that directly naming the numinous or the demonic is essentially conceptual; their felt qualities can be indicated only when the text requires to generate them by overcoming some cognitive anomalies.

Tennyson's imagery displays, then, a strong nightmarish affect; at the same time, a "psychological atmosphere of certainty" has been generated by the all too regular meter (mitigating the uncertainty of "nightmarish imagery").[5] This sense of control

4 See also his famous formulation "The ability to be in uncertainties, Mysteries, doubts, without any irritable reaching after fact and reason".

5 There are only two additional stresses to "soften" the impact of rhythm—at the least intolerant points, the beginnings of lines: "Cloud-towers" and "Dark bulks." Another possible source of weakening of metric shape is the allocation of the trisyllabic "shadowy" to two metrical positions, and of the bisyllabic "towers" to one position (provided that the performer does not elide a vowel adjacent to the *w*). All the strong positions have been actualised by lexical stresses, except, possibly, "half" in line 7, which may or may not bear lexical stress.

and security is reinforced by the closed symmetrical shape of the stanza, and the convergent use of alliteration as in "*lazy l*engths", where the repeated /l/ occurs at the onset of stressed syllables in strong position, with an intervening unstressed syllable in a weak position. Certain syntactic and semantic aspects of these quatrains tend to reinforce their strong metric shape. A series of items is enumerated here; each item stretches over a syntactic unit (clause or distinct phrase), which converges, exactly, with a line. There is only one exception to this rule, the enjambment at the end of line 3. As I have argued at some length (Tsur 1972), in an atmosphere of regularity and of "patent purpose," rather than weakening the shape of the verse, such an enjambment amplifies the requiredness of the next line; that is, the enjambment "arouses powerful desires for clarification" of the stanzaic shape, which are in this case straightaway gratified (and reinforced by the rhyme-scheme). Every image in the above description, every aspect pointed out in it, evokes a sense of insecurity and loss of control, increasing the nightmarish quality. Its regular metre and closed symmetrical stanza form, by contrast, evoke a sense of control and security, increasing its rational quality. These opposite qualities vie for dominance. The strong rhythmic shape keeps the irrational quality in tight control—up to an operationally undefinable point of relative strength. When the elements of insecurity exceed that point, the nightmarish quality abruptly gains dominion, and the rhythm is subordinated to it. Different readers may emphasise different elements in a text. That is why some readers do, while others do not, perceive a nightmarish quality in this passage, or recognise in *In Memoriam* in general the elegiac emotion it claims to have. For many readers, the rational quality of its strong metric shape moderates the irrational qualities generated by vagueness of diction and imagery. I suggested above that irrational contents frequently need some kind of reinforcement for overcoming the restraining effect of convergent metre. This can be done in one of two ways: either by foregrounding the energising potential of the convergent prosodic structures, or by weakening their restraining power. In Tennyson's nightmare there are no dancing rocks or daffodils but, rather, an accumulation of expressions suggesting lack of energy; and there are no syntactic complexities that would weaken the restraining power of the meter.

Let us turn now to Milton's "vague hell." It is impossible to do justice here to the infinite perspectives suggested by "bottomless perdition" or "At once as far as Angels' ken he views / The dismal situation waste and wild," etc. (I have discussed these at some length in Tsur 1977:180-185; 1992: 85–91; 1998: 256-264). Here I only wish to recapitulate the old commonplace that Milton's Hell is vague from the prosodic point of view, too (especially as compared with Tennyson's nightmare). Let us have a closer look at a description which has become by now a classic of metrical analysis:

4.   O'r mány a frózen, mány a fíery Álp,
     w   s ⌊w⌋ s w   s ⌊w⌋⌊s⌋ w s
Rócks, cáves, lákes, féns, bógs, déns, and shádes of déath,
w   s   w   s   w   s   w   s   w s
A úniverse of déath, which Gód by cúrse
w s w s   w s   w   s   w s
Creáted évil, for évil ónly góod,
ws w ⌊s⌋   w s w s w s
Where áll lífe díes, déath líves, and Náture bréeds
w   s   w   s   w   s   w   s   w   s
Pervérse, áll mónstrous, áll prodígious thíngs,
w   s   w   s   w   s   ws w   s
Abóminable, inútterable, and wórse (Paradise Lost, II. 620-626).
w s w ⌊s⌋ w s w ⌊s⌋   w   s

For the spiritual contents of the description, we find the cumulative impact of such "negative" words as "death, dies, curse, evil, perverse, monstrous, prodigious, abominable, worse...". Even words which do have positive connotations, such as "good, life, Nature," occur in such paradoxical constructions as "for evil only good", "life dies, death lives", so as to obscure any clear distinction between the opposites good and evil. Nor does the concrete scenery manifest any clear-cut shapes. The catalogue in line 621 is a muddle of items; none of them has a characteristic shape, and the little they may have has been blurred by the plural. In the next line, the description leaps to a far too abstract, shapeless "universe of death",[6] etc. (in lines 622–626, the most concrete and most specific item is the rather vague "things").

From the prosodic point of view, it may be observed that both regularity and clear-cut contrasts between prominence and nonprominence have been greatly blurred in these lines, resulting in an exceptionally weak rhythmic shape. So, dissimilar lines such as 620, 621 and 626 are a perfectly legitimate actualization of the same underlying metric pattern of regularly alternating weak and strong positions, ten in number. Each of these lines makes more than ample use of a perfectly "allowable" deviation (legitimised under the Halle–Keyser theory) (1966; 1971). Lines 620 and 623, surprisingly enough, are among the rare instances in Milton's work where stressed syllables occur in all strong positions and only in strong positions. Here, however, the metric pattern is obscured by three(!) and one instances, respectively, of positions occupied by two syllables each (notice that in these seven lines, six positions are occupied by two syllables each; in Tennyson's eight lines only two).[7] In line 621, the first six(!) positions are occupied by consecutive monosyllabics with

6   "Universe of death" is, conspicuously, a conceptual summary of the situation. As I have argued at length in chapter 5, such abstract expressions, when they occur in a concrete landscape description, may assume a diffuse emotional quality.
7   It is disputable whether "abominable" and "inutterable" in line 626 contain four or five syllables. I have elsewhere discussed at great length the performance and cognitive *raison d'être* of bisyllabic occupancy of metrical positions (Tsur, 1998: ch. 8).

equally heavy stresses (the relative prominence of certain syllables in some performances is completely gratuitous from the linguistic point of view).

It is remarkable in this line that whatever the uncertainties in the first six positions as to the regularity of meter, it is in the end "reconditioned" by the regularly alternating unstressed and stressed syllables in the last four positions. In contrast with this line, the next one begins with a syntactic group of six syllables. The stress of the fourth position is not realised here, leaving a series of three unstressed syllables in "A universe of death"; this "speeds up" the six syllables, and demands their emphatic grouping. In the last four positions, as in the previous line, regular alternation returns. (The analogy of "A universe of death" with its antecedents is ambiguous: in its structure it parallels "shades of death" whereas in its meaning it parallels the whole line). But the overwhelming metric contrast appears between line 621 and 626. In the latter only three stresses are actualized, with unstressed syllables heavily leaning backward. In both lines, contrasts between prominence and non-prominence are frequently leveled out—though by opposite means.

It is illuminating to compare Milton's technique of enumeration to Tennyson's. In Tennyson's description (excerpt 1), each item with its modifiers is "neatly spread out" so as to converge as much as possible on the prosodic unit rather than interfere with it. The sole run-on phrase, as we have seen, serves only to reinforce the closure of the stanza (counting towards strong shape). In Milton's line 621, a series of six equally stressed monosyllabics are "indiscriminately" lumped together, as it were, so that every other one is bound to fall in a weak position, blurring the contrast between prominence and non-prominence.

Line 624 is notable. It, too, "lumps together" five stressed syllables in positions 2–6, and then returns to regular confirmation of meter. It presents a pair of paradoxical statements: "Where all life dies, death lives". The strained emotive quality of this will be apparent when compared to the elegant, witty, rational quality of such pairs of paradoxical statements by Pope as:

> 5. Born but to die, and reas'ning but to err.
>   w   s w s w   s   w   s w s

The divergent–emotive and convergent–rational linkage exists in many ways. I submit that the strained emotive quality of Milton's paradoxes and the elegant rational quality of Pope's have to do with the weaker shape of the former and the stronger shape of the latter: their handling of metric regularity and the symmetry of the line. Pope's two paradoxes divide the line into two quasi-symmetric segments. Apart from the perfectly allowable "inversion" of the first foot, the metric structure of excerpt 5 is quite regular. The stress displaced to position 1 requires the reassertion of meter in position 4; the result is a stress valley, with a closed symmetrical shape, followed by an emphatic caesura. The somewhat lighter stress in position 8 (on "but") arouses a desire to seal up the witty statement, the line, the couplet (and thus it turns out to be functional). Milton distorts all sense of symmetry and balance by "lumping" together his two paradoxes in the first segment of the line. The strained quality is heightened, on the rhetorical level by asyndeton and on the metrical level by "neutralising" the contrast between prominence and non-prominence. As opposed to the clarity of Pope's pairs of paradoxes, there is some uncertainty in Milton's also regarding their meaning; i.e., whether the two paradoxical statements have the same meaning or not. In Pope we found that the division of his line into two "symmetrical" statements bestows upon it a balanced, rational quality (elsewhere I have shown [Tsur 1972; 1977:72–79; 1992a: 137–139; 1998: 121–123; see also Chapter 9 below] that a division into 4 + 6 is the most symmetrical division of an iambic pentameter line). Milton not only divides his line into three, but the third statement, "and Nature breeds," has positive, "life" connotations. The statement becomes akin to each of the preceding two statements when (distorting all sense of balance) completed:

> 6.   and Nature breeds
>   Perverse, all monstrous, all prodigious things...

   To conclude: vagueness of imagery and of rhythm may display a strong emotional quality, especially when they interact and enhance each other. In extreme instances, such vagueness may have a structure similar to mystic experiences (and reinforce such contents), or arouse anxiety and reinforce an "infernal" description. The emotional or non-emotional quality of a piece of poetry is the perceptual concomitant of the whole, which is determined by its sound-aspects as well as its meaning-aspects. In Milton and Pope these aspects join forces toward an emotional and a witty quality, respectively. The unemotional quality felt by some readers in Tennyson may be accounted for by the fact that the strong rhythmical shape of *In Memoriam* counteracts the emotional atmosphere generated by the imagery. We will see that strong rhythmic shape may enhance emotional qualities, when in other layers of the poem the energy level is high enough, or uncertainties marked enough, so as to subsume rhythm in a quasi-ecstatic experience. Such rhetorical schemes as parallelism and antithesis are double-edged. They may count toward convergence (strong shape) when focused on an unambiguous relationship, or when they reinforce the symmetry (or quasi-symmetry) of the segments into which the caesura divides the line. They may also count toward divergence (weak shape), when, for example, the structure and meaning of the same syntactic unit are analogous with different syntactic units, or when the rhetorical schemes run counter to the metrical segmentation. Referring to the grouping of lines, the couplet and the quatrain are closed and symmetrical; they count, other things being equal, toward strong shape.

Regular Rhythms

I suggested earlier that regular metre appears to be "double-edged". On the one hand, it tends to be rational, exhibiting definite directions and organising percepts into predictable orders; it has the psychological atmosphere of certainty. On the other hand, it may generate vigorous rhythms with an irrational, even ecstatic qualities, similar to a primitive drum-beat. In other words, regular metre shares important properties with conscious control and the exercise of will; at the same time, it is similar to certain fundamental involuntary physiological processes, many of which consist of regularly recurring events. Intense physical and emotional activities in humans and animals increasingly tend to possess regular rhythm and to transcend voluntary control. Consequently, one factor that differentiates between regular meter underlying a witty poem and that underlying an ecstatic poem is the energy levels perceived in other layers of the poem. Higher levels of energy will probably prevent or abolish any possibility of a witty effect. Another factor is the psychological atmosphere of certainty or uncertainty related to figurative language, rhetorical schemes, and the larger prosodic units; i.e, whether the length of lines and their grouping into stanzas is as predictable as in "An Essay on Man", or as unpredictable as in "Kubla Khan". Higher levels of uncertainty will encourage the perception of the regular metre as an emotional-hypnotic and even ecstatic quality.

It has been observed that the rhythm of some poems is more obtrusive than that of others; there is a small number of poems whose rhythm thrusts itself, so to speak, upon the reader or listener. Three factors lie at the root of this obtrusiveness: the delivery style adopted by the performer, the prosodic superordinates of meter, and the nature of the contents. The delivery style adopted—with respect to the conspicuity of meter—depends to a large extent on an arbitrary decision. Some performers give greater prominence to the metric pattern of the poem, some less. But—and this is more important than is usually realised—the nature of the text does have some bearing on the choice of the delivery style, or, at least, on some crucial points of the delivery instance. The crux of the problem is that in some poems one is more strongly inclined than in others to wrench the stress pattern of the words to adjust them to the metre, and so foreground metre through performance.

There are a number of factors which count toward the "wrenching" impulse; they may act separately or in any combination: (a) regularity; (b) trochaic meter; (c) short lines; (d) a high energy level indicated by contents (movement, emotion); (e) genre.

(a) When stress pattern and metre converge, that is, when a high proportion of strong positions are occupied by stressed syllables, and weak positions by unstressed syllables, readers are inclined to preserve regularity and wrench the stress pattern of a deviant word or phrase.

(b) It has been frequently noticed that the contrast between stress and unstress is more readily emphasized in the trochaic than in the iambic meter (cf., for example, Chatman 1965:141, n.). The reason lies in an intuitive, subtle manipulation of the acoustic cues for stress. In an "end-accented" metre like the iambic, there is a complex interplay between pitch, loudness and duration. In the trochaic, on the contrary, the inherent properties of "beginning-accented" metres demand the suppression of durational differences as an acoustic cue, and the bestowal of priority upon loudness (reinforced by pitch) in effecting stress—as demonstrated by Woodrow (cf. Chatman [1965: 26-27] and Tsur [1977: 88-90]). Chatman (1965: 79) quotes Brown, who "discovered an interesting difference between iambic and trochaic nonsense lines: ictus in iambic meter was from 2.1 to 2.9 times longer than non-ictus, whereas in trochaic meter, the ratio was profoundly different, the ictus ranging only .46 to 1.04 times the length of the non ictus". Thus, when performing a trochaic poem, readers tend to suppress durational differences and give prominence to loudness differences — even if there is an initial upbeat. Consequently, the trochaic has a more obtrusive nature; it has a "stronger shape" than the iambic.

(c) Likewise, tetrameter lines tend to compel greater regularity than pentameter lines (I have elaborated these themes in Tsur [1977, chap. 3]).

(d) Another means for "foregrounding" metre is a high energy level in the contents. Powerful emotions, such as terror, glee, ecstasy on the one hand, and vigorous physical motion on the other, tend to assimilate the "drum-beat" of regular metre, and to be enhanced by it. It may be accurate to say that regular metre and vigorous contents foreground and intensify each other. As for deviations from metre, there appears to be a kind of vicious circle. When the energy level is high, it tends to subdue stresses that occur in weak positions. The resistance of the wrenched stress, in turn, heightens the energy level of the poem. Consequently, a stressed syllable in a weak position is likely to have a different impact in "The Tyger" than in "An Essay on Man" and, in either, a different impact than in *Paradise Lost*. When the energy level of emotions or of physical motion drops, deviant stresses regain their tendency to weaken metric shape; metre returns to the background.

(e) Nursery rhymes, as a genre, demand a delivery style in which differences of stress-level tend to be straightened out (or sharpened), in such a way as to achieve maximum contrast between prominence and non-prominence.

The perceptual quality of verse will depend on several components, such as the underlying metre, the number of patterns organised in the sound structure of the line, their convergence or divergence, the relationship of smaller units to larger units and, last but not least, the relationship of prosodic shape to meaning.

Consider, for instance, the following pair of lines:

7.   Tackle, tackle, Mother Goose
8.   Tyger! Tyger! burning bright

The two lines exhibit quite a few identical features. Both are trochaic tetrameter, with the last weak position unoccupied; in other respects, both are perfectly regular. Both repeat, in their beginnings, a bisyllabic word that has a trochaic cadence, so as to emphasise at the very onset the metric pattern to be perpetuated. Both lines manifest a considerable perceptual unity, owing to the numerical impossibility of dividing them into symmetrical halves, by contrast, for example, with:

9.   Handy spandy Jack-a-Dandy,

Nevertheless, whoever reads the nursery rhyme and Blake's poem cannot help feeling that the regular metre of excerpt (7) is aimed, for the most, at a simplified mastery of reality, whereas the vigorous rhythms of excerpt (8) tremble sometimes on the brink of ecstasy. What is the source of the difference?

One difference lies in the number and kind of meanings conveyed by, and the number of patterns subsumed in, the respective sequences of sounds. We have seen that both lines achieve rhythmic regularity by the convergence of stressed syllables and strong positions. In Blake's poem, the prominence of stressed syllables is further enhanced by their convergence with two additional sound patterns: alliteration (b-r) and/or assonance (the diphtong [aj]); the two patterns converge in the last syllable (bright). Secondly, we have seen that at the onset of both lines, the repetition of the first "trochaic" word serves to reinforce the metric pattern. Besides this, the words "Tyger! Tyger!" emerge as syntactically ambiguous. Apparently three syntactic functions converge in them: (1) In the affirmative function, the two words "set the situation" ("there is a tiger there"); (2) it is a vocative phrase; and (3) it is an exclamation. The latter two functions set the tone of immediacy—even urgency—that pervades the whole poem, and both are emotionally loaded, that is, both carry energy. Likewise, *burning* has connotations of intense energy. The phrase "burning bright" consists of a syntagmatic sequence of two words; at the same time, they both suggest "light". The overwhelming emotive quality of the line has to do with its "loaded convergence": the direction of the emotion is set by a situation appraisal which involves thought processes, and is characterized by awe, admiration, etc. The absence of some of these renders the nursery rhyme much simpler, or even simplified.

I have said above that the words "Tyger! Tyger!" are ambiguous, and *apparently* three syntactic functions converge in them. The apparent syntactic ambiguity is disambiguated in lines 3–4, where the (rhetorical) question unambiguously suggests that "Tyger! Tyger!" is a vocative, not the subject, object or predicate of an elliptic sentence. The sentence stretches over the whole stanza and is perceived as weakening the line endings and the couplet ending—after the event. "Burning bright" is apparently a complete phrase; but the prepositional phrase "In the forests of the night" reopens it. All this generates loaded convergence in the perspective of the line or the couplet, and divergence in the perspective of the quatrain. Consequently, the microstructure generates certainty, whereas the macro-structure generates uncertainty. As I have suggested above, complex syntactic structures spread over several lines may weaken the restraining power of convergent prosodic structures, amplifying the effect of irrational elements in the contents, generating a hypnotic, ecstatic or similar quality. In excerpt 7, by contrast, the repeated "Tackle, tackle" is an immediately recognisable finite verb, and "Mother Goose" an undoubted vocative that helps to identify the subject of the verb. Thus, in excerpt 7 no syntactic tension builds up, and the repetition is perceived as "childish".

Schematically, then, one may speak of two distinctions between three types of rhythmic structures (though in practice one may expect to find any number of shadings between them). One distinction is between divergent and convergent style. The former, typical, for example, of Milton and Shelley, tends to have emotive overtones; the latter, typical of Pope, Spenser, and nursery rhymes, tends to be non-emotional: witty, rational, or simplifying. When convergence appears in a poem like *In Memoriam,* it mitigates the emotive quality. A second distinction may be made between simple and loaded convergence. Poems of this category are relatively rare. But when they do occur, they tend to tremble on the brink of the uncanny or ecstatic. The immense energy of "The Tyger," for instance, with uncertainties latent in other layers of the poem, renders the security given to the "Platonic censor in us" false. At the same time, the possible bodily appeal of its vigorous rhythm may render the emotional response more inclusive.

Obtrusive Rhythm and the Numinous

So, let us have a closer look at Blake's "The Tyger":

10.   Tyger! Tyger! burning bright
      In the forests of the night,
      What immortal hand or eye
      Could frame thy fearful symmetry?

      In what distant deeps or skies
      Burnt the fire of thine eyes?
      On what wings dare he aspire?
      What the hand dare seize the fire?

      And what shoulder, & what art,
      Could twist the sinews of thy heart?
      And when thy heart began to beat,
      What dread hand? & what dread feet?

      What the hammer? what the chain?
      In what furnace was thy brain?
      What the anvil? what dread grasp
      Dare its deadly terrors clasp?

      When the stars threw down their spears,
      And watered heaven with their tears,
      Did he smile his work to see?
      Did he who made the Lamb make thee?

      Tyger! Tyger! burning bright
      In the forests of the night,
      What immortal hand or eye,
      Dare frame thy fearful symmetry?

While the poem sets out with a certain, strong rhythmic shape, to satisfy the "Platonic censor in us," the "psychological atmosphere of security" is increasingly impaired. The second line, though not actively violating metre, deviates from the rhythm so emphatically established in the first line, and arouses a strong desire to wrench the stress pattern, to accent *"In* the forest *of* the night". In order to escape sounding childish, the performer is likely to adopt a "delivery-style" sufficiently ambiguous (in the sense of "complex") so that the prepositions do not appear unduly stressed and still confirm the strong metric expectations set in the first line. Thus, the beginning of the poem provides not only for intense trochaic metre, but also for complexity of performance. Some deviations from metre do enhance the contrast between prominent and non-prominent syllables, by adding a hypermetric unstressed syllable before the first strong position (increasing the number of stressed syllables between two unstressed ones), usually a conjunction ("and") or auxiliary verb ("could, did, dare"). Nevertheless, they weaken the psychological atmosphere of certainty; the performer can never be sure whether the next line will begin with a stressed syllable in a strong position, or an unstressed hypermetric syllable (see the second stanza of excerpt 15). In such instances, the reciter is likely to preserve the trochaic cadence of the verse by using loudness rather than duration as a cue for stress. But there are quite a few deviations in this poem that demand greater subtlety and complexity of delivery style.

It has been noticed that the trochaic violently resists "foot inversion" at line-onset, and even more in mid-line, as in:

> 11.   And whát shóulder, and whát árt.
>   s   w   s   w   s   w   s

Notice how easily Blake could have avoided this, by writing:

> 12.   Whát the shóulder, whát the árt.
>   s   w   s   w   s   w   s

In excerpt 11 the stress is displaced when the tendency to wrench deviant stresses is already well established. Consequently, high tension is generated, which makes a major contribution toward the energetic, emotional quality of the verse.

> 13.   Whát dréad hánd and whát dréad féet?
>   s   w   s   w   s   w   s

Not as in excerpt 11, trochaic cadence can rather easily be maintained in excerpt 13, where "dread," occurring twice in weak position, is preceded and followed by stressed syllables, to which it can be subordinated. Its relatively long duration, however, is hard to suppress. The contrast between the second and sixth (weak) positions and the adjoining strong positions has been levelled out to a considerable degree.

Constituting an elliptic clause, excerpt 13 introduces another element of uncertainty. One may only guess what is predicated about "dread hand" and "dread feet".

In an earlier version of this poem, lines 3–4 of stanza 3 read:

> 14.   What dread hand and what dread feet
>   Could fetch it from the furnace deep?

Regarding the syntactic error in line 4 of the final version, two different explanations may be suggested: first, the poet may have meant what he wrote; and second, when revising the poem, he may have overlooked the fact that the sentence remained syntactically incomplete. In the latter case, the overlooking may be treated as a downright failure, or as a happy accident that unintentionally assumed a desirable poetic function. Bloom (1954), for instance, adopts the "intentional" view: "Blake carefully revised so as to produce that last line, with its frightened leap in grammar" (36). In their College Survey of English Literature, in the annotations to this poem, Whiting et al. (1942, Volume one: 1103) adopt the "overlooking" view, but comment: "The *glorious* and startling grammatical error of line 12 was accidental" (my italics). In other words, they too admit that, intentionally or not, the line assumes a powerful effect. The "happy accident" view is more illuminatingly suggested in E.D. Hirsch's (1964: 249) reading: "As the astonished and uncertain mind of the speaker shifts alternatively from god to tiger he lapses into an incoherent confusion that makes no literal sense (The couplet is an unassimilated vestige from an earlier draft) but makes good dramatic sense".

I shall not go into the semantic aspects of the revision; rather, I will dwell only on some of its structural aspects. First, the rhyme in the revised version is more perfect. Second, the revised version introduces variation into a repeated structure that may otherwise have sounded monotonous. Consider the sequences "What the hammer? what the chain? / In what furnace was thy brain?", or "What the anvil? what dread grasp / Dare its deadly terrors clasp?", or "And what shoulder, & what art, / Could twist the sinews of thy heart?". In all these sequences, the odd-numbered line contains two parallel phrases, each of which contains the interrogative pronoun "what", superimposing a rhythmic repetitive pattern on the obtrusive rhythms of the poem. The ensuing even-numbered lines complete the sentence, by adding a single, longer verb phrase. The earlier version follows exactly this pattern; the revised version generates variation by inverting this order. Third, according to a well-established cognitive principle (see Chapter 9), in a series of parallel phrases or prosodic units the "longest unit comes last" is perceived as the well-ordered sequence. Accordingly, the order established in the foregoing excerpts has a "settling" effect; the inversion of this order in the revised version has an "unsettling" effect. It is this "unsettling" effect that is enhanced by the incomplete phrases "What dread hand? & what dread feet?", suggesting, as it were, a highly emotive exclamation.

Rhetorical questions typically display an atmosphere of highly definite direction and patent purpose. On the other hand, like exclamations, they load the utterance with high energy. The former aspect counts toward non-emotional quality, the latter toward emotional quality. In this poem, it is the emotional quality that prevails; the "psychological atmosphere of patent purpose" is latently loosened. One would assume that there is an implied answer to "What immortal hand or eye?"—God's, of course. One soon realises, however, that this answer does not suit such questions as "What the hammer", "In what furnace" or "On what wings dare he aspire?" Here we are in the domain of pagan mythology (Hephaistos? Icarus? Prometheus?). The last two questions plunge us into uncertainty. "Did he smile his work to see? (Was he happy with his wonderful accomplishment, or was he awe-strucken himself and could not even smile?). "Did he who made the Lamb make thee? (of course, yes; it is impossible).

Now consider the following two consecutive stanzas:

> 15. What the hammer? what the chain?
> In what furnace was thy brain?
> What the anvil? what dread grasp
> Dare its deadly terror clasp?
>
> When the stars threw down their spears,
> And watered heavens with their tears,
> Did he smile his work to see?
> Did he who made the Lamb make thee?

The first of these stanzas is fairly typical of the whole poem; the second is unique. There is a marked change of tone and rhythm from the first to the second. There is little change in metric regularity from one stanza to the next, but the straightforward vigorous rhythms give way to a "milder" rhythm (in spite of a natural tendency to perpetuate established rhythms). The first of these stanzas (indeed, the whole poem) is pervaded by an intense emotion of terror mixed with admiration, rendering the rhythm obtrusive, and it is the obtrusive rhythm that induces the urgency characteristic of the proximity of the numinous. The short paratactic units converge with the lines, or divide them, creating a distinct caesura; the short convergent perceptual units enhance the obtrusive quality of the metre. The enjambment beginning at the caesura of the third line has an impact similar to the one in excerpt 1; it prepares for emphatic closure. Metric tension is heightened in this stanza by two serious infringements of metre: the stress displaced to the right in "In what furnace was thy brain?" and the sequence of three stresses in "what dread grasp". The desire to wrench "in what" is strong, since the stress of "what" can be subordinated to "fur-", but not to "in". The resistance of "dread" to squeezing into a weak position is enhanced by its grouping, phonetically (and semantically), with "Dare," "deadly" (and, remembering that [t] is a voiceless [d], with "terrors"). Nonetheless, one is inclined to pronounce it as less prominent than the adjacent "what" and "grasp", so as to create tension and, at the same time, preserve the regular trochaic cadence until reaching the next line where the convergence of strong positions, stresses, and alliteration clearly contrasts with weak positions converging with unstressed syllables.

Here we might suggest a brief comparison of alliteration in "The Tyger" with Tennyson's passage. The typical alliterative pattern in convergent poetry, as I have said, consists of a repeated sound pattern coinciding with stressed syllables that coincide with metrical strong positions, with an intervening unstressed syllable in a metrical weak position the sounds of which are not part of a repetitive sound pattern, as in Tennyson's "*l*azy *l*engths", for instance. The same could be said of "*b*urning *b*right" in "The Tyger". However, "bright" is part of an additional sound pattern, that diverges from this one: the dyphthong [aj] recurs in this word after the repeated "Tyger". Thus, an element of divergence enters the convergent sound pattern. Or, consider the lines "What the anvil? what *dread* grasp / *Dare* its *dea*dly terrors clasp?", and compare them to Tennyson's "Cloud-towers by *g*hostly masons wrought, / A *g*ulf that ever shuts and *g*apes". In Tennyson's poem, the [g] recurs three times at the onset of stressed syllables in strong metrical positions. In Blake's, a more complex sound cluster is repeated three times, twice at the onset of stressed syllables in strong positions, once at the onset of a stressed syllable in a weak position *("dread")*. Thus, both poems are essentially convergent, with symmetrical stanzas. In Blake, convergence is heightened by such devices as repeated short phrase structures, and enormous emotional energies; at the same time, it is weakened too, by more complex alliteration patterns. That seems to be the reason that in Tennyson convergence tends to restrain the emotional quality, whereas in Blake it appears to enhance it.

In the next stanza of "The Tyger" one immediately feels that metre is relatively "backgrounded". There are three obvious changes which may account for this sudden change of mood and rhythm: (1) The vocative and the exclamation with their atmosphere of immediacy and urgency are replaced by a somewhat more relaxed mood. For the mood of powerful awe and admiration, a more moderate one has been substituted, introduced by a nature-description[8] (whatever the further implications of "the stars threw down their spears"). (2) The paratactic structure, so conspicuous throughout the poem, has been replaced by complex hypotactic structures. There are no complex sentences elsewhere in the poem, and in this stanza they have a remarkable effect (The only other attempt to generate a compound sentence, "And when thy heart began to beat", ends up in an elliptic fragment). The first complex sentence ("When...") is striking for its very length: the prediction of a main clause from the conjunction is only fulfilled in the third line. This weakens the shape of the lines considerably and softens their impact. Thus, a larger divergent structure is superimposed upon the convergent metric shape, splitting attention between the forward movement of the syntax and the need to remember a syntactic prediction whose fulfillment is delayed over a considerable stretch of text.[9] The second sentence is noto-

---

[8] As to the emotional effect of "seeing the place", see chapter 4.

[9] In chapter 9 we will encounter additional texts in different languages and different cultural traditions, which exploit similar syntactic structures for the same effects. This structure can also fruitfully be compared and contrasted to the structure of the first stanza, where too the vocatives of the first line "predict" the clause in lines 3–4; but here the "prediction" is realised only after the event: the emotional impact and the

rious for its great complexity. The syntactic subject of its main clause separates the auxiliary from the main verb ("Did . . . make thee?"). But the NP (e.g., "God") has been replaced by a relative clause serving as a periphrasis ("he who made the Lamb"). To make things "worse", two tokens of the same verb-type ("made", "make") are predicates in both clauses (once occurring in a strong, once in a weak metrical position), rendering the distinction between subject and predicate rather fuzzy. Such syntactic structures take up a relatively great deal of "mental space", blur prosodic shapes, and push metre into the background. (3) Two groupings of lines concur in this stanza, syntactic and phonetic: the first complex sentence groups lines 1–3 together and so overrides the symmetrical grouping of lines by the rhyme-scheme, which is conspicuous throughout the poem. By weakening the overall stanza-shape (as observed above), the mutual pressure of subordinate and superordinate shapes is loosened.

Finally, notice the impact of the extrametric syllable in the last line. Both of the last two lines begin with the words "Did he". In the third line, "Did" falls in a strong position, and the trochaic tetrameter thrusts a rather heavy accent upon it. In the next line, the same word constitutes a very lightly accentuated extrametric syllable, followed by a rank-shifted clause, thrusting a heavy accent upon "he". This reverses the relationship between the first two words, causing the psychological atmosphere of certainty to waver, and softening the rhythmic impact of the line. Notwithstanding this initial upbeat, the rigid trochaic nature of this last line may be (and usually is) preserved in performance, owing to the suppression of durational differences characteristic of the trochaic meter (as described above).

This last-but-one-stanza of "The Tyger" posed something of a problem to most commentators. Fortunately for them, Blake used the exact words "the stars threw down their spears" in *The Four Zoas* too. So, instead of coping with the unique quality of this stanza, they may introduce here the meanings discerned there, and be satisfied. But in this respect, too, there are substantial differences between critics. In his classical study of the romantic imagination, Sir Maurice Bowra demonstrates that he is no less good than others at finding the clue for this expression in the other work. But he keeps his commentary on a tolerably general level:

> The images of "The Tyger" recur in the prophetic books, but in the poem, detached from any very specific context, they have a special strength and freedom. The tiger is Blake's symbol for the fierce forces in the soul which are needed to break the bonds of experience. The "forests of the night," in which the tiger lurks, are ignorance, repression, and superstition. It has been fashioned by unknown, supernatural spirits, like Blake's mythical heroes, Orc and Los, prodigious smiths who beat out living worlds with their hammers; and this happened when "the stars threw down their spears," that is, in some enormous cosmic crisis when the universe turned round in

---

absence of a subordinating conjunction at the beginning generates a very different effect.

its course and began to move from light to darkness—as Urizen says in *The Four Zoas,* when he finds that passion and natural joy have withered under his rule and the power of the spirit has been weakened:

> I went not forth: I hid myself in black clouds of my wrath;
> I call'd the stars around my feet in the night of councils dark;
> The stars threw down their spears and fled naked away.

Harold Bloom, by contrast, reads specific meanings into the poem; he quotes the last two lines of this excerpt and quotes two more words from the next line "We fell". This quote allows him to introduce into this poem not merely a very general "enormous cosmic crisis" but a more specific theme which is nowhere hinted at in it: "So in *The Tyger,* the similar passage refers also to an abortive revolt of the angels. Unlike the Miltonic Angels, who fought well, the Angels of Experience cry like children" (37). For me, the interpretation of the lines "When the stars threw down their spears, / And watered heavens with their tears" boils down, in the final analysis, to the question of whether their main function is to evoke, visually, a nature description and thus to contribute to a sudden change of tone and rhythm, or to introduce the theme of the fall of the unmentioned rebellious Angels, who cry like children. My own position is that in language in general, and in poetry in particular (in good poetry, at least), the meaning of verbal elements is modified by the context and may mean very different things in different contexts. In this respect, I tend to embrace Bowra's next comment:

> If we wish to illustrate "The Tyger" from Blake's other works, it is easy to do so, and it adds much to our understanding of its background and its place in Blake's development. But it is first and last a poem. The images are so compelling that for most purposes they explain themselves, and we have an immediate, overwhelming impression of an awful power lurking in the darkness of being and forcing on us questions which pierce to the heart of life.

In this account I would only insert two additional words: "The images *and rhythms* are so compelling" etc. Now, considered "first and last a poem", what should we make of this last but one stanza? I am asking this question concerning both the new themes introduced, and the sudden shift of tone and rhythm.[10] As to the last two lines of the stanza, they suggest a new understanding, quite unexpected

---

[10]   The only discussion of these two lines that is similar to mine both in conceiving of them as of a nature description and in the assessment of their effect is E.D. Hirsch's: "These staccato beats of controlled fury are succeeded by a stanza of immense calm that enormously widens the imaginative range of the poem. It is a highly compressed and difficult stanza, but it is perhaps the finest moment in Blake's poetry" (Hirsch, 1962: 250).

after the foregoing exclamations: the unity of innocence and experience. To elucidate this new understanding, I fall back, again, upon Bowra:

> It was in such elemental forces that Blake put his trust for the redemption of mankind, and he contrasted them favourably with the poor efforts of the human intelligence: "The tigers of wrath are wiser than the horses of instruction." The wrath which Blake found in Christ, his symbol of the divine spirit which will not tolerate restrictions but asserts itself against established rules, was the means by which he hoped to unite innocence and experience in some tremendous synthesis.

For me, the most important part of this passage is its end: "the means by which he hoped to unite innocence and experience in some tremendous synthesis". It is not predicted by the preceding stanzas; but, prophesying after the event, it is implied by them, without importing too much from other works by Blake. The "innocence" aspect of this synthesis is further elaborated in *The Lamb, The Tyger*'s counterpart in the *Songs of Innocence*.

The nature description in the first two lines of the stanza combines, as we have seen, with a syntactic structure that splits attention between "incoming" information and unfulfilled syntactic predictions, and also blurs the symmetrical structure of the stanza. In this way, the stanza may preserve its vigorous convergent rhythms, giving security to the Platonic censor in us, while its overall structure is softened to a large extent, rendering the security *false*. This may evoke a sudden receptive attitude required for the insight suggested by this stanza. It is quite common in trance-inductive or ecstatic poems that some shapes of the imagery or of the prosodic structure are weakened toward the end, in the last or last-but-one stanza. In the present instance, it seems to have a double function. First, it effects a more receptive attitude toward the insight, the new understanding offered by the contents. Second, it enhances the closural force of the last stanza.

In her brilliant study *Poetic Closure,* Barbara Herrnstein-Smith explores how poems end, that is, how they suggest effectively that we have reached the end of a closed unit. Poems do not merely cease; they are closed. She devotes a long section to lyric poems that begin and end with the same stanza: they frame, so to speak, the poem. Now, to avoid some stale effect by a literal repetition, there is, most frequently, a slight, barely perceptible change in the last stanza. Indeed, in Blake's poem, the first and last stanza are identical—except for one word. The fourth line reads: "Could frame thy fearful symmetry?". The last line substitutes "Dare" for "Could". Beyond the closural quality, semantically, the opposition between the two auxiliaries suggests a *crescendo,* an amplification pattern of the enormous strength expressed in the poem. The fourth line suggests that only an exceptional god *could* frame such a fearful symmetry; the last line suggests that only an exceptional god god would *dare,* even if it could, frame such a fearful symmetry. This vigorous closure is greatly enhanced by an additional device, which I have demonstrated at a wide range of levels of poetry. When the unit preceding the closing unit is considerably

weakened in some structural respect, the requiredness of the closing unit is considerably heightened, and the final closure becomes more effective. Thus, the weakening
of the last-but-one stanza's structure has a double cognitive function: it increases receptivity to the insight toward which the whole poem leads; and it increases the requiredness of the last stanza and, by the same token, the closure of the whole poem.
The introduction of syntactic complexities and of the nature description unexpectedly
softens this last-but-one stanza.

Harold Bloom (1963) offers a radically different interpretation to this poem: "The
tone of the initial 'Tyger! Tyger!' is one of affrighted and startled awe only if you
dramatically attempt to project the poem's speaker as the self-duped creature he as-
suredly is; read aloud with understanding, the tone has a fierce and ironic joy" (36).
Morton D. Paley confesses that he "cannot help regarding [this bard] as entirely read
into the poem" (1969b: 73); nor can I. There is no way to *prove* the correctness of a
reading that assumes either the "overwhelming impression of an awful power lurking in the darkness of being", or a "fierce and ironic joy". An interpretation, as I
suggested above, cannot be true or false; it is merely a crucial recommendation what
to look for in a poem and how to look at it—to paraphrase Morris Weitz (1962). As
I said, I concur with Bowra in his claim that the images in this poem "are so compelling that [...] we have an immediate, overwhelming impression of an awful
power"; I even add "compelling rhythms" to the "compelling images". So, I cannot
prove that Bloom's interpretation is wrong; I can only point out the merits of a
"numinous" and "spell-weaving" reading, relying on the poem's compelling images
and obtrusive rhythms.

Morton D. Paley briefly surveyed the wide range of interpretations of this poem
during the past two centuries (Paley, 1969b: 69-74), and commented: "Writers on
the poem have continued to disagree about whether the Tyger is 'good', created by
the Lamb's creator; ambiguous, its creator unknown and the question of the poem
unanswerable; or 'evil,' created by some maleficent force" (ibid., 71–72). We cannot
prove or disprove any of these interpretations. As we have said, we can only point
out the merits of our own reading. An interpretation requires us to assume an
attitude toward the "merely possible" (As Else Frenkel-Brunswick [1968] demonstrated with reference to the intolerance of ambiguity, not all persons are capable of
doing that). The "merely" possible reading I am recommending here relies on two
conspicuous components: what Rudolf Otto called "the numinous", and what Snyder
called "hypnotic", or "trance-inductive", or "spell-weaving" poetry. The numinous
baffles the Platonic censor in us; the obtrusive rhythms give it a false security that
enables it to face the numinous. When the interaction of the two is realised, the
poem is perceived as trembling on the brink of ecstasy. We have discussed above at
considerable length the techniques by which this poem generates "loaded convergence", or "obtrusive rhythms". As to the numinous, one could quote here substantial parts from Otto's *The Idea of the Holy*. I will, however, point out only two of
the elements discerned by Otto in the holy: urgency or energy, and the element of
fascination.

There is, finally, a third element comprised in those of *tremendum* and *majestas,* awefulness and majesty, and this I venture to call the "urgency" or "energy" of the numinous object. It is particularly vividly perceptible in the *örge* or "wrath";[11] and it everywhere clothes itself in symbolical expressions—vitality, passion, emotional temper, will, force, movement, excitement, activity, impetus. These features are typical and recur again and again from the daemonic level up to the idea of the "living" God. We have here the factor that has everywhere more than any other prompted the fiercest opposition to the "philosophic" God of mere rational speculation, who can be put into a definition (Otto, 1959: 37).

I have pointed out the urgency suggested in the first line; and the poem is full, from the beginning to the end, with rhetorical manipulations to evoke an impression of "vitality, passion, emotional temper, will, force, movement, excitement, activity, impetus".

The daemonic-divine object may appear to the mind an object of horror and dread, but at the same time it is no less something that allures with a potent charm, and the creature, who trembles before it, utterly cowed and cast down, has always at the same time the impulse to turn to it, nay even to make it somehow his own. The "mystery" is for him not merely something to be wondered at but something that entrances him; and beside that in it which bewilders and confounds, he feels a something that captivates and transports him with a strange ravishment, rising often enough to the pitch of dizzy intoxication . . . (ibid, 45).

As to the element of fascination, all the rhetorical questions of this poem suggest awe and fascination.[12] I will briefly dwell here only on two expressions: "fearful symmetry" and "Did He smile his work to see?". The Merriam-Webster Collegiate Dictionary defines *symmetry* as "balanced proportions; also: beauty of form arising from balanced proportions". "Balanced proportions" is abstracted from a symmetrical body; and the "beauty of form" is abstracted from that abstraction. "Fearful symmetry" involves an oxymoron, the contradictory parts of which interact in a significant way. *Symmetry* suggests something beautiful, stable, that inspires calm. *Fearful* suggests the opposite. These are the elements of the *fascinans* in the numinous. The head noun of this phrase is an abstract noun. What adjectives and abstract nouns have in common is that both suggest, most frequently, attributes of objects. The difference between them is that abstract nouns are words that can occur in the referring

---

[11] Characterisitically enough, many critics of this poem quote from Blake the proverb "The tigers of wrath are wiser than the horses of instruction"; and Paley calls his essay "Tyger of Wrath".

[12] "While 'The Lamb' answers the questions it poses, 'The Tyger' consists entirely of unanswered questions. In this simple fact lodges much of the poem's richness (Hirsch, 1962: 244).

position of a syntactic structure, adjectives in a qualifying position. Psychologically, "fear", "dread", and "terror" are emotions that involve the heightening of mental energy. In this oxymoronic construction, the adjective transfers its enormous energy to the head noun which, by its very nature, suggests equilibrium, inspires calm. The two words *could* have occurred as two adjectives, *fearful* and *symmetrical,* for instance. In that case, they ought to have been subordinated to some concrete noun, e.g., *fearful and symmetrical body.* Such a construction would have kept the two attributes in control. Even the verb *frame* suggests "to construct by fitting and uniting the parts of a skeleton of (a structure)". Such a construal would prefer the concrete noun *body* as a head word. As it is, this verbal manipulation in *fearful symmetry* dissociates the dreadful and at once fascinating quality from the concrete tiger, and suggests its intense but disembodied presence.

In "Did he smile his work to see?", the effect of fascination is achieved by very different means: here the rhetorical question allows both a negative and a positive answer. In the former case, his work is perceived as awe-inspiring; in the latter—as inspiring an exciting feeling of achievement and satisfaction.

Simplified Mastery of Reality

The present chapter explores the effect of rhythmic structure on religious poetry. I take "rhythmic structure" here in its widest sense: the interaction of metre with the other sound patterns of language and syntax, and the interaction of these with theme and imagery. We have seen the obtrusive rhythm of "The Tyger", that underpins its overwhelming emotional quality. We have also seen the strong prosodic shape of a passage from *In Memoriam* which, on the contrary, tends to restrain the nightmarish quality of the imagery. Both kinds are varieties of *convergent rhythm.* Thus, convergent rhythm is double-edged: in different contexts it may give rise to different, even opposing, qualities. Regular metre may have a predictable, non-emotional (sometimes witty) effect; alternatively, under certain conditions, it may have an obtrusive, "trance-inductive", or "spell-weaving" effect. I have said that convergent rhythms can underlie another quality too: that of simplified mastery of reality. Poetry in ritual use frequently displays such a quality, for good functional reasons. In Chapter 2 I quoted the following paragraph from Kris and Kaplan:

> In ritual, form and content are strictly patterned, and repeated again and again with minimal deviation, on pain of losing the ritualistic efficacy. The ritualistic act is one of participation rather than creation: the response which the members of the group are required or expected to have is rigidly limited. As ritual becomes secularized, the priest gives way to the bard or poet. Conformity of reaction vanishes: interpretations are not rigidly confined to the institutional or doctrinal requirements, but proliferate in accord with the creative impulse of the individual artist. Poetry becomes ambiguous concomitantly with its emergence from ritual (Kris and Kaplan, 1965: 253).

Here we are interested in religious poetry not as ritual, but as aesthetic objects, with their concomitant complexities. Ostensibly, the simplifying function of regular rhythm should be irrelevant to the religious poem as an aesthetic object. In what follows we will have a look at a non-ritual, aesthetic object that conspicuously displays such a quality of simplified mastery of reality: Blake's "The Lamb". In this poem, regular metre and the simple couplet pattern of rhyming interact with the "innocent", childish point of view reinforced by extremely simple syntactic structures, inducing a nursery-rhyme quality. Now the "innocent" child–lamb situation can be observed from a higher point of view, that of "experience" or theology — yielding a variety of ironic perspectives. Thus, "conformity of reaction vanishes [when] interpretations are not rigidly confined" to a childish world-view.

16. Little Lamb, who made thee?
　　　 Dost thou know who made thee?
Gave thee life, & bid thee feed
By the stream & o'er the mead;
Gave thee clothing of delight,
Softest clothing, wooly, bright;
Gave thee such a tender voice,
Making all the vales rejoice?
　　　 Little Lamb who made thee?
　　　 Dost thou know who made thee?

　　　 Little Lamb, I'll tell thee,
　　　 Little Lamb, I'll tell thee:
He is callèd by thy name,
For he calls himself a Lamb.
He is meek, & he is mild;
He became a little child.
I a child, & thou a lamb,
We are callèd by his name.
　　　 Little Lamb, God bless thee !
　　　 Little Lamb, God bless thee!

I am not going to work out the ironic implications of these various perspectives. There is an enormous bulk of critical literature that does this. In this respect, my only contribution to interpretation could be to *reduce* the number of ironic implications attributed to the poem. I *will,* however, explore two issues that may be extremely important for our inquiry. First, how the simplifying potential of regular rhythm is activated in this poem; and second, how commonplace religious doctrine is turned into *insight*. First, then, compare the following two excerpts:

17. What the hammer? what the chain?
     In what furnace was thy brain?

18. He is meek, & he is mild;
     He became a little child.

The metre of both excerpts is trochaic tetrameter, with the last (weak) position unoccupied. Both excerpts contain three parallel syntactic units, two short ones followed by a longer one (that is, both conform with the rule "the longest unit comes last"). The parallel phrases in the first line of each couplet are arranged on either side of the caesura, increasing the rhythmic impetus of the lines. Nevertheless, the rhythm has very different effects in the two excerpts: in excerpt 17 it contributes to an unsettling, trance-inductive, effect; in excerpt 18 it tends to induce a sense of simplified mastery of reality. In what follows, I will point out some differences between the two excerpts. I claim that their cumulative impact may account for this perceived difference. (i) "hammer . . . chain . . . furnace" in excerpt 17 represent violent activity, immense energy or firm static resistance, as opposed to "meek" and "mild". These contrasting contents foreground, respectively, the vigorous and the gentle potentials in their strong metric shape. (ii) In excerpt 18, the short syntactic structures yield complete sentences (that have a subject and a predicate); in excerpt 17 they yield incomplete phrases (that have no finite predicate). The former structure has a "settling" effect, the latter an "unsettling" effect. (iii) The same holds true of their respective modes: excerpt 18 is in the affirmative mode (which has a settling effect), whereas excerpt 17 is in the interrogative or exclamative mode (which has a pointed unsettling effect). (iv) We have already discussed the stress displacement in "In what" in excerpt 17, which has no equivalent in excerpt 18. (v) In excerpt 17 the three parallel phrases constitute an incremental repetition, on the rhythmic level; in excerpt 18 they underpin a process set forth in the next paragraph. The phrases "He is meek, & he is mild" present two parallel perceptual units that are semantically synonymous, but syntactically independent. They present two independent features, as it were, which are *integrated* in one "little child" in the next line. These parallel phrases, then, affect poetic structure both by increasing the rhythmic convergence of the line, and by contributing to an iconic development of the imagery. These semantic and syntactic differences between the two excerpts foreground different potentials in the convergent structures and seem to account for their respective effects: the naive contents, for instance, actualise the simplifying potential of this particular metric shape which, in turn, reinforces the "innocent" contents of the poem.

Now for the second issue. When we follow the handling of the naive imagery of this poem, we come upon a sophisticated effect (which also has its origins in cognitive processes) that is no less important than the ironies regularly pointed out by almost every critic. Every image is a bundle of properties; each property is the source of some "combinational potential" that may be activated in poems. Most frequently, more than one such potential is activated. A lamb, for instance, has a gentle nature and behavior; has wool, has meat for cooking, has a tender voice, may serve as sacrificial animal, etc. The meat-for-cooking potential is not activated in this poem *(pace* Bloom!); the rest are activated to some extent or other. Interestingly enough, the list of the lamb's attributes in the first stanza does not include "meek and mild"; these are attributed to it only by analogy with Christ, *retroactively.* Three "agents" are mentioned in this poem: the speaker (the child), the addressee (the lamb), and the Creator (God). There is a culturally established analogy between child and lamb: gentleness, "innocence". The speaker begins his address by indicating a causal relationship between God and the Lamb ("who made thee?"); he then proceeds to point out an analogy between them: "He is meek, & he is mild". Thus, an analogy between child, lamb and God is generated. But then the analogy becomes identity: "He is meek, & he is mild / He became a little child". "For he calls himself a Lamb" may also suggest a less direct way of identification, presenting God, Lamb, and child as a single entity. Thus, the cognitive structure of the poem generates a process that results in experiencing an *insight*. A sense of insight occurs when multiplicity is suddenly perceived as unity. The reader is led to realise two crucial aspects of Christ: the child born in Bethlehem, and Christ the sacrificial Lamb, *Agnus Dei qui tollis peccata mundi.*

Such an insight is exactly what Stace identified as an extrovertive mystic experience;[13] "the Unifying Vision—all things are One" (Stace, 1961: 131-132). Horne (1978) elaborates on this:

> In the extrovertive experience, it seems, the mystic experiences the world as transformed, and discovers the unity which exists in a multiplicity of external physical objects. No matter what he observes, trees, grass, houses, or anything else, there has been a transfiguration, so that one Being shines through all the separate things (Horne, 1978: 23).

Unlike the introvertive experience—a pure unified consciousness, which requires purification of the mind from distractions and defects, contemplation and self-tuning (as in meditation techniques), Horne argues, "the extrovertive experience cannot be obtained via concentrating techniques: '... it happens spontaneously, as though it had occurred suddenly, without being sought'" (ibid.). The poem reproduces this original aspect of the experience, through such a sense of insight, towards which the reader is lead.

There is nothing new in the suggestion that in this poem the child, the lamb and Christ are identified with each other; the ground for this identification, too, is a commonplace in Christianity. Morton D. Paley, for instance, suggests that Blake condensed in "The Lamb" the meanings of such passages on Swedenborg's conception of Innocence as an inner state, as these: "In the Word also by *name* is signified the essence of a thing and by *seeing and calling by name* to know its

---

13   The distinction between introvertive and extrovertive experiences is propounded in Chapter 1, when discussing briefly the nature of the religious experience.

quality"; or "It is evident that all innocence is from the Lord. For this reason the Lord is called in the Word a 'lamb', a lamb signifying innocence"; or "The Lord himself is called a *child,* or a little *boy* (Isaiah ix, 6), because he is innocence itself and love itself" (Paley, 1969a: 3). What may be new in my argument is that this identification results from a cognitive process that evokes a sudden sense of insight: the old, familiar knowledge is experienced as a sudden insight.[14] HirschThe "sudden sense of insight"-effect helps readers to perceive the essential quality of these lines as a sensuous mystic experience, forced on the experiencer, rather than as a rational theological assertion or implication. This quality is perceived by the readers, who are not necessarily affected by such an insight the same way or to the same degree as the experiencing speaker, but can sense its effect. The repeated last line "Little Lamb, God bless thee!" suggests that the oneness of God and the Lamb does not necessarily abolish their "twoness", generating the paradoxical view of the one and the many, so typical of the extrovertive experience (Horne, 1978: 15).

This last aspect of the poem utilises, in an interesting way, the preceding aspect. The tone of simplified mastery of reality imposed on the poem by convergent metre leads the reader to expect anything but a sophisticated leap. The sequence "He is callèd by thy name, / For he calls himself a Lamb. / He is meek, & he is mild" focusses the reader's attention on the analogy between Christ and the Lamb, and discourages him from looking for an analogy between Christ and the speaker. Thus, the line "He became a little child" is highly unexpected before the event, but mobilises all our relevant knowledge about Christ and "falls into its proper place" after the event. Whatever the complexities of this poem in other respects, the immediate impact of its rhythm is one of childish simplicity. This is reinforced by the persistent symmetry of "thou–He," "I–thou," "we–He", although, in the final resort, these simple pairs amount to something quite sophisticated.

To Conclude

Traditionally, metrics engages in the description of metric patterns and, sometimes, in the judgement of "metricalness". This chapter has attempted to offer tools for dealing with a set of further aspects of metre: the interaction of metre with syntax and theme, which generates the typical perceived effects of metric shapes; these effects are the basis of their combinational potentials, and, by the same token, contribute to the overall poetic qualities of poems, such as mystic experience, the infernal, the numinous, or the naive-ironic. Metre is a prominent factor in constructing a cumulative impact of stability and control, that can be used as an indication of real simplifi-

---

[14] It is, again, Hirsch who comes nearest to the present conception. "The force of the poem is cumulative, and the sensitive reader will feel the victory of the child's mind over its superficially tame matter as it works its way to a conclusion which goes beyond its original thought. The new idea comes in at the line: 'He became a little child'" (Hirsch, 1962: 178).

cation, or as a rather superficial reassurance in the presence of divergent conflicting and confidence-undermining ideas.

The procedures used to find out whether the perceived effect of some verse tends to be ecstatic or rational are less reliable than those used to find out whether a given stressed syllable is a stress-maximum or not or whether it occupies a strong or a weak position (in short, whether a given verse-line is "metrical" or "unmetrical"). But this is perhaps not too high a price to pay for a more or less systematic discussion of how a given rhythmic shape may "count toward" or "count against" what Sibley calls "aesthetic qualities." If one wishes to go beyond the accumulation of "fool-proof" facts, one must sometimes abandon fool-proof methods.

Addendum

We have not sufficiently elaborated on the simplified nature of ritual participation as opposed to the simplifying metre of, e.g., Blake's poem "The Lamb". Above I quoted Kris and Kaplan saying that "The ritualistic act is one of participation rather than creation: the response which the members of the group are required or expected to have is rigidly limited". There are no possible additional contexts (and if there are, they are ignored) in which the text becomes ambiguous. It is the ritual situation rather than some texture or ambiguity in the text that determines the emotional tone of such a sentence as "Agnus Dei qui tollis peccata mundi miserere nobis". It is like the joke about the son who sent a telegram to his father with the words "Daddy send money". The father is angry: "how impudent of him, to demand bluntly 'Daddy! send money!'". The mother says "You are being unfair to the child; he is asking you so gently: 'Daddy... send... money....'".

Neither the ritual text, nor the telegram give sufficient information about their respective emotional context; all emotive interpretation is bound to be projective. The father and the mother add emotive texture by intonation contours. When Beethoven or Bach set those words to music, they supplied the emotional texture. In Beethoven's Missa Solemnis the tone can be described as "suppliant-anguished", in Bach's Mass in B Minor as "pensive-serene".[15] The different musics foreground different potentials of the text. In Blake's poem "The Lamb", the regular metre has a simplifying, naive effect; but the text also offers some doctrinal perspectives of which the speaker (the child) is possibly unaware, rendering the situation ironical.

---

[15] That seems to be the reason why composers frequently prefer to set to music texts that are poor from the aesthetic point of view. They can add, via their music, the concrete texture that is missing from the text.

Chapter 8

Visual and Auditory Ingenuities in Mystic Poetry

Permutation of Letters and the Mystic Experience

One of the central assumptions of the present study is that mystic or religious poetry not just formulates mystic or religious ideas: it somehow converts theological
ideas into religious experience, by verbal means. It somehow seems to reach the less
rational layers of the mind by some drastic interference with the smooth functioning
of the cognitive system, or by a quite smooth regression from "ordinary consciousness" to an "altered state of consciousness". In this way, the experience is affected
not only by its contents, but also by the perceived quality of the structure of the underlying mental process. This brings us to recognise that mystic or religious poetry
can be in vastly different styles. The present study distinguishes between two prototypes of such styles, those that are based on drastic and on smooth interference, respectively. The present chapter will examine poems based on a very special kind of
drastic disruption, of which George Herbert was the grand master.

In this chapter I will consider the relationship between mystic poetry and what
Willie van Peer calls "typographic foregrounding". In this relationship, I will
suggest, both mystic and aesthetic principles are involved. Let us begin with the
following anagram by George Herbert:

1. $\qquad$ *Ana-*$\begin{Bmatrix} \text{MARY} \\ \text{ARMY} \end{Bmatrix}$*gram*

> How well her name an *Army* doth present,
> In whom the *Lord of Hosts* did pitch his tent!

What is the mystic significance of a permutation of letters, such as
MARY→ARMY? On this issue, we might appeal to Gershom Scholem's discussion
of the doctrine of Abraham Abulafia, the great thirteenth-century Jewish mystic,
who expounds a peculiar discipline which he calls the "science of the combination of
letters". This is described as a "methodical guide to meditation with the aid of letters
and their configurations. The individual letters of their combinations need have no
'meaning' in the ordinary sense; it is even an advantage if they are meaningless, as
in that case they are less likely to distract us" (1961: 133). When mystics speak of
permutation of letters, it is not always clear whether they mean the written marks on
the paper or the speech sounds they signify. As we will see, there may be a significant psychological difference between them.

An anonymous disciple of Abulafia's gave an extended, masterful description of
his experience; I am going to reproduce here a short passage from it:

During the second week the power of meditation became so strong in me that I could not manage to write down the combinations of letters [which automatically spurted out of my pen], and if there had been ten people present they would not have been able to write down so many combinations as came to me during the influx. When I came to the night in which this power was conferred on me, and midnight—when this power especially expands and gains strength whereas the body weakens had passed, I set out to take up the Great Name of God, consisting of seventy-two names, permuting and combining it. But when I had done this for a little while, behold, the letters took on in my eyes the shape of great mountains, strong trembling seized me and I could summon no strength, my hair stood on end, and it was as if I were not in this world. At once I fell down, for I no longer felt the least strength in any of my limbs (Scholem, 1961: 150–151).

At this point of our inquiry we must ask two crucial questions about the foregoing two texts. First, what is the relationship between the meaningless combination of letters or speech sounds and the overwhelming experience of Abulafia's anonymous disciple? How is it that the contemplation of meaningless combinations can lead to such overwhelming emotional experiences? Second, what is the relationship, if any, between this process and George Herbert's curious punning on "Mary" and "Army"? To my great surprise, I had given the answer long before I became aware of the problem—as part of a discussion of musicality in verse and phonological universals.[1]

According to psychoanalytic theory, one of the possible sources of pleasure in human beings is the regression to a level of functioning characteristic of an earlier age. Kris and Gombrich (1965) contend that the scribbling style of caricature involves regression to the infantile pleasure in exploring articulate motor activities, just as punning and nonsense talk involve regression to prelanguage babbling. I assume that our mystic author may have meant both "scribbling" (letters) and "babbling" (speech sounds). It is plausible that the phonetic aspects of poetry afford pleasure in the exploration of meaningless sounds in a publicly respectable medium. Similarly, Ehrenzweig (1965) asserts that in painting and music there are articulate gestalts appealing to our "surface mind", and inarticulate, thing-free scribblings and sounds, appealing to our "depth mind". We may add with Roman Jakobson that in child language there are two distinct uses of sound: *referential,* which is nonemotional, and *expressive,* making use of sounds which are not yet utilised for "arbitrary linguistic signs". In poetic language we get both, mounted one on top of the other. Sounds are combined into words by a "syntagmatic" relationship (Jakobson, 1968: 70), "forming entities of linguistic value" (ibid., 25). At the same time there is a nonreferential combination of sounds, based on repetition, forming reference-free—

---

[1]   The next two paragraphs are taken from my book (Tsur, 1992b: 54-56).

thing-free, so to speak—qualities, exploiting not so much differentiated *contrasting features,* as similarities. Of unusually great interest are some of Jakobson's observations on the differentiation between denotative and expressive use of speech sounds. While a child proceeds with mastering the "arbitrary linguistic signs", selecting and contrasting sounds—being "inseparably linked to the sign nature of language"—it constantly resorts to the other sounds, still unmastered, for sound gestures (interjections and onomatopoeia).

The following problem arises in connection with regression to infantile pleasure in sounds: can we distinguish *mere* regression to infantile pleasure from a *structured* regression? Jakobson adduces some typical instances of phonological regression, some of which he dubs "deliberate infantilism". "Thus we find [...] a considerable number of babbling words in the vocabulary of all languages taken over from the 'nursery language'. It has been established repeatedly that a child in full control of his language can suddenly take pleasure in reverting to the role of a baby. [...] And [...] courting lovers quite frequently talk in child language [...]" (Jakobson, 1968: 16–7). Some of the cases suggest that they are emotionally charged to varying degrees. In my book I claim that poetic value can be attributed, in general, only to "structured" regression, and not to mere "deliberate infantilism". This may be the case, with the necessary changes, in respect of mystic experience as well. Structuring, in turn, depends in one way or another upon meaning and "good gestalts". Regression to an undifferentiated world is "mere infantilism", whereas underlying artistic pleasure we may find regression to an undifferentiated perception *by way of perceiving meaning, or differentiated or intensive gestalts.* Good gestalts, or referential meaning, satisfy the "Platonic censor" in us, so that it fails to suppress "offensive", undifferentiated or irrational information. This may apply, mutatis mutandis, to mystic experience as well.

I have quoted Gershom Scholem to the effect that "the individual letters of their combinations need have no 'meaning' in the ordinary sense; it is even an advantage if they are meaningless, as in that case they are less likely to distract us" (1961: 133). In light of the preceding two paragraphs this is not merely a matter of distracting us; we are switching to a different mode of experiencing speech sounds, the "babbling" mode. This is a regression to nonreferential combinations of speech sounds, released from "syntagmatic" relationships and "the sign nature of language". Such a regression is emotionally charged to a considerable degree. At the same time, the "Platonic censor" in us is satisfied too, so that it fails to suppress such "offensive", irrational information. As Abulafia's disciple reported, he "set out to take up the Great Name of God, consisting of seventy-two names, permuting and combining it". This renders the exploration of meaningless sounds publicly respectable; moreover, it may also invest this highly emotional activity with enormous cathexis (mental or emotional energy). In this way nonreferential, "babbling" speech sounds are permuted and combined; at the same time they are invested with the significance of God's name, and the process is even constrained by its letters. Another, related, way of appeasing the Platonic censor will be mentioned later.

There is, then, in early childhood a point when speech sounds serve in two different modes: as pleasurable, careless, nonreferential babbling; and as "arbitrary linguistic signs", combined into words by a "syntagmatic" relationship. In the former mode, they are emotionally charged; in the latter they are of a more rational and volitional nature. In our inquiry, a dichotomic spectrum has emerged from this polar dichotomy. In such words as "Mary" or "Army" speech sounds are combined into a "syntagmatic" relationship, and become "arbitrary linguistic signs" with conspicuous referential value. When the two words are put side by side, they assume some of the infantile pleasure in exploring articulate motor activities in mastering the sound inventory of all possible human languages. The punning on "Mary" and "Army" makes use of arbitrary referential linguistic signs, while the nonreferential sound patterns are only gratuitous additions to these publicly respectable verbal entities. Straightforward regression to pure babbling, by contrast, would be deemed as deliberate infantilism. So, we have found between pun and babbling a freer mode of experimentation with nonreferential speech sounds, constrained and rendered significant by God's name. This is what Scholem describes as "a methodical guide to meditation with the aid of letters and their configurations". Such literary devices as rhyme and alliteration are additional shadings on this spectrum.

Recently I found support for my conception in a neuropsychological study of God beliefs by Michael A. Persinger (1987). He claims that God experiences are associated with *temporal lobe transients,* which are electrical perturbations of the temporal lobe in the human brain (16). During such experiences, some people sometimes speak in gibberish. "The gibberish is often called 'speaking in tongues' and resembles the sounds emitted from young infants during the babbling stage" (30). In such extreme cases no publicly respectable excuses are used to appease the Platonic censor in us; it is just suspended. Such perturbations of the temporal lobe may also cause perceptual alterations which "are usually limited to the sudden expansion of visual and auditory images. Objects in the room may suddenly seem to grow very small and then increase in size again. Sounds may fluctuate from very faint and distant to very loud and near" (Persinger, 1987: 18). This conjunction would render the process particularly relevant to the experience of Abulafia's disciple, who reports: "behold, the letters took on in my eyes the shape of great mountains".

Expressive Devices Fossilized

It should be remembered, however, that Abulafia's disciple achieved this experience through weeks of intense exercise, at a special time of the night, and, perhaps under some "special grace". Thus, it would be unreasonable to suppose that Herbert would expect the single transposition of letters in his poem from MARY to ARMY to induce a similar experience. It would be more reasonable to suppose that by the time the device of letter transposition reached Herbert's poetry, it was fossilised into a mere stylistic device, one of the mannerisms of a great Metaphysical poet. In what

follows, I will offer a model adapted from Ehrenzweig that may account for the process of transformation from an experience such as the one described by Abulafia's
disciple to a poem of the sort of Herbert's "Anagram". This is a process that tends to
reduce the expressive force of highly affective devices into *style*. One of my
assumptions is that *précieux* devices such as Renaissance anagrams originate in
highly affective devices in which cognitive and psychodynamic activity has
fossilised. This is the source of ornamental art.

"There is in the human mind a strong reluctance", says Wilson Knight (1965:
XI), "to face, with full consciousness, the products of poetic genius". A similar conception was put forward by Anton Ehrenzweig (1965) in relation to music and the
visual arts. Ehrenzweig elaborates at great length on the defense mechanisms with
the help of which human society protects itself against the expressive force of artistic devices that have "too" strong an effect, and turns them into style, that is, harmless ornament. Ehrenzweig speaks of three stages in the evolution of artistic devices:
The first one is a stage when visual and auditory (or linguistic—we might add) patterns are perceived subliminally, so that they can strongly affect what he calls the
"depth mind". The more emphatic these devices, the stronger their emotional appeal,
provided that they don't become consciously perceptible. When they become semi-
consciously perceptible, they are considered to be in bad taste, cheaply emotional.
This is the second stage. At the third stage, these devices are turned into ornaments,
with drastically reduced emotional appeal. As long as the "inarticulate" glissandi and
vibrati of singers and the great masters of the violin are not consciously audible,
they have a strong and valued emotional appeal. When second-rate singers and vio-
linists exaggerate them so that they become semi-consciously audible, such devices
are considered "offensive", or "in bad taste". In the third stage, this offensive emotional force is eliminated, when these devices of ambiguous status are "sharpened"
into fully conscious, but rigid and lifeless ornaments.[2] The same actually happens
with an active metaphor. An active metaphor when just created is perceived as enhancing the depth of the language, through stimulating connotations, evoking individual associations and arousing private emotional possessions. When it becomes
half-known it is considered "in bad taste" (worn out metaphors). When it is completely known and becomes conventional, it functions as an additional lexical item

---

[2]   We do have some information about what happens to verbal material when it is
    hidden in the unconscious and when it is brought to full consciousness. Consider the
    case when one has a word on the "tip of one's tongue", unable to recall it. William
    James says of this phenomenon: "And the gap of one word does not feel like the gap
    of another, all empty of content as both might seem necessarily to be when described
    as gaps [...]". And again, "But the feeling of an absence is *toto coelo* other than the
    absence of a feeling [...]. The rhythm of a lost word may be there without a sound to
    clothe it [...]" (quoted by Ehrenzweig 1965: 10). The more information we have about
    this lost word, the more intense is that elusive feeling. When the lost word is
    recalled—that is, brought into full consciousness—that intense but elusive feeling
    disappears.

(idiom; the language becomes wider instead of deeper) and loses all emotional load. If there is any relationship between the mystic "science of the combination of letters" and anagrams in poetry (and in George Herbert's case, at least, one might reasonably surmise that there is), it must have been the result of some such process. In poetry, at least, a fourth stage may be added: when such "dead" ornaments (and idiomatic expressions) are revived through poetic manipulation.[3] In the present instance, the extremely emotional stage of the process is not related to some poetic device but, in the account of Abulafia's disciple, to some genuine mystic experience—one that causes the experiencer to tremble and his hair to stand on end.

Spoonerism and the Unconscious—Wit and Ecstasy

Permutation of speech sounds, and of even smaller phonetic entities, occur in real-life situations too, where they may or may not have deep unconscious significance. People are fascinated with phenomena related to the psychopathology of everyday life, such as slips of the tongue and the tip-of-the-tongue phenomenon, because they yield a glimpse into two kinds of unconscious processes, to which one has no direct access: the unconscious "Freudian" processes, and the organisation of semantic and phonetic units in long-term memory. We retrieve words from long-term memory with amazing ease, without noticing the cognitive mechanisms involved. In the tip-of-the-tongue phenomenon, the semantic and phonetic information retrieved is somehow prevented from "growing together" into one word; in slips of the tongue, some of this information is transposed. I suggested (Tsur, 1987a: 273–288; 1992b: 69–70, 144–153) that the unconscious mind on the one hand, and poetic language on the other, may exploit the disturbance of the smooth working of these mechanisms for pyschopathological and aesthetic purposes, respectively. It would appear that the same mechanism may be exploited for inducing varieties of mystic states of mind. The permuting of letters and phonetic units for psychopathological purposes, for witty effects, and for inducing a mystic state of mind, testifies to their intimate relationship with the unconscious mind. I will argue that in mental processes as well as in literary texts one of the major differences between "witty" and "mystic" permuting of letters and speech sounds resides in the amount of mental energy invested. Mystic permuting involves much higher cathexis than witty permuting.

There is good evidence, then, that the permuting of phonetic entities and of letters (slips of the tongue and, more rarely, slips of the pen) may be intimately related to the unconscious mind. That is one conclusion we may draw from Freud's two classical books, *Wit and Its Relation to the Unconscious,* and *The Psychopathology of Everyday Life.* That is why spoonerisms (certain kinds of "Freudian" slips of the tongue) are sometimes so funny. Spoonerism is the transposition of initial or other sounds of words, usually by accident, attributed to the Reverend W. A. Spooner, as

---

[3]   I demonstated (Tsur, 1992a: 305–316) the third and fourth stages in the ballad "Edward".

in "a blushing crow" for "a crushing blow", "our queer old dean" for "our dear old queen"; or, chiding one of his students, "You have hissed all the mystery lessons; indeed, you have tasted the whole worm".

In a linguistic study, Victoria Fromkin (1973) explored what kinds of linguistic units may be transposed in real-life "slips of the tongue". She brought to light a wealth of evidence concerning the psychological reality of a great variety of linguistic rules. An interesting aspect of the more than 6000 speech errors that she collected, involving substitution and permutation of various segments of sound, concerned the type of speech units that are affected. It is important for our purpose that the process itself is involuntary and inaccessible to conscious introspection. Besides such consciously accessible items as words or clusters of speech sounds, speech units of which the speaker is unaware may also be involved. Here I will mention only one such unit: the distinctive features of speech sounds, as in *glear plue sky* for *clear blue sky*, where the feature [+VOICED] is transferred from the initial phoneme of "blue" to the initial phoneme of "clear". "When a person says *cedars of Lemadon* instead of *cedars of Lebanon,* the nasality features of the [b] and the [n] are reversed. The intended oral labial [b] becomes a nasal labial [m] and the intended nasal alveolar [n] an oral alveolar [d]" (ibid., 114). There are very few language users who would be aware of the fact that the pairs of consonants b/m and d/n respectively share the same distinctive features, except for [±NASAL]. It is by now a commonplace that such slips are frequently related to the unconscious. Unlike *Lemadon,* in such cases the substitute word is usually meaningful. I will adduce here only one more instance, to show how the slip-of-the-tongue phenomenon works on the level of units smaller than phonemes, where only the distinctive feature [+VOICED] is permuted. In a graduate seminar in Hebrew literature, a promising young poet wanted to say *məvakrim* (critics), but inadvertently said *məfagrim* (mentally retarded). These two words contain the bilabial fricatives [f] and [v] and the velar stops [k] and [g]. Phonetically, the speaker transposed the values of the feature [VOICED] of the [v] and [k] in *məvakrim*. By the same token, his unconscious mind revealed its attitude toward critics. In addition to the possible Freudian import, such slips of the tongue increase the weight of phonetic features in the compact speech sounds, their "babbling" nature relative to their sign nature.

Mystic experiences of great force (such as the one reported by Abulafia's disciple), have been induced by both the manipulation of the speech sounds and of the letters of God's names, or of some meaningless speech sound sequences. While in Herbert's anagram it is the *letters* that are manipulated, in e.g. Hopkins' poetry, *clusters of specch sounds* are exceptionally foregrounded, far beyond what is acceptable in ordinary alliteration. Consider such notorious densely packed phrases as "Heaven-Haven", or "I caught this morning morning's minion, kingdom of daylight's dauphin, dapple-dawn-drawn Falcon" ("The Windhover"), or the following stanza from "The Sea and The Skylark":

2.   Left hand, off land, I hear the lark ascend,
     His rash-fresh re-winded new-skeinèd score
     In crisps of curl off wild winch whirl, and pour
     And pelt music, till none's to spill nor spend.

I claim that when invested with enormous cathexis (that is, mental or emotional energy), the unconscious processes involved may be experienced as highly emotional, even ecstatic, rather than witty. Most significantly, Abulafia's disciple reports that "the power of meditation became so strong in me that I could not manage to write down the combinations of letters [which automatically spurted out of my pen], and if there had been ten people present they would not have been able to write down so many combinations as came to me during the influx". In addition to reasons mentioned so far, I will later point out further reasons for which I assume that ecstasy based on the manipulation of letters may demand greater mental energy than ecstasy based on the manipulation of speech sounds. In Hellenistic or Renaissance anagrams, the letters rather than the speech sounds are manipulated; and the enormous charge of emotional energy is eliminated. This process is nearer to wit than to ecstasy: the expressive means are frozen into frivolous word games. I will argue that in Herbert's poem this frozen literary device is taken one step further, to the fourth stage mentioned above.

We have related both wit and ecstatic experiences to the unconscious. I have suggested that similar verbal devices may underlie both. This inevitably raises two crucial questions. First, if they are so similar, why do wit and ecstasy appear to the consciousness as such different experiences; and second, how can we distinguish between bold stylistic devices (such as paradox or the permutation of letters) that generate wit and those that generate an ecstatic quality in poetry. I have used the psychoanalytical term "cathexis" (investment of mental or emotional energy). The greater the charge of cathexis, the less witty, the more passionate the audacious expression appears to be. The author of the Hellenistic treatise on rhetoric *Peri Hypsous* (On the Sublime) attributed to Longinus (second or fourth century A.D.), was not familiar with this Freudian notion. But he propounded a similar conception of "sublime passion" in the verbal arts. "Wherefore a figure is at its best when the very fact that it is a figure escapes attention" *(Peri Hypsous,* chapter 17). This may be true of the elevated poetry "Longinus" admired; its reverse, however, seems to be true of Donne's, Herbert's, Eliot's, or Ibn Gabirol's poetry. Such Metaphysical poets achieve a witty effect by deliberately drawing attention to their figures and metaphors. The treatise discusses some of the means by which attention may be directed away from the figures. In chapter 32 (paragraphs 3–4) of *Peri Hypsous,* "Longinus" speaks of mitigating "audacious expressions" in terms that are entirely compatible with our foregoing conception of witty devices that become ecstatic when invested with cathexis: "but still for number and boldness of metaphors I maintain, as I said in dealing with figures, that strong and timely passion and noble sublimity are the appropriate palliatives. For it is the nature of the passions, in their vehement rush, to sweep and thrust everything before them, or rather to demand hazardous turns altogether indispensable. They do not allow the hearer leisure to criticise the number of metaphors because he is carried away by the fervour of the speaker".

"False Wit", Mysticism, and Metaphyscial Poetry

Regarding Herbert's "Anagram", this kind of poetry has always been something of a problem for literary critics of classicist taste, who considered it as "false wit". Thus, for instance, "in Spectator 60 (May 9, 1711), Addison remarks that '[t]he Acrostick was probably invented about the same Time with the Anagram, tho' it is impossible to decide whether the Inventor of the one or the other were the greater Blockhead'" (Rothman, 1997). As we have seen with reference to Longinus's generalizations, however, what is bad classicism may be excellent mannerism or metaphysical poetry.

There are two opposite ways out of this dilemma. One is based on the assumption of an unwritten contract between poet and readers to treat such poems seriously *in spite* of their frivolous playfulness. The other approach assumes that those visual ingenuities are functional in some significant way. I will adopt here a combination of the two approaches. The first approach is propounded by Joseph Summers (1968: 138):

> We may see the poems which derive from the Elizabethan acrostics and ana-grams in a different light. Aside from the courtiers to whom any exercise in ingenuity was welcome, this type of poem had its serious religious adher-ents in the seventeenth century. If biblical exegesis demanded the solution of anagrams, and if the good man was truly "willing to spiritualize every-thing," the composition of such poetry was a logical result. With due ap-preciation of the wit involved, the good man was likely to treat such poetry seriously. The seriousness depended on a religious subject and on the as-sumption that the poet would draw "true" meanings from his word-play.

Such a conception, when brought to its extreme, is problematic: "if the good man was truly willing to spiritualize everything", then it really would not matter what the poet did. Nevertheless, I do agree that the seriousness of such verse "depended on a religious subject and on the assumption that the poet would draw 'true' meanings from his word-play". But, I claim, this is only a small—and not the most interesting—part of the story. Metaphysical poetry may be treated seriously not *in spite* of its wit, but *because* of it. Wit, being an effective adaptation device, may be a very serious matter. I base my alternative conception on two assumptions derived from Steven T. Katz in a slightly different context (1992: 7–8): the shock caused by the mystics' paradoxes, and the mystic or magical effects of the permutation of letters.

Such linguistic ploys exist in many places throughout the world, usually connected with the conscious construction of paradoxes whose necessary violation of the laws of logic are intended to shock, even shatter, the standard epistemic security of "disciples," thereby allowing them to move to new and higher forms of insight/ knowledge. That is, mystics in certain circumstances know that they are uttering nonsensical propositions, but in so doing they intend, among other things, to force the hearers of such propositions to consider who they are—to locate themselves vis-a-vis normal versus transcendental "reality". The object of such exercises is existential rather than propositional (though this practice involves propositional claims that are inherent in the respective metaphysical systems of which such linguistic practices are a part).

I would like to make a few observations on this passage. First, metaphysical poetry, too, typically involves the conscious construction of paradoxes. Second, one of the main cognitive principles pointed out by the present study is based on the smooth but heightened functioning of the orientation mechanism (as in the "composition of place" in Jesuit meditation) or, alternatively, on drastic interference with its smooth functioning. Orientation is the ability to locate oneself in one's environment with reference to time, place, and people. In this respect, Katz speaks of shocking, even shattering, the standard epistemic security of disciples, and then forcing them to *locate* themselves [reorientate] vis-a-vis normal versus transcendental reality. Third, Wiley Sypher describes mannerism (including metaphysical poetry) in almost exactly the same terms: "The center of psychological gravity has been displaced, and when the force of the poem or painting has been diverted toward us, we are compelled, willy-nilly, to make a double adjustment: first, to meet the shock of the diversion, and second, to regain some distance and disengage ourselves from the situation in which we have been involved" (1955: 145).[4] So, there appears to be some coincidence between the principles of mysticism and of metaphysical poetry. We should not be surprised, therefore, that there is a metaphysical version of mystic poetry.

I claim that those visual ingenuities of poems like Herbert's anagram (or pattern poems) are, too, "intended to shock, even shatter, the standard epistemic security" of the readers. What is, then, the relationship between the "violation of the laws of logic" and "typographic foregrounding"?

---

[4]   Sypher uses the term "mannerism" in a sense from which all pejorative implications are expunged: "Thus mannerism has two modes, technical and psychological. Behind the technical ingenuities of mannerist style there usually is a personal unrest, a complex psychology that agitates the form and the phrase".

Typographic Foregrounding and Disorientation

In two versions of a paper on pattern poetry focussed on Herbert's "Easter Wings", I argued (Tsur, 1997; 2001) at great length that such typographic foregrounding is the logical extension of a deep-rooted poetic principle and, at the same time, the violation of some no less deep-rooted cognitive principles that may account for its shocking quality. There seems to exist a general consensus as to the artificiality of the graphemic patterning of pattern poems, as compared to the relative naturalness of the various kinds of phonetic patterning prevalent in all kinds of poetry. But only very few people actually ask why graphemic patterning should be less natural than phonetic patterning. And those who do, give a different answer from mine. The answer to this question is based on a semiotic model on the one hand, and on research in speech perception on the other.

Human culture consists of long series and hierarchies of signifiers and signifieds. Man seems to be programmed to reach the last link of the chain of signifiers and signifieds as fast as possible. Such a programming has considerable survival value. If a certain noise is "a sign of" some predator, knowledge of the predator has greater survival value than knowledge of the noise. In verbal magic and mysticism, the signifier is frequently indistinguishable from the signified. God, and the name of God, have sometimes the same powers. The sounds of the name of God, and the letters that signify those sounds (e.g., the tetragrammaton), have sometimes the same magic power.[5] In this respect, poetry is diametrically opposed to verbal magic. In a complex cultural situation of human society in which the automatic identification of signifiers with their signifieds may be the source of maladaptive behaviour, the signifiers and signifieds must be properly kept apart. It is here where poetry comes in.

> "The function of poetry" wrote Jakobson in 1933, "is to point out that sign is not identical with its referent": why do we need this reminder? "Because", continued Jakobson, "along with the awareness of the identity of the sign and the referent (A is A_1), we need the consciousness of the inadequacy of this identity (A is not A_1)".
>
> This antinomy is essential since without it the connection between the sign and the object becomes automatical and perception of reality withers away (Erlich, 1965: 181).

---

[5] The impious Cassius puts this conception to ironic use:

> Brutus and Caesar: what should be in that 'Caesar'?
> Why should that name be sounded more than yours!
> Write them together, yours is as fair a name;
> Sound them, it doth become the mouth as well;
> Weigh them, it is as heavy; conjure with 'em,
> 'Brutus' will start a spirit as soon as 'Caesar'. *(Julius Caesar,* I. ii. 141–146)

Thus, poetic language is contrasted both to magical and to ordinary language, in different ways. In a magical context, sign is frequently identical with its referent. In the nonpoetic use of language we tend to "attend away" from the signifier to the signified. In poetic language we tend to attend to the signifiers more than in ordinary, nonpoetic language, where sometimes we remember the information, but not the exact words in which it was conveyed; sometimes we can't even tell in what language we received the information, or whether it was in the verbal medium at all. Mysticism sometimes uses magical language; but sometimes its use of language more resembles poetic language. As Deikman pointed out (2000: 77, quoted above in chapter 3), mystic perception involves deautomatisation; "as a consequence, sensuousness, merging of boundaries and sensory modalities became prominent". Likewise, Jakobson suggests that the deautomatisation of the linguistic sign is needed, so as to prevent reality from withering away.

Poetic language compels us to "linger" at the signifier or, rather, at ever higher signifiers in a hierarchy of signs: rhyme, meter, alliteration arrest the reader at the strings of phonological signifiers which signify semantic units; figurative language, parallelism and other semantic manipulations arrest the reader at the string of semantic components, which eventually signify the extra-linguistic referents. In this perspective, we might expect to find some patterning of the typographic signifier as well. Such patterning, however, is relatively rare in poetry. The reason for that seems to be that the nature of the graphemic signifier is fundamentally different from that of the phonological signifier. Speech is "special": not only an earlier acquisition than writing, but also different from it.

Speech is normally transmitted by a stream of inconstant, rapidly and continuously changing sounds, which specify the articulatory gestures that produced them, resulting in invariant and discrete speech categories. This is "the motor theory of speech perception". This process, says Liberman, is biological, "precognitive". He contrasts this conception with the "received view", according to which the perceived speech categories "are the end products of a cognitive translation that converts auditory percepts into a form appropriate to language. Getting from speech signal to the primary level of language is, therefore, a two-stage process: evocation of an auditory percept in the first stage, followed by conversion to a phonetic representation in the second" (Liberman, 1992: 110). In this important respect, the rival view "implausibly makes perceiving speech no different in principle from perceiving Morse code or, for that matter, the letters of the alphabet" (110). "Unlike a Morse code operator or writer, a speaker is directly using motor representations that are inherently linguistic. There is no need to connect a nonlinguistic act (pressing a key or writing an alphabetic character) to some linguistic unit of a cognitive sort" (111). This may explain why the semantic elements of poetry fuse more easily with phonetic categories than with either musical tones, or letters on the page.

There is, then, a substantial difference between phonetic signifiers in the auditory mode, which are inborn, and graphemic signifiers in the visual mode, acquired at a relatively late age. But there is also an enormous difference within the auditory mode itself, between the speech mode and the nonspeech mode, both inborn, or acquired at a very early age. The former appears to be of a far higher psychic economy than the latter, handled by a specialised inborn mechanism. The nature of this psychic economy can be understood with reference to two of its characteristics: parallel transmission (that one piece of acoustic stimulus may give information about two successive phonemes), and a distinction between the acoustic and phonetic stream[6] (in the phonetic stream, a vast amount of acoustic information is recoded into a small number of unified phonetic categories). We listen to a stream of abstract phonetic categories, made amenable to the resolving power of the human ear by parallel transmission. At the same time, at a lower level, and subliminally, we may attend to the rich, precategorial acoustic information, which may affect the perceived quality of poetic language in a variety of ways. This could be called the "poetic mode". For our present business, one thing is important: there is a subtle interplay in the background, on a very minute scale, between this rich, precategorial acoustic information and the fine-grained semantic components. Obviously, such interplay cannot take place between the visual design superimposed upon the line arrangement and the patterns of signs at the phonetic, semantic, syntactic and thematic levels.

Typographic patterning violates, then, the smooth functioning of our cognitive system in two different ways. First, it disrupts the process of reaching the last link of the chain of signifiers and signifieds as fast as possible. If in poetic language we typically attend back to the semantic and phonological signifiers, typographic patterning forces us to linger at an additional string of signifiers, one more step removed from the referent. Second, lingering at this additional string of signifiers is less natural than lingering at, e.g., the phonetic string. Hence, Philip Thomson's comment on Christian Morgenstern's brilliant word plays seems to be applicable to such poems as Herbert's visual patterns as well: they are "devious devices of alienation, and at their most radical succeed in producing in the reader a strange sensation—making one suddenly doubt one's comfortable relationship with language—not unlike the sense of disorientation and confusion associated with the grotesque" (Thomson, 1972: 165). In Katz's description, they may "shock, even shatter, the standard epistemic security" of the readers of such pattern poetry, forcing them "to consider who they are—to locate themselves vis-a-vis normal versus transcendental reality".

The second principle derived from Katz concerns the more specific effects of such permutations of letters as MARY→ARMY. He discusses, as paradigmatic, the theur-

---

[6]   One aspect of this distinction by Liberman and his colleagues is available for listening online in the sound files displayed following figure 2 in my article (Tsur, 2001):
http://www.trismegistos.com/IconicityInLanguage/Articles/Tsur/default.html *or*
http://www.tau.ac.il/~tsurxx/Cuckoo_onomatopoeia.html

gical[7] and contemplative manipulation of letters found in the *Sefer Yetzira* (an early Jewish mystical text). But, he says, "Pythagoreans as well as Muslims and individual Christian mystics engaged in these sorts of explorations" (p. 18). Gershom Scholem (1961: 78) points out that "these theurgical doctrines form a kind of meeting-place for magic and ecstaticism". According to this conception, "the letters of the Hebrew alphabet, out of which words are composed, are the fundamental building blocks of creation. The letters have ontic capacity and can be—indeed, have been—employed by God to create the world and everything within it. In this reading, the creation accounts wherein 'God speaks' are taken with extreme, if original, literalness. The process of creation resides in the manipulation of the alphabetical ciphers" (Katz, 1992: 16).

In this passage, the creative decree (wherein "God speaks") underwent a curious metamorphosis. Such phrases as "Let there be light", or Milton's

> 3.   "Silence ye troubled waves, and thou deep, peace!"
>   Said then th'Omnific Word, "Your discord end!"

exploit the semantic component of the Word to perform the Act of Creation, in a *possible world* where the forces of Chaos do obey imperative verbs. In the magic-ecstatic use of mysticism, the creative power of the Word is displaced from the semantic to the graphemic component. Katz quotes a short passage from *Sefer Yetzira* that describes such "meaningless" manipulation of letters:

> 4.   How did He combine them, weigh them and set them at opposites?
>   Aleph with all of them, and all of them with Aleph,
>   Bet with all of them, and all of them with Bet.
>   It rotates in turn, and thus they are in two hundred and thirty-one gates.
>   And everything that is formed and everything that is spoken goes out from one term.[8]

But he also provides an account of the MARY→ARMY type of permutation.

---

[7]   Theurgy is the art or technique of compelling or persuading a god or beneficent or supernatural power to do or refrain from doing something.

[8]   Cf. Lancaster (2001: 243) for a different translation and discussion of this passage. In this translation the passage ends with "emerges from one Name". This connects the passage with our earlier discussion of permuting and recombining the letters of God's name. But, as I hinted above, the very systematic recombination of letters is an additional way to appease the Platonic censor in us and make it accept the toying around with nonreferential, quasi-babbling speech sounds.

5.   Twenty-two letters are the foundation: He set them in a wheel, like a kind of wall, with two hundred and thirty-one gates. And the wheel rotates forward and backward. And the sign of the thing is: there is no goodness above pleasure (=ᶜoNεG [ayin – nun – gimεl]) and there is no evil below pain (=NεGaᶜ [nun – gimεl – ayin]).[9]

Multiple Relationship

Now such a permutation as MARY→ARMY or ᶜoNεG→NεGaᶜ is not too remarkable an achievement. Children play at it in games, and the computer version of the Merriam-Webster Collegiate® Dictionary offers such a feature too. This is not the ground for Herbert's poem to have claims for mystic or aesthetic value. Beardsley (1958) speaks of "multiple relationship", Wheelwright (1968) of "multivalence" in relation to such more traditional poetic devices as metaphor. In Herbert's "Anagram", permutation is embedded in a thick texture of "multivalence", or "multiple relationship". On the children's-game or computer-feature level the permutation from MARY to ARMY is trivial, even if we assume that the change of word entails a change of nature, as in Wallace Stevens' "Ordinary Evening in New Haven": "When the mariners came to the land of the *lem*on trees, [...] / They said, 'We are back once more in the land of the *elm* trees [...]' / [...] an alteration / Of words that was a change of nature". While the change from *lem*on trees to *elm* trees is founded on a shared superordinate category, at first sight there appears to be no meaningful relation between *Mary* and *Army*. No more, apparently, than between the items of Louis Carrol's catalog "Of shoes—and ships—and sealing wax— / Of cabbages— and kings". It will be noticed, however, that a rather roundabout relationship is established via "In whom the *Lord of Hosts* did pitch his tent". "Host" is a synonym of "Army", and a "stock-epithet" of the Lord; and armies are associated with pitching tents for lodging. "Pitch" suggests "fixing firmly"; "pitch a tent" suggests "lodging". The metaphor suggests, then, that God chose to lodge in Mary, perhaps temporarily, as in a tent; but it also connotes firmness. Now even this multiple relationship may be considered rather laboured; but it becomes quite elegant if we provide an additional piece of information, which may have been known to Herbert's readers: for some reason, the Virgin Mary was regarded as the patroness of the armies (since Byzantine times, at least).[10] Returning now to Addison's value judgment, in No. 62 of his Spectator Papers he gives an evaluation that has greater descriptive contents than his passage quoted above: "Mixt Wit"—as compared to "True Wit" and "False Wit"—"is therefore a Composition of Punn and true Wit, and is more or less perfect as the Resemblance lies in the Ideas or in the Words". In the juxtaposition of "Army" and "Mary", the resemblance lies only in the letters of the words; what

[9]   In Hebrew, only the consonants are written (and permutated).
[10]   I am indebted for this information to Professor Itamar Grünwald.

Herbert did, was to elaborate his image in a way that suggests an intense network of "Resemblance of Ideas", generating unity in variety.

As I have suggested in chapter 7, a sense of insight occurs when multiplicity is suddenly perceived as unity. In the foregoing analysis I have demonstrated how a multiplicity of apparently unrelated entities are suddenly perceived as closely inter-woven. The magical formula of permuted letters is only one item in this unified complex, though it may be considered by some adepts as an adequate "methodical guide to meditation with the aid of letters and their configurations". To this we may add the cumulative effect of typographic foregrounding "to shock, even shatter, the standard epistemic security of disciples", so as to force them "to consider who they are—to locate themselves vis-a-vis normal versus transcendental reality". Thus, to use Summers' words, the serious religious subject and the "true" meanings drawn by the poet from his word-play become the object of a powerful insight.

The Poem as Hieroglyph (Emblem)

Herbert critics frequently emphasize the visual element in his poetry in both the se-mantic and the typographic treatment of the poem. In this context, they speak of the poem as a hieroglyph (Summers, 1968; Rickey, 1979; Brown and Ingoldsby, 1979), or as an emblem (Freeman, 1979). Some of the paradigmatic cases of these critics are the same, whether they call them a hieroglyph or an emblem. In this chapter I will discuss only the typographic aspect (I have discussed the semantic aspects in chapter 5). As Rickey (1979: 314) pointed out, "if one conceives a hieroglyphic poem as one the physical shape of which reinforces its actual meaning, he doubtless associates the hieroglyph primarily with *The Altar* and *Easter Wings*". This hiero-glyphic conception involves a half-truth; as all half-truths, it is a half-lie, too. It should be complemented with the conception propounded above. The manipulation of the poem's typographic arrangement enhances both the unity and the variety of the text: it does not only *reinforce* its actual meaning; by the same token, it shocks, even shatters, the reader's "standard epistemic security", as discussed above.

In some of Herbert's poems, the typographic manipulation yields no mimetic shape; Rickey (1979: 314) describes these as "semi-hieroglyphic". Here, too, she emphasizes their reinforcing rather than their baffling aspect. Among the new poems in *The Temple,* she says, Herbert has six of the semi-hieroglyphic type, among them "Anagram of the Virgin Marie" ("How well her name an *Army* doth present, / In whom the Lord of Hosts did pitch his tent"); and "The Water-course", "where the shape of the last lines of the two stanzas is at least mildly suggestive of its subject":

> 6.   *The Water-Course*
> Thou who dost dwell and linger here below,
> Since the condition of this world is frail,
> Where of all plants afflictions soonest grow;

If troubles overtake thee, do not wail:

For who can look for lesse, that loveth $\begin{cases} \text{Life?} \\ \text{Strife?} \end{cases}$

But rather turn the pipe and waters course
To serve thy sinnes, and furnish thee with store
Of sov'raigne tears, springing from true remorse:
That so in purenesse thou mayst him adore,

Who gives to man, as he sees fit, $\begin{cases} \text{Salvation.} \\ \text{Damnation.} \end{cases}$

Rickey, I suppose, means that the typographic arrangement of the words *Life* and *Strife* or *Salvation* and *Damnation* reflects the alternative courses men may take on earth, or God's sovereignty to decide on reward or punishment. It should be pointed out, however, that the disruption of the smooth reading process in these verse lines is more radical than in any one of the other instances. Herbert's experimentation with typographic arrangements here is baffling indeed. The last word of each verse line can be one of two words rhyming with each other, that have opposite meanings or emotional tendencies (Life–Strife; Salvation–Damnation). Thus, the verse lines convey opposing meanings that cannot be expressed simultaneously, as would be the case in a metaphysical pun, for instance. Here we may point out different degrees of the same kind of effect. The metaphysical pun produces "in the reader a strange sensation—making one suddenly doubt one's comfortable relationship with language—not unlike the sense of disorientation and confusion associated with the grotesque". Such visual devices that convey conflicting meanings may produce a higher degree of the same kind of feeling—but only in a certain kind of mental performance, as explained in the next section.
Hieroglyph Emblem

Psychological Reality and Diminishing Rhymes

In light of the foregoing deliberations, the visual ingenuities discussed here can be perceived either as playful "mannerisms" or disorienting disruptions of the smooth functioning of the cognitive system. These different perceptions result from different mental performances. We sometimes fortuitously choose one or the other mental performance; but the structure of texts on the one hand, and the reader's cognitive style on the other, may have a crucial influence on this choice. I wish to emphasise that the phrase "disruptions of the smooth functioning" is not a mere empty token to fill in the syntactic structure of the theoretical statement, but refers to processes that have considerable psychological reality. I propose to consider a linguistic mechanism underlying reading, which in some performances of certain typographic arrangements may be fully activated; in others—by-passed. I claim that the effects concerned arise only in certain kinds of mental performance. Consider George

Herbert's poem "Paradise", where typography becomes a formal element: the second and third rhymes of each stanza are formed by "paring" off the first consonant of the preceding rhyme. Summers observes on this poem: "The device is artificial in the extreme, and it requires some wrenching of orthography. As an abstract form it is hardly satisfactory. But Herbert never used forms abstractly, and we are left in no doubt as to the reason for the form of this particular poem":

> 7. I blesse thee, Lord, because I   GROW
>   Among thy trees, which in a   ROW
>   To thee both fruit and order   OW.
>
>   What open force, or hidden   CHARM
>   Can blast my fruit, or bring me   HARM
>   While the inclosure is thine   ARM.
>
>   Inclose me still for fear I   START.
>   Be to me rather sharp and   TART,
>   Then let me want thy hand &   ART.
>
>   When thou dost greater judgements   SPARE,
>   And with thy knife but prune and   PARE,
>   Ev'n fruitfull trees more fruitfull   ARE.
>
>   Such sharpnes shows the sweetest   FREND:
>   Such cuttings rather heal then   REND:
>   And such beginnings touch their   END.

Summers does observe, then, that "the device is artificial in the extreme", and I agree with him. But I would like to add that it is so artificial that it may, in some mental performances, baffle the reader, even shatter his "standard epistemic security". What is more, unlike the preceding example, there is a third (in fact first) kind of possible mental performance for this poem: one may read the poem and enjoy the sheer musicality of the rhyme, without noticing its "pruned" structure. Summers, at any rate, proceeds by describing the harmonious interplay between the device and the contents.

> The "pruned" rhymes do compel the reader to "see" what the poem is saying concerning the positive function of suffering. The meaning is traditional, of course. The fate of the "unprofitable vineyard" was destruction rather than pruning. By changing the image from the vine to the English orchard, Herbert related the "pruning" more immediately to his readers' experience, but the point is the same: the surgical knife is necessary for the order which produces fruit. The final line of the poem is "naturally" ambiguous. For the

religious man of the seventeenth century "end" nearly always implied purpose as well as finality. "And such beginnings touch their END" means that
God's pruning causes the fruits of righteousness which are the end of man's
creation. It also implies that the cutting away of the fruitless branches images the final "cutting away" of the body and the release of the soul at death
(Summers, 1975: 139).

Incidentally, we happen to have some experimental knowledge about the demand
such a task may exert on our "standard epistemic security", when performed "in a
flash". This demand concerns our command of phonetic coding. When we emit
strings of speech sounds, we obviously have recourse to phonetic coding. It is much
less obvious that phonetic coding is a major resource in the performance of a wide
range of cognitive operations, among them reading. Researchers at the Haskins
Laboratories (e. g., Liberman and Mann, 1981: 128–129; Brady et. al., 1983: 349–
355; Mann, 1984: 1–10) in their research on the possible causes of reading difficulties in children have revealed a deficiency in the use of phonetic coding by poor
readers; good readers, by contrast, seem to make an excellent use of it. In one experimental task, poor readers had greater difficulty than good readers in tapping once or
three times in response to the number of syllables in such spoken words as *pig* or
elephant, or once, twice or three times in response to the number of phonemes in
such words as *eye, pie* or *spy*. This has been interpreted as a deficiency in the use of
phonetic coding. Notice that the latter task is based on materials that are exactly like
the "pruned" rhymes. In another task, they had to memorise groups of words—either
rhymed or unrhymed, as in the following ones:

8.	chain	train	brain	rain	pain
	cat	fly	score	meat	scale

Good readers did consistently better with both kinds of groups than poor readers.
However, with the rhymed groups, their performance seriously deteriorated. While
their reliance on phonetic representation increased their overall performance, the similar sounds of the rhyming words seem to have caused confusion in their acoustic
memory. Thus, this experiment reveals an intimate relationship between rhyme and
the cognitive mechanisms involved in certain memory tasks. There was no difference
in IQ between the two groups (in fact, in one of the experiments the average IQ of
the poor readers was insignificantly higher). In nonverbal memory tasks the poor
readers were as good as the good readers (in fact, insignificantly better). It was only
that the good readers made efficient use of phonetic coding. Since the poor readers
made inefficient use of the acoustic information in short-term memory, they were
not penalised by the similar sounds of the rhyming words. Virginia Mann advances
two plausible explanations for these experimental results. "On the one hand, poor
readers might not resort to phonetic representation at all, relying instead on semantic

or some other modes of representation. On the other hand, they may attempt to employ phonetic representation but for some reason their representations are less effective" (1984: 8).

What can we learn from these experiments about the psychological reality of rhyme in general and "pruned" rhymes in particular? I have suggested above that in the "speech mode" we listen to a stream of abstract phonetic categories; in the "poetic mode", at the same time, subliminally, we may attend to the rich, precategorial acoustic information. In these experiments, we may suppose that these same auditory characteristics, held for several seconds in an echoic sensory register, provide good readers with rich, precategorial information that enables them to attend, with relative ease, to the phonological structure of the words: the number of syllables in the words "dog" or "elephant"; or the number of speech sounds in the words "eye, pie, spy". The same rich, precategorial information reverberates in the good reader's "echoic sensory register", enabling him to attend simultaneously to a number of rhyming words, the acoustic traces of which enhance each other. Briefly, this rich, reverberating precategorial information is an efficient means to hold verbal material in active memory for longer, making it available for increasingly complex processing: for recognising the correspondence of letters and speech sounds in reading, or the disruption of automatic correspondence in the various kinds of typographic foregrounding discussed in this chapter, or the decreasing length of words in "pruned rhymes", or Morgenstern's "brilliant word plays" (I certainly do not mean counting the number of syllables or phonemes in the rhyme words, but rather performing any additional processing required).

When repeated sound clusters follow one upon the other, their precategorial acoustic informations fuse, and confusion occurs. In poetry, this may render the effect exceptionally strained, as in Hopkins' sound patterns. When there are intervening words (verse lines) between these rhyming words, their precategorial acoustic informations fuse and a smooth musical quality results. This mechanism may account, then, for cognitive phenomena on two levels. First, it may account for our ability to hear a musical fusion of the rhyming words; and second, it suggests that the rich, precategorial information renders the phonological structure of the words available for additional processing. This latter ability may be called "meta-awareness".

People seem to differ with respect to the efficiency with which they employ phonetic representation. Phonetic reperesentation relies on rich, precategorial information reverberating in echoic memory. There is some experimental evidence that poor readers employ semantic instead of phonetic coding. The above experiments have revealed an interesting fact. Reading is a skill that demands the efficient handling of strings of letters. But this skill, we have discovered, requires the efficient use of phonetic representation. Such tasks of meta-awareness as tapping for each speech sound in the words "eye, pie, spy" seem to exceed the capability of some children; and some tasks of poetry processing—that of some grown-ups.

Turning now to readers of George Herbert's poetry, we must take it for granted that all of them would count as very efficient readers by the criteria of the foregoing experiments. Nonetheless, those experiments may illuminate the mechanisms underlying reading, as well as the response to rhyme in general, and to "pruned" rhyme in particular. "Pruned" rhymes require the ability to fuse the sound information of rhyme words, as well as to exploit them for additional processing. Moreover, it may suggest a possibility that even among expert readers there may be considerable differences of cognitive style; and that one of those differences may concern relative readiness to rely on phonetic coding. An examination of the published works of professional critics and academicians seems to support such a possibility.

For readers who make full use of phonetic representation and their acoustic correlates, we may postulate the following process. Letters signify speech sounds; speech sounds are combined into words which, in turn, signify meaning units which combine into syntactic units which, in turn, refer to extra-linguistic referents. In order to work all this out, the acoustic information that carries the speech sounds must reverberate for a considerable time in the reader's short-term memory. When similar-sound words occur with some regularity, the acoustic information related to them fuses into a quality perceived as harmonious musicality. Such a fusion delays, but does not disrupt the chain of signs extending from letters to extra-linguistic referents. It may, in fact, even enhance it. This is one way in which Herbert's "pruned-rhyme" poem may be read—without the reader noticing that there is something unusual with these particular rhymes. This is what I mean by the smooth functioning of the cognitive system in language processing. Readers who do notice the "pruned" structure of the rhyme words are forced to disrupt this chain at its very beginning. They must notice the diminishing length of the strings of letters in the rhyme words. What is more, if they are reading the poem according to Summers' interpretation, they must relate these observations to the underlying theme of the poem. To enable this extra processing, they will attempt to stretch the period of the speech sounds' availability in their acoustic short-term memory. If they fail, they will experience it as a drastic disruption, sometimes followed by an attempt at readjustment.

Readers who make less efficient use of phonetic coding may be penalised at some point at the very beginning of this process. The musical fusion of precategorial acoustic information in rhyme may impress itself less powerfully on their perception; this may drastically limit their ability to process all the sign information while the precategorial sounds are actively present. As experiments with efficient and poor readers suggest, in some extreme cases readers may rely on semantic rather than phonetic coding, which would involve them in piecemeal guesswork rather than fluent information processing. In the present context, "semantic coding" is a euphemism for "guessing instead of reliable processing". The extra tasks will not impose an extra load on the working memory of such readers; they will perform the processing in a step-by-step fashion. Such readers will perceive the physical shape reinforcing the poem's actual meaning as little more than a playful "mannerist" ornament.

Rhyme consists in the harmonious fusion of precategorial sound information. This is the simplest and most natural processing of rhyme words. There may be, however, an indefinite number of levels of additional processing, resulting in varying degrees of unnaturalness. Thus, between "mere" harmonious fusion (where the effect is achieved on the precategorial level) and "pruned" rhymes (where the effect is achieved on the graphemic level) there may be, for instance, echo rhymes (where the effect is achieved on the phonological level). I compared (Tsur, 1992b: 131–132) the more than usually musical fusion of rhymes in Rimbaud's sonnet "Voyelles" and a very different effect of very similar structures in George Herbert's echo poem "Heaven". Both poems rely heavily on echo rhymes; but while in Rimbaud's sonnet the effect is smooth musical fusion, in Herbert's poem it is sharp and witty. Echo is a repetition of sounds where there are two rhyming words, the second of which is wholly included in the first, as *light* in *delight*, or *leisure* in *pleasure* in the ensuing poem:

9.   O who will show me those delights on high?
             echo   I.
      Thou Echo, thou art mortall, all men know.
             echo   No.
      Wert not thou born among the trees and leaves?
             echo   Leaves.
      And are there any leaves that still abide?
             echo   Bide.
      What leaves are they? impart the matter wholly.
             echo   Holy.
      Are holy leaves the Echo then of bliss?
             echo   Yes.
      Then tell me what is that supreme delight?
             echo   Light.
      Light top the minde: what shall the will enjoy?
             echo   Joy.
      But are there cares and business with the pleasure?
             echo   Leisure.
      Light, joy and leisure; but shall they persevere?
             echo   Ever.

In "Voyelles",[11] there is only one pair of rhyming words, neither of which is wholly included in the other: *voyelles* and *cruelles*. As for the rest, *latentes* is in-

---

[11]   A noir, E blanc, I rouge, U vert, O bleu: voyelles,
        Je dirais quelque jour vos naissances latentes:
        A, noir corset velu des mouches éclatantes
        Qui bombinent autour des puanteurs cruelles,

        Golfes d'ombres; E, candeurs des vapeurs et des tentes,
        Lances des glaciers fiers, rois blancs, frissons d'ombelles;
        I, pourpres, sang craché, rires des lèvres belles
        Dans la colère ou les ivresses pénitentes;

cluded in *éclatentes, tentes* in *pénitentes, latentes* and *éclatentes; belles* is included in *ombelles, rides* in *virides, yeux* in *studieux*, and *Anges* in *étranges*. The cue for the opposing perceptual qualities in these two poems may be found in Longinus' formulation quoted above: "Wherefore a figure is at its best when the very fact that it is a figure escapes attention". When, as in Herbert's poem, the word *echo* draws attention to the sound repetition, it is perceived as an ingenuous, "mannerist", witty play on words. What strikes the reader in "Voyelles" is that a similar device fuses here in a pleasant, harmonious texture, yielding musicality rather than intellectual play. Suppose that before each one of Rimbaud's rhyme words the word *rhyme* were printed — it would have "spoiled" the smooth fusion, and would have rendered the effect witty. Now suppose we omit from Herbert's poem the tokens of the word *echo*. We will still perceive a crucial difference between the two poems. Rimbaud's rhyme words are overdetermined by the semantic and syntactic structures of their local context; the rich precategorial sound information is active only in the back of the reader's mind. In Herbert's poem, by contrast, the similarity of speech categories as related to meanings (rather than precategorial information) is involved; and it *must* be pushed into the focus of attention. There is no possibility to predict on syntactic or semantic grounds the word "I" from the first line "O who will show me those delights on high".

In Herbert's echo poem, the last speech sounds are extracted from the end of the preceding line. Even though these echo sounds are perceived as part of the preceding word, a different referent is assigned to them. This drastically interferes with the phonemic structure of the word. In the above terms, additional processing is forced on the reader, which contradicts the phonemic nature of language. The additional (incompatible) meaning assigned to the extracted speech sounds forces the reader (or listener) to keep the sign vehicles apart in consciousness, and prevent smooth fusion.

Echo became a favoured embellishment in Baroque secular music and poetry. Now echo (like shadows in visual perception) is a prototypical instance of thing-free qualities that impress themselves on the senses. This feature of it was exploited by Baroque music and poetry as a conventional means to indicate a pronouncement issuing from a supersensuous transcendental presence. In the fourth Cantata of Bach's *Christmas Oratorio,* for instance, the echo is used to reinforce the believer's attitudes.

U, cycles, vibrements divins des mers virides,
Paix des pâtis semés d'animaux, paix de rides
Que l'alchimie imprime aux grands fronts studieux;

O, suprême Clairon plein des strideurs étranges,
Silence traversés des Mondes et des Anges:
— O l'Oméga, rayon violet de Ses Yeux!

10. **Aria (Sopran mit Echo)**
Flößt, mein Heiland, Flößt dein Namen
auch den allerkleinsten Samen
jenes strengen Schreckens ein?
nein, du sagst ja selber nein!

Sollt ich nun das Sterben scheuen?
nein, dein süßes Wort ist da!
oder sollt ich mich erfreuen?
ja, du Heiland, sprichst selbst ja!

Could, my Saviour, could your name implant/ even the smallest grain/ of terror in me?/ no, you yourself say: no! [Echo: no!]

Should I dread now Death?/ no, your sweet Word is here!/ or should I rejoice?/ yes, you yourself, my Saviour, say yes! [Echo: yes!]

It will be illuminating to compare Bach's use of echo to Herbert's. In Bach, the music does all the interesting work. The text is much more simplistic in the Oratorio. First, we are supposed to know who hides behind the echo's voice: the Saviour. In Herbert's poem there is considerable uncertainty as to the identity of the "speaker". Second, in Bach's text the echo repeats a whole word with the same meaning as the original speaker. In Herbert's poem the echo word is entirely included in the preceding word (with a few exceptions) and emerges from it as a new phonological and semantic entity. Third, in Bach's text the speaker tells the echo what she wants to hear; the echo merely repeats the last word "nein" (no), or "ja" (yes). In Herbert's poem, by contrast, the echo imparts new knowledge to the speaker, sometimes contradicting his expectations, even if eventually it turns out to be highly conventional.

Briefly, Herbert's echo poem generates, in contrast to Rimbaud's smooth fusion of echo words, a sharp witty quality. As compared to the echo play in Bach's Oratorio, it baffles the reader by shattering the phonological nature of language and assigning new, incompatible meanings to the extracted sound fragments, thus making him suddenly doubt his comfortable relationship with language. Such bafflement may force readers "to consider who they are—to locate themselves vis-a-vis normal versus transcendental 'reality'". On the level of content, too, the echo attempts to shock the reader's "standard epistemic security". In Baroque secular poetry there is a considerable corpus of echo poems in which the phonemic chunks that constitute the echo are handled in a way that is more similar to Herbert's poem than to Bach's Oratorio. In these poems the effect is *précieux,* playful. In Herbert's echo play, by contrast, the supersensuous transcendental presence indicated by the echo may arouse a feeling of contact with the invisible world of the "beyond".

"Easter Wings"

George Herbert's pattern poem "Easter Wings" is, according to Gross (1997: 16), "arguably the most famous example in the history of English literature". Summers (1968), Rickey (1979: 314) and Brown and Ingoldsby (1979) treat it as the prototypical hieroglyphic poem, Freeman (1979: 221) as the prototypical emblem poem. Van Peer (1993) discusses the poem under the heading "typographic foregrounding"; I disucuss the poem (Tsur, 1997; 2001) within a theoretical framework that is the precursor of the framework expounded in the present chapter. I have quoted Rickey (1979: 314) saying "If one conceives a hieroglyphic poem as one the physical shape of which reinforces its actual meaning, he doubtless associates the hieroglyph primarily with *The Altar* and *Easter Wings*".

11.   *Easter wings*

Lord, who createdst man in wealth and store,
Though foolishly he lost the same,
Decaying more and more,
Till he became
Most poore:
With thee
O let me rise
As larks, harmoniously,
And sing this day thy victories:
Then shall the fall further the flight in me.

My tender age in sorrow did beginne:
And still with sicknesses and shame
Thou didst so punish sinne,
That I became
Most thinne.
With thee
Let me combine,
And feel this day thy victorie;
For, if I imp my wing on thine,
Affliction shall advance the flight in me.

I have pointed above to the notions "multivalence" or "multiple relationship" between technical ingenuities and the other aspects of a poem as a possible source of aesthetic excellence. If we combine what some earlier critics wrote about this poem, we may see how multiple relationship works in it. Joseph Summers points out the resemblance not only between the visual design of wings and the "wings" and "flight" mentioned in the contents, but also the structure of this design and the thinning and expanding structure of the the visual design and the "thinning and expanding" presented by the contents.

> The pattern is successful not merely because we "see" the wings, but because we see how they are made: the process of impoverishment and enrichment, of "thinning" and expansion which makes "flight" possible. By

that perception and by the rhythmical falling and rising which the shaped lines help to form, we are led to respond fully to the active image and to the poem.

Willie van Peer pointed out some evasive aspects of the verbal level that reinforce these correpondences:

> [T]he title explicitly refers to a subject matter corresponding to the typographical form. The wings symbolise man's elevation resulting from his belief in Revelation: note also the reference to the divine wings ('imp my wing on Thine') and to the lark, yet another explicit topicalisation of the motif of the wing ('With Thee/ O let me rise/ As larks'). More important still is the fact that each stanza displays a typographical form which closely mirrors the development of the theme. This can be seen quite clearly from the verbs and their distribution across verse lines. Each time the length of the line shrinks, verbs occur which refer to a process of diminution: 'lost' (line 2), 'decaying' (line 3), 'became poore' (lines 4-5), 'became ... thinne' (lines 14-15). When the width of the verse line increases, verbs belonging to a semantic field indicating increase and growth are used: 'rise' (line 7), 'further' (line 10), 'combine' (line 17), 'imp' (line 19), 'advance' (line 20). This pattern is reinforced by the change of tense occurring in each stanza: past tense in the first half of each stanza, when the lines start to grow shorter: 'createdst' (line 1), 'lost' (line 2), 'became' (line 4), 'did' (line 11), 'didst (line 13), 'became' (line 14); *via* present tense when the lines begin to increase in length: 'let' (line 7), 'sing' (line 9), 'let' (line 17), 'feel' (line 18), 'imp' (line 19); to the future in the final line of each stanza: 'shall further' (line 10), 'shall advance' (line 20) (55-57).

I accept this conception of a multiple relationship; but, in harmony with the approach propounded in the present chapter, I insist that the visual patterning has opposing effects here: on the one hand it reinforces the "hieroglyphic" correspondence between the linguistic, thematic, figurative and typographic strata of the poem; on the other hand, it disrupts the smooth transition in the hierarchic chain of signs, at the most sensitive stage, the transition from the graphemic to the phonemic stratum. In some readings, at least, this may evoke a process of disorienting shock and readjustment—very much in the manner I have pointed out in the foregoing examples.

These critics touch upon an additional problem: some picture poems (such as Herbert's "Easter Wings") are generally treated in criticism as "major poems", some as justly-forgotten minor ones. Van Peer quotes an occasional wing poem by Mellin de Sainct-Gelais' "On the Recovery of our Lady, Mother of François the I[st]". This poem, he says, had it *not* been composed in the form of two wings, would presumably lose little of its effect. In the case of George Herbert, however, typography and theme form a symbiotic whole, the aesthetic value of which would be affected if the wing-pattern were disrupted. In this sense, typographic forms of foregrounding may contribute in a specific way to the quality of poems (57).

Summers too adopts a functional conception of aesthetic value in pattern poetry.

Both before and after 1633 the literary quality of most of these poems was notoriously low. The poets seemed usually to consider the shapes as a superficial or frivolous attraction for the reader. As the Renaissance poets and critics never tired of reiterating, pleasure *could* be made a bait for profit, but a superficial conception of the "bait" often resulted in very bad poems. Many of the patterns depended largely on wrenched typography, and it was a common practice to compose a poem in ordinary couplets, then chop the lines to fit the pattern (140).

What Van Peer and Summers suggest here is, precisely, that bad or mediocre pattern poems result from the absence of such a multiple relationship as proposed above between the visual arrangement of the lines and the various aspects of the verbal structure of the verse. In this respect, their analysis supports our assumption that Herbert's use of the pattern poem is in a sense a rather logical extension of more conservative aesthetic principles. In our terms, when there is no such multiple relationship between the wing-arrangement of lines and the verbal structure, the two can be contemplated in isolation, with no attempt to integrate them, and no emotional shock arises. The emotional shock would arise only when the multiple relationship serves as an incentive for the integration of the hard-to-integrate dimensions of the poem.

In the beginning, I adopted this approach to the evaluation of pattern poems. Then, however, I encountered a Hebrew poem (copied in 1768) called "Palm Tree" (Ilan Tamar) by **R**abbi **M**ordechai **T**ama, quoted by Pagis (1977: 27). In this poem, the motto is taken from *Proverbs* 3/18: "She is a tree of life to those who lay hold of her" (the Hebrew word for Palm, *tamar,* yields an anagram of the author's initials). The poem offers a variety of routes of reading, which yield different poems, with different metres and rhyme patterns; the MS (reproduced here) also provides the various outcomes of the various readings. The very existence of this undisputedly minor poem poses a serious problem for the foregoing conception, since here too "typography and theme form a symbiotic whole". Nevertheless, in this case too, "to a modern reader, the text is little more than a manneristic game", to use Willie van Peer's words.[12]

---

[12] On the other hand, to a modern reader such a "multi-route" poem might be quite familiar from contemporary interactive, "mobile" art.

12. שרש האילן

Perhaps two not incompatible solutions can be offered to this riddle. First, as I suggested above, when there is no multiple relationship between the graphic arrangement of lines and the verbal structure, the two can be contemplated in isolation, with no attempt to integrate them, and no emotional shock arises. In Rabbi Mordechai Tama's tree poem, on the contrary, there seems to be too much multiple relationship, exceeding the reader's ability to integrate it: the same words can be related to each other in four different ways, at least. Consequently, the resulting texts *must* be contemplated in isolation.

The emotional shock would arise only when the multiple relationship serves as an incentive for the integration of the hard-to-integrate dimensions of the poem; so, again, no emotional shock arises. Thus, it would not necessarily be the "symbiotic whole" formed by "typography and theme" that would constitute the criterion for poetic excellence, but rather a graspable balance between complexity and simplicity. Secondly, picture poems may have, after all, inherent poetic values prior to the graphic patterning. Herbert's wing-poem, for instance, occurs in the manuscripts in the ordinary line-below-line arrangement, and only in the first (1633) edition of *The Temple* are the lines printed vertically. Thus, Herbert's poem may have an inherent poetic value which Mordechai Tama's poem perhaps lacks.[13]

An Alternative Proposal

This article presented a cognitive approach to mysticism related to the contemplation of speech sounds and the letters that signify them, as they appear in poetry. After having written this chapter I ran into Brian Lancaster's (2000) article which also explores "linguistic mysticism" from a cognitive point of view. His interest is only in the cognitive foundation of linguistic mysticism, not the literary process. But the comparison between our approaches becomes intriguing because he too has recourse to Abraham Abulafia's "Science of the Combination of Letters", and he too quotes from the admirable account of Abulafia's anonymous disciple of his overwhelming mystic experience. Furthermore Lancaster quotes exactly the same passage from *Sefer Yetzira* which I have quoted (through Katz). Lancaster too is engaged in an attempt to point out the cognitive foundations of "linguistic mysticism" found in these writings.

Lancaster discusses the effects of ordinary language, its disintegration and reintegration on mystic experience. To the extent that a goal of mystical practice is that of transcending distinctions and gaining direct experience of the oneness said to characterise ultimate reality, language is often viewed as an impediment on the path, since language specifically compartmentalises experience (237). In the language mysticism of ecstatic kabbalah, by contrast, the major intent was to deconstruct words to their constituent letters — individual letters were to be visualised, and chanted together with other letters, with little or no concern for semantic content. In this sense, language was used effectively to transcend the compartmentalisation of meaning normally ascribed to language (245). An equally forceful emphasis is on the "reconstructive" use of language. This is evident in the appeals to a higher, or more inclusive, view of language, especially with regard to the divine Name and

---

[13] In his anthology *The Meditative Poem* Louis Martz provides (pp. 154–155) facsimile reproductions of "Easter wings" as printed on facing pages in the first edition of Herbert's *Temple,* 1633, but in the text he prints the verse lines (p. 156) horizontally, and comments: "The manuscripts present these emblematic verses horizontally, but the vertical form of 1633, here reproduced, seems more effective visually" (p. 535).

God's own use of language in creation. Lancaster conjectures that by reconnecting deconstructed language elements with the various (and elaborate) permutations of the Name, the mystic is effectively substituting the all-encompassing divine Being into the role normally played by "I"-tags (247).

We are engaged here in the cognitive explanation of those aspects of mysticism that exploit letters and speech sounds. Such an explanation must rely on two sets of information. On the one hand, it must examine what the mystics have to say about letters, speech sounds, and the mystic process. On the other, it must provide models of the best information available from psychology and psycholinguistics about the contribution of manipulating letters and speech sounds to the mystic process. The focuses of these two articles, I believe, complement each other. Lancaster provides a "macro" pattern of three stages of language use which is most essential for an under-standing of the process: compartmentalisation (required for ordinary consciousness), deconstruction, and reconstruction (that are indispensable for the mystic experience). My paper was more than sketchy about this macro structure of the process, which was taken care of mainly by what I had to say about satisfying the Platonic censor in us.

Lancaster, on the other hand, was too sparing at the middle stage of the process. The little he had to say on letters and speech sounds mainly relied on the study of mysticism, almost nothing has been said about the cognitive side of the equation. When he speaks of "preconscious" processes, he diverts attention from phonetic to semantic and other nonphonetic elements (such a tendency is most common in literary criticism as well). Even when he asserts that in language mysticism the major intent was to deconstruct words to their constituent letters, he suggests that the purpose of this was effectively to transcend the compartmentalisation of meaning normally ascribed to language.

> The model assumes that a sensory stimulus triggers multiple representa-
> tions preconsciously. In the case of spoken polysemous word stimuli, for
> example, Pynte *et al.* (1984) and Swinney (1979) have demonstrated that a
> word's multiple meanings are activated simultaneously within 250 mil-
> liseconds. Depending on context, a single meaning subsequently enters
> consciousness, at which point the other, competing meanings seem to be
> inhibited. An instructive insight into the multiplicity at the preconscious
> level is also given by the syndrome of synaesthesia, in which sensory
> modalities become confused — as when someone hears colours (243).

Lancaster concludes from the foregoing that "the syndrome is evidence for the view that prior to their articulation as stable, meaningful objects and events in con-sciousness, preconscious images and thoughts are represented in multiple fashion" (244). I find this conclusion most illuminating for our topic. In all probability, mystic experiences *are* associated with an influx of sensory information, for which cognitive theory must account. But this does not change the fact that nothing has been said of letters or speech sounds. The present article, by contrast, elaborates at great length on the cognitive aspects of the phonetic and graphemic signifiers. I have distinguished between two modes of using speech sounds in infancy, babbling and referring. The former is emotionally charged, the latter is characterised by volitional control. Lancaster's "deconstructional" phase seems to involve regression to the babbling mode in a publicly respectable manner. I have pointed out that depth psychology as well as cognitive and neuropsychological studies conceive similarly of such phonological regression. I have also drawn attention to a psycholinguistic mechanism that manipulates and rotates speech sounds and even smaller phonetic features, sometimes meaninglessly, sometimes in all sorts of bizarre combinations with conscious and unconscious meanings. I have suggested that Freudian slips, witty Spoonerisms and the anagram are products of this mechanism, in varying degrees of consciousness. These phenomena constitute a decreasingly fluid scale of combinations of meanings with permuted speech sounds and phonetic features. For people who make efficient use of phonetic coding, the rich precategorial sensory information related to speech sounds enable subliminal diffuse perceptions as well as higher-level language processing, by preserving the phonetic information longer in active memory.

To Sum Up

Poetry is not meant to arouse a mystic or ecstatic process in the reader. At most, it may display certain structural properties that are sufficiently similar to the structure of mystic or ecstatic mental processes, so as to have the reader *detect* a mystic quality in the text (cf. Hepburn, 1968). In this account I do not say anything about how similar "sufficiently similar" must be. It varies from one poetic system to another, and it depends, among other things, on the elements available in the system, and their "fine-grainedness" (see "Introduction", and chapter 9). Perhaps, "sufficiently similar" is that which chooses those options available in the system that are most similar to the mental processes concerned. Cognitive poetics assumes that the response to poetry involves adaptative devices turned to aesthetic ends. With reference to mystic poetry I assume two different modes: one that involves the more or less smooth application of orientation mechanisms, and one in which the reader or observer is compelled to make a double adjustment: first, to meet a staggering shock, and second, to regain some balance. Mannerism in art in general, and metaphysical poetry in particular, offers a stock of artistic devices to baffle the reader or observer—ranging in poetry from the grotesque, through paradox, the metaphyscial puns and conceits, to typographical manipulation of the text. This poetic double adjustment is tailor-made for the verbal imitation of a mental process characterised by Katz as follows: "mystics in certain circumstances know that they are uttering nonsensical propositions, but in so doing they intend, among other things, to force the hearers of such propositions to consider who they are—to locate themselves vis-a-vis normal versus transcendental 'reality'". In this chapter I have explored the account of an overwhelming mystic experience resulting from systematic permutations and recombinations of the letters of God's names on the one hand and, on the other, visual and auditory "mannerisms" in George Herbert's poetry. I adopted Ehrenzweig's conception of the psychological origins of such "mannerisms". They are said to originate in unconscious processes, in which they have exceptional affective force. When brought to the light of full consciousness, they loose their emotional force and become "harmless" stylistic ornaments. In certain circumstances, these "harmless" ornaments can be used to shock the reader into the afore-mentioned process of double adjustment, possibly reviving some of their unconscious roots. I have also argued that the boundary between the two prototypes can be blurred: when the "baffling" stylistic devices are invested with huge quantities of mental or emotional energy, they may generate an ecstatic rather than disorienting effect.

Chapter 9

Oceanic Dedifferentiation, "Thing Destruction", and Mystic Poetry

Oceanic Dedifferentiation

Ordinary consciousness organises percepts into objects that have stable shapes with clear-cut boundaries between them. It is intimately associated with voluntary control. Altered states of consciousness consist of withdrawal from the achievements of ordinary consciousness. This may turn out to be difficult to achieve, because it involves the voluntary abandonment of voluntary control. Religion, meditation and mystic experience involve such altered states of consciousness, in this mounting order of difficulty. Hypnosis, dream and the hypnagogic state (drowsiness preceding sleep), too, are altered states of consciousness. They involve withdrawal, to some degree or other, to a lowly-differentiated state of mind, the relinquishing of conscious control. Such states of consciousness are not easily accessible to the arts, least of all to poetry, the medium of which is conceptual language. In relation to music and the visual arts, Anton Ehrenzweig speaks of "thing-destruction", "suspension of boundaries", "thing-free" and "gestalt-free" qualities, and of a "secondary elaboration", or a "superimposition", of an organising pattern on the resulting diffuse qualities. These critical terms seem to have considerable descriptive content, since they enable the critic to point out the source of those "unspeakable" effects. Ehrenzweig relates these notions to Freud's notion of "Oceanic Dedifferentiation" (or "Undifferentiation"), and to Bergson's "Metaphysical Intuition". In some of his writings Ehrenzweig uses the term "dedifferentiation", in others "undifferentiation"; the former suggests a process, the latter the resulting state. In the poems discussed below the emphasis will be more on the process of dedifferentiation, on strategies for releasing objects from their stable configuration, rather than on the resulting state of undifferentiation. According to Freud, some religious and mystic experiences are intimately related to what he calls "Oceanic Dedifferentiation". In a paper on "Oceanic Dedifferentiation and Poetic Metaphor" (Tsur, 1988b) I applied this notion to metaphors of a certain type, both religious and secular. In this chapter I wish to broaden it not just to a certain kind of metaphor, but also to other means that may approach such an effect to some degree or other. Bergson, as quoted by Ehrenzweig, claims that such an effect (without calling it "Oceanic Dedifferentiation") is a useful instrument to get intuitive access to the inner self (Ehrenzweig, 1965). Ehrenzweig himself describes it as producing a "flexible unconscious fantasy" (Ehrenzweig, 1970: 261).

In this chapter I will briefly present that theory and illustrate it *via* the use of imagery in the Hindu Upanishads and in *Faust;* then I will elaborate it in additional directions needed for the present chapter. Finally, I will apply the theory to three poems written in three languages, in three very different cultural traditions and periods: one of them Jewish, one Christian, and one that uses religious symbolism to generate a mystic-ecstatic quality in a secular love poem. My first example will be from the "Hekhaloth Books", one of the oldest Jewish mystic texts. My second example will be a devotional poem by the seventeenth century English poet, Richard Crashaw. The third one is a love poem called "Hymne" by the French Symbolist, Charles Baudelaire. I will end with a brief discussion of Baudealaire's poem "Le Léthé", throwing some light on the frequently-observed affinity between sexual imagery and the expression of a feeling of mystic experience.

My point of departure for this discussion is the following argument by Anton Ehrenzweig (1970: 135), who speaks of "a creative ego rhythm that swings between focussed gestalt and an oceanic undifferentiation":

> The London psychoanalysts D.W. Winnicott and Marion Milner, have stressed the importance for a creative ego to be able to suspend the boundaries between self and not-self in order to become more at home in the world of reality where the objects and self are clearly held apart (Ehrenzweig, 1970: 135).

Seen in this way, the oceanic experience of fusion, of a "return to the womb" (as Ehrenzweig describes it) represents the minimum content of all art; Freud saw in it only the basic religious experience. But it seems now that it belongs to all creativity (ibid.).

> As the ego sinks towards oceanic undifferentiation a new realm of the mind envelops us; we are not engulfed by death, but are released from our separate individual existence. We enter the manic womb of rebirth, an oceanic existence outside time and space (ibid., 136).

Why should such a rhythm help man "become more at home in the world of reality"? A cognitive explanation would point out that hard-and-fast categories (that eventually amount to *cognitive stability)* are indispensable for such elementary abilities as recognising a person or a place as the same person or place, or identifying a series of vastly different sound-stimuli emitted by different speakers as the same word. But this cognitive stability is bought at the price of relinquishing subtle and minimal precategorial cues, perceivable only by intuition, which are equally indispensable for survival. What is crucial for our present inquiry is the opposition *focused gestalt ~ undifferentiation*. One of man's greatest achievements is his cognitive differentiation. This accomplishment, however, plays the tyrant to him: the less differentiated processes become less accessible to him, as well as less reliable. The passages quoted from Ehrenzweig imply, in fact, that religion, art, and creativity in general, are among the means that may yield a heightened consciousness of these less differentiated processes.

The suspension of the boundaries between self and not-self by the creative ego is thus said to lead to oceanic undifferentiation. In this state, we are said to be released from our separate individual existences; as such, it is similar to death. On the other hand, in this state, energy may be revived and released, which leads to the opposite extreme, the state of ecstasy. Kenneth Burke (1962: 850) speaks of the mystic oxymoron, "the identification of the infinitesimally frail with the infinitely powerful"; we have here the fusion of a deathlike state with enormous energy. This might bring about an intense feeling of communion with "Infinity", "Eternity", or "Nothingness". Ecstasy may be said to consist in a state of oceanic undifferentiation, loaded with enormous energy; which is why in ecstatic poetry we so frequently encounter death-imagery loaded with undifferentiated energy (cf. Chapter 3).

From the point of view of available verbal techniques, I suggest, abstractions, gases and liquids are among the most prototypical natural symbols in our conceptual system to suggest a state in which the boundaries between objects are suspended.[1] From the point of view of the resulting mental states, say Newberg et al. (2001: 6–7), this is exactly, how generations of Eastern mystics have described their peak meditative, spiritual, and mystical moments. In the words of the Hindu Upanishads,

1.   As the river flowing east and west
Merge in the sea and become one with it,
Forgetting that they were ever separate rivers,
So do all creatures lose their separateness
When they merge at last into

In the afore-mentioned paper (Tsur 1988b) I discussed at considerable length such poetic metaphors as "But ye loveres, that bathen in gladnesse" (Chaucer, *Troilus & Cresseyde,* I.), and "Steep'd me in poverty to the very lips" (Shakespeare, *Othello,*

---

[1]   According to Scholem's (1961: 131) account, the thirteenth-century Jewish mystic Abraham Abulafia propounds a view that is very similar to the present conception of "ordinary consciousness" and "Oceanic undifferentiation":

> There are certain barriers which separate the personal existence of the soul from the stream of cosmic life [...]. There is a dam which keeps the soul confined within the natural and normal borders of human existence and protects it against the flood of the divine stream, which flows beneath it or all around it; the same dam, however, also prevents the soul from taking cognizance of the Divine. The "seals," which are impressed on the soul, protect it against the flood and guarantee its normal functioning. Why is the soul, as it were, sealed up? Because, answers Abulafia, the ordinary day-to-day life of human beings, their perception of the sensible world, fills and impregnates the mind with a multitude of sensible forms or images (called, in the language of mediaeval philosophers, "natural forms"). As the mind perceives all kinds of gross natural objects and admits their images into its consciousness, it creates for itself, out of this natural function, a certain mode of existence which bears the stamp of finiteness.

IV. ii.); these metaphors are of the shape [IMMERSED in an ABSTRACTION], which tend to cause an heightened effect of precisely this kind. In many instances, metaphors of this structure are used in mystic or Romantic poetry to arouse an intense feeling of communion with "Infinity", "Eternity", or "Nothingness", as suggested above. In certain circumstances, especially when placed in a context of the expanse of vast space, such metaphors may be perceived as a direct intuition of the "oceanic undifferentiation"-pole of the "creative ego rhythm that swings between focussed gestalt and an oceanic undifferentiation", of which Ehrenzweig speaks. Bearing in mind Wayne Booth's (1961: 211–240) distinction between *telling* and *showing,* this technique may be as good as any for "showing", so to speak, an altered state of consciousness, or a "peak experience" by verbal means.

At this point, it is important to make a very clear distinction between the *perception* of such a quality in a poetic text, and certain of its *interpretations* in the psychoanalytic tradition. Some critics, among them Ehrenzweig himself, are prone to take some image with a focused gestalt and construe it as an image of "oceanic undifferentiation" of some kind, as we will see in the following.

Oceanic Imagery in Faust: *Ehrenzweig against Ehrenzweig*

Ehrenzweig refers several times to the Homunkulus-episode in *Faust Part Two* as "oceanic" imagery. This episode seems to have an enormous grip on Ehrenzweig's imagination; as he says himself, "Nowhere in literature is there a more condensed image of the self-creating and self-scattering womb, or rather the divine parentless child identified with the womb from which he delivers himself in a threefold act of birth, love and death" (Ehrenzweig, 1970: 215). Since Homunkulus appears as a *dramatis persona,* rather than as a literary or linguistic figure in *Faust,* a *persona* furthermore who engages in dialogues and longer speeches over substantial stretches of time, I shall quote here only one of Ehrenzweig's several summaries of the episode:

> The chemical manikin, Homunkulus, achieves his own suicidal rebirth in love. I have already mentioned the extreme oceanic undifferentiation of the episode. Homunkulus is still unborn, enclosed in a glass phial which can become incandescent and lift itself into the air (this is an additional phallic symbolism). The manikin achieves rebirth by shattering his glass in a fiery explosion at the feet of the sea goddess, Galatea, amidst a general scene of orgiastic self-abandon (Ehrenzweig, 1970: 215).

We must distinguish in this account between the *immediate presentation* of an undifferentiated state, and the *differentiated idea,* or the *differentiated image,* of that undifferentiated state. Had Ehrenzweig characterised only the events conveyed in the last sentence of this quotation as "oceanic undifferentiation", we might have accepted his account as a description of the achievement of such a state. But when he concerns himself with the image suggested in the last sentence but one (including the suggestion of "phallic symbolism"), or when he speaks of Homunkulus as of the man-made manikin "who is still unborn and encased in the glass womb he carries about" (ibid., 199), we may regard it at best as the differentiated idea of an undifferentiated existence in the womb, that is, an allegory of an oceanic state.

This conclusion is warranted by Ehrenzweig's own account of the oceanic experience as quoted above. My argument rests mainly on the opposition between "oceanic undifferentiation" and "focused gestalt". The stable glass case with a characteristic human shape in it may, perhaps, represent a "return to the womb", and thus *stand for* "oceanic undifferentiation"; but it also *presents* the audience or the reader with a focused, well-differentiated gestalt. Thus, far from being an "experience of fusion", of suspending "the boundaries between self and not-self", this image of Homunkulus represents a state in which "the objects and self are clearly held apart", the glass case serving to enhance this separation. From such a focused, stable shape one may perhaps abstract the idea of the "return to the womb"; but this shape cannot be perceived as the experience of fusion and undifferentiation. The image is basically allegoric in character.

Thus, there appear to be two alternative ways of introducing "oceanic" imagery into a poem. Either *via* a *differentiated stable visual shape,* as in the image of the encased Homunkulus, from which a visual resemblance to the unborn child in the womb may be inferred, or by some *dedifferentiation* process that "suspends many kinds of boundaries and distinctions; at an extreme limit it may remove the boundaries of individual existence and so produce a mystic oceanic feeling" (Ehrenzweig, 1970: 304). Earlier, I have mentioned one kind of metaphorical construction as a technique of obtaining such a suspension of boundaries; and Goethe, in *Faust,* had recourse to this technique. Here, I only want to quote a single passage of this work, in which a crucial metaphor concerns immersion in an abstraction, apparently leading to mystic insight.

> 2. The spirit-world no closures fasten—
>   Thy sense is shut, thy heart is dead;
>   Disciple, up! untiring, hasten!
>   to bathe thy breast in morning-red!
>   (*Faust Part One,* 443-446, trans. Bayard Taylor).

Stuart Atkins comments on this passage: *"Dawn's first red* a favorable hour for successful mystic intuition or experience (here apparently figurative: Faust has momentarily gained a mystic insight)" (315). In excerpt (2), the undifferentiated experience of being immersed in a "dense", thing-free and gestalt-free entity is reinforced by two aspects of the metaphorical abstraction. First, by canceling the material aspects of the colorless substance *water* (as in "bathe"), the abstraction process allows the experience to have a sensory attribute: color (as in "redness"). Hence, one of its effects here is to increase the "dense texture" of the thing-free entity into which one is to be plunged, and so intensify the resulting undifferentiated sensation. Second, this abstraction itself is part of a large-scale spatial scene. Perhaps the most conspicuous condition in which abstract nouns may assume a lowly-differentiated character is when they occur in the description of a concrete, specific landscape, in which the speaker (or the perceiving consciousness) is in an intensive relation to the environment (cf. above, Chapter 4). In excerpt (2), the redness of the morning both provides the abstraction and indicates the concrete landscape, without mentioning any object that may have a stable, characteristic visual shape. In my paper on oceanic dedifferentiation (Tsur, 1988b), I distinguished between "rapid" and "delayed" categorisation. The former leaves the perceiver with as short a period of indecision as possible, and thus spares him the discomfort of uncertainty. The latter requires a considerable period of uncertainty; by the same token, it allows the perception of low-structured sensory information, and a more reliable judgment. In the case of Ehrenzweig, an alternative way to handle his two kinds of interpretation would be to suggest that with reference to the Homunkulus episode, the interpretation concentrates on focused gestalts and enables rapid categorization; with reference to the immersion in "morning-red", the interpretation focuses on diffuse, unstructured gestalts, requiring delayed categorization; at the same time, it allows for the perception of a diffuse state that is not unlike oceanic undifferentiation.

"Metaphysical Intuition"

Ehrenzweig makes insightful use of the terms "thing-destruction", "thing-free", "gestalt-free", applying them mainly to music and the visual arts. In the past thirty years or so, I have made some effort to explore the insights they yield in poetry criticism. Apart from oceanic dedifferentiation, he found that these terms are also highly illuminating of what Bergson calls metaphysical intuition. Since I found his discussion most stimulating for my present inquiry, I am going to quote from it at some length.

> What Bergson calls metaphysical intuition is a gestalt-free vision, capable of superimposed perception. Let us hear his own masterful description of surface and depth vision:

> "When I direct my attention inward to contemplate my own self [...] I perceive at first, as a crust solidified at the surface, all the perceptions which come to it from the material world. These perceptions are clear, distinct, juxtaposed or juxtaposable one with another; they tend to group themselves into objects. [...] But if I draw myself in from the periphery towards the centre [...] I find an altogether different thing. There is beneath these sharply cut crystals and this frozen surface a continuous flux which is not comparable to any flux I have ever seen. There is a succession of states each of which announces that which follows and contains that which pre-

cedes it. In reality no one begins or ends, but all extend into each other"
(Ehrenzweig, 1965: 34–35).

Bergson recognises that juxtaposition is essential for surface perception, but not
for depth perception. He gives a practical recipe to achieve intuition: he recommends
one to visualise at the same time a diversity of objects in superimposition.

> "By choosing images as dissimilar as possible, we shall prevent any one of
> them from usurping the place of the intuition it is intended to call up, since
> it would then be driven away at once by its rivals. By providing that, in
> spite of their differences of aspects, they all require from the mind the same
> kind of attention [...] we shall gradually accustom consciousness to a
> particular and clearly defined disposition" (ibid.).

It seems quite clear that while it is possible "to visualise at the same time a
diversity of objects in superimposition", it is impossible to imagine a diversity of
verbal expressions in superimposition. All verbal expressions are received in succession, "in juxtaposition". One remedy for this state of affairs would be "to visualise
at the same time the diversity of objects" denoted by the phrases of the text "in
superimposition". This, however, would hardly be consistent with the process of
speech reception. Another possible remedy, more consistent with the conception of
the poem as a verbal artefact, would be that the information conveyed by the
succession of phrases of the catalog may, under certain conditions, result in a
cognitive overload on the reader's processing space; in such a case, one might
assume, the reader is compelled to handle this information by collapsing it into an
undifferentiated mass (very much in the manner in which perceptual overload is
handled by "dumping" the excess of perceptual information into an undifferentiated
background mass). Given the conceptual and sequential nature of language, the latter
is a difficult achievement. Let me elaborate this issue at some length.

Following William Empson, literary criticism in the English-speaking world was
dominated for decades by ambiguity-hunting in poetry. My own work is no
exception. But here a crucial distinction must be added. The rival meanings may
interact in two opposite ways. They may vie for dominance, so as to establish
themselves in the reader's perception; as a result, each one is perceived more clearly,
frequently yielding a sharp, witty effect, as in Metaphysical poetry. Or, they may
blur each other, yielding a relatively undifferentiated mass, as, in extreme cases, in
Symbolist or Impressionist poetry. Art historians imported the terms "soft" and
"sharp" focus from optics (indicating thereby that we are up against a perceptual
phenomenon). Renaissance, Baroque and Romantic painting, for instance, display
soft focus. I have borrowed these terms from art history, and applied them to poetry,
later changing them into "split" and "integrated" focus. In an essay, "The Structure
of Figurative Language in Shakespeare's Sonnets", Arthur Mizener (1964) provides
an illuminating linguistic description of the phenomenon (by way of the line "If my

dear love were but the child of state"). He discusses over seven meanings of the word "state" in the context of the sonnet.

> Nothing, I think, could show more clearly than these three lines the difference between Shakespeare's figurative language and that of a metaphysical poem. For no single one of the meanings of *state* will these lines work out completely, nor will the language allow any one of the several emergent figures to usurp[2] our attention; it thus becomes impossible to read the lines at all without making an effort to keep all the meanings of state, all the emergent figures, in view at once. That is, the purpose is to make the reader see them all, simultaneously, in soft focus; and the method is to give the reader just enough of each figure for this purpose (142).

This provides, I believe, an operational description of how "a cognitive overload on the reader's processing space" may be generated in poetry. Now, as I said, not all ambiguity results in soft focus; some of it results in sharp focus, the metaphysical pun, for instance. What are, then, the conditions in which ambiguity results in soft focus? I will mention three of them. The first two were implied by Mizener's discussion: first, the greater the number of meanings, the more it is likely that "the language [will not] allow any one of the several emergent figures to usurp our attention"; and second, "the purpose is to make the reader see them all, *simultaneously*". I am adding a third condition, that the imagery should not have recourse to stable objects with well-differentiated boundaries, which might resist fusion.

So, there is yet another efficient technique to generate a fluid perception, to present the universe in "flux". In chapters 3, 5 & 7 we have distinguished between two kinds of space perception: shape perception and orientation. The former presents the consciousness with clear-cut, stable visual shapes, with well-differentiated boundaries, clearly separating the things and shapes from one another. Orientation, by contrast, consists of a stream of fluctuating, undifferentiated, ever-changing information lumping together a variety of sensory inputs. Now Bergson characterises percepts in "surface perception" as "clear, distinct, juxtaposed or juxtaposable one with another; they tend to group themselves into objects". The stable boundaries between differentiated shapes and objects are essential for juxtaposition. The poet may resort to verbal techniques which suspend in one way or another the boundaries between objects so as to prevent the objects from exerting resistance; and to some other techniques that would encourage them to extend into each other. Overload might be one of them.[3]

---

2   Notice that both Bergson and Mizener use the verb "usurp", for exactly the same purpose.

3   Indeed, in the psychological laboratory, two major ASC [Altered States of consciousness]-induction procedures have been found, those of perceptual overload [...] and perceptual deprivation (Glicksohn, 1989: 12). Perceptual deprivation will be discussed in chapter 6.

An Ancient Merkabah Hymn;

Gershom Scholem wrote in "Merkabah Mysticism and Jewish Gnosticism" that the first phase in the development of Jewish mysticism is also the longest. Its literary remains are traceable over a period of almost a thousand years, from the first century B.C. to the tenth A.D. (Scholem, 1961: 40). Most of the tracts are called "Hekhaloth Books", i.e., descriptions of the *hekhaloth,* the heavenly halls or palaces through which the visionary passes and in the seventh and last of which there rises the throne of divine glory (Scholem, 1961: 45). "There is little hope that we shall ever learn the true identity of the men who were the first to make an attempt, still recognizable and describable, to invest Judaism with the glory of mystical splendor" (ibid, 41).

> The Greater Hekhaloth presents us with a large number of Hebrew hymns, which it treats in an unusual manner: the very same hymns are characterized by the text as representing two different types of songs. On the one hand, the hymns are addressed to the throne and to Him who sits upon it, and are described as celestial songs of praise sung by "the Holy Living Creatures" *(Ḥayyoth ha-Kodɛš)* who, in Ezekiel 1:5 ff., are the bearers of the throne. On the other hand, these same hymns are the ones the mystic is instructed to recite before and during his ecstatic ascent to heaven (which, in a very curious and so far unexplained change of phraseology, is always referred to in this text as a *descent* unto the Merkabah). The hymns describe, in a plethora of solemn phrases, the spirit of majesty and solemnity that permeates the heavenly realm, "the Palaces of Silence" in which God's Shekhinah dwells (Scholem, 1960: 20).

Before turning to the poetic text itself, I propose to perform two short semantic exercises concerning two phrases in the last sentence of this paragraph: "the Palaces of Silence" and "God's Shekhinah". A Palace is a large, impressive and majestic building of imposing magnificence; it is usually the official residence of a sovereign, bishop, or other exalted personage. A huge hall of a palace casts on the perceiver self-specifying information that makes him feel extremely small (precisely that appears to be the reason why ancient sovereigns chose such buildings for residence and elevated thrones for seats: to inspire their subjects awe). Great silence may reinforce such a feeling. "Palaces of Silence" may then suggest real palaces dominated by great silence, casting self-specifying information of smallness. As we have argued at great length in Chapter 4, it is the orientation mechanism that handles such self-specifying information, involving a ready integration of many inputs at once and producing a diffuse output. This has an intense nonrational effect which, when heightened, generates a quality similar to altered states of consciousness, such as meditation and mystic experience. However, in a figurative construal

"Silence" may be the referring expression. In this case, the conflicting terms of the metaphor delete such physical and visual features of "palaces" as [+STABLE SHAPE], transferring to "silence" such features as <+IMPRESSIVE +MAJESTIC +IMPOSING MAGNIFICENCE +SELF-SPECIFYING SPATIAL INFORMATION>. The result is the intense but diffuse presence of an engulfing thing-free and gestalt-free quality.

Scholem sometimes uses the Hebrew term "God's *Shekhinah*" in the English text. But in one of the hymns (Scholem, 1960: 21), for instance, he translates "Shekhinat ha-Shekhinah" as "the presence of Presence". The nickname "Presence" for "God" can be accounted for by two Chomskian transformations of such an expression as "God is present": the adjective is turned into an abstract noun, and manipulated into the referring position of the phrase. I have called this stylistic device *Thematised Predicate*, or *Topicalised Attribute*. The phrase "presence of Presence" reflects a double transformation of this kind. This device is most widespread when conceptual language is required to convey a nonconceptual experience such as altered states of consciousness, meditative, mystic or ecstatic. In poetry, thing-destruction and thing-free or gestalt-free qualities readily contribute to the impression of such an experience.[4] In Crashaw's poem below there is an instance of this device, in the line "To drowne the *wantonnesse of* this wilde thirst". In Baudelaire's poem there is another one: "le goût de l'éternel", and some more in Gryphius' and Wordsworth's sonnets in Chapter 5. I have elsewhere shown at great length that this is one of the most effective stylistic devices that distinguish Whitman's "meditative catalogue" from his "illustrative catalogue" (Tsur, 1992: 416–428).

In chapter 4 of his book, Scholem provides three short texts which, he claims, are outstanding paradigms of what Rudolf Otto called "Numinous Hymns" (1960: 21–22). I reproduce and briefly discuss one of them here:

> 3.   From the praise and song of each day,
> From the jubilation and exultation of each hour,
> And from the utterances which proceed[5] out of the mouth of the holy ones,
> And from the melody which welleth out of the mouth of the Servants,
> Mountains of fire and hills of flame
> Are piled up and hidden and poured out each day.

As Scholem insisted, nearly nothing is known about the origins of this poetry. One remarkable thing about it is that already its earliest known representatives are frozen into rigid formulae. There are, for instance, long catalogs of songs and

---

4   The fact that *Shekhina* is so frequently personified supports my contention that a quality of intense thing-free presence is hard to tolerate. The phrase "presence of Presence" compels the reader to face this difficulty.

5   The grammatical form of the Hebrew verbs for "proceed" and "welleth forth" is more like the present participle than a finite verb.

praises; and most visible things are described as made of fire and flames. We know almost nothing about the people who wrote these poems; even less do we know about their psychodynamic or cognitive processes. In Chapter 8 we took up one of Ehrenzweig's many illuminating insights, concerning the origin and evolution of artistic ornaments and fossilised formulae. Ehrenzweig claims that ornaments and frozen formulae in the arts result from the application of defence mechanisms against artistic devices that have too much expressive power.[6] The reiteration of rigid formulae is meant to have a strong hypnotic effect. That, indeed, may be the case for the initiated. However, as I argued in the chapter "Poem, Prayer, and Meditation", the uninvolved outsider, the *reader of poetry,* may need much more in order to detect in the poem the kind of devotional experience felt by the initiated. As for this specific hymn, I will argue that when it switches from one rigid formula to another, from the reiteration of "praise and song" to the reiteration of "Mountains of fire and hills of flame", an overwhelming feeling of oceanic dedifferentiation may suddenly be experienced.

Certainty and Uncertainty

In my earlier works I discussed at great length "obtrusive rhythms" in syllabo-tonic verse that generate what Snyder has called "hypnotic", or "spell-weaving", or "trance-inductive" poetry.[7] (In chapter 7 I argued that a very regular rhythm induces security, and may have several kinds of effect: that of a simplified mastery of reality (as in nursery rhymes); or a rational-witty effect (as in the neo-classical couplet), or a hypnotic effect (as in Poe and Coleridge). In the former two the security induced is "genuine", reinforced on the stanza level as well as on the syntactic and rhetorical levels. In the latter, the security induced is "false". In the "hypnotic" poems security was generated by obtrusive rhythms reinforced on the metrical, syntactic and thematic levels; in quite a few of them cairtain rigid formulae were also reiterated. At the same time, insecurity was generated by an irregularity on the stanza level, or by a syntactic arrest. This "false" security seems to be required for relinquishing rational control when facing some of the most irrational experiences in poetry. In two of the

---

[6]   In a Hebrew paper (Tsur and Eynath-Nov, forthcoming) we claim that the frozen formulae of the Merkabah hymns became even more rigidly formalised in later mediaeval poetry. In the light of Ehrenzweig's hypothesis, the rigid formulae of this poetry may still have had too much expressive power for the later poets.

[7]   In English poetry I discussed Coleridge's "Kubla Khan" (Tsur, 1987a) and works by Blake, Wordsworth and Poe (1992a: 431–454; see above, chapters 1 and 7); in Hebrew poetry I discussed Alterman, Ratosh and Strauss (Tsur, 1988); in Hungarian poetry, Babits and Kosztolányi (Tsur, 1994). In chapter 4 above we suggested that altered states of consciousness such as meditative and hypnotic states presuppose "high absorption", that is, a propensity to adopt an "experiential" rather than an "instrumental" set. In Glicksohn et al. (1991) we report an experiment which demonstrates that high-absorption readers responded to a hypnotic poem, as expected, differently from low-absorption readers.

texts discussed in the present chapter we find strikingly similar techniques of incantatory reiteration coupled with a syntactic arrest outside syllabo-tonic verse, in a Merkabah hymn and in a Baudelaire poem. In the Merkabah hymn quoted above there seems to be a significant interaction between the two reiterated formulae mentioned in the preceding paragraph. The rigid, formulaic reiteration of "praise and song" would be meaningless without the ensuing feeling of oceanic dedifferentiation; but this feeling could not be "overwhelming" were it not preceded by some incantatory reiteration.[8]

The first four lines are different at the immediately observable level, but synonymous on a higher level: they all contain expressions of glorification. This structure directs attention to the common elements, *away* from the individuating elements, of each line. Syntactically, all are parallel prepositional phrases, introduced by "from". There is also some extra parallelism within each pair of lines. This excessive repetition has a magical, incantatory effect. The first two lines offer smaller-scale repetitions as well. The first line contains two parallel nouns that suggest glorification: "praise and song". The second line, too, has two parallel nouns that suggest ecstatic joy: "jubilation and exultation". The Hebrew phrase translated as "each day" literally says "day and day"; the phrase translated as "each hour" literally says "times and times". Such an incantatory device may have some limited quasi-hypnotic effect, but in itself it would be insufficient for evoking an ecstatic quality. The "descenders unto the Mercabah" claim that in their adventures they encounter great dangers. This straightforward, obtrusive rhythm gives some security to the "Platonic censor" in us. But there is a syntactic device in this hymn (shared, *mutatis mutandis,* with the first stanza of the Baudelaire poem below) that makes this rhythm less "straightforward", rendering the security "false". The four-times-reiterated preposition "from" generates *suspense* in two different senses: "holding in an undetermined or undecided state awaiting further information", and "mental uncertainty, anxiety". The parallel prepositional phrases do generate a straightforward rhythm; but, by the same token, they impede the straightforward movement of the sentence, delaying the predicate required for clarifying its structure. In fact, the subject phrase causes an additional delay, and the predicate "piled up" (syntactically but not semantically predicted by the prepositional phrases) occurs only in the last line.[9]

When I first read Scholem's book thirty years ago, I had a strong intuition that after the four incantatory lines there was a switch to some overwhelming quality that powerfully engulfed me. At that time I couldn't account for it. Today I know that it had to do with the dynamics of oceanic dedifferentiation. The last two lines, contain-

8   In Chapter 4 we quote Newberg et al. (2001: 87) to the effect that "These slow rhythmic behaviors stimulate the quiescent [parasympathetic] system, which, when pushed to very high levels, directly activates the inhibitory effects of the hippocampus", eventually depriving the orientation area of information "and, ultimately, blurring the edges of the brain's sense of self".

9   In other works I demonstrated at great length similar structural devices (that induce certainty and uncertainty at the same time) in what Snyder called "hypnotic", or "spell-weaving", or "trance-inductive" poetry.

ing the subject and the predicate phrases, also shift the poetic strategy of the hymn. "Fire" and "flame" in the last-but-one line continue the pattern of obtrusive reiteration. But, by the same token, they introduce a gestalt-free, unstable, threatening entity, radiating excessive energy. From the figurative point of view, the genitive phrases "Mountains of fire and hills of flame" may be construed similarly to the genitive phrase "Palaces of Silence". When "fire" is the referring member of the phrase, "Mountains" suggests "enormous mass"; the feature [+STABILITY] is deleted.[10] However, "Mountains" and "hills" reinforce in each other their literal meaning; when they are the referring members, they indicate a vast landscape to which the perceiving self may relate itself, activating the orientation mechanism. The three parallel verb phrases "[are] piled up and hidden and poured out" not only recapitulate the incantatory effect: the contrast between the absence of finite verbs in the first five verses and the sudden pile-up of three consecutive finite verbs in the last verse introduces much movement; by the same token, the meaning of the verbs indicates intense fluctuation of a stable scenery. "Poured out" is associated with liquids (in fact, the Hebrew verb suggests both pouring and alteration from a solid to a liquid state, usually by heat); and the sequence as a whole subverts, as it were, the surrounding landscape with its self-specifying information. The landscape itself is unstable: it comes into existence, disappears and reappears.

Finally, the whole presentation has an interesting existential aspect. The syntactic agents ("holy ones", "Servants") are conspicuously inactive. It is the praise, the song, the jubilation, the exultation, the utterances, the melody that are active, that display a voluntary or spontaneous impulse to act, employing "linguistic devices that shift the [agent] to a non-volitional role" (cf. Balaban, 1999: 259). The praise, the song, the jubilation, the exultation, the utterances, the melody happen, as it were, of themselves.[11] Such a consistent syntactic strategy indicates a suspension of voluntary control. Now "Mountains of fire and hills of flame", as we have said, serve as referential terms for the self's orientation; but, at the same time, they have no objective existence at all: they issue from, or their pile-up is caused by, the praise, the song, the jubilation, the exultation, the utterances, the melody, which, in turn, issue *from the mouth of* the agents.

;

[10] Leo Spitzer argued that the plural has a contour-blurring effect.

[11] In chapter 4 we quoted Tellegen's distinction between experiential and instrumental set. In the former set, "experiences have a quality of effortlessness, as if they happened by themselves, and in that sense, of involuntariness". Recent neuropsychological studies of altered states of consciousness throw interesting light on such depersonalization. Michael A. Persinger (1987) claims that God experiences (as well as some pathological conditions) are associated with *temporal lobe transients,* which are electrical perturbations of the temporal lobe in the human brain (16). A characteristic of such states "is an alteration in the description of the self. Depersonalization is typical" (Persinger, 1987: 18).

Crashaw's Fluid Universe

Richard Crashaw's poem, "Our Lord in his Circumcision to his Father" *(Poems,* 98-99), offers another illuminating example of generating a fluid universe:

4.   To thee these first fruits of my growing death
        (For what else is my life?) lo I bequeath.
        Tast this, and as them lik'st this lesser flood
        Expect a Sea, my heart shall make it good.
        Thy wrath that wades here now, e're long shall swim
        The flood-gate shall be set wide ope for him.
        Then let him drinke, and drinke, and doe his worst,
        To drowne the wantonnesse of this wilde thirst.
        Now's but the Nonage of my pains, my feares
        Are yet but in their hopes, not come to years.

        The day of my dark woes is yet but morne,
        My tears but tender and my death new-borne.
        But may these unfleg'd griefs give fate some guesse,
        These Cradle-torments have their towardness.
        These purple buds of blooming death may bee,
        Erst the full stature of a fatall tree.
        And till my riper woes to age are come,
        This knife may be the speares *Preludium.*

There are only six nouns in this poem that denote objects with stable characteristic visual shapes: "flood-gate, Cradle, buds, tree, knife, speares"; the rest denote thing-free or gestalt-free entities: abstract nouns, psychological abstractions and fluids. The semantic field of fluids looms large in the first stanza: "flood; Sea; wades; swim; flood-gate; drinke and drinke; drowne; thirst", generating a psychological atmosphere of fluid objects and lack of boundaries. You cannot juxtapose two liquids, unless they are in containers with stable boundaries. Otherwise they mingle and loose their identity as in excerpt 1. There is another salient semantic domain, which may perhaps be described as "growing, coming of age". These are processes that do not consist of discrete stages, but of "a succession of states each of which announces that which follows and contains that which precedes it. In reality no one begins or ends, but all extend into each other". Related to this domain there is another group of words (as we shall see, highly functional), which in one way or other denote beginning: "first fruits; Nonage; morne; tender; new-borne; unfleg'd; Cradle; not come to years". An interesting variant of this is the phrase "in their hopes", here meaning "in their prime", but yielding an oxymoron with "feares". These words indicate the tender age of the baby Christ, but join the oxymora that blend beginning and end.

   Another conspicuous semantic field belongs to trees. One aspect of trees is "growing"; they have their "buds" and "fruits", they "bloom", too. But they also have stable characteristic visual shapes. The phrase "fatall tree" becomes, in a very important sense, the crux of the poem. It is very much like the notorious Neo-classical poetic diction, a stock phrase with a stock epithet serving, conspicuously, as a periphrasis for some object. However, when we try to figure out what the referent of this stock phrase is, we are faced with two equally plausible, even equally obvious referents: the "tree of knowledge", that is, "that forbidden tree whose mortal taste brought death into our world", and the cross on which Christ was to die. Even the word "mortall" suggests here two fairly different meanings: causing death, and resembling fate in proceeding in a fixed sequence, determining one's fate. The meaning "causing death" applies to both referents, but in quite different senses. The meaning "proceeding in a fixed sequence" applies to the fate of Christ's, who was predestined to be crucified. And, perhaps, it applies to the forbidden tree, too: if there were no original sin, there could be no redemption, either. The conflict of stable visual shapes, of the forbidden tree and the cross, is backgrounded: we are not presented with the different objects, but with a stock phrase that refers to both. Thus, to paraphrase Bergson's words, "the beginning and the end extend into each other" (the beginning of the human race, and Christ's end; original sin, and redemption therefrom).

Neo-Classicist critics such as Joseph Addison would have deplored this kind of solution as "false wit": it relies on a resemblance of words, not ideas. As I argued in many of my publications, bad classicism can be excellent Metaphysical poetry; in our case, it may yield a remarkable metaphysical pun. Notwithstanding, this "false wit" does not sound here as a witty Metaphysical pun. There seem to be two quite different reasons for that. First, there is a theological system behind this pun, a system of *types,* that is, a person or thing (as in the Old Testament) believed to foreshadow another (as in the New Testament). This underlying system appears to justify the pun and integrate the focus of perception: the forbidden tree "prefigures" the cross, just as the knife prefigures the spear. Second, this verbal pun that conceals conflicting visual shapes is embedded in a fluid, gestalt-free and sometimes thing-free context, which prepares the readers to accommodate it in a soft focus. What is more, the underlying theme of the whole poem is that "the beginning and the end extend into each other". This idea is repeated in a wide range of images; but, not as with the cross and the forbidden tree, in the other instances this is illustrated by images that have no conflicting characteristic visual shapes, no rigid boundaries that resist fusion.

According to Aristotle's conception, the acorn already contains the grown oak; likewise, the bud already contains the bloom; the oak and the bloom are the full realisation (entelecheia) of the acorn and the bud, respectively. In this way the beginning (the bud) contains the end (the bloom). The phrase "blooming death" foregrounds two of the meanings of "blooming": supporting abundant life—yielding a powerful oxymoron; and maturing into the achievement of one's potential—realising the "entelecheia" process. "Purple bud" may be understood literally, suggesting the natural hue of the bud, but it may also suggest majesty. Above all, it may act as a "simple replacement", as a periphrasis, for blood. In this case, "bud" serves, syntactically, as the referring noun of the phrase; but, figuratively, it qualifies "purple", i.e., the phrase suggests something purple that is not yet mature or at full develop-ment. Now blood may be spilt at the circumcision as well as at the crucifiction; in Chrstian theology, the former blood is the *type* of the latter. However, unlike the cross and the tree of knowledge, or the knife and the spear, blood is a liquid, and has no stable visual shape or rigid boundaries: the two bloods may mix imperceptibly. Again, the beginning and the end are inseparably blended.

"Bud" connotes, then, beginning; "blooming"—a *full-blown* state but also *pros-perity,* yielding an oxymoron: "blooming death". This oxymoron runs through the poem, e.g., "these first fruits of my growing death", or "my feares / Are yet but in their hopes", and so on. "In their hopes" means "in their first stages" (as opposed to "the full stature" in line 16); ironically, it suggests here *hopelessness:* "the more I grow, my fears grow with me, and my death draws nearer". But there is more to it: Christ's birth and circumcision get their very significance from his death; they are, in fact, necessary preparations for that supreme moment of *fulfilment.* Thus, the moments of the two extremes are telescoped into one mysterious vision. Another implication is strongly emphasised throughout the poem: Christ's tragic fate. Un-like other children—from his very infancy, every act and event of his life is but pre-paration for torture and death.

In lines 15–16, then, there are two concrete nouns which are, in general, associ-ated with characteristic shapes, and are metonymically related to each other: buds and tree. Two other nouns are abstract: death and stature. This sparing framework sug-gests a greater than usual range of meanings which *must* be realised; otherwise the poem remains meaningless and falls apart. Since there are many important rival—sometimes contradictory—implications of which characteristic shapes form a negligible part, or clash with one another, three important effects result: (1) there is here a very soft focus (indeed, almost "smeared"); (2) the clashing shapes and meanings of high importance produce high tension and evoke intense emotional response; (3) utterly incompatible things are viewed as a shapeless whole, in an impassioned state of mind—a mystic truth is glimpsed.

Viewed against the background of Christian myth, "blooming death" may refer not only to Christ's future death, but also to the present state of death of fallen hu-manity, from which it is to be delivered by Christ's death. In this context, "fatall tree" is a periphrasis for two extremes of one all-important process, of the fall and redemption: the forbidden tree and the cross. The buds and blooms of death, too, are then related with both trees. In this light we should now consider lines 5–6. "Wrath" is no mere psychological abstraction here, but, remembering that it is God's Wrath, it is an all-powerful, thing-free, disembodied force. It introduces the numinous qual-ity into this poem.

> The referring of this feeling of numinous tremor to its object in the numen
> brings into relief a property of the latter which plays an important part in
> our Holy Scriptures, and which has been the occasion of many difficulties,
> both to commentators and to theologians, from its puzzling and bafffing na-

ture. This is the örgé, the Wrath of Yahweh, which recurs in the New Testament [...], and which is clearly analogous to the idea occurring in many religions of a mysterious *ira deorum*. [...] But as regards the "wrath of Yahweh", the strange features about it have for long been a matter for constant remark. In the first place, it is patent from many passages of the Old Testament that this "wrath" has no concern whatever with moral qualities. There is something very baffling in the way in which it "is kindled" and manifested. It is, as has been well said, "like a hidden force of nature", like stored-up electricity, discharging itself upon anyone who comes too near. It is "incalculable" and "arbitrary" (Otto, 1959: 32).

"Wades", then, is ironical in some respect as a predicate for "Thy wrath": it connotes physical difficulty. By the same token, however, it connotes energetic beginning, or proceeding slowly. There are two contrasts involved in this couplet, upsetting proportions. One contrast is between "wades" and "swim". The former verb suggests "walking with labour and difficulty through substance impeding motion"; the latter one suggests "moving along through a liquid substance, while the raising flood *carries one away*". The former appeals to the motor sense mainly, the latter—both to the motor sense and a smooth sensation on the whole skin.

"Wades" connotes also *mud,* as opposed to "the flood-gate . . . wide ope". This indicates further a contrast between the flood and the few drops of circumcision blood. Now, it is worth noticing that "wrath" is and is not identified with "blood" at one and the same time. *Blood* is, traditionally, a metonymy for *anger*. According to line 5, *wrath* "e're long shall swim", but in line 6 the image is imperceptibly fused into another image: "The flood-gate shall be set wide ope *for him"*—wrath is not personified as it has been, *swimming* in the flood; now it *is* a flood, shapeless, rising, threatening.

There is much to say about the passionate, excessive Baroque quality of this poem, compelling a soft focus on the powerful oxymora—the skeleton of this poem—rather than letting them split the focus in Metaphysical wit. I want only to point out that the overwhelming flood image helps to establish—among other things—a fluid, *shapeless* universe, evoking an impassioned, receptive attitude rather than an actively organising intelligence (in the Metaphysical fashion). Drinking and thirst are associated with formless liquid, also with the relatively low-differentiated gustatory sense, with craving and with passive *taking in*. No wonder, then, that some of Crashaw's best mystic poetry combines oxymoron and imagery of liquid things, abolishing the tough control of the conscious mind, and sometimes arousing intense passions that "drowne" all consciousness and geometric shapes, offering a glimpse into unknown things, in a moment of self-oblivion.

Finally, I wish to make a few microstructural observations on lines 7–8: I will scrutinise an instance of syntactic transformation, and examine some prosodic structures, in an attempt to understand their contribution to the fluid, gestalt-free universe of the poem. "Drowne" can be associated with "drinke" and "flood" in the preceding lines. After "doe his worst" its distructive power is emphasized. "Wantonnesse" and "wilde" emphasize the tremendous intensity of *thirst*. "To drowne", apart from indicating excess, creates high metaphoric tension by joining a concrete vehicle with an abstract term. It applies a concrete verb to an abstract object. The tension has been heightened by a device which elsewhere (Tsur, 1987b: 128–143; 1992: 421–428; see above, chapter 5) I have called *Thematised Predicate,* or *Topicalised Attribute* (a device more familiar from the mid-nineteenth century on). "Wantonnesse" ought to have been an attribute of "thirst", e.g., "wild, wanton thirst". Through the processes of *nominalisation* and *thematisation* "wantonnesse" is manipulated into the referring position, and so it is an abstraction from an abstraction that is to be drowned by the concrete flood.[12] This device is most widespread when (conceptual) language is required to convey a non-conceptual experience such as altered states of consciousness, meditative, mystic or ecstatic. In poetry, thing-destruction and thing-free or gestalt-free qualities readily contribute to the impression of such an experience.

Couplets are symmetrical prosodic structures, and as such have an exceptionally strong prosodic shape. In this poem they may serve to balance and to "hold together" the fluid universe discussed above. Notwithstanding this, they are softened to a considerable extent by conflicts between sentence and verse structure. I will resist the temptation to discuss the various degrees of enjambment and their effects, and will concentrate only on one illuminating case. The cumulation of verbs in the line "Then let him drinke, and drinke, and doe his worst", foregrounded by the polysyndeton, may impress the reader as a gradation of mounting intenseness. In another manuscript of the poem, the line runs (according to the Oxford edition):

     5.   Then shall he drinke: and drinke shall doe his worst

From the metrical point of view, the changes are very slight: "shall he" has been changed into "let him", and "shall doe" into "and doe". Yet the other version strikes us as more balanced, more stable. Although the line is divided into two parts of unequal length, it nevertheless strikes the reader as symmetrical; this impression is enhanced by a paratactic structure, the symmetry of syntactc parts, and the occurrence of "drinke" in both clauses (once as a verb, once as a noun). The accepted version, with its gradation of verbs and hortatory "let", seems to enhance the fluidity, the irrational sweep of Baroque excess in the poem.

This comparison between the two versions of this line points up an interesting prosodic aspect of its perceived fluidity. As I have argued elsewhere at great length (for instance, Tsur, 1992a: 134–139; 1998: 118–123), verse lines that contain more than seven ("plus or minus two") metrical positions must be divided into two equal

---

[12] "Topicalised Attribute" is fairly widespread in our corpus in widely different cultural traditions, because it solves a linguistic-cognitive problem. Ehrenzweig speaks of "thing-destruction" in the arts; but in poetry, words can denote only compact things and concepts. In concrete things and in concepts, the attributes are *grown together*. This stylistic device *abstracts* an attribute from a compact thing or concept and, by manipulating it into the referring position, the attribute gains some independent existence.

parts for a clear-cut perception. Unlike the iambic tetrameter (4 + 4 positions) and the iambic hexameter (6 + 6 positions), the iambic pentameter cannot be divided into two parts of equal length and equal structure. If we divide it into 5 + 5, we obtain one part that begins and ends with a weak position; and another part that begins and ends with a strong position. Alternatively, we can obtain parts that both begin with a weak position and end with a strong position, if we divide the line into 4 + 6, or 6 + 4. For excellent cognitive reasons, when no preference interferes, of two parallel entities the longer must come last (consider, for instance, some of the names of the categories and sub-categories in the Yahoo portal: Arts & Humanities, Business & Economy, News & Media, Chats and Forums, Finance and Investment).[13] Thus, the 4 + 6 division is the more natural, "unmarked" one. When we read the line "Then let him drinke, and drinke, and doe his worst" in sequence, two alternative mental performances are available. If the words "drinke, and drinke" are grouped together as one perceptual unit, the end of the phrase confirms a caesura after the sixth position, resulting in a "marked", less natural division. If, however, the reader receives the words in sequence, not knowing that "drinke" will be doubled, the major syntactic juncture following the unit "Then let him drinke," effectively confirms the caesura after the fourth position. When he realises that "drinke" is redoubled, he must reopen the already closed perceptual unit, generating a sense of perceptual fluidity. In the alternative version of the verse line, the end of the first clause (marked by a semicolon) unambiguously confirms the caesura after position 4, generating a sense of symmetry and stable balance. This sense is reinforced by the resulting coordinate sentences.

We have followed the process of generating a fluid universe in this poem. We have observed the stylistic strategies by which the text smoothly fuses the beginning and the end, while avoiding stable boundaries of the fused images. There is one conspicuous instance in which this principle of gestalt-free qualities is blatantly violated: "This knife may be the speares *Preludium*". Here, "knife" and "spear" have stable characteristic visual shapes; what is more, they have different sizes and shapes, and smooth fusion becomes impossible. Now this "blatant violation" does not infringe upon the stylistic character of the poem; quite the contrary, in fact. The fluid sequence leads up to a stable point. Since this point occurs at the end of the sequence, it does not *disturb,* but *organises* it; it serves as what Barbara Herrnstein-Smith calls "poetic closure". Now even this stability is not completely conclusive; the text undermines it to some extent. One typical thematic device for closure is "closural allusion": the occurrence of some such word as "end" or "death" in the last line. In this poem, on the contrary, the last word is *Preludium*.[14]

[13] Thes examples have been collected by Motti Benari, replacing some of my more conservative examples.

[14] I have not invented these possibilities for saving this specific interpretation of this specific poem. This is, for instance, how the typical Miltonic passage works, though in Milton's poetry both fluidity and stability are achieved by prosodic rather than thematic means (cf. Tsur, 1992a: 148–153; 1998: 243–265). In many sonnets, too, that is the function of the concluding couplet (see, for instance, Baudelaire's

Oceanic Dedifferentiation in Baudelaire's Spiritual and Sensuous Love
Baudelaire's "HYMNE"—Cliché or Masterpiece?

6.   A la très-chère, à la très-belle
       Qui remplit mon cœur de clarté
       A l'ange, à l'idole immortelle,
       Salut en immortalité!

       Elle se répand dans ma vie
       Comme un air imprégné de sel
       Et dans mon âme inassouvie
       Verse le goût de l'éternel.

       Sachet toujours frais qui parfume
       L'atmosphère d'un cher réduit,
       Encensoir oublié qui fume
       En secret à travers la nuit,

       Comment, amour incorruptible,
       T'exprimer avec vérité?
       Grain de musc qui gis, invisible,
       Au fond de mon Éternité!

       A la très-bonne, à la très-belle
       Qui fait ma joie et ma santé
       A l'ange, à l'idole immortelle,
       Salut en immortalité!

To the very dear, to the very beautiful (one) / Who fills my heart with light, / to the Angel, to the immortal idol, / Greetings in immortality!

She pervades my life / Like air impregnated with salt / And into my insatiable soul / Pours the taste of the eternal.

Sachet always fresh that perfumes / The atmosphere of a dear recess, / Forgotten censer that smokes / Secretly through the night,

How to express you truly, / Incorruptible love? / Grain of musk lying invisibly, / At the bottom of my Eternity!

To the very good, to the very beautiful (one) / Who gives my joy and my health, / to the Angel, to the immortal idol, / Greetings in immortality!

"Correspondance"—Tsur, 1992a: 455–470). As for the poetic sabotage of the closure, Herrnstein-Smith devoted an entire chapter to "anti-closure".

This poem (HYMNE) is on the boundary of the cheap cliché and the masterpiece. The masterpiece seems to do to cheap clichés what, according to Sir John Davies quoted by Coleridge on imagination, the spirit does to bodies.

> 7.   Doubtless this could not be but that she turns
>   Bodies to *spirit* by sublimation strange,
>   As fire converts to fire the things it burns,
>   As we our food into our nature change.

The ensuing close reading will attempt to substantiate this claim; in so doing, I will draw liberally upon the theoretical framework expounded above. The import of some of the key expressions in the first and last stanza can simply be looked up in the dictionary: "très-chère", "très-belle", "très-bonne" are unqualified praises, single-minded superlatives attributed by the least-sophisticated lovers to the objects of their desire. In a religious context, ANGEL means a spiritual being, or celestial attendant of God; IDOL means a deity other than God. In the context of love poetry, the relevant meaning of ANGEL suggests, according to the *Random House College Dictionary,* a person who performs acts of great kindness, or whose actions and acts are undeviatingly virtuous; the relevant meaning of IDOL suggests any person or thing excessively or devotedly admired. According to *Le Petit Robert,* ANGE means a perfect person; IDOLE means a person or thing that is the object of some kind of adoration. As compared to these clichés, the clichés of Petrarcan love poetry are highly sophisticated poetic expressions.

The single-mindedness of these expressions is reinforced and, at the same time, greatly qualified by the syntactic and prosodic structure of these two stanzas. There are some conflicting syntactic-prosodic cues in these stanzas. Consider the first line: "A la très-chère, à la très-belle". Prosodically, it is eight syllable long, subdivided into two segments, four syllable long each. Syntactically, the segments contain two parallel phrases. The third line too contains two parallel phrases, beginning with the same function words as those in the first line, but of unequal length. Such short parallel segments reinforced by the anaphora "à la très" may be perceived as hypnotic re-iteration, displaying fast alternation of roughly equal units. This sets the structure underlying the poem's joyful, enthusiastic or ecstatic tone. Such a structure may arouse a feeling of certainty; coupled with the appropriate contents, it may generate a "witty", "joyful", "enthusiastic" or "ecstatic" quality. This straightforward structure, however, is qualified by a typically divergent device, splitting the cognitive processing by syntactic means. The poem begins with a preposition, "à la", repeated four times(!), predicting a predicate ("salut"), which occurs only in the fourth line. In the meantime, the reader goes along with the text, but must still remember the beginning, and bear in mind that the syntactic predictions of the reiterated preposition have not yet been fulfilled. The expected predicate turns out to be an exclamative formula, not a finite verb, that has the psychological atmosphere of greater than usual security, definite direction and patent purpose. The exceptionally long syntactic uncertainty undermines this security, renders it "false security", bestows on it something of the more diffuse kinds of emotion.[15]

Several words in this poem are derived from the domain of religion. Most of them occur in a wider than the religious sense. We have already mentioned the more general meanings of "ange" and "idole". "Hymne", too, means a song of praise to God or a deity, but also suggests a song expressing joy and enthusiasm, celebrating a person or a thing. SALUT in the Judeo-Christian religions and in Buddhism means "eternal bliss"; in the Roman Catholic Church it may refer to several kinds of ceremonies; in this poem it serves as an exclamative formula by which one may wish someone health and prosperity. ENCENSOIR is introduced into the poem for the effects of the odour and smoke of the incense; but, for the same reasons, it is one of the props of religious ceremonies too. "Immortelle, immortalité, l'éternel, Éternité" have meanings with religious connotations. Now all these words are neutral from the aesthetic point of view, and fairly banal as metaphors of love. But when they enter into this poem, they become part of a verbal imitation of a mystic-ecstatic experience, which is the text's aesthetic quality. In other words, in Baudelaire's poem, conceptual language conveys, or evokes in the reader's imagination, an experience that is very far from conceptual.

We have already seen how the straightforward words in the first and last stanza are amplified and diffused by the cognitive processing of the prosodic-syntactic structure. In order to gain a better understanding of the emotive and aesthetic significance of the semantic structure of stanzas 2–4, I will rely on my above discussion of Oceanic Dedifferentiation. In Baudelaire's "Hymne" we do find, indeed, a state of suspension of "the boundaries between self and not-self", in which the speaker feels "released from [his] separate individual existence". The central poetic device for this is what Ehrenzweig calls "thing-destruction" and "shape-destruction". "L'air" and soluble salt in stanza 2 are shape-free substances (salt having *dissolved* and lost its shape). "Vie, âme, le goût, l'éternel" imply a lack of constant shape (abstractions, or liquid and gaseous states), "inassouvie" and "goût" connote taste, whereas line 2 of the stanza

---

[15] A conspicuous English instance of a poem beginning with a preposition is *Paradise Lost*. Here the predicate that governs the initial "of" is "Sing" at the beginning of the sixth line.

> *Of* Man's first disobedience, and the fruit
> Of that forbidden tree, whose mortal taste
> Brought death into our world, and all our woe,
> With loss of Eden, till one greater Man
> Restore us and regain the blissful seat,
> *Sing,* Heav'nly Muse ...

The complex emotional effect of such split attention can readily be seen by contrasting this word order to a more *straightforward* one, in which the preposition follows immediately the verb, as e.g., in "Heav'nly Muse, *Sing / Of* Man's first disobedience, and the fruit ...", etc.

suggests taste and smell. The thinglessness and complete merger of these qualities contribute to the almost ecstatic passion dominant in the poem. "L'éternel" has the force of the sublime, enhanced by "verse"—connoting a powerful action. "Mon âme inassouvie" suggests a powerful craving (for eternity? or for the qualities represented by "elle"?, or for the liquids connoted by "verse" and "inassouvie"?), while the abstract noun eliminates, so to speak, the physical ingredient of the verb "verse". "Le goût de l'éternel", in turn, denotes two abstractions (of different orders), removing, again, the physical ingredient, leaving a supersensuous intense experience.

"Le goût de l'éternel" evokes a feeling of fulfilment and heavenly pleasure, but, again, it is only the taste, not eternity itself, that is poured into the soul (this is, again, a *topicalised attribute*). Taste and scent are less differentiated senses than sight and sound. When we speak of an abstraction or of the domain of a higher sense in terms of a less differentiated one, we foreground a less differentiated aspect of the target domain, inaccessible to straightforward conceptual language. Taste and scent suggest in this poem the immediate experiencing of lowly-differentiated sense information bringing the experiencer into contact with an inaccessible, more real reality (this is the case, as well, in the ensuing stanzas with "Sachet toujours frais", "Encensoir oublié", and "Grain de musc qui gis, invisible, / Au fond de mon Éternité!". Thus, "le goût de l'éternel" presents the imagination with an intuitively perceived, nonconceptual aspect of eternity.

"Elle" refers to a flesh-and-blood woman; "elle se répand" is bound to eliminate her *solid shape,* retaining an idealised, airy *essence* and refreshing quality. The salty air could have spread in "my body" (expanding a fresh and acute awareness of every bit of the body, or bringing life like blood); the speaker could also have said that there is a mystic communion, by fusing *her* and *my* soul. Instead, he uses a metonymic transfer, "dans ma vie", suggesting all these implications; but, in addition, he uses the least concrete relevant noun. It enhances the shapeless, thing-free quality, indispensable for the immediate "melting with emotion", but it has a long-term significance too: "she has changed my life, my very inner self"; "her influence is present in all my actions"; "she *fills* me and my life with meaning". The receptive disposition of the speaker is enhanced by the facts that (1) the activities "se répand" and "verse" are done by "elle", and (2) they mean "expanding" and "pouring *into* ...".

Elsewhere (Tsur, 1992: 299-300) I discuss the use of perfumes and jewels in Mediaeval Hebrew *précieux* poetry, as opposed to metaphysical poetry.

> A possible (extreme) means for creating what may be regarded as "cheap or easy effects" is the use of jewellery, or of sophisticated perfumes as metaphoric vehicles. This we find, typically, in the Mediaeval poetic genre devoted to the triple theme of drinking, love, and the description of the garden in which these activities take place. Pagis (1970: 257), in his study of the poetics of Mediaeval Hebrew secular poetry, says: "The poet neglects many details of reality; on the other hand, he brings up typical details whose metaphoric presentation suggests the luxuries of a refined culture: the odour of blossoming is like rare perfumes, the wine is like a ruby set in

crystal; flowers, too, resemble a variety of gems, the whole garden itself is like rich embroidery or jewels of pure flattened gold". Artistic pleasure typically arises when some emotional or perceptual tension is replaced, or rather resolved, by a structure that induces a feeling of stability. Jewels, rare perfumes, rich embroideries, "gold to airy thinness beat" are paradigms of pleasurable sensations with no need to undergo first the experience of perceptual or emotional tensions.

In a term borrowed from Gombrich (1963: 15) I said that jewels and fragrances provide "direct gratification". Mediaeval poets use perfumes and jewellery to suggest some directly achieved and intense pleasure, to amplify natural sights and odours. Baudelaire, too, has excessively frequent recourse to olfactory imagery; and he, too, uses them to suggest the amplification of sensations. But he goes far beyond this. Consider, for instance, the sestet of his famous programmatic sonnet, "Correspond-ances":[16]

> 8.   Il est des parfums frais comme des chairs d'enfants,
>   Doux comme les hautbois, verts comme les prairies,
>   — Et d'autres, corrompus, riches et triomphants,
>
>   Ayant l'expansion des choses infinies,
>   Comme l'ambre, le musc, le benjoin et l'encens,
>   Qui chantent les transports de l'esprit et des sens.

First, of the three adjectives "corrompus, riches et triomphants" (corrupted, rich and triumphant), the last two could occur in the Mediaeval poets' nature descriptions too; but not the first one. Baudelaire's odours are not only ripe, but sometimes overripe; he indulges not only in direct gratification through pleasurable sensations, but also in painful excesses. In one of the Jeanne Duval poems of sensuous love, "Le Léthé" (see below), he writes:

> 9.   Dans tes jupons remplis de ton parfum
>   Ensevelir ma tête endolorie,
>   Et respirer, comme une fleur flétrie,
>   Le doux relent de mon amour défunt.

Sensuous indulgence for Baudelaire involves corruption too. RELENT means persisting bad odour; "Le doux relent de mon amour défunt" suggests a sophisticated "after-scent" of a no-longer-existing ambivalent emotion; "ét respirer, comme une fleur flétrie" suggests indulgence in such an "after-scent".

---

[16] I have discussed this sonnet at great length elsewhere, emphasising those aspects in it that might be directly relevant to our present discussion (Tsur, 1992a: 455–470).

Second, for Baudelaire (but not for the Mediaeval poets), the olfactory sense is a lowly-differentiated sense;[17] indulgence in it leads to regression from the more rational modes of experiencing the world. In other words, indulgence in odours and perfumes constitutes a regression from rational consciousness in two respects: there is a regression from well-organised gestalts to gestalt-free and thing-free qualities; and from the more differentiated senses (like sight and sound) to a less differentiated one. These sensations are evasive, diffuse, yet exceptionally intense. Third but not least, in Baudelaire the indulgence and regression do not occur for their own sake; they are subordinated to an "altered state of consciousness"; in "Correspondances", for instance, "l'ambre, le musc, le benjoin et l'encens" lead to a peak experience, "Transport of the spirit and the senses"; in "Hymne", exposure to the beloved one leads to a mystic fusion of ego with non-ego.[18]

Now "Hymne" is one of the poems idealising Madame Sabatier, characterised by a pure spiritual attitude; its odours too are pure, fresh and uncorrupted. And its tone, though highly enthusiastic, cannot be said to be "ecstatic". It suggests a more evasive kind of altered state of consciousness, an *attenuated variety* of a peak experience. As I have already suggested, in the second stanza "I" and "she" are turned, through semantic manipulations, into thing-free and gestalt-free entities, experiencing a merger, a "mystic communion", so to speak. Two of the perfumes mentioned in "Correspondances", "le musc" and "l'encens" occur in "Hymne" too. But, again, they undergo certain semantic manipulations. Consider the ambiguity of "atmosphère". In this poem it suggests the air that fills "a dear recess", as well as the dominant mood or emotional tone of some place or a work of art. This ambiguity is not accidental; "atmosphère" is *the* gestalt-free and thing-free quality *par excellence,* that fills all the space around, and whose presence is perceived but one does not know how. The

---

17 This statement should not be construed as support for the intentional fallacy; it does not refer to Baudelaire's or the Mediaeval poets' private fantasies, but to publicly accessible rhetorical manipulations in their poems. Baudelaire's lines "Et respirer, comme une fleur flétrie, / Le doux relent de mon amour défunt", serve to foreground some nameless feature of love that is not immediately associated with its stereotype, and refers to the indulgence in diffuse sensations originating in love, when love itself is no longer accessible. The major part of my discussion of "Hymne" is concerned with similar rhetorical manipulations. The Mediaeval poets, by contrast, use the artificial or prototypical fragrances to describe and amplify natural scents, or such social interactions as fame, rumour, friendship; they use these fragrances to present pleasant sensations as more pleasant, and outstanding experiences as more intense. They amplify the stereotypic features of those notions and sensations.

18 Newberg et al. (2001: 89) provide information on ritual that may illuminate the combination of hypnotic rhythms and appeal to the olfactory sense in this poem. "These feelings of awe can be further augmented by the sense of smell, which might account for the customary use of incense and other fragrances in religious rites. The middle part of the amygdala receives nerve impulses from the olfactory system, so strong smells could stimulate the watchdog to generate alertness or a mild fear response. [...] When rituals combine fragrances with marked actions and repetitive sounds [...] the resulting stimulation to the amygdala might result in an intensification of the sense of religious awe".

various perfumes, too, are prototypical thing-free and gestalt-free qualities, and serve to "saturate" the atmosphere (in both senses) with intense, pleasurable sensations, just as the air *impregnated* with salt is saturated with pleasurable sensations.

"La nuit" too, in the third stanza, is a thing-free and gestalt-free quality that fills the entire space around, and also renders sight, the most differentiated (most rational) sense ineffective. But one can perceive the *scent* of the hidden "encensoir" that secretly smokes across the night. In other words, the more differentiated sensations are rendered impossible; only the less differentiated ones are accessible. Now it should be noticed that this "encensoir" is not only at some far away, unspecified place, imperceptible to the eye: it is also forgotten; it is the source of intense but invisible, diffuse information that fills all the surrounding space, and is devoid of any possible purposiveness (that is what "oublié" suggests here). Thus, we are presented with a verbal imitation of feeling, or intuiting, rather than knowing, our environment and some inaccessible remote reality.

I have said that "Hymne" conveys an attenuated variety of a peak experience, or, if you like, an attenuated romanticism. I have elsewhere quoted Bowra on the Romantic imagination. The Romantic poets sought to discover, with the help of their *imagination,* the transcendental order inaccessible to the senses, in nature, that *is* accessible to the senses. In English Romanticism, says Bowra (1961: 271), "five major poets, Blake, Coleridge, Wordsworth, Shelley, and Keats, despite many differences, agreed on one vital point: that the creative imagination is closely connected with a peculiar insight into an unseen order behind visible things". The Romantic poets call the unlimited reality with which they seek communion "Infinity", "Eternity" or "Nothingness", rather than "God";[19] sometimes they merely seek *integration* with surrounding Nature (Tsur, 1992: 412). The evasive, undifferentiated, diffuse scents in Baudelaire's poem give information about some remote, invisible, inaccessible, unspecified reality; they yield "a peculiar insight into an unseen order behind visible things". "Mon Éternité" is a curious expression. "Éternité" is an unqualified, absolute existence; the possessive pronoun renders it particularly private, subjective; it is, perhaps, infinity somehow internalised. Romantic poets would like that, perhaps: it suggests the sublime as an internal experience. The "grain of musk" is infinitesimally small, and "lies still" at the *bottom* of my eternity, at the remotest, least accessible point (as at the *bottom* of the sea). Yet the speaker experiences it most intensely.[20]

---

[19] This practice is most familiar with the religious mystics as well.

[20] Bowra characterises the Symbolists' attitude as follows:

> To this belief they clang with a conviction which can only be called mystical because of its intensity, its irrationality, its disregard for other beliefs and its reliance on a world beyond the senses. Symbolism, then, was a mystical form of Aestheticism (Bowra, 1943: 3).

Baudealaire's "Hymne" and Wagner's Liebestod

I said in chapter 1 that Spitzer's analysis (1962) of Isolde's *Liebestod* in Wagner's music-drama most powerfully anticipates my conception of oceanic dedifferentiation in poetry. But a brief comparison with Baudelaire's "Hymne" may also foreground the difference between the two texts.

> But though there is here, as with Juan de la Cruz, a suggestion of "todos los sentidos suspendidos {all the senses suspended}", the ecstasy which Wagner is describing differs in one most essential point. The union for which Isolde yearns is a union no longer directly with Tristan (who is lost sight of after l. 32), but with the elements into which he himself has dissolved: the emanation of perfume, breath, and sound elicit from Isolde the desire for a similar dissolution *("mich verhauchen"* {to dissolve in a breeze; "to breeze away"}) in the scented, breathing, sounding medium [...] which is figured as a sea: "untertauchen {to dive, to submerge} /.. . . / In des Wonnemeeres {sea of blissfulness} / wogendem Schwall {the billowy, undulating flush} / ... / ertrinken-- {to drown} / versinken {to sink}". Here we have the pantheistic idea of the melting into the universe of two souls who have consumed themselves in longing for each other. In the words of Isolde--which we hear sung in a deep contralto--there is no suggestion of upward movement (two souls mounting heavenward in an apotheosis, as at the end of the Flying Dutchman); rather, that of sinking, ever deeper, into the sea of nothingness (Spitzer, 1962: 175).

"This sea of nothingness is not that void described by Jacopone and other mystics (including Juan de la Cruz): an emptiness created by the soul in order that it may be filled by God; it appears as a turbulent mass of waves, perfumes, breaths [...] ruled over not by a personal God, but by the violent forces of Nature" (ibid., 176). Both poems evoke a sense of union with the beloved one. Both texts (Baudelaire's poem and Wagner's music drama) do this through semantic transformations that indicate dissolution of the lovers into gestalt-free and thing-free entities suspending the boundaries between self and not-self, so as to enable an imperceptibly smooth fusion

---

Indeed, Bowra senses the undifferentiated nature sometimes to be found in French Symbolist poetry as part of its religious quality:

> For the undivided attention which the enraptured worshipper gives to the object of his prayers and the sense of timeless contentment which he finds through them are not entirely different from a pure aesthetic state which seems to obliterate distinctions of time and place, of self and not-self, of sorrow and joy (ibid., 6).

between them. But Baudelaire's poem has recourse to mostly artificial, highly refined, elusive scents, whereas Wagner's text is transfused with "violent forces of nature", culminating in overwhelming ecstatic transport.

Baudelaire uses in "Hymne" such uninteresting love clichés as "angel, idol", and
such straightforward superlatives as "dearest, most beautiful, best". He also has recourse to perfumes and odours which in *précieux* poetry are used to suggest easy, direct gratification, rather than overcoming some difficulty which is the essence of
artistic creation. But these "cheap" devices of love poetry are turned into a masterpiece through prosodic and syntactic organisation, and the semantic manipulation of
the words. The single-minded exclamatory formula of the first and last stanzas assumes a more diffuse and complex emotional quality by splitting the direction of its
cognitive processing by prosodic and syntactic means. The poem conveys the mystic
union of an ego with a non-ego, through the suspension of boundaries and the abolishment of gestalts through semantic manipulation. In mystic poetry, love and sexual relationship serve as metaphors for the mystic union of ego with non-ego. In
Baudelaire's poem, the infusion of ego with non-ego as a gestalt-free quality with
suspended boundaries performs the mystic union of love. The use of excessive artificial perfumes serves to amplify sensuous indulgence; but these are also treated as diffuse information about a remote, inacessible and invisible reality—that is, they act
as the verbal imitation of some mystic experience.

Baudealaire's *"Le Léthé"*

"Hymne" is one of Baudelaire's Madame Sabatier poems that celebrate spiritual love.
But even in the Jeanne Duval poems that express the pangs of sensuous love Baudelaire sometimes resorts to oceanic imagery to indicate the state of self-abandonment
leading to self-oblivion that typically characterises mystic experience at its height.
Let us consider the following poem.

> 10.   Viens sur mon coeur, âme cruelle et sourde,
>   Tigre adoré monstre aux airs indolents;
>   Je veux longtemps plonger mes doigts tremblants
>   Dans l'épaisseur de ta crinière lourde;
>
>   Dans tes jupons remplis de ton parfum
>   Ensevelir ma tête endolorie,
>   Et respirer, comme une fleur flétrie,
>   Le doux relent de mon amour défunt.
>
>   Je veux dormir! dormir plutôt que vivre!
>   Dans un sommeil aussi doux que la mort,
>   J'étalerai mes baisers sans remords
>   Sur ton beau corps poli comme le cuivre.

Pour engloutir mes sanglots apaisés
Rien ne me vaut l'abîme de ta couche;
L'oubli puissant habite sur ta bouche,
Et le Léthé coule dans tes baisers.

A mon destin, désormais mon délice,
J'obéirai comme un prédestiné;
Martyr docile, innocent condamné,
Dont sa ferveur attise le supplice,

Je sucerai pour noyer ma rancœur,
Le népenthès et la bonne ciguë
Aux bouts charmants de cette gorge aiguë
Qui n'a jamais emprisonné de coeur.

Come upon my heart, cruel and deaf soul,/ adored tiger, monster with an air of indolence;/ I want to plunge for long my trembling fingers/ in the thickness of your heavy mane.

To bury my painful head/ in your petticoats filled with your perfume,/ and breathe in, like a withered flower,/ the sweet (musty) odour of my deceased love.

I want to sleep! sleep rather than live!/ In a slumber as sweet as death,/ I will spread out my remorseless kisses/ upon your beautiful body polished like brass.

To swallow up my appeased sobs/ nothing equals the abyss of your bed,/ powerful oblivion dwells on your lips,/ and the Lethe flows in your kisses.

To my destiny which from now on is my delight,/ I will obey like a predestined person; / docile martyr, innocent convict,/ whose fervour fans the flames of torture,

I will suck, to drown my resentment,/ the nepenthe and the good hemlock/ at the charming tip of your sharp breast/ that has never imprisoned a heart.

I will not discuss here the religious overtones of "martyr" and "predestined person" in stanza 5. Let me comment only on what I consider the tenor of this poem: self-oblivion and undifferentiation. Its title is "Le Léthé", a river in Hades whose water caused forgetfulness of the past in those who drank of it. In stanza 4, too, we find "the Lethe flows in your kisses". It is not only the "forgetfulness"-ingredient in "Lethe", but it also has an oceanic aspect: "Lethe" is a river, and the abstraction (forgetfulness) is presented as active (flowing).[21] In the last stanza the speaker proposes to suck nepenthe and hemlock from the breast of his beloved. "Breast" is that part of the female body from which nurslings suck fluid food, while males derive sexual pleasure from female breasts by similar lip movements. In

---

[21] On other occasions too, Baudelaire associated sensuous pleasure with Lethe, as in characterising Rubens' paintings in "Les Phares": "Rubens, fleuve d'oubli, jardin de la paresse,/ Oreiller de chair fraîche où l'on ne peut aimer..." (Rubens, river of oblivion, the garden of indolence,/ Cushion of fresh flesh, where one cannot love).

Baudelaire's poem the male sucks different fluids, Nepenthe and hemlock, which by a metaphorical process turn into the abstractions forgetfulness and death. Nepenthe is "a drug or drink used by the ancients to bring forgetfulness of sorrow or trouble"; or, "anything inducing a pleasurable sensation of forgetfulness". Hemlock is a drug or lethal drink prepared from the poisonous plant of the same name. In this sense, sexual pleasure at its peak induces an extreme degree of self-oblivion. This is followed by a punch line that contains a powerful "metaphysical" conceit, switching from one aspect of "breast" and "heart" to another: in "that has never imprisoned a heart"—"breast" changes its meaning to the cavity in which the heart and lungs lie; the absence of a flesh-and-blood heart in this cavity assumes the metaphorical meaning "absence of feelings".

In the third stanza, the speaker expresses his wish "to sleep! sleep rather than live!", achieving "a slumber as sweet as death"—all these expressions suggest the reduction of differentiated mental activities, the dissolution of ordinary consciousness. "Abyss" does not merely threaten with annihilation, but also suggests the dissolution of gestalts, and evokes the intense presence of absence. Here its function is to transfer those features to the woman's bed, suggesting the annihilation of the speaker's self, furthering the dissolution of the self and focused gestalts at the peak of sexual union.

From the perspective of oceanic dedifferentiation in stanza 4, some verbal features in the first stanza become significant, after the event. The phrase "plonger [...] dans l'épaisseur" is an instance of the IMMERSION in the ABSTRACTION construction. The abstraction "thickness" in this construct has been derived from some such phrase as "I want to plunge my trembling fingers in your thick and heavy mane", by two transformations: nominalisation and topicalisation. The qualities "thickness" and "heaviness" belong to the least differentiated sensory mode, the tactile. The tactile sense is reinforced by the trembling fingers. The semantic ingredient of "thickness" and the fingers plunging in it turn the abstraction into an intense, undifferentiated presence. Finally, consider the verse line "powerful oblivion *dwells* on your lips" (instead of, e.g., *"is* on your lips"). The verb "dwells" substitutes a predicate of action for a predicate of state. Both "is" and "dwell" suggest occupying some place; but the latter verb suggests greater mental activity. Thus, the presence of the imperceptible abstraction ("oblivion") becomes more intensive; this quality is reinforced by "powerful".

It is a commonplace that sexual imagery is exceptionally suitable to express, even evoke, a feeling of mystic experience. For years I have been inclined to interpret this association between sexual and mystic union as a means to evoke a perception of the *unio mystica* by figurative language. I assumed, in harmony with Rudolf Otto's position, that sexual union is the nearest experience in our normal life that may suggest heightened emotional activity, self-oblivion and self-abandonment for a verbal re-creation of mystic experience. The physical union of ego with a non-ego foregrounds the nonconceptual and experiential nature of the spiritual union of ego with a non-ego. Leo Spitzer's discussion of three ecstatic poems strongly supports such a theological and literary assumption. Newberg et al., however, view the issue in a neurological and evolutionary perspective, addressing an additional difficult but fascinating question: Why would the human brain, which evolved for the very pragmatic purpose of helping us survive, possess such an apparently impractical talent for transcendence! What evolutionary advantage would a mystically gifted mind provide? (p. 123) Evolution, after all, doesn't plan ahead. It gropes impartially for potential, with no idea where that potential might lead. (p. 124)

> We believe, in fact, that the neurological machinery of transcendence may have arisen from the neural circuitry that evolved for mating and sexual experience.[22] The language of mysticism hints at this connection: Mystics of all times and cultures have used the same expressive terms to describe their ineffable experiences: *bliss, rapture, ecstasy,* and *exaltation.* They speak of losing themselves in a sublime sense of union, of melting into elation, and of the total satisfaction of desires. (p. 125)

Baudelaire proceeds in the opposite direction: he too speaks of losing himself in an abyss—but as part of a sexual experience. Perhaps he elaborates on that oceanic element in sexual relationships that renders sex and love such an apt metaphor for mystic experience.

---

[22] This is an instance of a more general principle adopted by cognitive poetics: once you develop some neural circuitry for one pupose, it can be exploited for additional purposes of less immediate survival value. Thus, for instance, brain lateralisation seems to have evolved in humans in order to afford them different right and left hand skills for the performance of complex actions in, e.g., toolmaking. This circuitry, in turn, enabled humans to develop speech.

Chapter 10

The Infernal and the Hybrid
Bosch and Dante

Throughout the present work we have been exploring interferences with the smooth functioning of cognitive processes in the course of reading poetry, interferences that produced effects regularly associated with religious, mystic, and meditative experiences. That is what I am going to do in this chapter, too, but this time with reference to the demonic and infernal, not the divine, aspect of the otherworldly. In Chapter 7 we briefly considered the relationship between the vague and the infernal; here we will discuss the hybrid and the infernal at considerable length. In chapter 7 we remained with a debt toward Dante; in this chapter I am going to repay it. The chapter will be divided into two parts: the image of the Devil and Hell in the visual arts, and the infernal in Dante's *Inferno*.

The Demonic and the Grotesque

We are not concerned here with the *idea* of the devil and the evils he stands for; nor with a knowledge that he belongs to a world beyond the absolute limit. In some representations, at least, the devil or the demonic are *immediately experienced* as causing discomfort, pain, distress, or anxiety. It is not that we infer some threat from his appearance: the mere perception of his appearance induces painful cognitive or psychodynamic processes. Now notice this: in some representations of Hell, people are tortured in ways that are not different in kind from the tortures by the Inquisition, or the Gestapo, or the KGB. These interrogators were sometimes far more imaginative and inventive than what is traditionally attributed to the devils. Devils may also assume postures or facial expressions or have body parts that threaten with a painful or destructive act. But, in some representations at least, the devil is experienced as immediately causing discomfort, pain, distress, or anxiety, even if he has no lion's head or eagle's foot. I submit that the key term for this response is "grotesque". Consider figures 1 and 2. In the latter, the demon has a wide range of threatening features: he is lion-headed, eagle-footed, and holds dangerous weapons in his hands. The minor devils, demons, satyrs and hobgoblins in figure 1, by contrast, have no such features; two of them even play musical instruments. These creatures are painful to look at not because of what they can do to you, but because they are visually disconcerting. I will claim that it is in this way that Hieronymus Bosch's infernal creatures capture the very core of the infernal in the visual medium.

Figure 1 Minor devils, demons, satyrs and hobgoblins.
From Olaus Magnus' *Historia de gentibus septentrionalibus,* Rome, 1555.[1]

I propose to introduce my discussion of the grotesque by two observations: first, that devils and fiends are sometimes represented as extremely fearsome creatures, but sometimes as clowns and buffoons; second, that traditionally fiends and devils are represented as having a human body with goatlike horns and hooves; and sometimes they have tails. In time, the goat hooves turned into horse hooves; not a significant difference. Historically, this tradition can be accounted for by the fact that pagan fertility deities became demons in Christian mythology; and that goats were intimately associated with fertility cults.[2] Now the average believer is deprived of this historical knowledge; and his priests are not very eager to enlighten him in this respect. So, one must look elsewhere for the source of the effectivity of these representations. I submit that this source is to be found in their grotesque effect. This will also explain the fearful and laughable appearances of the devil. In Freudian terms, the ambivalent figure is split into a fearsome and a laughable one. According to Thomson, "What will be generally agreed upon [...] is that 'grotesque' will cover, perhaps

---

[1] Figures 1 and 2 are reproduced here from Lehner and Lehner (1971). I am indebted to Dr. Yona Pinson for this reference.

[2] Figure 2 points at a different origin of such hybrids: the limbs and head of a human figure are replaced by the most typically dangerous members of the most typical beasts of prey. Such an origin would suggest a process in which the hybrids of figure 2, for instance, lost their directly-threatening features for some reason.

among other things, the co-presence of the laughable and something that is incompatible with the laughable" (1972: 3). The "other things" include the suspension of the boundaries between the categories "human, animal, plant", or an independence of the members of the human body; or the flouting of taboos—renewal of infantile interests forbidden by early socialisation.

The grotesque, as described by Thomson, is a quality that, in the first place, is "hard to take". In the grotesque, there is a clash between incompatible responses— the laughable on the one hand, and the horrible, the disgusting, or the pitiable on the other. The element that is so "hard to take" is the uncertainty, the emotional disorientation, the indecision in the face of a threat. Making a decision in one or the other direction provides, according to some psychologists, a defense against the threat, whereas indecision causes discomfort, pain, distress, or anxiety. Consequently, the grotesque stays grotesque—according to Thomson—as long as the reader (or the observer) is capable of staying exposed to incompatible emotions, without seeking relief in one of these "secondary responses" or "rationalisations" that resolve the conflict in favour of the laughable, the disgusting, or the pitiable. This kind of "secondary response" appears to be an instance of a wider aesthetic-psychological process active in cultural history. In chapter 8 we have discussed a process pointed out by Ehrenzweig: people apply defense mechanisms against artistic devices of great expressive force, turning them into ornaments or frozen poetic formulae. Now what about the horns and hooves of the devil? Artists and art historians have long realised that "hybrid creatures" have a grotesque effect. Gombrich, for instance, quotes Horace and St. Bernard de Clairvaux deploring such visual compositions, and then aptly points out the cognitive source of these effects: "What these texts have in common is the reaction of exasperated helplessness provoked by hybrid creatures, part plant, part human; part woman, part fish; part horse, part goat. There are no names in our language, no categories in our thought, to come to grips with this elusive, dream-like imagery in which 'all things are mixed' (to quote Dürer)" (Gombrich, 1984: 256). Devils are just such hybrid creatures, part humans, part goats. I submit that the grotesque presentation of the devils has one overwhelming function: the grotesque is so affective because of its *immediate* ambiguity.

Not only horns, tails and hooves have been associated with the demonic, but even the very notion of the grotesque. This point deserves some consideration. Kayser (quoted by Thomson, 1972: 18) suggests that "the grotesque is an attempt to control and exorcise *('zu bannen und zu beschwören')* the demonic elements in the world". While this may be a correct observation, it should be kept in mind that in order to "control and exorcise", the grotesque must also *conjure up* "the demonic elements in the world". Gombrich's inspiring discussion of the grotesque would strongly support both claims. Still, I believe, Thomson's reservation is well taken: "We may object also to the somewhat melodramatic over-emphasis on the 'demonic', which totally removes the fearsome aspect of the grotesque to the realm of the irrational—almost supernatural" (Thomson, 1972: 18–19). To this, I would add that the relegation of the grotesque to the supernatural is an all too easy way of handling it. As I said above, the grotesque is so affective precisely because of its *immediate* ambiguity, even before questions may be raised concerning the possible existence of the creatures involved. Grotesque creatures leave us defenseless, threatened, irrespective of the question which side of the ultimate limit they inhabit. In fact, the present position is an outright reversal of Kayser's. Rather than relegating the fearsome aspect of the grotesque to the realm of the irrational—almost supernatural, it is a means to present in this world the discomfort caused by the demonic or infernal.

Figure 2 The lion-headed, eagle-footed Assyrian-Babylonian demon
of disease and evil, holding the mace of wounding and the dagger of killing.
After a wall carving at Nineveh.

Ernst Kris (1965) speaks of the "double-edgedness" of the comic. When the defense against the threat is dismantled, the ridiculous stops being ridiculous and becomes painful (for instance, a man who suspects his wife of being unfaithful will not find a comedy about a cuckold funny at all, but rather painful or distasteful). The comic, just like the sublime, originates in a threatening event, which is observed at a sufficient distance from the danger for the observer to feel safe. An observer who does not feel sufficiently safe will respond in an opposite manner. What characterises the grotesque, according to some psychologists and literary theorists, is *a disruption of alternativeness*. Instead of deciding unambiguously in favour of one or another defense mechanism, the grotesque leaves the observer in an intermediate state, in uncertainty, in a state of indecision. He has a sense of "emotional disorientation". Many people find such an emotional state difficult to bear. For these people a comic, or even a fearsome devil would be more tolerable than this state of emotional disorientation. So they are likely to suppress one of the conflicting emotions, achieving an unambiguously fearsome or unambiguously funny devil.

The first step to this disambiguation is already built into Gombrich's account above: "There are no names in our language, no categories in our thought, to come to grips with this elusive imagery". In the case under consideration, the hybrid creatures do have a name or category: *the devil*. Such a name in language (or category in thought) incapacitates the disorienting power of the grotesque.

The foregoing analysis may throw some light on Hieronymus Bosch's infernal creatures, for instance: they are hybrid figures, but do not fit into any category such as "the devil". Moreover, they are made up of parts that are neither functional (as in figure 2), nor conventional (as in figure 1). They have no names, and the categories mixed in them have never been seen together. Consider figure 3. I will quote only a few brief passages from a very detailed description of it:

> The focal point of Hell, occupying a position analogous to that of the Fountain of Life in the Eden wing, is the so-called Tree-Man, whose egg-shaped torso rests on a pair of rotting tree trunks that end in boats for shoes. His hind quarters have fallen away, revealing a hellish tavern scene within, while his head supports a large disc on which devils and their victims promenade around a large bagpipe. The face looks over one shoulder to regard, half wistfully, the dissolution of his own body (Gibson, 1973: 97).

Furthermore, at the bottom of figure 3, from left to right, one nude figure is attached by devils to the neck of a lute; another is helplessly entangled in the strings of a harp, while a third soul has been stuffed down the neck of a great horn (ibid., 96). These are not different in kind from the torments in earthly torture chambers. But the huge musical instruments turned to torture instruments inspire the observer not only with awe, but with emotional disorientation, too.

Another possible source of the grotesque is when members of the human body become conspicuously independent and/or disproportionately big (Gogol's "Nose", for instance). Near the "Tree-Man" in figure 3 there is a pair of huge human ears (pierced with arrows?). Gibson describes it as follows:

> A huge pair of ears advances like some infernal army tank, immolating its victims by means of a great knife. The letter M engraved on the knife, which also appears on other knives in Bosch's paintings, has been thought to represent the hallmark of some cutler whom the artist particularly disliked, but it more likely refers to Mundus (World), or possibly Antichrist, whose name, according to some medieval prophecies, would begin with this letter (ibid, 97).

Figure 3 Hieronymus Bosch: *Tree-man and buildings burning in Hell* from *Garden of Earthly Delight* (tryptych, right wing).

Much learning has gone into the explication of Bosch's symbolism and icono-graphy in this and other paintings. But notice this: on this detail, even when the ex-plicator offers an explication, as with the letter M, he offers three of them, none of which is more plausible than the others. Concerning, however, the ears themselves, he can do little better than venture a rather loose metaphor: "infernal army tank". I would prefer to rely on the disconcerting, grotesque effect of the image. The two ears are erect and parallel exactly as they would be on the two sides of a human head; but there is no head between them, only the blade of a knife, in a conspicuously phallic position. The huge pair of ears does not merely immolate its victims or run them over. It is independent of any body, and *acts* independently.

Such an image renders erudition desperately helpless, but has an exceptionally strong appeal to direct perception. It affects the observer with its disorienting power rather than with its meaning. Likewise, Gibson comments on the tree-man: "The meaning of this enigmatic, even tragic figure has yet to be explained satisfactorily, but Bosch never created another image that more successfully evoked the shifting, insubstantial quality of a dream" (ibid., 98). We can only hope that art historians will fail to explain satisfactorily the meaning of this enigmatic figure: part of its enormous effect is derived precisely from its lack of meaning. In Gombrich's words, "There are no names in our language, no categories in our thought, to come to grips with this elusive, dream-like imagery in which 'all things are mixed'". We have mentioned above Ehrenzweig's conception according to which human society applies defense mechanisms against artistic devices that have "too" strong an emotional impact. And one obvious publicly respectable way of defending society would be to apply scholarship to explain all the obscure elements in art and literature. This is how Wilson Knight, the great Shakespeare critic, described this tendency:

> There is in the human mind a strong reluctance to face, with full conscious-ness, the products of poetic genius; and this often takes the form of an at-tempt to reduce them to something *other* [...]. This, our natural academic tendency, is of appalling, and insidious, strength. [...] Such scholarship receives a ready, if ephemeral, acclamation denied to the more authentic and comprehensive approach. [...] All would clearly be well were it not for the uncomfortable suspicion that it is too often the very essence of poetry, the liquid fire of its veins, which we are asked to suppress (Knight, 1965: xi-xii).

The grotesque appears to be one of the most extreme instances of art where a "satisfactory explanation" would be totally devastating, for its very essence is "a sense of confusion and emotional disorientation". This reservation does not apply to what Knight's phrase "more authentic and comprehensive approach" may refer. This expression I take to refer to an approach that does not explain what this or that ob-scure detail means, but points out the overall structure of the work, so as to facili-tate the experiencing of the whole.

Figure 4 Bird-headed monster complementing figure 3 at lower right

Bosch exploits additional sources of the grotesque. Consider figure 4, presenting a bird-headed monster at the lower right of his *Hell* who, according to Gibson,

> gobbles up the damned souls only to defecate them into a transparent chamber pot from which they plunge into a pit below. He recalls a monster in the *Vision of Tundale* who digested the souls of lecherous clergy in a similar manner. [...] the glutton is forced to disgorge his food, while the proud lady is compelled to admire her charms reflected in the backside of a devil (ibid, 98).

Again, Gibson is at pains to account for the enormous effect of this detail. The comment that "He recalls a monster in the *Vision of Tundale* who digested the souls of lecherous clergy in a similar manner" is characteristic of his scholarship. He can point out only additional instances of a principle, but not the principle itself. One of the possible sources of the grotesque I designated above as "the flouting of taboos— renewal of infantile interests forbidden by early socialisation". The punishments described by Gibson are associated with excretions (feces, disgorged matter), and the orifices of the human body (the monster's beak protruding and wide open, its anus discharging bodily waste, the glutton's mouth discharging the contents of his stomach, and the devil's backside reflecting the lady's charms). The damned souls are not just annihilated by being swallowed; they are turned into feces.

Gibson's conception is in headlong collision with the one propounded here. I believe that all historical information may be very useful, as long as it is kept in the proper proportions and does not usurp the place of other legitimate explanations. Historical research may come up with illuminating information about, e.g., verbal puns which, as we will see, are processed by cognitive and psychodynamic mechanisms of considerable aesthetic interest. Gibson, by contrast, denies outright the relevance of psychological explanations:

> The tendency to interpret Bosch's imagery in terms of modern Surrealism or Freudian psychology is anachronistic. We forget too often that Bosch never read Freud and that modern psychoanalysis would have been incomprehensible to the medieval mind. What we choose to call the libido was denounced by the medieval Church as original sin; what we see as the expression of the subconscious mind was for the Middle Ages the promptings of God or the Devil. Modern psychology may explain the appeal Bosch's pictures have for us, but it cannot explain the meaning they had for Bosch and his contemporaries. Likewise, it is doubtful that modern psychoanalysis can help us to understand the mental processes by which Bosch developed his enigmatic forms. Bosch did not intend to evoke the subconscious of the viewer, but to teach him certain moral and spiritual truths, and thus his images generally had a precise and premeditated significance. As Dirk Bar has shown, they often represented visual translations of verbal puns and meta-

phors. Bosch's sources, in fact, should rather be sought in the language and folklore of his day, as well as in the teachings of the Church (ibid, 12).

This argument from an outstanding Bosch scholar is thoroughly fallacious, confusing "meaning" and "appeal". It is the history of ideas that ought to explain the meaning Bosch's pictures had for Bosch and his contemporaries, or for us. At the same time, modern psychology may explain the appeal they have for us, or for Bosch and his contemporaries. Historical research must reveal as much as possible of the cultural materials handled by the psychological processes. Psychology must reveal those psychological processes that handle them. That "Bosch never read Freud" proves nothing, just as the fact that he didn't know that the blood circulated in his body doesn't prove that it didn't. Gibson himself admits that Freud's and the medieval Church's terms may have the same referent within different idea systems, as in "what we choose to call the libido was denounced by the medieval Church as original sin". We are interested here not so much in the terms as in the world of referents. Consequently, such a statement only suggests that this "libido" was very active and threatening to the Church and its values. Or, consider the statement "what we see as the expression of the subconscious mind was for the Middle Ages the promptings of God or the Devil". Such a formulation suggests its obverse too: what for the Middle Ages was the promptings of God or the Devil is, for Freudian psychology, the expression of the subconscious mind. Freudian psychology does not deny the mediaeval ideas about the promptings of God or the Devil; it only attempts to account for them. Thus, a piece of the history of ideas is explained in psychological terms. Historical research *may* refute the relevance of Freudian psychology: not by producing ideas incompatible with modern conceptions, but by producing evidence that it didn't apply to the psyche of mediaeval man. The taboos flouted by the grotesque were taboos for Bosch too, and may have had an effect for Bosch that is not entirely unintelligible to us.

For the time being, Bakhtin's study of the grotesque may prove illuminating for this last issue. He places his discussion in a historical and semiotic, non-Freudian, perspective. In the sixteenth century, he says, a major change of the bodily canon took place in Western art, intimately related to the rise of individualism.

> The new bodily canon, in all its historic variations and different genres, presents an entirely finished, completed, strictly limited body, which is shown from the outside as something individual. That which protrudes, bulges, sprouts, or branches off (when a body transgresses its limits and a new one begins) is eliminated, hidden, or moderated. All orifices of the body are closed. The basis of the image is the individual, strictly limited mass, the impenetrable façade. The opaque surface and the body's "valleys" acquire an essential meaning as the border of a closed individuality that does not merge with other bodies and with the world (1968: 320).

No isolated quotation can do justice to Bakhtin's magnificent study. This paragraph is indicative of its opposite too, the old bodily canon. Only in the old canon the grotesque was possible, because "Of all the features of the human face, the nose and mouth play the most important part in the grotesque image of the body [...] The grotesque is interested only in protruding eyes [...] It is looking for that which protrudes from the body, all that seeks to go out beyond the body's confines" (316). [...] The grotesque face is actually reduced to the gaping mouth; the other features are only a frame encasing this wide-open bodily abyss (317). The mouth gaping with laughter is replaced in the new canon by the Madonna smiling with closed lips. As to their relative importance, "Next to the bowels and the genital organs is the mouth, through which enters the world to be swallowed up. And next is the anus. All these convexities and orifices have a common characteristic; it is within them that the confines between bodies and between the body and the world are overcome [...] Eating, drinking, defecation and other elimination (sweating, blowing of the nose, sneezing), as well as copulation, pregnancy, dismemberment, swallowing up by another body—all these acts are performed on the confines of the body and the outer world" (317)[3]. Accordingly, the grotesque quality of the treeman in figure 3 is derived not only from the absence of names in our language or categories in our thought "to come to grips with this elusive imagery", nor only from the emotional disorientation generated by the face regarding half wistfully the dissolution of his own body—but also by the blatant violation of the confines between the disintegrating body and the outer world.

From the preceding paragraph one may draw one of two opposite conclusions for our business. One possibility is that the taboos concerning the orifices of the human body were established only toward the end of the sixteenth century. In this case, Gibson would be certainly right in suggesting that modern psychology cannot explain the appeal Bosch's pictures had for his contemporaries. Alternatively, one may suppose that the taboos existed long before the sixteenth century; but in the seventeenth century they became so strong that they could not be violated any more in the arts. In this case, modern psychology can be quite useful in giving some idea of the appeal Bosch's pictures had for his contemporaries. In the present state of knowledge it is reasonable to suppose that the latter is the case.[4] At any rate, Gibson's

---

3 This would suggest a fascinating possiblity for the present study: both in mystic experience and the grotesque confines are overcome—between self and not-self, and between the body and the world, respectively.

4 Compare this, for instance, to a linguist's testimony: "The conceptual areas affected by verbal taboo vary through space and time. The interdictions are generally centered on a few topics, such as sex, bodily functions, death, illness, and aggressive impulses. The semantic sphere of these topics may be more or less extensive. In seventeenth-century French salons the domain of obscene words also contains such 'vulgar' terms as marriage, to eat, and to sleep according to the Dictionary of abbé de Somaize ([1660] 1856). The verbal procedures of avoidance, however, were essentially the same across space and time" (Fónagy, 2001: 268).

statement "what we choose to call the libido was denounced by the medieval Church as original sin" strongly supports such a supposition.

Finally, consider: "As Dirk Bar has shown, they often represented visual translations of verbal puns and metaphors". This information is extremely valuable from the aesthetic point of view. But its aesthetic significance has psychological roots. First, verbal puns are, according to Freudian theory, intimately associated with unconscious processes: they save mental energy (by giving two things in one), and renew the infantile pleasures in babbling (Kris and Gombrich, 1965: 197). And second, as Thomson pointed out, such a process of "smashing" language, of visualising verbal puns and metaphors, may cause a sense of confusion and emotional disorientation: it arouses a strange sensation, making one suddenly doubt one's comfortable relationship with language, that most habitual part of one's life. Why else should have Bosch bothered to give us visual translations of verbal puns and metaphors? Historical research may, indeed, reveal Bosch's sources in the language and folklore of his day, as well as in the teachings of the Church. But no amount of source-hunting can, without the help of stylistic and psychological research, account for the effect of the realisation of verbal puns and metaphors on us, or on Bosch's audience, or on Bosch himself.[5]

The Infernal in Dante's Inferno

I have quoted (in Chapter 7) Alan Sinfield who quotes Tennyson saying: "Milton's vague hell is much more awful than Dante's hell marked off into divisions". I suggested that, taken at its face value, Tennyson's aphorism does injustice to Dante, who achieves *his* awful effects by different techniques. We may add that he achieves them in ways that are not unlike Bosch's. Furthermore, Sinfield quoted two versions of a nightmare description by Tennyson, and observed that the revised version is, indeed, semantically vaguer. I pointed out that the substitution of one phrase for another renders the stanza not only semantically, but also prosodically vaguer, and that this, too, has a decisive effect on the perceived quality. In this section I will elaborate on both the painful cognitive structure of the thematic and figurative elements in Dante, and the fluid, uncertain nature of the *terza rima*.

True, Dante's hell is marked off into clear divisions. But, in some instances at least, Dante blurs the boundaries on a much deeper cognitive level, between conceptual categories, with a violence unimaginable in Milton, generating no mere "vagueness", but what Thomson (1972) calls "a sense of confusion and emotional disorientation". In an important sense, Dante uses a verbal equivalent of Hieronymus Bosch's visual techniques to represent Hell. I suggested that in some representations at least, the devil (or the infernal) is experienced as immediately causing discomfort, pain, distress, or anxiety resulting not only from the meaning of the image, but also

---

5   In the next section we will encounter another conflict—between source-hunting and Leo Spitzer's stylistic explorations in Dante.

from an interference with the smooth functioning of cognitive processes. I claimed that not only numinous, mystic, and meditative qualities can be conveyed in poetry by interference with the smooth functioning of cognitive and psychodynamic processes, but demonic and infernal qualities as well. I quoted Gombrich on "the reaction of exasperated helplessness provoked by hybrid creatures, part plant, part human; part woman, part fish; part horse, part goat. There are no names in our language, no categories in our thought, to come to grips with this elusive, dream-like imagery in which 'all things are mixed' (to quote Dürer)" (Gombrich, 1984: 256). In an infernal situation, such a feeling of exasperated helplessness reinforces similar qualities arising from the gross contents. I will argue that Dante displays and amplifies such exasperated helplessness provoked by hybrid creatures, for similar effects, with some consistency.

Years ago I perceived this exasperated helplessness with reference to the "speech" of the flame-man in Canto XXVII of the *Inferno* (1-9). Later I discovered that Leo Spitzer (1965) had done the same with reference to the plant-men in Canto XIII. I will briefly discuss both sections. To do justice to Spitzer's subtlety, one ought to quote his entire essay; here I will quote or paraphrase only parts of it, with some shifts of emphasis. In Canto XIII, people whose sin had been suicide were turned into plants. Traditional Dante critics have pointed out that such ancient poets as Virgil and Ovid also described metamorphoses from human to plant. Spitzer argues that such a conception is simplistic; that there are differences that one cannot ignore. Dante gives us

> something unknown either to Ovid or Virgil: a plant that bleeds and speaks. This creature is "very man and very plant": [...] this plant not only bleeds (this in itself and other similar phenomena may be found in Ovid), but reveals the anguished workings of a human mind and heart. It represents, then, something quite different from the creations of Ovid [...]: with the latter we have to do only with a plant that was once a human being; there is no painful insistence that this creature, after its metamorphosis, is both plant and human. [... The] hybrid creation of Dante is more monstrously hybrid than anything to be encountered among the ancients (Spitzer, 1965: 81).

According to the present conception, such painful insistence that a creature is both plant and human is prone to baffle the reader, to cause a sense of confusion and emotional disorientation. Spitzer's approach combines a stylistic with a general culture-historical framework. Accordingly, he claims that such hybrid creatures conflict with Dante's Christian values.

> [T]o the medieval Christian poet the concept of hybridism is, in itself, repellent. The Christian system does not recognize "evolution of species": the species are neatly delimited [...]. Hybrid creation is outside of the natural plan of God; and, at the hands of Dante, it becomes [...] a symbol of

sin and punishment—of punishment for the "antinatural" sin of suicide by which the God-willed connection between body and soul has been broken (Spitzer, 1965: 82).[6] ;

For me, the repellence of hybridism has much deeper, cognitive roots. Dante's passages are very effective for modern, post-Darwinian readers as well; they need not go to the mediaeval world-picture to experience it. I claim that it is the violent blurring of cognitive categories that is so offensive, making one suddenly doubt one's comfortable relationship with one's own cognitive system, to paraphrase Philip Thomson (1972). Such hybrid creatures cause a cognitive bafflement as voiced by Gombrich above; and Horace too, long before Christianity, objected to the conflicting emotional tendencies arising from such hybrid creatures. But the "Christian system" as invoked by Spitzer may further enhance this sense of confusion. A similar disconcerting effect is found in Kafka's *Metamorphosis,* where Gregor Samsa is suddenly turned into a giant obnoxious insect. What is hard to bear in this story is not the violation of traditional Christian concepts, but the sustained divided emotional response forced on the reader by Gregor's human consciousness enclosed inside a repellent insect body. We are faced with an obnoxious insect that "reveals the anguished workings of a human mind and heart". Thus, Dante's plant-men and flame-men are nearer to Kafka's *Metamorphosis* than to Ovid's.

An illuminating aspect of this man-plant condition in Dante is when human activity and the plant state restrict each other, and give rise to conflicting responses both in the hybrid creature and the reader. An animistic conception of nature would see nothing extraordinary in a spirit that dwelled in a tree calling out in human language. In this respect, the tree is merely a dwelling place for a spirit capable of speech. Dante, by contrast, wants us to understand literally the complete identification of man and plant. The man wants to cry out, but the plant has no mouth to serve as an outlet for man's cry. That is a most desperately hopeless state of affairs. Pain that finds no outlet in crying is unbearable. Here "outlet" must be understood literally, as a physical orifice for letting out speech or emotions. We repeatedly en-

---

6   "By the creation [...] of this monster which combines the human and the non-human, the poet succeeds in demonstrating the gulf that exists in nature between the human and the non-human. Thus the whole spirit of the Dantean metamorphosis is opposed to that of Ovid: the pagan poet with his pantheistic love for nature [...], who could discover a nymph in every fountain, a dryad in every tree, was able to see in metamorphosis only the principle of the eternal change of forms in nature [...]. It could be said that in Ovid the (gradual) transformation of a human into a vegetal being seems to take place almost naturally; but with Dante the link between nature and man has been broken by a tragic-minded Christianity; where Ovid offers to our view the richness of organic nature, Dante shows the inorganic, the hybrid, the perverted, the sinful, the damned" (Spitzer, 1965: 82). Notice that Spitzer's last phrase vaguely echoes Milton's "Nature breeds, / Perverse, all monstrous, all prodigious things" quoted in Chapter 7.

counter in this Canto that breaking the branches creates such an outlet; but, by the same token, it causes pain to the human-in-the-plant.

But this is only part of the story. Consider the following three excerpts:

1. Come d'un stizzo verde, che arso sia
   da l'un de' capi, che da l'altro geme,
   e cigola per vento che va via;
   si de la scheggia rotta usciva inseme
   parole e sangue . . .

[As from a green branch that is burning at one end and drips and sputters from the other with escaping vapor, so from that broken stick words and blood came out together . . .]

2. Allor soffiò il tronco forte, e poi
   si converti quel vento in cotal voce.

[The branch then blew hard and the breath then changed to a voice.] (p. 85)

3. e menommi al cespuglio che piangea,
   per le rotture sanguinenti, invano.

[And he led me to the bush that was weeping in vain from its bleeding rents.]

According to excerpt 1, "from that broken stick words and blood came out together". Blood is the fluid part of humans, that circulates through their vascular system, just as sap is the watery solution that circulates through a plant's vascular system. In Dante's verse, when you break the branch, blood instead sap comes out, sensitising, so to speak, the plant, or de-humanising the man. A sense of extreme helplessness results from having a human consciousness of pain, but a plant's ability to avoid pain. Furthermore, the verb "issue" originally denotes physical movement in space generating — by virtue of a trivial grammatical change — a powerful but informal synaesthetic metaphor. Spitzer points out that "in the single phrase *usciva inseme parole e sangue* [words and blood came out together] the two sense-data are fused together: there gashes forth a stream of 'speech-endowed blood,' of 'bleeding screams' — a hideous revelation of the hybrid, which we must accept as a unit-manifestation, because of the singular verb *usciva"* (Spitzer, 1965: 84). By the same token, however, the conjoining of blood and words revives the element of spatial movement in the metaphoric verb "issue", generating a conflict between the spatial process of the blood's appearance, and the non-spatial process of the words' appearance. All this is reinforced by "drips and sputters [...] with escaping vapor" that suggests letting out liquids, plus intense but inarticulate noise and diffused visual matter. Since these sputters are felt to have an intrinsic, independent force, they reinforce the "humanness" of the action. In terms of case grammar semantics, the inanimate physical processes "drips and sputters" and "escaping vapor", are self-moving processes characteristic of animate things, and make noises like inarticulate but intentional and purposeful speech produced by a human (cf. Doležel, 1976: 133; Lyons,

1977: 483). Inarticulate "drips and sputters" imply here ex–PRESSION at its lowest. The inarticulate noise of "drips and sputters" as a substitute for speech suggests extreme helplessness. In excerpt 2 the blowing breath suggests an inanimate, self-moving processual force and an animate human action at the same time. The rival occurrence of unintentional and intentional processes in both excerpts may evoke, again, a divided response.

As I have said, the lack of outlet or the need to "translate" the expression of pain to a different medium is one of the most effective cognitive means for evoking a feeling of exasperated helplessness. An extreme instance of this is pointed out by Spitzer in excerpt 1: "Dante chose to describe a hissing, guttering fire-log by way of characterizing the genesis of speech in his *uomini-piante*". In a footnote he refers the reader to an additional instance of such "translation", where no hybridity is involved. In Canto XIX those who made material profit of spiritual goods are half-buried in small holes in the earth, head down. "From the mouth of each [hole] projected the feet of a sinner and his legs as far as the calf, and the rest was within" (XIX: 22–24; trans. Singleton). Dante spots one "who writhes himself, twitching more than all his fellows" (31–32; trans. Singleton). A few lines later we read *piangeva con la zanca* [was weeping with his shanks] *(Inf.* XIX: 45; trans. Spitzer) to which Spitzer refers as "the 'dehumanized' weeping of the pope" (p. 85n).

In the same footnote Spitzer criticises the Italian scholar Torraca, who pointed out parallel similes in Provençal poetry, in which the "'weeping' of a fire-log is compared to the weeping of a poet lover; he overlooks the fact that this particular simile is meant to throw light on weeping that is precisely non-human". Here again Spitzer objects to influence-and-motive hunting in Dante, and focuses on the unique effects of poetic expressions.

In the ensuing passage I will discuss again the effects of hybridity, of seeking an outlet for a painful cry, of translating a human cry into an unsuitable medium. This time I will discuss both the hybrid creatures and the effects of the *terza rima* in light of our discussions of blurring the boundaries between categories, and of the changing effects of fluid metric structures (in Chapter 7). Let us have a look at the following passage from Canto XXVII of the *Inferno*:

4.   Già era dritta in sù la fiamma e queta
     per non dir più, e già da noi sen gia
     con la licenza del dolce poeta,

     quand' un'altra, che dietro a lei venia,
     ne fece volger li occhi a la sua cima
     per un confuso suon che fuor n'uscia.

     Come'l bue cicilian che mugghiò, prima
     col pianto di colui, e ciò fu dritto,
     che l'avea temperate con sua lima,

mugghiava con la voce de l'afflitto,
si che, con tutto che fosse di rame,
pur el pareva dal dolor trafitto;

così, per non aver via né forame
dal principio nel foco, in suo linguaggio
si convertïan le parole grame.

Ma poscia ch'ebber colto lor vïaggio
su per la punta, dandole quel guizzo
che dato avea la lingua in lor passaggio,

udimmo dire ... (282–284) 1–19.

The flame was already erect and quiet, having ceased to speak, and, with the consent of the gentle poet, now went away from us, when another that came on behind it made us turn our eyes to its tip for a confused sound that came from it. As the Sicilian bull (which bellowed first with the cry of him — and that was right — who had shaped it with his file) was wont to bellow with the voice of the victim, so that, though it was of brass, yet it seemed transfixed with pain: thus, having at first no course or outlet in the fire, the doleful words were changed into its language. But after they had found their way up through the tip, giving it the same vibration that the tongue had given in their passage, we heard it say (283–5).

We are, of course, in a part of Hell where sinners are punished by being turned into "tongues" of flame. "Sicilian bull" alludes to the brazen bull invented by the Athenian artisan Perillus, as reported by several ancient Latin authors, Orosius, Pliny , Ovid, and Valerius Maximus whose account follows:

> There was a savage fellow who invented a brazen bull in which victims were enclosed and a fire kindled beneath; they suffered a long and a hidden torture for he so arranged it that the moans that were torn from them sounded like the lowing of a bull, since if they sounded at all like human voices, they might plead for mercy from the tyrant, Phalaris. Now, since he was so anxious to torment the unfortunate, the artisan himself was the first to experience the efficiency of his hideous invention (Singleton, vol. I, 2: 473).

No amount of familiarity with poetic conventions will help us interpret this image. It *does* require considerable erudition; but once the allusion is identified, the reader can process its natural features quite easily: its relevant features are "no course or outlet" for crying, extreme pain, torture, flames, de-humanisation, and some kind of "natural" justice.[7] In Dante's passage the brazen-bull image is introduced, apparently, only as a simile for "having no course or outlet" for crying. But once introduced, all the afore-mentioned features connect to elements in the target image. Spitzer used above the word "outlet" as part of his metalanguage; in this passage, "having at first no course or outlet in the fire" becomes one of the central terms of the poetic text, turning the victim shut up in the bull into the prototypical situation of terrible pain and lack of outlet for it. *No outlet* suggests not merely the physical barrier, but also that any pleading for mercy in the verbal medium would be doomed to failure, would be perceived in the outside as the bull's bellowing. Here de-humanisation must be understood literally.

Here we are confronted with hybrids of flame-men. I will not repeat here all that I have said about the hybrids of plant-men, and will only focus on one key expression of the passage. Consider the tercet "thus, having at first no course or outlet / in the fire, into its [the fire's] language / the doleful words were converted". There is here a drastic deviation from normal cognitive functioning; in normal cognitive functioning speech or crying are perceived through the aural sense. Being shut up in a red-hot container, and having no course or outlet for one's shrieks is a desperately helpless situation. But it is still in the domain of the "what", and the conversion is from human shrieks into bull's bellowing—still within the auditory mode. When the painful cries and shouts are translated into a different medium and perceived, visually, as the vibrations of a sensitive, flickering tongue of flame, they produce in the reader a strange sensation, making one suddenly doubt one's comfortable relationship with one's own cognitive system. But this is not the whole story.

It can be objected that the verses merely *portray* such a shift of sensory modes, but do not *interfere* with the functioning of the reader's cognitive apparatus. The portrayal of this shift of sensory modes, however, entails here a powerful synaesthetic metaphor: "into [the fire's] language / the doleful words were converted". Being exposed to it, the reader must *process* the synaesthetic metaphor, turning from observer to an experiencer of the cognitive shift. To be sure, we are facing a "possible world" in which such conversion may be literally true; nevertheless, interpretation of the phrase involves processing that is characteristic of figurative language.

This metaphor has been haunting me for the past forty years or so. During this period I have acquired theoretical tools that may account for its exceptionally strong appeal, relying on the mechanisms underlying synaesthesia, caricature, and the grotesque as discussed above. Such features as "high potency", or "extremely painful" are transferred from one sensory mode to another (from fire to doleful words)— amplifying the intenseness and painfulness of the doleful words. The supposed literal truth of the statement in this possible world reinforces rather than mitigates these qualities. Throughout the present study I have insisted that language is a highly conceptual tool, and that poets search for ways to escape the tyranny of conceptual

---

7   Some authors explicitly comment on this justice. Ovid, for instance, comments: "Both were just; for there is no juster law than that contrivers of death should perish by their own contrivances" (Singleton, I2: 473).

thought. One way to do this is through synaesthetic metaphor. First, synaesthetic metaphor blurs the boundaries between the clear-cut sensory modes into which ordinary consciousness is marked off; and second, when you convert a relatively differentiated sense ("doleful words") into a less differentiated sense (heat), conceptual differentiation is toned down, and a more intuitive mentation is promoted.

Kris and Gombrich's discussion of the principles of caricature may account, with the necessary changes, for some sources of pleasure derived from this painful metaphor. First, Kris "adopted one of the earliest, and frequently neglected, thoughts of Freud [...] the suggestion that under certain conditions man may attempt to gain pleasure from the very activity of the psychic apparatus" (Kris, 1965: 63). Second, the human tongue and the "tongue of fire" involve a verbal pun as well as a visual pun, as in caricature. Kris and Gombrich (1965) argue that puns and caricatures derive pleasure both from the saving of mental energy, and the renewal of some infantile pleasure. These authors mention caricatures in which politicians or types are presented as animals, or a series of four caricatures showing the "metamorphosis" of Louis Philippe into a pear. Such caricatures give two things in one, exploiting the similar contours in fusing the widely different entities. The result is "very pear and very man". In addition, puns and the scribbling style of caricatures derive pleasure from regression to the babbling sounds and inarticulate movements of the infant, respectively (Kris and Gombrich, 1965: 197; cf. above, Chapter 8).

Dante's image revives the dead metaphor "tongue of fire": the "tongue of fire" and the speaker's tongue have similar shapes and similar vibrating "tips"; it is for this reason that they are called by the same name. The realisation of the "tongue" image is reinforced by the end of the excerpt: "But after they had found their way up through the tip, giving it the same vibration that the tongue had given in their passage, we heard it say". Speech is produced here not by the vibrations of a human tongue, but by similar vibrations of the tip of the "tongue of fire". The fusion of the shapes, of the activities, and of the "tips" of both kinds of tongues results in the saving of mental energy. By the same token, such a process of realisation may cause, according to Thomson, a sense of confusion and emotional disorientation: it arouses a strange sensation, making one suddenly doubt one's comfortable relationship with language, this most habitual part of one's life. This is what renders these lines one of the most powerful passages in the *Inferno*.

The *terza rima* was invented by Dante. Traditional criticism has pointed out that it gives "an effect of linkage to the entire composition"; that "the symbolic reference to the Holy Trinity is obvious"; and that "the intricate harmony which Dante achieves through his mastery of the form gives to the poem a structure at once massive and subtle, a structure which can only be suggested by any passage taken out of context" (Preminger, 1974: 848). I wish to point out a perceptual aspect of this "massive and subtle structure". The *terza rima* is one of the most fluid, least stable stanza forms. The couplet and the quatrain are symmetrical and closed, hence of the strongest gestalt, whereas the *terza rima* is asymmetric and "open". It has no stable closure: a "loose end" is left, insofar as the second line arouses expectations for a rhyme which are fulfilled only in the next stanza. The next stanza leaves another "loose end", tied up in a third stanza, and so forth indefinitely. After 130–150 verse lines there is a lonely line that "ties up" the last loose end, bringing the sequence to a relatively stable halt but constituting no compelling closure for the Canto.

In fact, the structure of the *terza rima* is double-edged, like the other versification structures considered in Chapter 7. It may arouse a vague uncertain feeling, but can also be described, as presented in Chapter 7 and 9, in the words Bergson used to describe the mental flux underlying metaphysical intuition: "There is a succession of states each of which announces that which follows and contains that which precedes it. In reality no one begins or ends, but all extend into each other". Notice, however, that Bergson speaks of a succession of objects, whereas I am speaking here of a succession of prosodic units. One can also view this instability differently. Many sentences in Dante's poem run-on from one line to another, from one tercet to the next one, blurring the line ending and the tercet ending. When you print Dante's text (as some editors do) as a single continuous block of verse lines, you might tend to group one *terza rima* and the subsequent line into an a-b-a-b quatrain; but then there follows a line that must be grouped forward, and yet another that must be grouped backward, intruding upon the symmetrical closed unit: the whole grouping falls apart. Furthermore, as Barbara Herrnstein-Smith pointed out, the *terza rima* has no "self-generated" end; there is no strong sense of stable closure in it; it just ceases to continue without leaving a loose end. The fluidity of this structure is sometimes enhanced by run-on sentences that begin near the end of the line.[8] Consequently, it can be expected to exert less vigorous resistance to the pressure of enjambment. Thus, both syntactic and prosodic units may be blurred rather than enhanced when tension arises.

Notice the a-b-a, b-c-b, c-d-c etc. rhyme pattern in excerpt 4, as described above. In the fore of perception there is a fluid mass consisting of a blend of rhythmic, syntactic, and semantic structures, in which the rhyme pattern is backgrounded. The fluidity of the passage is enhanced by the extremely long and complex sentences. The first sentence, for instance, runs from the first to the sixth line of the passage, blurring the line endings and the stanza ending. Behind this smoothly moving mass, in the background, the rhymes are "clicking in" in the back of the listener's mind, articulating, so to speak, the line endings. In the first two tercets syntactic anticipation is kept to a minimum. The first tercet is occupied by two co-ordinate clauses that make no further syntactic predictions. What is more, the first two lines are apparently end-stopped: the utterance "The flame was already erect and quiet" appears to be complete; only after the event the adverbial "by saying nothing" re-opens, so to speak, the closed unit (something similar can also be said about "and already went

---

[8]   As I have pointed out elsewhere (Tsur, 1972; 1992: 139–148), the sequence of *terzinas* in Shelley's "Ode to the West Wind" is strewn with such run-on sentences, rendering it exceptionally fluid. At the same time, not as in Dante's poem, this sequence is "jointed" into brief "divergent passages" the beginning of which is exceptionally fluid, but are sealed off by a *couplet* that constitutes an exceptionally stable closure.

away from us, / with the consent of the gentle poet"). Only the conjunction "quand'" at the onset of the next tercet indicates a further, unpredicted, subordinate clause. In the next three tercets, by contrast, great tension is generated. These tercets are occupied by one single compound-complex sentence, made up of several main and subordinate clauses, arousing strong suspense, by both syntactic and figurative means. The most notable of these is the long epic simile introduced by the conjunction "As", in the sense of "in the same way that". The epic simile involves the comparison of one composite action or relation with another. But it is distinguished not only by its length and elaborateness, but also by the order of presentation: in the epic simile the "source" image as a rule precedes the "target" image, generating a period of extended anticipation. Thus, the conjunction "Come" introduces a two-tercet-long image, alien to the immediate context; and predicts another image, relevant to the context, which occurs only in the third tercet. In the meantime, the reader is left in ignorance, uncertainty, and suspense as to the target of the simile.

In the third tercet of this passage I wish to point out only two more devices that increase tension—one of acceleration, the other of suspense—and contribute to the backgrounding of the rhyme pattern. First, the phrase "prima / col pianto di colui" ("first / with the cry of him") begins only two positions before the line ending, yielding an exceptionally strained enjambment, and giving a strong forward impetus to the flow of the utterance. Second, the sentence "As the Sicilian bull [...] was wont to bellow with the voice of the victim" provides the main information of the image, straddled over two tercets. This sentence is interrupted by a digression in the parentheses "which bellowed first with the cry of him [...] who had shaped it with his file"; and there is another digression-within-digression: "and that was right".

Thus, the awfulness of Dante's hell is induced, pace Tennyson, by the fluid sequence of prosodic structures further blurred by elaborate syntactic structures and epic similes, combined with the effects of interference with the smooth functioning of the cognitive system on the thematic-figurative level.

It may be objected that the same prosodic and syntactic structures also underlie the *Paradiso;* therefore their vagueness cannot account for the awfulness of Hell. This objection poses no real difficulty to my argument. Rather, it encourages a further development of it. As I claimed in Chapter 7, both strong and weak shapes are "double-edged". The same verbal strategies that generate vagueness in Milton's Hell can be used to generate a variety of altered states of consciousness that involve "Oceanic dedifferentiation", such as mystic experience, varieties of ecstasy and meditation. The same verbal strategies are used in poetry to generate these mystic qualities as to render Milton's Hell vague. What is more, as I have pointed out in several of my writings, the same verbal strategies are used to generate emotional qualities in poetry that are not necessarily of a religious nature.

The same uninterrupted succession of *terza rima* stanzas continues throughout the three books of the Divine Comedy, giving an effect of "interrelatedness" and "linkage" to the entire composition. The present suggestion is that much more than "linkage" is involved. The pilgrimage through Hell, Purgatory and Paradise constitutes not merely a complex whole, but also an emotional pattern. Maud Bodkin speaks of the emotional patterns of the "Death and Rebirth Archetype", and the "Archetype of Heaven and Hell". In Coleridge's work, for instance, we find the former in "The Rime of the Ancient Mariner", as an underlying "pattern of rising and sinking vitality, a forward urge and backward swing of life, reflected in an imagery deployed in time", whereas in "Kubla Khan" we find the latter, as "an emotional pattern of somewhat similar character presented statically, in imagery of fixed spatial relation—the mountain standing high in storm and sunlight, the cavern unchanging, dark, below, waters whose movement only emphasizes these steadfast relations of height and depth" (Bodkin, 1963: 114–115).[9] Dante's journey unfolds both in space and time: Hell, with all its emotional correlates, constitutes the earliest stages of his journey, Paradise the latest. Between them we find Purgatory, the place of expiatory purification. This constitutes not merely a mapping of the other world, but also an emotional pattern.[10] Bodkin analyses at some length the imagery of super-sensuous light and heavenly ascent in the *Paradiso* in an attempt to account for the verbal presentation of super-sensuous joy. I submit that the imagery of the *Inferno* and that of the *Paradiso* exploit and realise different potentials of the same prosodic-syntactic structure. In this way, the underlying prosodic-syntactic structure reinforces not only the mere unity of the composition, but also a changing emotional pattern unfolding in time.[11]

To Sum Up

The present study proposes to account for the varieties of religious experience by assuming that their idea-contents alone cannot account for their effects. They need to be enhanced by the effects of the disruption of cognitive processes related to ordinary consciousness. Bosch and Dante resort to similar techniques, in their respective media, to evoke an immediate perception of the infernal. The demonic or infernal in visual representation may result from a disconcerting presentation of the infernal creatures. The grotesque causes confusion and emotional disorientation (resulting in discomfort, pain, distress, or anxiety) by two conflicting defense mechanisms disrupting each other's activity, or the suspension of boundaries between established cate-

[9] Significantly, Wilson Knight speaks of "Coleridge's Divine Comedy".

[10] "A few words may be said concerning the relation of the image of Hell or Hades, as here considered, to the 'night journey' stage within the pattern of Rebirth. The horror of Dante's Hell is made bearable for the reader by the fact that interest is concentrated upon a forward movement. The torments of the damned are described as unending, but they have their effect as incidents in a journey—a transition from darkness to light, from the pangs of death to new life" (Bodkin, 1963: 136) By the way, this passage has entirely different presuppositions from Tennyson's as to the awfulness of Dante's Hell.

[11] Unfortunately, I cannot elaborate here on this issue, and must be necessarily sketchy. I have discussed related issues at greater length in my book on "Kubla Khan" (Tsur, 1987b).

gories. I have established a three-stage scale in visual representation stretching from a conceptual to a perceptual causation of painful awareness. The hybrid creature of figure 2 is dominated by dangerous body parts: the head and limbs of a human figure are replaced by those members of a beast of prey and a bird of prey that most typically serve to seize or devour their victims; this direct threat is reinforced by deadly weapons in its hands. paradoxically, the explicit threat alleviates the discomfort and uncertainty caused by the mixing of categories. In figure 1 the images violate our established thought categories, suspending the boundaries between the categories of "human" and "goat". The confusion caused by these images is strongly mitigated in two ways: the mixed elements are highly conventional, and there *are* names and thought categories for these creatures: "devils", "demons", etc. In Bosch's painting, the emotional and perceptual disorientation or exasperated helplessness are the highest, because they are effected by the unconventional mixing of a large number of elements into creatures for which there are no precedents in art, or names in our language, or categories in our thought. Another way to achieve this disorienting effect is the blatant flouting of taboos. In Dante, despite all the differences, we encounter surprisingly similar devices to arouse emotional disorientation: hybrids consisting of plants or flames that reveal "the anguished workings of a human mind and heart". The phrase "the doleful words were changed into the fire's language" suggests both a pun and a synaesthetic metaphor, arousing an exceptionally powerful semantic and perceptual process.

This chapter has touched upon some methodological issues too. In the study of Bosch I found support for Wilson Knight's claim that sometimes certain kinds of scholarship are used to suppress the painful experience evoked by great art. Leo Spitzer too found that source-hunting scholarship is not the most illuminating way to handle Dante's mastery. Briefly, I attempted to face the issue of anachronism by considering the relative merits of historical research (including source-hunting) and psychological explanation.

Chapter 11

Let There be Light and the Emanation of Light
The Act of Creation in Ibn Gabirol and Milton

Thou art wise; and wisdom, the source of life, flows from Thee, / and every man is too
  brutish to know Thy wisdom.
Thou art wise, and pre-existent to all pre-existence, / and wisdom was with Thee as
  nurseling.
Thou art wise, and Thou didst not learn from any other than Thyself, / nor acquire wisdom
  from another.
Thou art wise, and from Thy wisdom Thou didst send forth a predestined Will, / and made it
  as an artisan and a craftsman,
To draw the stream of being from the void / as the light is drawn that comes from the eye,
To take from the source of light without a vessel, / and to make all without a tool,
Cut and hew / and cleanse and purify;
That will called to the void and it was cleft asunder, / to existence and it was set up, / to
  the universe and it was spread out.
It measured heavens with a span, / and its hand coupled the pavilion of the spheres / and
  linked the curtains of all creatures with loops of potency; / and its edge of the curtain
  in the coupling.
  (Solomon Ibn Gabirol, *The Kingly Crown*, IX. translated by Bernard Lewis)[1]

In this chapter I propose to compare the poetic treatment of Creation in Milton's
Paradise Lost and Ibn Gabirol's *The Kingly Crown*. Many people may have doubts
as to the legitimacy of such a comparison. If a person believes that as a precondition
to such a comparison one must first prove poetic influence, s/he is bound to regard
this as a dubious enterprise: there is no doubt that Milton did not read Ibn Gabirol's
poetry. Indeed, Ibn Gabirol wrote in Hebrew in eleventh-century Moslem Spain;
Milton, by contrast, wrote in English, in the seventeenth century, in a very different
cultural setting. One poet was a devout Jew, the other—a devout Christian. Yet,
from the thematic point of view, there appears to be some firm ground for
comparison. Both poets wrote in the Biblical tradition; and both were strongly

---

[1] London, 1961. I have inserted oblique lines in the text, to indicate the end of rhymed
   units, and occasionally re-arranged the passages, so as to indicate the groups of
   "verses" rhyming on the same ending. This I have done in accordance with Professor
   Schirmann's edition of the Hebrew text in his *Hebrew Poetry in Spain and Provence*,
   Jerusalem and Tel-Aviv, 1961, Book I. Part I., pp. 262–3. My reservations on details
   of the translation have been indicated in the course of my discussion of the work.

influenced by Neo-Platonic philosophy. The need to fuse these two traditions posed a peculiar aesthetic (and perhaps also a philosophical-theological) problem to both poets. Though there is no direct continuity between the two traditions, both are related with the classical tradition of rhetoric, which may account for certain similarities in their handling of figurative language. But all these things considered, the two poetic traditions still differ widely.

Furthermore, these two poetic treatments of Creation occur in very different poetic genres. Milton's poem is an epic, recounting the story of "Man's first disobedience" and, within that story, the act of Creation. Ibn Gabirol's poem is lyrical, combining a philosophical contemplation of God's attributes and of the created universe with a confession, probably composed for ritual performance in an actual service.

The question that arises is how can one compare the poetic structures of works so disparate? Such a comparison requires critical categories general enough to be applicable over a wide cultural and conventional gap, and still not too general to make meaningful distinctions within and between particular works. We claimed in Chapter 1 (and *passim*) that in translating effects from one semiotic system to another—or, as in the present instance, in comparing effects in one poetic system to effects in another—equivalences are shaped and constrained by the options available in the respective systems. The point is to find categories that may relate general impressions, "regional qualities", to their respective texts in a reasoned manner. I have already provided one such pair of categories, "convergent and divergent style" (Chapter 7); now I will add another, "split and integrated focus", and test both. This method affords us great flexibility in our study. There is no single element whose presence is a necessary condition for any of these qualities; and not all the elements present necessarily contribute to the same quality. Nor can the absence of any element refute the general impression. Only one property is indispensable for each one of these qualities: a minimum degree of unity. In the next section I will give some examples of the divergent style with its guiding principles in Milton's poetry. The CONVERGENT~DIVERGENT distinction in Ibn Gabirol's poetry will be discussed in the section "CONVERGENT vs. DIVERGENT Style in *The Kingly Crown*".

Divergent Style in Milton

Poems can be compared from the point of view of convergence/divergence (as I did in Chapter 7). The blank verse and the syllabo-tonic versification system underlying *Paradise Lost* are more fine-grained than the rhymed prose of *The Kingly Crown,* and offer a greater variety of options; but both can display the CONVERGENT~DIVERGENT opposition. Both are based on convergence or lack of convergence of linguistic and versification units. The former consists of a series of verse lines of equal length and structure whose ends converge (or fail to converge) with the ends of such syntactic units as phrase, clause, or sentence; and strings of regularly alternating weak and strong metrical positions converging (or failing to converge) with strings of regularly or irregularly alternating stressed and unstressed syllables. The rhymed prose of *The Kingly Crown* consists of a series of rhymed units of unequal length whose ends correspond (or fail to correspond) to the ends of syntactic units. Metrical position, syllable stress, syllable length or syllable counting are irrelevant to this system.[2]

"Convergent" style is marked by clear-cut shapes, both in contents and structure; it is inclined toward definite directions, clear contrasts (prosodic or semantic)—toward an atmosphere of certainty, a quality of intellectual control. "Divergent" style is marked by blurred shapes, both in contents and structure; it exhibits general tendencies (rather than definite directions), blurred contrasts, an atmosphere of uncertainty, an emotional quality. Convergence appeals to the actively organising mind, divergence to a more receptive attitude. The two are not solid categories, the differences are of degree, shadings are gradual, along a spectrum. In one style the various linguistic aspects *tend* to act in convergence, in the other in divergence. This may be reinforced by aspects of the imagery: whether the things mentioned have solid characteristic shapes, or the nouns refer rather to "thing-free" abstractions, shapeless masses; or by syntactic structure; convergent poems tend to have a larger number of finite verbs, divergent ones a larger number of nouns and adjectives. The difference of perceptual quality in the two styles is striking. Thus, for instance, in the convergent style sound repetitions tend to be salient and sometimes playful or witty. In divergent style repeated sounds tend to fuse with the dispersed elements, to heighten the emotional quality of the passage, to be perceived as musicality. Let me illustrate this distinction.

In Chapter 7 I claimed that both convergent and divergent structures are "double-edged". In different contexts they give rise to different perceived qualities. In Chapter 7 we found convergent structures underlying hypnotic-numinous qualities as in Blake's "The Tyger" or simplifying qualities as in his "The Lamb"; or mitigating the nightmare quality in a Tennyson passage. Convergent sequences are rare in Milton's poetry. In excerpt 1 it reinforces a nonemotional, "factual" tone. What generations of poetry readers and critics perceived in Milton's poetry and characterised by the epithet "Milton's miraculous organ voice" can be described in structural terms as divergent poetry rich in sound patterns. In Chapter 7 I argued that the divergent structure was associated with the awful uncertainties of "Milton's vague hell". In excerpt 2 below, by contrast, it evokes the perception of a fluid universe and the sublime perspectives of creation.

Our main concern in Milton will be, of course, Book VII of *Paradise Lost*. Here occasionally we find convergent passages, such as

---

[2] It will be remembered that in Chapter 9 we already encountered a similar comparison: the Mercabah hymn and Baudelaire's "Hymne" consist of similar repetitive schemes and syntactic predictions, based on similar prepositional phrases; but the latter is based on a more fine-grained versification system than the former.

1.   Thús Ádam his illústrious guést besóught
       w   s w s   w s   w   s   w s
       And thús the gódlike ángel ánswered míld... (109-110)
       w   s   w s w s   w s   w   s

The repetition of "thus" and the pair of verbs "besought"—"answered" present the two lines as symmetrical. This strong shape is reinforced by the convergence of line and clause; all the lexically stressed syllables but one converge with a strong position (the exception being the first *Thús),* and all the strong positions but one converge with a lexically stressed syllable (the exception being *his* in a strong position). Line 110 is one of the very rare lines in *Paradise Lost* in which stressed syllables occur in all strong positions and only in strong positions (in the first 165 lines there are only two such lines). The repeated sound cluster *st* converges with strong positions and stressed syllables, sharpening the contrast between prominent and non-prominent syllables (illú*st*rious gué*st* besóugh*t*). But even here, convergence is slightly mitigated by the syntactic inversion in line 109; and by the occurrence of the stressed syllable *thus* twice, first in a weak and then in a strong position. This entails a fairly complex sound pattern: in the words *Thús ... illústrious ... thús* the repeated sound cluster occurs twice in a strong position reinforcing the overall convergence of the passage, but once in a weak position, still mitigating it.

Unlike the nearby passages, the business of these two lines is to report quite factually "who told whom". But when the description mounts in intenseness and sublimity, its style becomes increasingly divergent. More precisely, emotion (underlying sublimity) *is* a perceptual corollary of divergence. The increasingly divergent passage is usually sealed, as it were, with a forceful, solid ending (cf. Tsur, 1977: 175-189; 1992a: 148-153, 455-470; 1998a: 243-250, 256-264). The following passage is fairly typical:

2.   On heavenly ground they stood; and from the shore
       They viewed the vast immeasurable abyss
       Outrágeous as a séa, dárk, wásteful, wíld,
       w   s   w   s w s   w   s   w s
       Up from the bottom turned by furious winds
       And surging waves, as mountains, to assault
       Héaven's híghth, and with the cénter míx the póle.
       w   s   w   s w s w   s w s   w s
       Silence, ye troubled Waves, and thou Deep, peace,
       Said then the Omnifick Word; your discord end!   (210-217)

I said "fairly typical", because the typical Miltonic passage has more compelling schemes of phonetic repetition and a greater number of rhythmic deviations. Notwithstanding, here too there are such alliterations—though rather diffuse—as "They viewed the vast immeasurable abyss"; two consonants of "vast" are anticipated in "stood" and repeated in the next line in "wasteful, wild" (and again, two lines later, in "assault")—diverging from its conspicuous alliteration with "wild". "Wild" forms

a "consonant-rhyme" with "winds" at the end of the next line. "From" in an unstressed syllable alliterates with "furious" in a stressed syllable in a strong position.
The nt and nd clusters recur, rather diffusely, in "turned", "winds", "mountains",
"center", "end", and so forth. Notice also how the contrast between prominent and
non-prominent syllables in lines 212 and 215 is blurred by stress deviation. The
passage has a strong onset: it starts at the beginning of a line and there are two finite
verbs in the first two lines (though none of them verb of action). The next finite
verb, however, does not occur before the last word of the quotation. From the middle
of line 210, one single clause runs to the end of line 215. Longer phrases are articulated only by line-endings, breaking them up into segments, whereas lines are sometimes segmented by short phrases. The first point where line-ending converges with
the end of the clause is line 215. The softening effect of a run-on sentence, even in a
rather tame case, enhanced by a mild syntactic inversion, can be noticed if one observes how more straightforward and purposeful is the impact of quote 3:

> 3.   They viewed the vast immeasurable abyss

than of quote 4:

> 4.   ... and from the shore
>   They viewed the vast immeasurable abyss
>   Outrageous as a sea ...

The relatively conclusive tone of the isolated line in quote 3 becomes somewhat
suspensive, hesitant, indecisive in quote 4. Here a complex set of forward-and-
backward directed attention is generated. The prepositional phrase *from the shore*
necessarily anticipates a subject and a predicate. At the same time, the reader must
split his attention in two directions: he must follow the string of words, but bear in
mind, at the same time, that a "loose end" has been left at the beginning of the
clause, the preposition "from", predicting the verb in the next line. The isolated line
in quote 3 converges with what appears to be a clause; its word order is the most
natural one possible: subject + predicate + object phrase, with no inversion of word
order, or interpolated delaying phrase, or prediction of additional syntactic elements.
Hence its conclusive tone and decisive effect of being closed. The post-nominal
adjective phrase in the next line reopens, so to speak, the conclusively closed unit.
The bi-directional attention and the violated stop at the end of the middle line
generates a less "single-minded", more "complex" feeling. A more strained instance
of split attention we find in *Paradise Lost* Book I: 1–6; the poem begins with the
preposition "Of", predicting the verb "Sing" in line 6 (I discussed this instance at
great length in Tsur, 1978, reprinted in Tsur, 1992a: 100–103).
    An intense feeling of violent *quality* is generated by the fact that *actions* sugges-
tive of movement are turned into *conditions* suggestive of movement: violent events
are not expressed by finite verbs but by adjectives as "outrageous ... wasteful, wild",

past participle as "up.... turned by", present participle as "surging" and, finally, the infinitive "To assault" and, governed by the same particle, "mix". Thus, the fluid structure is gradually solidifying only towards line 215. The Divine Decree in the next two lines forms a powerful closure. The command itself has an "atmosphere of patent purpose"; the chiastic structure of line 216 imposes upon it a balanced, closed quality; the end of each of the two lines converges with the end of a syntactic unit. Notice, however, that even this forceful, convergent utterance is softened by divergence on the phonetic and syntactic level, adding to it, in Oras' phrase "the dimension of depth". Line 216 is broken up into no less than four "purposeful" segments, whereas line 217—into only two, alternating direct and reporting speech.

Furthermore, notice the sequence

> 5.   and thou déep, péace,
>   w   s   w   s

blurring the contrast between prominent and non-prominent syllables. The chiastic repetition of *-eep pea-* emphasises two consecutive stressed syllables, in a weak and a strong position. It also creates a "jam" between the last two syntactic units, compelling the reader to slow down. Some critics feel that this bestows some forceful weight upon the sublime creative decree. At any rate, Neo-classical critics with a strong convergent (rational) bias "amended" the phrase into "and peace, thou deep", creating an unusually strong contrast between prominence and non prominence. From the syntactic point of view, the first two commands ("Silence.... peace") are, still, expressed by nouns (it should be granted, however, that such "elliptic clauses" are double-edged; they can equally corroborate convergence and divergence; in the present case—convergence). Only the third command ("end") is a proper imperative verb. "Your discord end" constitutes a salient inversion of word order. In line 217 there is an internal "rhyme": *word—discord,* muted by the fact that one member occurs in a stressed syllable in a strong position at the end of a clause, the other in an unstressed syllable in a weak position, in the middle of an inverted clause. In addition, there are no less the seven <u>d</u>s irregularly scattered in lines 216-217.

But, in fact, the shapeless quality is most conspicuous in the contents of the passage. The only solid (though shapeless) entities mentioned in the passage occur in 210, "ground" and "shore" ("mountains" in 214 is of liquid substance, and functions to indicate impetuous motion). "Centre" and "pole" (215) which may connote clear spatial organisation, definite directions, symmetry, balance, order, are only introduced to serve as direct objects of "mix". Being abstract nouns, they are particularly suitable for takig part in the process of "shape-destruction".

Concerning the command in line 216, Douglas Bush refers the reader to *Mark* 4.39: "And he awoke and rebuked the wind, and said to the sea, "Peace, Be still". This miracle performed by the Son in his human incarnation, can be conceived as of the *type* of his Creation decree. But, beside the illuminating similitude, the difference between the two is even more noteworthy. First, such a comparison emphasises that the forces involved in the act of creation are far more sublime even than those which Christ rebuked in the Sea of Galilee. Secondly, the waves beating into the boat are, indeed, of a shapeless fluid substance, whereas the waves concerned in this passage on Creation are of an "immaterial substance". The Hebrew word for "abyss" *(Tehom)* can mean also ocean, immense water, while the English word primarily refers to an immense void (derived from the Greek word for "bottomless"), which is only "outrageous *as* a sea". Thus, on the one hand, there is a much higher tension between abstract and concrete; on the other hand, one may experience an intense feeling of a supersensuous presence oscillating between existence and non-existence, if one remembers that it is the "troubled waves" and "furious winds" of *nothingness* that have to end their discord. This is enhanced by what I have called throughout the present study a "transferred attribute" or "nominalised predicate". Instead of "to assault / High Heavens" we have here "Heav'ns height" an adjective turned into an abstract noun manipulated into the referring position. So the object of the assault is an abstraction from an abstraction.[3] This shapeless quality is reinforced, as we have seen, by the strained enjambment and metric deviation.

Metaphysical Poetry and Conflicting World Pictures

Sir Herbert Grierson mentions a small group of rare poems which he calls "Metaphysical Poetry, in the full sense of the term". It

> is a poetry which, like that of the *Divina Commedia,* the *De Natura Rerum,* perhaps Goethe's *Faust,* has been inspired by a philosophical conception of the universe and the rôle assigned to the human spirit in the great drama of existence. These poems were written because a definite interpretation of the riddle, the atoms of Epicurus rushing through infinite empty space, the theology of the schoolmen as elaborated in the catechetical disquisitions of St. Thomas, Spinoza's vision of life *sub speciae aeternitatis,* beyond good and evil, laid hold on the mind and the imagination of a great poet unified and illumined his comprehension of life, intensified and heightened his personal consciousness of joy and sorrow, of hope and fear, by broadening their significance, revealing to him in the history of his own soul a brief abstract of the drama of human destiny (Grierson, 1921: XIII).

Although Grierson is uncertain whether the term in its full sense can be applied to *Paradise Lost,* he has no doubt that Milton, too, "was, or believed himself to be, a philosophical or theological poet of the same order as Dante" (ibid., XV). Without going into this distinction between Dante and Milton, I have no doubts that Ibn Gabirol's *The Kingly Crown,* too, belongs to this category of "Metaphysical Poetry, in the full sense of the term". Nevertheless, in Ibn Gabirol, just as in Milton,

---

[3]   It will be noticed that in many chapters of the present study I have repeatedly pointed out such constructions throughout our corpus.

the "definite interpretation of the riddle" has not been founded on sufficiently solid foundations. The solutions offered by these two poets contain systems of a conflicting nature. Their philosophical poetry is characterised by religious, philosophical and astronomical systems that are sometimes incongruous with one another. We are confronted with "the most heterogeneous ideas yoked together by violence"—not as a mere literary device, but as the solution to a scientific-philosophical problem. The seventeenth century was when the great geographical and astronomical discoveries of the preceding centuries gradually destroyed the coherent world picture of the Middle Ages and the Renaissance; likewise, the religious disputes and wars undermined the unified scale of values. Ibn Gabirol, on his part, lived in Spain, where the three major monotheistic religions (Jewish, Christian, and Moslem) met.

Incompatible elements or ideas may occur together in one of two different ways. They may blur each other, generate ambiguity, uncertainty, or they may conflict, trying to "preserve their warring identity", in James Smith's famous formulation. An illuminating example would be the violent yoking together of the geocentric and heliocentric conceptions of the world in one poem. In Book VIII of *Paradise Lost,* Adam asks Raphael about the movement of the stars; Raphael gives a long lecture presenting the Ptolemaic world picture, as described by Ibn Gabirol as well, existence within existence, orb within orb:

> 6.   Cycle and epicycle, orb in orb: (84)

However, in line 122, Raphael switches to the rival possibility:

> 7.   What if the sun
> Be center to the world; and other stars,
> By his attractive virtue and their own
> Incited, dance about him various rounds? (122–125)

Raphael does not prefer any one of these theories: it seems to him that neither can explain the true nature of Creation, which "From Man or Angel the great Architect / Did wisely to conceal [...] / [...] who ought / Rather admire". All these models seem to him ridiculous; and from this point of view there is little difference between them (lines 70–79). There is no reliable evidence as for which one of them is right; moreover, the very existence of opposite theories proves that it is impossible to understand the wonders of Creation. In this example, the conflicting models do not generate a witty quality; they arouse wonder and admiration in the face of what is beyond understanding. Milton's contemporary, John Donne, by contrast, presented in his Holy Sonnet "I am a little world" the two world pictures side by side, sharpening their conflict as much as possible, and untuning "the harmony between microcosm and macrocosm", so as to achieve metaphysical wit (see above, Chapter 6).

This example shows how poems can be compared along the axis *split* and *integrated* focus. Dr. Johnson said of metaphysical wit that in it the most heterogeneous elements are violently yoked together. I argue that every image yokes heterogeneous elements together. The difference between split and integrated focus lies not in the disparity of the elements, but in their different rhetorical manipulation (cf. Chapter 13, below). The same elements can occur in different hierarchical orders, or they may strive for dominance, failing to achieve a hierarchic order. One of the techniques for "yoking together the most heterogeneous ideas by violence" is relevant here. Sometimes a metaphysical poet ("metaphysical" both in the wider and the more restricted sense) may wish to solve a paradoxical problem of philosophy, or "yoke together" two incompatible philosophical ideas in a more or less arbitrary manner. Then, sometimes, the poet resolves the paradox by relying on the resemblance of words and not the resemblance of ideas. That is what the neo-Classical critics called "false wit". Let us take the following verse from Section I of Ibn Gabirol's "The Kingly Crown" (I will discuss this verse in a slightly different context in Chapter 12):

8.   Yours is the reality whose light's shadow generated all existent
        things / of whom we said: under his shadow we shall live.

The philosophical-theological problem which both Ibn Gabirol and Milton must face is how to fuse the Neo-Platonic conception of Creation by light emanation with the Biblical conception of a personal God. Ibn Gabirol was preoccupied with this problem not only as a poet, but also as a philosopher (cf. Guttmann, 1973: 114). One of the solutions in *The Kingly Crown* (but, as we shall see, not the only one) is to be found in the verse under consideration. The word *shadow* occurs in it in two different senses: the phrase "light's shadow" refers, according to commentators like Schirmann and Yarden, to light emanation. Light and shadow are usually perceived as opposites; but here they are conceived of as of successive stages in one continuous process: the shadow is a relatively less spiritual, more physical stage in the process of emanation. In the next image there is a drastic shift: "his shadow" suggests something like Divine Providence or protection, implying a personal God. The phrase "under his shadow" is idiomatic, a dead metaphor; but its juxtaposition with "light's shadow" revives it. "Of whom we said: under his shadow we shall live" is a verbatim quotation from *Lamentations* IV: 20, where "he" refers to flesh-and-blood, "the Lord's annointed" who "was taken in the pits" of "our pursuers"; "live" suggests here "dwelling among the nations", whereas in Ibn Gabirol's text it suggests "being one of all living things". Thus, Ibn Gabirol's "under his shadow we shall live" involves a drastic shift of meaning both from his own earlier image and from the Biblical verse. The conflicting conceptions of the godhead are reconciled here in a verbal pun, in one verbal signifier that signifies two incongruous notions.

"Shadow" has, then, two meanings in Ibn Gabirol's poem, incongruous not only in their referents, but also in their emotional tendencies: in its first meaning, it refers to a state of being that is less pure than the one referred to by "light"; in its other meaning, it serves as protection against (excessive) light. Accordingly, "light", too, has a pure and a harmful meaning in this verse. Metaphysical conceits exploit one after the other various, usually incongruous, potentials of the underlying image.

In the next verse, Ibn Gabirol resorts to a talmudic common-place; but as an additional meaning potential of the foregoing image, it is unforeseen:

9.   Thou hast the reward which thou hast hoarded and concealed for the righteous, / and saw it was good and hast hidden it.

Among other sources for this verse, Dov Yarden quotes the following from *Ḥagiga* 12: "The Light which The-Holy-One-blessed-be-He created on the first day [...] he concealed. [...] And for whom did He conceal it? For the future righteous men, for it has been said *(Genesis* 1.4) And God saw that the light was good, and there is nothing as good as a righteous man, for it has been said *(Isaiah* 3.10) Tell the righteous that it shall be well[4] with them". This is, then, one of the efficient ways prevalent in Metaphysical poetry to yoke together heterogeneous ideas in an arbitrary if not violent manner, resolving them on the verbal level only. This is one of the ways to generate split focus (in our discussion of Section 9 of *The Kingly Crown* we will see another, less arbitrary way of combining the two conceptions of the Creator).

Divergent style may integrate the perception of discordant elements, generating what some art critics and historians call "soft focus". On the other hand, when the various aspects of language converge along two lines, the focus is split (some art critics and historians call its perceptual quality "sharp focus"), usually generating wit or irony.

The focus of incongruous elements can be integrated, e.g., by subsuming them in a descriptive scheme, such as *chronographia* or *topographia*, in a landscape, a coherent situation, a sustained mythical image, a continuous epic or dramatic action. This perceptual phenomenon may be explained by one of two perceptual mechanisms which I have expounded elsewhere at great length, or both. Michael Polányi (1967) discerned the cognitive mechanism that generates *tacit knowledge.* Such knowldge may be generated when attending away from the *proximal term* of the tacit knowledge to its *distal term,* which bestows a meaning upon the *whole.* In the present instance, the verbal pun is the proximal term, the descriptive scheme—the distal term. The other cognitive mechanism concerns space perception: the schemata of *chronographia* or *topographia* activate cognitive mechanisms that are similar to the orientation mechanism, which organise semantic information as diffusely as possible (cf.Chapter 4, above). On the other hand, focus can be split, to mention only a few possibilities, by a sudden leap from one universe of discourse to another, by "domesticating" a sublime theme, or by the unexpected introduction of a characteristic stable shape into a context of fluid diffuse impressions, of vague, shapeless masses, thing-free qualities.

As I suggested earlier, both sets of terms, convergent/divergent and split/ integrated, refer to overall impressions, to "regional qualities" of poems. This has a par-

---

4   Thus the Revised King James Version; the Hebrew text literally translated says "Tell the righteous that [he is] good".

ticular advantage for our inquiry. No particular element is required to be present for any of these qualities; and not all elements present contribute to the *same* quality (hence the complexity of poems). The absence of no element can refute the over-all impression. There is only one single property that is required for *all* these qualities, a *minimum degree of unity*. On the other hand, every element that occurs will count toward either convergence, or divergence, either split, or integrated focus. Thus, for instance, we have seen that in Milton's epic the iambic line frequently plays a decisive part in its divergence from syntactic units and lexical stress pattern. Ibn Gabirol's *The Kingly Crown*, on the other hand, is written in rhymed prose; so, metre can have no influence on the quality of the poem. This is not necessarily so in all of Ibn Gabirol's poems. The main bulk of his poetry is rhymed and measured (in strict quantitative metre), sometimes with a strongly divergent tendency. But, whereas in Milton's blank verse formal rhyme can have no decisive function, in Ibn Gabirol's rhymed prose it is *the main prosodic feature*. Here, the end of a prosodic unit cannot be predicted; it is wholly arbitrary where the rhyme will fall, with two restrictions: that the successive members of one rhyme may not be interrupted by members of another rhyme; and that the rhyme word must occur at the end of what may be considered a syntactic unit, whether a clause (in which case the balance is tilted in the direction of convergence), or a more or less independent nominal phrase (in which case the balance is tilted in the direction of divergence). Another consideration may concern the structure of the syntactic unit. We have seen that in Milton clauses frequently have a strongly divergent impact by heightening their "predictive load". In Section IX of *The Kingly Crown* clauses are usually short, and their predictive load minimal. Nevertheless, we will observe in this section some very significant syntactic variation, where a nominal style is substituted for a verbal style—at points that are by no means accidental. As we shall see, these syntactic variations may considerably affect the divergent or convergent character of the passage.

The Vague and the Precise: Donne's and Milton's Compasses

One important device for splitting focus, for achieving a quality usually associated with metaphysical wit, is the "domestication" of great themes. According to Alexander Pope, "True wit is Nature to Advantage dress'd". Metaphysical poets normally prefer to treat the sublime themes of poetry in terms of something less sublime, everyday activities, niceties and precision being the antithesis of the sublime—dress it "to disadvantage". Man-made instruments—instruments of precision, in particular— may have such a "domesticating" effect, especially when unexpectedly introduced in an elevated or spiritual context (see Ibn Gabirol's "bucket" below). I wish to illustrate split and integrated focus by considering the way Donne and Milton handle the same image, of compasses. Donne, in his "Valediction forbidding Mourning" deals with a problem that "resembles ontological problems of the one and the many", to use James Smith's phrasing, in "Our two souls, therefore, which are one". I shall point out only two related devices that make the poem witty rather than sublime: (1)

Donne treats spiritual reality in terms of an instrument of precision, dwelling on exact details; (2) in order to appreciate all the spiritual implications of the image, the reader must carefully *visualise* the details of the image.

> 10.   If they be two, they are two so
>   As stiffe twin compasses are two,
>   Thy soule, the fixt foot, makes no show
>   To move, but doth if th'other doe.
>
>   And though it in the centre sit,
>   Yet when the other far doth rome,
>   It leans and hearkens after it,
>   And growes erect as that comes home.

Milton uses the compass image very differently (VII. 224–231). He, too, introduces his instrument in a context of shapeless and sublime masses and abstractions. But unlike Donne (1) he does not "domesticate" the spiritual and the sublime and (2) he makes the transition from visual shapes to shapeless entities as smooth as possible, making them continuous with one another rather than using similitudes and overt statements about those similitudes. The theme of Donne's poem is the lovers' souls and the compass is a simile, speaking of the spiritual in terms of the "domestic"; whereas in Milton, the theme is the Supreme Architect with his compasses.

The compasses occupy a higher place in the hierarchy of Milton's poem than in Donne's. They are no "mere" figure of speech, the vehicle of a domesticating transfer; they are conceived as part of a sustained mythical image, really existing in the context of the possible world of an architect creating a universe. The shapeless masses are not presented in "warring" opposition to it, but subsumed into it. The shapelessness of Chaos is an extension of the Architect's image, who gives shape to everything. Secondly, the description proceeds from the instrument to the sublime and shapeless, and not, as in Donne, from the spiritual and shapeless to the exact and domestic instrument. Thirdly, Milton's instrument is anything but "domesticated". He adapts it to its sublime task well in advance, so that the transition should not be too abrupt.

> 11.   Then stayed the fervid wheels, and in his hand
>   He took the *golden* compasses, *prepared*
>   In God's *eternal* store, to circumscribe
>   The universe and all created things (VII. 224-227, my italics).

In line 228 attention is focussed on the exact use of the compasses (threatening with the domestication of the Sublime Act): "One foot he centered, and the other turned...". But, the design drawn by the golden compasses is not allowed to solidify into a definite circle (as in Donne). The second foot is lost in the vague and infinite and shapeless, or even matterless, so to speak:

12.   One foot he centered, and the other turned
       Round through the vast profundity obscure... (VII. 228-229).

(Notice the diffuse perception of the sound cluster n-t-r-d in ce<u>nter</u>ed, <u>tur</u>ned, <u>rou</u>nd, <u>pro</u>fu<u>nd</u>ity and f-t in <u>foo</u>t and <u>pro</u>fundity). Unlike *the Deep* which may denote "sea, Ocean", especially in the Miltonic vocabulary, its synonym, *profundity,* is a purely abstract noun. Its two epithets, *vast* and *obscure* indicate vagueness, indistinctness, lack of understanding, immaterial qualities — as opposed to the exactitude of compasses and circumscription, which are related with the rational shapes of geometry. From line 232 on, Milton elaborates on the shapeless as the background for Creation. Notice my italics in the following passage, concentrating on shapeless matter and abstract nouns. Most illuminating is the transferred epithet "wat'ry calm"; it substitutes an abstract for a concrete noun "calm waters" — itself denoting a shapeless substance:

13.   Thus God the heav'n created, thus the earth,
       Matter unformed and *void. Darkness* profound
       Cover'd *th'abyss;* but on the *wat'ry calm*
       His brooding wings the *Spirit* of God outspread,[5]
       And vital *virtue* infused, and vital *warmth*
       Throughout the *fluid mass*... (VII. 232–237; my italics).

---

[5]   A comparison between Milton's and Wordsworth's use of "brood" may indicate how romantic poetics involves, in some respects, the amplification of Baroque poetic devices. Compare

                    on the wat'ry calm
       His brooding wings the Spirit of God outspread
and
       The gentleness of heaven broods o'er the Sea

Both texts use poetic diction to manipulate attention away from some Gestalt-free entity to one of its Gestalt-free and thing-free attributes, to roughly the same effect ("wat'ry calm", "gentleness of heaven"). But whereas in Milton "brood" is applied to the concrete noun "wings" (the traditional representation of the Holy Ghost) in its familiar literal sense "to cover with the wings", in Wordsworth's pantheistic Calais-Beach sonnet it is applied to an abstraction ("gentleness") in one of its psychological senses (e.g., "sit quietly and thoughtfully"), or in the sense of "hover, loom", increasing the supersensuous "energeia" of the perceived quality (cf. above, Chapter 5).

"Existence out of Nothingness" or "Existence out of Existence"

Both Ibn Gabirol in Section IX of *The Kingly Crown* and Milton in Book VII of *Paradise Lost* give an account of Creation. Both use two not easily compatible sources. Like Milton, Ibn Gabirol sets himself to the poetic task of reconciling the traditional Biblical view with a Neo-Platonic conception (see also Kostandin of Erznka in Chapter 12). But the solution he offers is rather unlike Milton's. I propose to examine two aspects of this problem, as these two poets handled them. I shall argue that both were consistent in their treatment of both aspects: Milton accommodated his sources in divergent, integrated focus; Ibn Gabirol—by splitting the focus.

One aspect is the question "What was the world created of?" According to the Book of *Genesis,* God created the world out of Chaos. Abraham Ibn Ezra, the 12th century poet and Bible commentator explains: *"Creation* means to derive Existence out of Nothingness". The Neo-Platonic view of Creation through the emanation of light is not strictly compatible with this view; it postulates the pre-existence of a purer substance out of which the physical world was derived. In this respect, the relevant passage in Milton is

> 14.   Boundless the deep, because I am who fill
>   Infinitude, nor vacuous the space.
>   Though I uncircumscribed myself retire,
>   And put not forth my goodness, which is free
>   To act or not, necessity and chance
>   Approach not me, and what I will is fate.
>
> *(Paradise Lost* VII: 168–173)

Douglas Bush comments on this passage: "In brief, Milton rejects the orthodox view that God created the universe out of nothing and argues that he created it out of himself: God fills all space, although he has not yet exerted his creative power ("goodness") upon the disordered elements of Chaos (cf. *Timaeus* 53) and this he now, through the Son, proceeds to do. The Creation is a voluntary act, not necessitated...". This seems to imply that Milton takes the easier way. By rejecting one of the two incompatibles (the Biblical view of Creation), Milton's account becomes consistent.

Nevertheless, the first two lines of the above quotation *do* sound paradoxical to the poetically sensitive ear. The reason for this can be explained by the difference between logical and poetic discourse. In logical discourse, the negation of a negative is the perfect equivalent of an affirmative. In poetic discourse, conversely, both the negative concept and its negation are perceptual parts of the utterance, Thus, "nor vacuous" is not a perfect equivalent of "I am who fill". It asserts both the possibility of vacuity and its negation (that is, both *vacuity* and *fullness);* so, the idea of "fullness" (in "I am who fill") is less complex than the negation of the negative concept. It is characteristic of Milton that he does not leave such ambiguities dubious and casual. He reinforces, as here, both opposing implications—usually by some way of repetition. In the present case, the positive implication of "nor vacuous" is reinforced by "I am who fill"; the negative aspects—by other negative notions, as *"In*finitude" and "bound*less* the deep". So, while on the logical surface these lines assert an unambiguous positive idea, their poetic deep structure suggests an oxymoron, equating nothingness with allness; or, to put it otherwise, God and vacuous space are presented as one and two at the same time. As it happens, this oxymoron is widespread in Mysticism, as Gershom Scholem assures us:

> I shall not go into the difficulties with which the orthodox theologians found themselves whenever they tried to preserve the full meaning of this idea of creation out of nothing. Viewed in its simplest sense, it affirms the creation of the world by God out of something which is neither God Himself nor any kind of existence, but simply the non-existent. The mystics, too, speak of creation out of nothing; in fact, it is one of their favourite formulae. But in their case the orthodoxy of the term conceals a meaning which differs considerably from the original one. This *Nothing* from which everything has sprung is by no means a mere negation; only to us does it present no attributes because it is beyond reach of intellectual knowledge. [...] In a word, it signifies the Divine itself, in its most impenetrable guise. And, in fact, creation out of nothing means to many mystics just *creation out of God*. Creation out of nothing thus becomes the symbol of emanation, that is to say, of an idea which in the history of philosophy and theology, stands farthest removed from it (Scholem, 1955: 25).

We should approach the language of Milton and Ibn Gabirol as *poetic use of language*. "'Literature' is well defined as 'discourse with important implicit meaning'" (Beardsley, 1958: 127). The reader has to realise the interplay of the explicit and implicit meanings. Milton achieves a smooth, even surface by what seems to be a "rejection of the orthodox view". In truth, it is an integrated soft focus: one extreme of a mystic oxymoron is explicitly stated, but the account receives a more accurate meaning if the reader realises the incongruous implications (as suggested by Scholem). Ibn Gabirol's strategy is diametrically opposed to Milton's. His basic device is the oxymoron. And not only as a last resort where no better solution can be found. As I hope to show below, he stresses the incompatibility of elements even where he could easily avoid it. Thus, the over-all perceptual quality of the passage is a deliberate split focus.

Unlike Milton, Ibn Gabirol makes the surface of his poem deliberately rough and illogical. He uses the oxymoron: "And it called upon Nothingness—and it was cleft asunder". The verb "cleft asunder" requires some material substance for subject. In other words, the predicate "cleft asunder" is attributed to a subject (Nothingness) which most conspicuously cannot be cleft. This logical inconsistency is sharpened by the fact that the Hebrew verb *nibhqa*ᶜ can be interpreted as *active* intransitive as in

Numbers 16. 31–32: "The ground under them *split asunder;* and the earth opened its mouth and swallowed them up". So *Nothingness* is implicitly turned into an active agent. This logical contradiction can be settled by referring to the mystic equation of nothingness with infinite matter and the Divine itself (or, in Scholem's words, "Creation out of nothing thus becomes the symbol of emanation"). That is, in both poems the reader has to realise some aspect of the mystic oxymoron, either to create it (in Milton), or to settle it (in Ibn Gabirol). In Ibn Gabirol's work, this conception is reinforced by verbal associations. Schirmann, who is noted for his "one word— one meaning" explications, comments on *nibhqaᶜ* (cleft asunder): "It seems to refer to the emanation of light", according to *Isaiah* 58.8, where the same verb is used in "Then shall your light *break forth* like the dawn". Bernard Lewis, by contrast, obviously opted for the allusion to *Numbers*. In my conception of the work, two Biblical "allusions" are condensed in one word; the allusion to *Numbers* generates an oxymoron by splitting Nothingness; the allusion to *Isaiah* enhances the emanation aspect of a more complex metaphor of Creation. The next clause restates the oxymoron by implicitly equating *being* with *becoming*. According to this clause, creation consists of an (existing) substance being pitched, thrust or fastened (into its proper place). This wording implies two incompatible conceptions at one and the same time. Creation suggests the derivation of existence *(the is)* from non-existence *(the isn't);* or, possibly, that a fluid substance is being solidified.

It might be pointed out that Ibn Gabirol's philosophical conception of the physical world created by emanation is fundamentally paradoxical.

> Sensual reality is, at one and the same time, the last link in a uniform series of emanations, and, the absolute opposite of the suprasensuous world. There is a manifest clash here between the monism of the metaphysical view of the world, and the dualism of its theory of values (Guttmann, 1973: 106).

Guttmann thinks that this poses a fundamental problem to Ibn Gabirol's philosophical system; he then adds:

> Even apart from this difficulty, the attempt to bridge the gap between material and spiritual existence, and to convert this essential difference into one of degree, never gets further than vague and metaphorical language. In the last resort, Gabirol, too, could not solve this fundamental problem (ibid.).

This is precisely what Metaphysical poetry is about. Sypher (1955: 122) speaks of "Donne's false and verbal (perhaps false? perhaps verbal?) resolutions—his incapacity to commit himself wholly to any one world or view" (122). "The resolution is gained, if at all, only rhetorically, not [through] reason" (123). As I have suggested elsewhere, both seventeenth century English Metaphysical poetry and eleventh century Hebrew Metaphysical poetry apply paradoxical phrasing to a paradoxical mode of existence (Tsur, 1992: 294).

A few verses earlier the oxymoron is stated most explicitly: "To draw out the stream [or continuity, or substance] of existence from nothing". It occurs in a passage preoccupied with the emanation of light. Here, again, the logical contradiction is most obvious. It can be settled in a similar way to the one discussed above. And here, too, the handling of the verbal material adds to the complexity of the expression. Hebrew *limsokh* means "to draw" in the sense of "to cause to change place in a particular direction, usually in the causing agency's direction"; it may also mean "to pull or pull out or attract or take from". The meaning of the verb includes the idea of continuity. If the *change* and *cause* constituents of the verb's meaning are emphasised, the expression may be conceived of as of an orthodox theological statement. At the same time, if the ingredients of continuity and stretching are emphasized too, it can be conceived as of a sensuous representation of emanation. The expression is further complicated by the obscurity of the noun *mesekh*. Even-Shoshan's Dictionary explains the word as a gerund of *limsokh* (to pull or draw) and quotes the present verse from *The Kingly Crown*. Schirmann draws upon the obscure verse *Job* 28.18, where this noun occurs, and suggests that here it might mean "matter". If this sense is to be accepted, it cannot cancel the usual meaning of the root, three times repeated here in close succession. Yet it can corroborate the matter-aspect of this process which is presented as a sudden miraculous act and, at the same time, as a gradual emanation, from infinitely attenuated matter unfolding as physical reality (very much like Milton's "spun out the air"(*Paradise Lost* VII: 241).

The next verse presents a remarkable simile: "As the light being drawn out from the eye". This simile enhances the continuation aspect of the previous image, on a small scale. Schirmann (1961: 262) explains it: "The Greek philosopher Empedocles explained the power of vision on the assumption that the stream of light comes out from man's eye and it is united with the stream that comes towards him from the object, at which it looks". But, he also adds: "The poet attempts to describe the wonder of creation of existence out of nothing". In other words, the simile reinforces the traditional "wonder" of Creation, and also the implications of continuity. It anticipates, as well, the paradox of equating existence with nothing; the "object" which emits these "invisible rays" is nothingness. From the philosophical point of view, the creation of *existence out of nothing* necessarily requires, then, a great leap entailing, as indicated by Gershom Scholem, severe logical difficulties. From the poetic point of view, by contrast, the transition from nothingness to light emanation is more gradual. The most salient property of "nothing" is that it is a thing-free and gestalt-free quality. As such, the transition to the stream of light—which, at its source, is infinitesimally thin—is quite natural; it involves no big leaps, and there is no clear point at which *nothingness* becomes *something*. In this respect, the continuous change of place serves as a metaphor for continuous change of essence. This aspect of the simile is emphasised by what I said above about the verb *masakh*: contrary to the verb *push*, for instance, the verb *draw (masakh)* focusses attention on the point at which the moving cause is placed, toward which the spatial movement is directed; its starting point may remain vague or indefinite. This vagueness is actualised by the starting point: "nothingness". In this way, the reader may experience the intuition (or, a verbal imitation of the intuition) of existence emerging from nothingness.

Personal Creator or Neo-Platonism: Split and Integrated Focus

The other aspect of the "reconciliation" of incompatible sources by the two poets is connected with the conception of God, the Creator. The Bible presents us with a personal God who created man in his own image. The anthropomorphic conception is further emphasized in the New Testament by the idea of incarnation. The Neo-Platonic account of creation by emanation or through the *Logos* suggests a completely different conception of God. This is not only a theological or philosophical problem. The Neo-Platonic and the Biblical images have contrasting stylistical potentials. The stylistic problem that arises concerns the effective combination of the two. An anthropomorphic God with a personal awareness is not easily converted into a shapeless quality, into a fluid, emanating mass. Such a conversion runs the risk of sudden leaps in transition; or else, it requires deliberate stylistic manipulation to make it more acceptable. According to the kind of manipulation, the work may be seen in integrated soft focus, or in split sharp focus. In the present works, I argue, there is a difference of hierarchical organisation. In *Paradise Lost,* as we have seen, there is a sustained, even surface of definite shapes, into which the fluid masses are subsumed. In *The Kingly Crown,* as in Donne's poem, the primary objects of description are shapeless qualities; definite shapes are introduced as subsidiary discordant elements.

James C. Smith's (1932) definition of metaphysical poetry has become classical: Metaphysical poetry presents problems which resemble such ontological problems as the One and the Many, or time, space, eternity, while the discordant elements preserve their warring identity. In his edition of Milton, Douglas Bush comments on *Paradise Lost,* VII 224–550: "Also, unlike many thinkers and poets, [Milton] feels no conflict between the Many and the One; the Many manifests the One". It is not far-fetched to suggest that it is the *reader* who feels no conflict between the Many and the One. It is a matter of stylistic manipulation whether "the Many manifests the One", or "preserve their warring identity". The ontological paradox of the one and the many, of identifying the *Logos* with God on the one hand and with life and light on the other is already suggested in the New Testament:

> In the beginning was the Word, and the Word was with God, and the Word *was* God. He was in the beginning with God; all things were made through him, and without him was not anything made that was made. In him was life, and the life was the light of men. The light shines in the darkness, and the darkness has not overcome it *(John* 1.1–5).

The question is what the poets do with this ontological paradox. Milton violently yokes together some of the most heterogeneous ideas. But he conceals his violence under silken gloves. Take, for instance, the ideas of the Word and the Son. The one is a typically Platonic concept, the other a typically anthropomorphic conception. Theologically, it may be completely legitimate to identify them. Poetically, however, there may arise the problem of how to join them so that they do not split the focus. I shall briefly consider three instances where Milton identifies the Word with the Son. He never explicitly states that they are identical. In VII 163 Milton implies their identity by juxtaposing them as two vocative phrases which, at first sight, may or may not address the same addressee:

15.   And thou, my Word, begotten Son...

I would like to make two additional comments on this expression. First, "begotten" is a recurring epithet of "Son", and each of the two words implies what the other denotes. So, the adjective does not carry much information. Still, it has here the function of emphasising the flesh-and-blood identity of the Son, as distinct from the abstract Word. Secondly, the continuation of the utterance can apply equally to both:

16.   by thee
          This I perform; speak thou, and be it done.

Thus the reader, though aware of their separateness, feels no acute contrast between the Many and the One.

In VII 174–175 the two notions appear again together, this time as apposite subjects of the same verb:

17.   So spake th'Almighty, and to what he spake
          His Word, the Filial Godhead, gave effect.

Here, though still separate notions, the contrast between abstraction and visual shape is eliminated. The Son idea is turned into an adjective which qualifies an abstract noun; the two yield a periphrasis of the Son: "The Filial Godhead", removed one step further from the concrete shape.

The next instance of identification is at the height of the sublime act of Creation:

18.   "Silence, ye troubled waves, and thou deep, peace,"
          Said then th'Omnific Word, "your discord end".

Apparently, only the all-creating Logos is mentioned here; and this may be so from the theological point of view. Rhetorically, however, this may be a transferred epithet as well (so frequent in Milton's epic style), meaning: "Said the Word of the

omnific God (or Son)". In this case, Word would be a metonymy for the entire decree. Thus, in the phrase "omnific Word" the disparate notions of *Logos* and *begotten Son* are condensed with no explicit contradiction. Thus, we may see, Milton apparently introduces (in both quote 17 and 18) certain constructions merely for the
sake of seventeenth century poetic diction, but in fact exploits them by also for
imperceptibly fusing the Neo-Platonic *Logos* with the personal Son as creators.

Ibn Gabirol has the task of fusing the conception of a personal, omniscient, and
"self-conscious" God, with the image of light emanation. He resorts to the most
obvious solutions, some of which were later to serve also the Kabbala Mystics (cf.
Scholem, pp. 217–221). What is remarkable in Ibn Gabirol's solution is the powerfully smooth transition from the personal to a "fluid" Godhead on the one hand, and
his persistent violation of his own achievement on the other.

The transition from a personal God to a shape-free entity is performed, most
smoothly, by means of metonymic transfer. One of the attributes of the personal
God is Wisdom. And if God cannot be *smoothly* dissolved as part of a continuous
emanation, His Wisdom is certainly a shapeless abstraction. This transfer is significantly enhanced by certain Biblical allusions, mainly to the Book of Proverbs. In
Proverbs 8.22 ff.[6] Wisdom is presented as created before anything else, being with
God throughout the act of Creation. In the Kabbala, Ḥokhma (Wisdom) is intimately associated with the creative principle of the Godhead (see Scholem, ibid).

In *Proverbs* 19.14 we find the crucial expression "the teaching of the wise is a
fountain of life". Here *fountain* has, in the first place, the meaning of "origin, the
principle of". In Ibn Gabirol's text the expression *has* all these meanings but, in addition, the visual implications of the image are continuously and directly stressed by
the predicate "welling forth" applying to "Thy Wisdom" and a few verses later by the
threefold occurrence of the root *m-š-kh* (draw), and *š- ʾ-bh* (draw water) with the noun
deli (bucket). Yet, notice the two opening verses of the passage (in a literal
translation):

> 19.   Thou art wise — and Thy Wisdom, the Fountain of Life, from Thee
>   welleth forth,
>   And Thy Wisdom — every man is too stupid to comprehend it.

The second of these verses contains a literal quotation from *Jeremiah* 10.14. But
the difference between the two contexts is most significant. In *Jeremiah* the expression occurs immediately after a short description of God's wisdom as revealed in the
created Universe, and as opposed to the impotence of the idols. The actual phrase occurs in a verse preoccupied with man's stupidity in ignoring such obvious signs, and
in creating the idols: *"Every man is stupid and without knowledge;* every goldsmith
is put to shame by his idols; etc...". In *The Kingly Crown* the expression refers to

---

[6]   It is interesting to notice that Milton, too, draws precisely on this chapter, as
Douglas Bush comments on VII. 225 (where he gives further reference to Dante).

transcendental Wisdom, beyond man's understanding, a mysterious creative principle, the source and initiator of emanation, far removed in space and time but, by the same token, existing outside any relation of space and time.

The next two verses press on with the elaboration of the thing-free qualities (by way of drawing upon *Proverbs* 8. 22–31):

> 20.   Thou art wise and pre-existent to all pre-existence,
>   And Wisdom was with Thee as a nurseling.

The very last word breaks this movement in the abstract sphere rather unexpectedly, suddenly leaping to the concrete, by personifying Wisdom as a nurseling. In fact, the surface is not completely smooth. The focus that has been split by the sudden leap is reinforced by the paradoxical implications of "pre-existent to all pre-existence". This method seems to be persistent throughout the present section. Thus, in the following, the poem achieves a powerful Gestalt-free vision:

> 21.   To draw out the stream of being from the void
>   As the light, being drawn from the eye,
>   And it draweth from the Fountain of Light...

But the passage ends, again, on a discordant note:

> 22.   And it draweth from the Fountain of Light *without a bucket*
>   And doth all without a tool.

Dan Pagis devotes an important discussion to the type of construction "to do (metaphoric) action without a (concrete) tool", and calls it "negative metaphor".

"In the sentence 'the inhabitant of this world flies without wings and returns to vain', a part of the image itself appears to be negated. When Ibn Ezra describes the pen which 'flies without a wing' or wine which is 'tempting without a tongue' he adds to these images a rational characteristic, for he points not only to a quality common to the theme and some implicit 'simile' (man or pen fly like a bird etc.), but also to the incongruence of the two universes of discourse. Thus he emphasises that the metaphoric words (fly, tempt...) are really metaphorical, and removes the reader from all animistic identification" (Pagis, 1970: 73).

One could restate this observation in the terminology of the present work (indicating the possibility of further distinctions), saying that the "rational characteristic" is one possible corollary of the fact that in a convergent style the negative metaphor is an efficient means to reinforce split focus.

Pagis observes that in the secular poetry of Moshe Ibn Ezra (who was more fond of this figure than any of his predecessors), "negative metaphor" has the impact of "feigned wonder", "whereas in his Divine poetry (and the secular poems related to it) the negation is founded upon a philosophical conception; God is 'ḥaqiqa', the absolute reality, and negative metaphors are not meant to describe Him, but the impossi-bility of describing Him [...]. In the Divine poems the negative metaphor is a sug-gestion of the real wonder rather than of feigned wonder" (ibid., 78).

From the theological point of view, it is a real commonplace that God always acts without instruments. But from the poetic point of view the recourse to this im-age is remarkable indeed. The metaphor occurs when the image of light emanation of light is well on its way, after having solved the problem of transition from the traditionally anthropomorphic God to a powerful, gestalt-free vision. The immediate effect of the introduction of an everyday man-made tool with a characteristic shape is far from that of yet another conventional metaphor. It most effectively splits the focus of vision. The sublime is domesticated; the result is witty. And how easily this could have been avoided, had Ibn Gabirol wanted to. A poet like Milton would have, simply refrained from adding "without a bucket". (In Bernard Lewis' translation, the "shock" is unduly mitigated by the use of a more generic term, *vessel,* for *bucket).* Once introduced, the image is exploited for additional functions. When we use a metaphor, we abstract from the image certain qualities relevant to the context, and eliminate the irrelevant ones. In "It draweth from the Fountain of Light", the metaphor eliminates the physical and human factors of drawing water. Paradoxically enough, by adding "without a bucket", the poem reminds the reader of the anthropomorphic conception of God, where it has been painstakingly eliminated. Thus the image explicitly reinforces the shapeless conception of God; but by the same token, it associates God with human type of activities and tools. In fact, it is a sophisticated example of the rhetorical device "preterition", which consists of drawing attention to something while pretending not to (far be it from me to draw attention to the fact that...). The order of statements should be noticed too. Had "And doth all without a tool" preceded the bucket image, the sequence would have been less startling. "Doth all" is a superordinate of "draweth water"; and "tool" is more generic a term than "bucket". Interpolation of the more generic terms would have evened the transition, toned down the sharp, abrupt effect.

Convergent vs. Divergent Style in The Kingly Crown

I have said that in this section of *The Kingly Crown* rhymes fall at the end of syn-tactic units, a factor counting toward convergence. But even within such a structure there is room for contrasts, for greater or lesser convergence. The first six rhymes fall at the ends of *clauses;* what is more, this part of the section is predominantly clausal; in the first six rhymed units there are no less than nine predicates. In the passage where shapeless quality is at its amplest, the poem shifts to phrasal struc-ture, yielding emphatic support to it. The proportion of predicates suddenly drops to two in four rhymed units (condensed in the first of them), as follows:

> 23.   Thou art wise, and from Thy wisdom Thou didst emanate a
>   predestined Will,

> As an artisan and a craftsman,
> To draw out the stream of being from the void
> As the light being drawn out from the eye.

When the sudden occurrence of "bucket" splits the focus, clausal structure with its finite verbs returns, reinforcing the "convergent" shape:

24.   It *draws* from the Fountain of Light without a bucket / and *makes* all without a tool / and it *cut* and *hewed* / and *cleansed* and *purified*...

So, syntactic structure most emphatically reinforces the peak of the shapeless qualities contrasted with the preceding part, and then with the next part that splits the focus.

Jefim Schirmann (1962 I. i.: 184) ends his preface to Ibn Gabirol's poems with the following remark: "...he succeeds in a verbal description of what we could never make felt with the help of cold logic: the creation of the world—existence out of nothing—through emanation:

25.   And it called upon Nothingness—and it split asunder
        And upon existence—and it thrust in,
        And upon the world—and it spread out".

וַיִּקְרָא אֶל הָאַיִן – וְנִבְקַע

וְאֶל הַיֵּשׁ – וְנִתְקַע

וְאֶל הָעוֹלָם – וְנִרְקַע!

He gives no indication wherein lies the special force of this passage.

It should not be very surprising that at the dramatic peak of the creating decree, Ibn Gabirol—like Milton—strongly increases the convergent impact of the passage. And—also as in Milton—a thick tissue of divergent elements underlies the convergent command; hence its more than usual impetus and its more than usually vivid "dimension of depth" (though, not as in Milton, the command is given in third person, reported speech). In the first place, one should notice the steep increase of finite verbs as compared with the earlier passages. Most of the following verbs connote violent force:

26.   And it hewed and cut / and-cleansed and purified,
        And called upon Nothingness—and it split asunder / and upon existence / and it thrust in / and upon the World—and it spread out [was hammered out].

From the beginning of the section (in Hebrew) up to here there are only seven fi-nite verbs, as against thirty nouns and adjectives (pronouns not counted). In this pas-sage the proportion is reversed: eight finite verbs as against three nouns, and no ad–jectives (pronouns are implicit). Elliptic phrases and clauses (like word-repetitions) are double-edged: they are powerful means to reinforce either convergence or diver-gence as the context may be. In the present case, they obviously enhance conver-gence. The three Hebrew verbs are near-homonyms: *nivqaꜥ, nithqaꜥ* and *nirqaꜥ*. At the end of the elliptic sentences, they have a strong unifying, convergent, straightfor-ward impact.

Earlier in the present chapter we have seen the oxymora involved in this sequence. One of the means by which the two oxymora become so compelling is that the verbs seem to belong together both phonetically and semantically The second verb denotes "thrust or drive into" (as, e.g., a peg—cf. *Judges* 3.21; 4.21). This seems to be connected with the first image. The thing being thrust (e.g. peg) is driven into the cleavage; or alternatively, the cleavage might have been caused by the thrust. By a small metonymic transfer, the verb came also to mean "to put up a tent" (as in *Genesis* 31.25; hence Bernard Lewis' translation, "it was set up"), giving rise to divergent complementary meanings.

The third verb of the triad is used in the Bible in the sense of spreading, stretch-ing out the earth by God *(Isaiah* 42.5; 44.24; *Psalms* 136.6), and in the sense of hammering out gold (as in *Isaiah* 40.19; *Exodus* 39.3; *Numbers* 17.4). In the first sense, it is noteworthy that Ibn Gabirol attributes this predicate to an abstract sub-ject, *world* (instead of earth). The second sense of the verb seems to be here of no less importance (enhancing the connotations of violence in "hammering out" on a cosmic scale). Schirmann explicates the beginning of this passage: *"And it hewed and cut* are expressions taken from *The Book of Creation* 2.2, and primarily refer to the production of metals; and purified and refined *(Mal'akhi* 3.3.) primarily refer to gold". So, "and upon the World—and it was hammered out" becomes the fifth item in the earlier string of four verbs in the semantic field of metal works.

Subsequently, the description relaxes this unified vision somewhat, creating again a "metaphysical" split focus. As in metaphysical poetry, the *various* implications of the tent-image are further developed one after the other. There are allusions to two dissimilar Biblical passages: *Isaiah* 40.22: "Who stretches out the heavens like a curtain, and spreads them like a tent to dwell in". This verse indicates the visual impression the skies make. According to Ibn Gabirol's (and Milton's; remember: "Cycle and epicycle, orb in orb") Ptolemaic world picture, the heavenly spheres are arranged one within the other. This aspect is taken care of by allusion to *Exodus* 96.17, where the Tabernacle is made curtain within curtain.

Let us quote the next passage from *The Kingly Crown*:

> 27.   It [the Will] measured the heavens with a span, / and its hand
>   coupled the pavilion of the spheres, / and linked the curtains of all
>   creatures with loops of potency.

"Loops of potency" takes up another aspect of the Biblical Tabernacle: "And he (Bezalel) made fifty loops on the edge of the outmost curtain of the one set and fifty loops on the edge of the other connecting curtain" *(Exodus* 36.17). The last clauses complete the process of emanation which welled forth at the beginning of the section from God's Wisdom and reaches at the end "as far as the lowest ebb of creation". So, the image of the tent, introduced by driving in a peg, followed by being set up, spread out like the sky, indicating the visual form of the sky and its arrangement layer within layer, being held together by loops (of potency), reaching down at the Horizon, now completes its task by indicating the hierarchical Great Chain of Being which also reaches down to the lowest creature (by the same token, the process of emanation also reaches down to the lowest creature).

The figures of speech are such as to split the focus between abstract and concrete. "Measured the heavens with a span" is an unmistakable allusion to *Isaiah* 40.12. But in the present context the image undergoes two significant changes. First, from an anthropomorphic God, span is transferred to abstract Will. Secondly, should one be inclined to eliminate the concrete flesh-and-blood aspects of span (as proper in metaphoric constructions), the next phrase reinforces precisely those aspects: "and its [the Will's] hands coupled...". How easily one could put it "and it coupled..."!

Tension between abstract and concrete is carried further by "loops of potency". Dan Pagis calls such constructions "genitive of concretion" (op. cit. pp. 64-70). He observes that such genitives, paradoxically, have rather an abstract, rational impact. It seems to me that this construction is what Christine Brooke-Rose called "pure attribution", which consists in an artificial split of one idea into two. It seems to me, again, that the "rational" impact is a perceptual corollary of the split focus. This tension is extended by an elaborate phrase with two abstract nouns "strength" and "creation", which ends with a literal quotation from the description of the Tabernacle: "the edge of the outmost curtain in the coupling".

Split and Integrated Focus: Milton vs. Milton

Earlier I suggested that the two types of style cannot be accounted for in a satisfactory manner merely with reference to the kinds of the material the poets used. We have found that Donne tended to treat the compass-image in a sharp split focus, as against Milton's soft integrated focus. Furthermore, one could profitably compare the strategies Milton himself uses in treating the same images in, say *Paradise Lost* and the Nativity Ode. In this way, one may make quite significant distinctions between almost "minimal pairs" of images, to which the phrase "other things being equal" can most specifically be applied. This also shows how quite unforeseen, evasively minute differences can be handled fruitfully by our present model, as will be demonstrated forthwith.[7]

---

[7]   This section was reproduced in Tsur, 1992: 97–100.

There is a wide range of sometimes incompatible definitions of the *Baroque*. As may be apparent by now, *Paradise Lost* complies with those definitions of the Baroque in which "divergent" structure and "integrated soft focus" are among the dominant stylistic principles. "Metaphysical", by contrast, applies to a style most conspicuously marked by a "sharp split focus". Herbert Grierson included "On the Morning of Christ's Nativity" in his anthology of Metaphysical poets, making, by the same token, an implicit statement about its style. Helen Gardner, on the other hand, excluded this poem from *her* anthology, supporting her decision as follows: "I differ from Grierson in not including the 'Nativity Ode', a poem too epic in conception and style" (Gardner, 1972: 316). One should not, therefore, be too much surprised to find, e.g., that Milton treated the same images in slightly different manners, manipulating them in ways that in *Paradise Lost* typically count in the direction of integrated focus, and in the 'Nativity Ode' toward split focus. I shall confine my discussion to comparing one stanza of the Ode to parallels of its imagery in *Paradise Lost*. One may on first sight recognise no significant differences. Yet, the small "insignificant" differences gain significance by virtue of their contribution either to split or integrated focus. It would perhaps be more accurate to say that the slight differences between the two poems can be placed alongside a spectrum on which the device in *Paradise Lost* is nearer to the INTEGRATED end, whereas in the 'Nativity Ode' it is nearer to the SPLIT end.

> 28.   Such music (as 'tis said)
>   Before was never made,
>   But when of old the sons of morning sung,
>   While the Creator great
>   His constellations set,
>   And the well-balanced world on hinges hung,
>   And cast the dark foundations deep,
>   And bid the welt'ring waves their oozy channel keep.
>
>   (lines 117–124).

The hanging of the well-balanced world recurs in *Paradise Lost:*

> 29.   [...] then founded, then conglobed
>   Like things to like, the rest to several place
>   Disparted and between spun out the air,
>   And earth self-balanced on her center hung. (VII. 239–242).

Hinges and harmonious sound occur together in

> 30.   [...] Heav'n opened wide
>   Her ever-during gates, harmonious sound
>   On golden hinges moving.   (VII. 205–207).

First, let me make some general observations: syntactically, a single hypotactic sentence runs through the stanza in quote 28; the reader is required to follow, at the same time, both this complex sentence and a complex stanza form with lines of changing length. In *Paradise Lost,* on the other hand, the length of blank-verse lines is unchanged through hundreds of verses. The syntactic structure of the verses in quotes 29–30 from *Paradise Lost* is basically paratactic. This, in itself, can be insignificant. But these two structures can reinforce split and integrated focus, respectively. Hypotactic sentences running through stanzas with lines of changing length form, indeed, a structure much favoured by metaphysical poets like Donne and Herbert; the reader seems to be "compelled" to split his attention between two consistent ways of proceeding.

Second, the parenthesis in line 117 of the Ode ("as 'tis said") seems to be a deliberate device for "domesticating" the sublime. The sublime is experienced *directly.* The verbal imitation of the sublime may involve no "hearsay".

Third, a comparison of some images of the Ode with those of their Biblical source would show how Milton "distorted" the latter in the direction of the concrete and exact, limiting, as it were, their sublime imagination. "He stretches out the north over the void / and hangs the earth upon nothing. / He binds up the waters in his thick clouds [...]" *(Job,* 26: 78). This description is exquisite for its delicate manipulation of shape-free and diffuse entities covering and supporting, so to speak, the earth. In the Nativity Ode, Milton presents the same elements with an emphasis on fixed shapes and stable positions. Instead of upon *nothing,* he hangs the earth on *hinges,* whereas in *Job,* paradoxically, the solid earth is firmly kept in its place by airy nothing. Likewise, he "bid the welt'ring waves their oozy channel keep": in the Nativity Ode, the "welt'ring waves" are contained, nay securely canalized, in their solid channels. The sublime has been brought under control. This domestication of the "welt'ring waves" is apparent, not only as compared to "He binds up the waters", resulting in shapeless "thick clouds", but even when compared to "Let the waters under the heavens be gathered together into one place" *(Genesis,* 1: 9). "Be gathered together into one place" is vaguer than "their oozy channel keep".

In the present stanza of the Ode the first three lines give an account on a consistent level of discourse, of thing-free aural harmonies (with no reference to visual shapes). The rest of the stanza gives an account, also on a fairly consistent level of discourse, of things that have, primarily, a visual appeal and, usually, stable and characteristic visual shapes. The metaphorical possibilities on such consistent levels of discourse are rather restricted. The main effect of the passage comes, indeed, from the drastic shift from the shape-free aural appeal to the predominantly visual shapes which, inevitably, splits the focus.

In VII. 205–207 of *Paradise Lost,* the changes of level are more flexible. Also, the focus appears to be integrated, because the shifting levels are subsumed under one dominant, coherent image. The utterance begins on what Wimsatt calls "the substantive level": "Heav'n opened wide / Her ever-during gates". In what follows, there is tension between two attributes of the opening gates, one less stable, less concretely defined, appealing to the sense of hearing ("harmonious sounds") and the other more concrete (as compared to the "substantive level"), viz., the elaborate visual detail ("golden hinges"). Notice that the description might still remain meaningful — but the focus split — if the integrating over-all image were omitted:

31.   [...] Heav'n opened wide,
          Harmonious sound on golden hinges moving.

The image could be even further domesticated, if "iron" were substituted for "golden.

A word must be said about how the diffuse and shapeless entities are united, brought together in an over-all visual image in lines VII. 239–242 of *Paradise Lost.* The verbs *founded* and *conglobed* refer to the act of taking shape and to stability. An important semantic ingredient of *conglobed* is "globe", one of the most perfect geometrical shapes. But this shape is not *contrasted* to diffuse matter as if we were dealing with two incompatible states. The verb's semantic ingredients include also the process of BECOMING, of transition from one state to another. Its object still suggests a multiplicity of entities upon which oneness is imposed: "conglobed / Like things to like". The rest of the lines 240–241 emphasise precisely the diffuseness of substance, even after having shapes imposed upon it.

I would like, further, to point out the difference between "And the well-balanced world on hinges hung", and "And earth self-balanced on her center hung". The former leaves nothing insecure. The world itself is *well*-balanced, and is hung on stable, solid hinges (Here, some domesticating tension is derived from the abstract *world* being hung on concrete *hinges)*. While *well*-balanced suggests symmetry and perfect organisation, *self*-balanced enphasises rather the lack of stable outward support. Here the earth is kept in a state of rest; a state not due to some solid hinges, but to its placement in the center, that is, to invisible forces that counteract each other. This invisible support is enhanced, so to speak, by the underlying substance, the air "spun out" between the solid bodies. Even the word order corroborates the respective qualities of the two utterances: "And the well-balanced world", with the compound adjective preceding the noun, has the straightforwardness and sense of security of rational discourse, while in "And earth self-balanced", though syntactically legitimate, the adjective following the noun has a quality of less certainty, of hesitation, of afterthought, so to speak. This hesitant quality, coupled with a caesura (which may or may not be observed) precisely after the fifth position, becomes an icon, as it were, of the precarious balance of the earth.

The Effect of Genre: Combination and Selection

It may be remarked that the over-all impact of the literary genre may contribute toward one or other type of style in the two works. The unfolding epic scheme of *Paradise Lost,* with its coherent situations and actions, is likely to integrate the focus even where logical contradictions — as in metaphor and oxymoron — are conspicuous.

In *The Kingly Crown* there is an underlying meditative situation. The speaker addressing God, with the basically paradoxical philosophical and theological argument on the one hand, and passionate devotion on the other, may contribute to what Herbert Grierson (1965: xxxiv) described as "a strain of passionate paradoxical reasoning" which is, he says, the essence of metaphysical poetry. Roman Jakobson in some of his writings insisted upon two structural principles in a great variety of human activities (including linguistic), combination and selection. Construction along the combination axis yields a continuous whole; the selection axis consists in the juxtaposition of parallel (similar or contrasting) entities (see Jakobson, 1956; 1960). The difference between the two works may be profitably expressed in terms of this distinction. Milton's complex structures are subsumed under a sustained mythical image, as well as a continuous epic action. Being continuous, they tend to integrate the focus of the poem in spite of the occasional discordant elements which constitute it. To use Polányi's term, we tend to "attend away" from the incongruous figures to the continuous epic action. The over-all organising principle of *The Kingly Crown* is that of selecting parallel entities. Each of sections I–IX consists of a series of passages which begin with the same word or group of words, according to the theme of the section. The first four passages of section IX are analogous in that they begin with the words "Thou art wise", and then elaborate some aspect of His Wisdom. On one level, analogy heightens the sense of unity of a text; on another level, however, it is marked for its discontinuity. Thus, the principle of analogy that organises the section both heightens its intensity and enhances its split focus.

However, one cannot insist too much on the principle that both the continuous mythical image and the discontinuous rhetorical address derive their respective poetic forces from the fact that they are superimposed upon smaller-scale elements some of which are discordant, and some—reconciled on various levels.

Chapter 12

Light, Fire, Prison

A Cognitive Analysis of Religious Imagery in Poetry

This chapter explores the use of spatial imagery in poetry in general, and religious and mystic poetry in particular. It recapitulates two observations from earlier chapters. First, that language is highly differentiated and conceptual; it is, therefore, ill-suited to convey lowly-differentiated, nonconceptual experiences, such as mystic experiences. Nevertheless, it has been observed that mystic poetry can sometimes convey not only the *differentiated idea* of mystic experiences, but also something that feels like the undifferentiated experience itself. In my various writings I have explored a great variety of techniques by which poets sometimes manage to overcome this cognitive limitation. The present chapter is yet another attempt to do so. Though these techniques are applicable to a wide range of nonconceptual—perceptual, emotional, mystic or ecstatic—experiences, in the present context I explore their application to problems that typically arise in religious poetry. Second, it has been observed that mental processes most frequently make use of visual, concrete, spatial imagery. I will explore some cognitive reasons for this tendency. As a bonus, I will have some comments on three central notions of literary criticism, allegory, symbol and archetypal patterns.

I am assuming here the position of an "empathetic" atheist, trying to show how some mystic poetry, by its very structure that is handled by the cognitive system in certain ways, may have certain effects on believers and nonbelievers alike, by offering them a verbal imitation of a mystic insight. As for the varieties of mystic-religious poetry, I will address two central issues. First, from Chapter 3 I will take up Gordon Kaufman's claim in his book *God the Problem* that we use "God-language" in dealing "with experiences that are beyond the *absolute limit* of our experience, construed by analogy with the relative limits of our every-day life". Much mystic poetry, and much of its secular version in romantic poetry is an attempt to get a glimpse of that other, more real reality. In this respect, I will explore the potential contribution of two spatial images: light and prison. Why precisely these two images? There are many reasons for that, but one of them is this: "prison" is a convenient metaphor for the absolute limit; and "light" is a convenient metaphor for suggesting a source beyond that absolute limit.

Secondly, I will further elaborate on an issue discussed at length in Chapter 11. This is the theological and poetic problem with which Mediaeval and Sixteenth-Seventeenth Century Jewish and Christian poets were sometimes confronted, namely, how to fuse the Biblical personalistic conception of God with a Neo-Platonic conception of light emanation, or of "in the beginning was the Word". In the present chapter I intend to examine the poetic issues involved in such a fusion, in a brief excerpt from Ibn Gabirol's *Kingly Crown,* and in the short masterpiece "Here Comes the Sun" by the Thirteenth Century Armenian poet, Kostandin of Erznka.

As for poetic style, I will recapitulate from earlier chapters the distinction between two types of structure in figurative language, with their respective perceived qualities: split and integrated focus. Coleridge described the dominant property of poetic imagination as "the balance or reconcilement of opposite or discordant qualities". In integrated focus, greater emphasis goes to "the balance or reconcilement"; in split focus, to "opposite or discordant qualities". I will demonstrate split focus in Metaphysical and Modern poetry (Ibn Gabirol, Donne, Eliot); integrated focus in Renaissance and Romantic poetry (Sir Philip Sidney and Wordsworth). I will explore the different strategies in assigning unrelated or even incompatible meanings to the images "light" and "fire". The perceived effect of integrated focus is typically emotional, sometimes arousing the impression of "the verbal imitation of an intuition". The perceived effect of split focus is typically witty, sometimes involving "a strain of passionate paradoxical reasoning", generating a heightened awareness of the paradoxical nature of existence. Finally, I will recapitulate the suggestion that integrated focus sometimes exploits orientation mechanisms to arouse an impression of intuitive processes, whereas split focus, at its extreme, at least, arouses a feeling of confusion and emotional disorientation.

Cognition and Spatial Imagery

Let us begin, then, with the observation that there is a general human tendency to treat mental states and processes, social relationships and various kinds of abstractions in terms of spatial imagery. The language of such primary processes as dreams consists of a sequence of spatial images. Kenneth Burke proposed a "dramatic" approach to the analysis of human motives, including "the principle whereby the scene is a fit 'container' for the act, expressing in fixed properties the same quality that the action expresses in terms of development" (Burke, 1962: 3). George Lakoff (e.g., Lakoff, 1993) and his associates reinvented Burke's notion that there is a tendency to speak of purposeful activities in terms of motion in space, the purpose being expressed by the goal of the journey. Mental states or moral qualities are expressed in terms of staying in a certain place. According to Lakoff, such idiomatic expressions as "he spilled the beans" and "he blew his stack" can be traced back to the generative metaphor "the body is a container". He speaks of such generative metaphors as "understanding is seeing" and "life is a journey". But such conceptual metaphors are only a small part of the whole story. There is much empirical evidence for a significant correlation between mental representation and creativity. Students whose knowledge is represented in a spatial code have been found to make more creative use of it than those whose knowledge is represented in a verbal code (Walkup, 1965). In a paper on theory construction, J.J.C. Smart points out the enormous usefulness of spatial models in explaining physical laws. With reference to the Kinetic Theory of Gases, "we proceed to connect the gas laws with ideas, roughly speaking, of the behaviour of things like billiard balls" (Smart, 1966: 231). The theory is explanatory "because it shows the analogy between a gas and a swarm of particles, and in putting forward the analogy it has created some entirely new ideas, such as that of gas particles" (ibid., 234). At considerable variance with general belief, Smart suggests that "a failure to fit the facts may in certain circumstances be additional reason for accepting the theory as being essentially sound" (ibid., 236). As Smart's example indicates, the reason for this resides in the nature of spatial models. The failure to fit the facts draws attention to an additional, hitherto ignored potential of the spatial model, that can be related to the observational facts. This may generate new, productive ideas about the domain explored.

In some of my earlier writings I pointed out several reasons for this predominance of spatial imagery, one of them being that spatial images can encode many kinds of information efficiently. In the chapter "The Concrete and the Abstract in Poetry" of my book *On Metaphoring* I have discussed at great length this aspect of the use of concrete images. The word "concrete" is derived from a Latin word meaning "grown together". In a concrete noun a large number of features are "grown together". Every such feature is a "meaning potential" of the spatial image. It also holds the potential to combine with other meaning potentials in the context. This I call "combinational potential". This efficient coding enables one to manipulate a large amount of information, without overburdening the system, and to move from one potential of the image to another, granting one great flexibility. Hence the relationship between spatial coding and creativity. This conception may illuminate the relationship between poetic symbol on the one hand, and such notions as allegory, or Lakoff's conceptual metaphor on the other. Symbols are the efficient coding of a wide range of usually unrelated or even incompatible sets of information. This may include allegorical meaning as one set of information, conceptual metaphor as another. But the very essence of symbol is to include a much wider range of sets of information. In what follows, I shall illustrate this at great length.

In the chapter "Some Spatial and Tactile Metaphors for Sound" in my *What Makes Sound Patterns Expressive—The Poetic Mode of Speech Perception* (1992b) I point out some additional reasons for the dominance of spatial imagery in human cognition. One of these reasons is the need to overcome certain limitations of the human cognitive system. Thus, for instance, instrumental music makes use of at least three dimensions of sound: pitch, volume and tone-colour. The last two dimensions are rather elusive. We can quite reliably, without instruments, distinguish a wide variety of pitches, and remember their order for years as a tune. But how many degrees of volume can you reliably distinguish, and then remember their sequence in, let us say, a recording of a Beethoven symphony, or, to make it easier, its first twenty bars? And for how long? Pitch, by contrast, is recoded into a spatial template that resembles, roughly speaking, a ladder: it reaches upward, and is divided into discrete steps. As a result, we are capable of remembering quite reliably long successions of tunes, for instance. But this ability is bought at the price of losing irrecoverably much elusive "precategorial" information. In the present chapter, an opposite possibility will be explored: that spatial imagery can be used in mystic poetry to escape the tyranny of the clear-cut categories of conceptual language.

Potentials of Light

Let us begin our inquiry with Lakoff's short discussion of the opening lines of Dante's Divine Comedy:

> In the middle of life's road
> I found myself in a dark wood.

> "Life's road' evokes the domain of life and the domain of travel, and hence the conventional LIFE IS A JOURNEY metaphor that links them. "I found myself in a dark wood" evokes the knowledge that if it's dark you cannot see which way to go. This evokes the domain of seeing, and the conventional metaphor that KNOWING IS SEEING, as in "I see what you're getting at", "his claims aren't clear", "the passage is opaque", and so forth (Lakoff, 1993: 237).

The main bulk of the present chapter will be devoted to an exploration of the figurative uses of fire, light and related images, such as darkness, clouds and shadow. Lakoff's discussion does, in fact, explore some of the more obvious potentials encoded, according to the foregoing discussion, in light: light affords seeing and finding the right way. Darkness deprives you of this ability. In some circumstances it is justified perhaps to equate with understanding this ability to find one's way, or to judge what is presented to one's perception. This is certainly one conspicuous potential of light, and we shall encounter it time and again in the course of our inquiry. But light has many other potentials as well, frequently exploited in poetry, religion and philosophy. Consider the first ten lines of one of Sir Philip Sidney's "Certain Sonnets":

> Leave me, O love which reachest but to dust;
> And thou, my mind, aspire to higher things;
> Grow rich in that which never taketh rust,
> Whatever fades but fading pleasure brings.
> Draw in thy beams, and humble all thy might
> To that sweet yoke where lasting freedoms be;
> Which breaks the clouds and opens forth the light,
> That doth both shine and give us sight to see.
> O take fast hold; let that light be thy guide

> In this small course which birth draws out to death,

I have already briefly referred to this sonnet in chapter 6. I will resist the temptation to discuss the other images, and will confine myself to the light image only. The phrase "let that light be thy guide" exploits, certainly, a meaning potential similar to the one the opposite of which we encountered in Dante. But, in addition, "Draw in thy beams" seems to suggest here something very similar to its sequel: "humble all thy might". "Fade" in line 4 means "to become dim as light, or lose brightness of illumination"; here it refers to the opposite of "that which never taketh rust"—gold on the one hand and spiritual things on the other which, in turn, suggest "being valuable". Line 7, "Which breaks the clouds and opens forth the light", exploits an additional, very frequent and important potential of light: light can put us in contact with worlds inaccessible to us; it can travel to our place from far beyond our reach. In this case, it reaches us from some place that is not only inaccessible for our body; we cannot even see its source, it is hidden by the clouds. In Gordon Kaufman's terms, light in this case helps us to deal "with experiences that are beyond the *absolute limit* of our experience". Line 8 exploits two additional potentials of light: "shines" suggests splendour, perhaps of that inaccessible reality. And last, but not least, light may "give us sight to see", literally. For Sidney, then, light is a bundle of many features, and he exploits them one after the other to suggest changing meanings that are not necessarily compatible with one another. By this he achieves what in some aesthetic theories is called "unity-in-variety".

Some additional potentials of light that are of great religious significance we may find in an ancient Egyptian inscription, Akhnaton's prayer to the sun, quoted by Maud Bodkin (1963: 141), in her discussion of light symbolism in Dante's *Paradiso:*

> With seeing whom may my eyes be satisfied daily when He rises in this temple of Aton in the city of the Horizon, and fills it with His own self by His beams, beauteous in love, and lays them upon me in life and length of days for ever and ever.

This passage may illustrate three of the issues extensively discussed in the present chapter: the conception of light as a bundle of attributes grown together; conception of the aesthetic context as one that realises in one image a variety of meaning potentials based on those attributes; and conception of the spatial image as a vehicle for conveying an experience that escapes conceptual language. With reference to this passage, Bodkin speaks of the idea "of Light as a symbol of supreme well-being—the organic factor of heightened vitality blended in it with the delight of the eyes, and both with subtler cravings of the spirit"—quite a wide range of meaning potentials. I would like to point out an additional aspect in this passage, which not only increases the multiple relationship of this image, but also illustrates its potential to serve as an apt perceptual vehicle for a crucial aspect of the mystic experience. In Chapter 9, on "Oceanic Dedifferentiation", I spoke of liquids as one of the most prototypcal natural symbols in our conceptual system to suggest a state in which the boundaries between objects are suspended, implying the loss of individual identity. In Akhnaton's hymn it is the sun-god that "fills [the city] with His own self by His beams",—an effective visual image suggesting the suspension of boundaries between self and not-self, by way of filling the entire available space.

Or take the Neo-Platonic image of the Creation as Light Emanation. The two most conspicuous potentials of light exploited in this image is that it is a thing-free and shape-free substance, and that the further away it travels from its source, the less intense, the fainter it becomes. There is an interesting trace of the KNOWING IS SEEING ingredient in this image. The stronger the light, the more "spiritual" it is. Near its source, it is purely spiritual; the further away from its source, it becomes less spiritual, more grossly physical. The shadow, according to this model, is purely physical, devoid of all spirituality. This generates an interesting paradox pregnant with poetic possibilities: the shadow is continuous with the emanating light; at the same time, it is its opposite as well. "Sensual reality is, at one and the same time, the last link in a uniform series of emanations, and the absolute opposite of the suprasensual world. There is a manifest clash here between the monism of the metaphysical view of the world, and the dualism of its theory of values" (Guttmann, 1973: 106). The element of inaccessible reality is also present in the light-emanation image. Human beings have access only to the last stages of emanated light. At any rate, poets may choose to foreground the "uniform series of emanations", or the absolute opposition between light and shadow, or the "manifest clash" between the two conceptions. By the way, Jungian psychology exploits three obvious potentials of "shadow": it is the opposite of "knowing", it belongs to the "unconscious"; it represents the "darker", more sinister part of our personality; and it can easily be "cast" on objects to which it inherently does not belong.

Or consider the stars: they are sources of light. They are small, they are far away, inaccessible, steadfast. "Bright Star! would I were steadfast as thou art!" says Keats. For Shakespeare, too, Love "is an ever-fixèd mark/ That looks on tempests and is never shaken"; but, in addition, it is also "the star for every wandering bark", showing the right way. But, in much poetry, stars make us feel, again, that we are in contact to some degree or other with some inaccessible reality. They do this in two different ways. First, they send forth the light from afar; and second, they set behind the horizon: we see them setting "there", but don't know where. In fact, we *see* them setting "beyond the *absolute limit* of our experience", thus bringing us into some contact with that "beyond".

In chapter 3 we discussed at length Coleridge's passage concerning "the first range of hills, that encircles the scanty vale of human life": "On *its* ridges the common sun is born and departs. From *them* the stars rise, and touching *them* they vanish". In Wordsworth's Immortality Ode we read: "The soul that rises with us, our life's star / Hath had elsewhere its setting". The Roumanian Symbolist poet, Mihai Eminescu, in his poem "La Steaua" (To the Star), draws upon an additional potential of stars, that became available to him only through modern astronomy. Stars are thousands of light years away from us, and have their own life cycle. When we see the light of a star, it may be long extinguished and thus, something which no longer exists may be influencing our lives, like our extinct loves. Now stars have an additional feature, of very significant meaning potential. In the night sky they are very clearly discernible; but when the day breaks, they become fainter and fainter, finally disappearing in daylight. For present-day astronomers, the Star of Bethlehem may have been a supernova: a star that exploded, doubling the light of our galaxy, and became strong enough to be visible in daytime. For the authors of the New Testament, it was a miracle that the star could overcome this law of nature, that the smaller light disappears in the bigger light. In the Hellenistic treatise on rhetoric and poetics *Peri Hypsous* (attributed to Longinus) we find the following simile: "For just as all dim lights are extinguished in the blaze of the sun, so do these artifices of rhetoric fade from view when bathed in the pervading splendour of sublimity". The same is true, with the necessary changes, of fire. Russell (1987: 122), speaks of "the Zoroastrian belief that the greater fire can overwhelm and vitiate the power of the smaller".

Some literary critics are inclined to regard the realisation of the potentials discussed above as "conventions". There is, indeed, no reason on earth why we should not store all those conventions in memory, except for parsimony. My position is that the ability to move from one potential of an image to another is the basis of creativity both in poets and readers, and can account for their ability to handle unforeseen situations. This can also explain where conventions come from (when those potential meanings turn into conventions). There would be precedence for my conception in the way we use images in everyday cognitive tasks. Consider such questions as "Is a ping-pong ball smaller or bigger than an egg?", or "What is the colour of the bee's head?" We do not usually store in advance the verbal answers to such questions in our memory. When the question comes, unexpectedly, we retrieve the image from memory, assess the relevant features, and generate an answer (we would not call it a "convention", even though the odds are that most people who can answer those questions will generate roughly the same answers). The issue at stake is whether we are willing to grant poets and readers a considerable degree of creativity in changing circumstances, or prefer to regard them as conditioned by unchanging conventions.

Light *and* Fire: *Split and Integrated Focus*

The dichotomy "Split and Integrated Focus" is a most serviceable tool in the analysis of poetry. On the one hand, it is general enough to make generalisations across poems, or poetic styles and periods. On the other hand, it has sufficient descriptive contents to make subtle distinctions within the micro-structure of one poem. The methodology involved is rather complex, but operationally well-defined. Description must be done on two levels. One must describe the perceived quality of a stretch of text, ranging from one line to a whole poem, as emotional, witty, intuitively smooth, disorienting, and the like. Then one must look for elements in the text that "typically count toward" or "against" the quality perceived. There must be a third stage, explicitly stated, or lingering in the background: a theoretical framework within which one may justify that a certain feature typically counts toward or against some perceived quality.

I have insisted throughout the present work that language is highly differentiated and conceptual, and is therefore ill-suited to convey lowly-differentiated, nonconceptual experiences, such as mystic experiences. In this and the next two paragraphs I will consider some linguistic and cognitive devices that are prone to increase the compact, linear and logical-conceptual character of language or, on the contrary, its diffuse, global and emotional-intuitive character. These devices are independent variables, and may act in a text in harmony, reinforcing each other's effect, or may conflict, mitigating or overriding each other's effect. Of the many possible variables, I will present here only three intimately related ones (though I may touch on additional ones in the course of my specific analyses): modes of space perception (shapes or orientation); modes of verbal presentation (description or argument); types of background (specific or universal scene, or no background at all).

For our present purposes we may point out two different mechanisms for space perception: shape perception and orientation (cf. Chapter 4). The two are located in different brain centres, and when one is damaged by brain injury, the other one may still function flawlessly. The two mechanisms are opposed in almost all respects. Shape perception dissociates the perceiving self from the thing perceived; it picks up visual information, analyses and organises it into stable well-differentiated relationships. Visual shapes display stability, definite directions, and frequently generate closed areas. Orientation, by contrast, is defined by the *Random House College Dictionary* as "the ability to locate oneself in one's environment with reference to time, place, and people". Consequently, it picks up from one's environment a wide range of diffuse information in all sensory modes, specifying the environment as well as self-specifying relative to the environment. It effects fast integration of diverse, fluid and diffuse information. While shape perception is precise, analytic and determines specific directions, orientation is much faster, less precise, determining general tendencies only, but capable of coping with rapidly changing conditions. In my paper "Aspects of Cognitive Poetics" (Tsur, 2002) I claimed that emotions are efficient orientation devices. In figurative language, nouns that denote objects with stable characteristic visual shapes (that is, that have stable boundaries) are hard to fuse, tend to conflict with one another and are prone to split the focus of perception. The result is frequently witty or grotesque. Abstract nouns, by contrast, and nouns that denote thing-free and Gestalt-free entities, may fuse more easily and more imperceptibly. When an enclosing or surrounding open space is indicated by the text, with a perceiving consciousness in its centre, that is, when the orientation mechanism is activated by imagination, thing-free and Gestalt-free entities are perceived as more diffuse, more fluid, less stable, less logical. From this distinction other distinctions can be derived. A persuasive argument has a beginning, middle and end, and displays a patent purpose and definite directions. A landscape description, by contrast, refers to an entity that has no beginning, middle or end, and has no definite direction or patent purpose. At the same time, it may serve as the immediate environment in which orientation takes place. Sometimes an immediate environment, a concrete situation defined "here and now", centering around a perceiving consciousness, may be indicated by some deictic device, without mentioning concrete objects with stable characteristic visual shapes, turning the thing-free and Gestalt-free entities into emotionally loaded diffuse information, as in:

> It is a beauteous evening, calm and free,
> The holy Time is quiet as a nun,
> Breathless with adoration...

or

> Oh listen! for the vale profound
> Is overflowing with the sound.

By contrast, when the thing-free and Gestalt-free entities are displayed against a general background, or no background at all, the abstract nouns and the thing-free and Gestalt-free entities tend to preserve their compact, conceptual nature. By selecting the images mentioned in the title of this chapter, I have loaded the dice in favour of integrated focus: light and fire are thing-free qualities that have no stable characteristic visual shapes; and in the prison not its shape is emphasised, but rather the enclosing space and one's own relationship to the physical limitation. Notwithstanding, as we will see, poets sometimes overcome this integrating potential of *light* and *fire* and split the focus.

Coming back to Sir Philip Sidney's sonnet, some of its conspicuous elements typically count toward split focus, and some toward integrated focus. There are two elements in this poem that we might typically expect to occur in a Metaphysical poem. First, there is a vigorous argument attempting to persuade "Love" and "my mind" to behave in a certain way, displaying a psychological atmosphere of patent purpose and definite direction. This would count, doubtless, toward a rational, logical-conceptual attitude in the poem. Furthermore, light in this poem is treated very much in the way of the Metaphysical Conceit. It is treated as a bundle of features by virtue of which a variety of unrelated meanings are encoded in it. Very much in the way Donne does with his notorious compass image (or Quarles with his rib hieroglyph, see Chapter 5), Sidney enumerates these meanings one by one, placing them in the "sharp focus" of the reader's contemplation. Nonetheless, the poem is not perceived as a witty Metaphysical poem, because these features of the poem are overridden by other features that typically count in the opposite direction, indicating

rather a mild emotionally charged quality of "insight". First, very much like romantic poetry, the poem makes "less use [than metaphysical poems] of the central overt
statement of similitude which is so important in all rhetoric stemming from Aristotle and the Renaissance" (Wimsatt, 1954: 109). Second, the various meanings encoded in "light" are unrelated, but not conspicuously incompatible; they can be—and
are, in fact—accommodated in one situation. Third, while the compass, e.g., has a
stable characteristic visual shape and the various figurative meanings attributed to it
can be understood only through a careful visualisation of its various aspects, the
light and the clouds are thing-free and Gestalt-free entities. Finally, the line "Which
breaks the clouds and opens forth the light" evokes an unlimited landscape, with a
perceiving consciousness locating itself with reference to the clouds and the light.
This is reinforced by the "life as a journey" metaphor: "let that light be thy guide /
In this small course which birth draws out to death". The "small course", though
used metaphorically, has an additional function here: it helps to evoke the consistent
landscape with the situation defined "here and now". The light breaking through the
clouds indicates some reality beyond one's reach; the thing-free and Gestalt-free nature of "clouds" and "light" enhances the non-conceptual nature of the experience indicated; the orientation mechanism evoked by the situation amplifies the diffuseness
of these entities; this diffusing effect is mitigated but not cancelled by the persuasive
argument pervading the poem, displaying a psychological atmosphere of definite direction and patent purpose.

The next two short examples are due to the great eleventh-century Hebrew poet in
Spain, Shlomo Ibn-Gabirol, from his monumental philosophical-liturgical work,
The Kingly Crown, written in rhymed prose (cf. Chapter 11). Compare Sidney's use
of the light image to that in the following excerpt:

> Yours is the reality whose light's shadow generated all existent things / of
> whom we said: under his shadow we shall live.

In Neo-Platonic philosophy there is a partial identity between light and shadow
on the one hand, and spiritual and physical existence on the other. Light is perceived
as a metaphor for some supersensuous reality. This metaphor has been developed so
thoroughly that it must be meant literally: sensual reality is conceived of as the last
stage in the process of emanation and, at the same time, as the outright opposite of
supersensuous reality. This metaphor is meant to bridge the gap between the
spiritual and the physical world, and to substitute a difference in degree for the
difference in kind. Some aspects of shadow, however, are irrelevant to this
metaphor; a shadow may, for instance, arouse a pleasurable feeling, by keeping
away the heat of the sun. Precisely this property of the shadow is exploited in the
next segment of this excerpt. At the same time, Ibn Gabirol uses this image to
bridge another "unbridgeable" abyss, between the Neo-Platonic conception of creation by way of light emanation, and the monotheistic conception of a personal creator. Ibn Gabirol is not content with an easy solution, conceiving the light or the

reality as the Creator's possession ("Yours is the reality"); he resorts to a typical device of seventeenth-century English Metaphysical poetry. The phrase "of whom we said: under his shadow we shall live" is a literal quotation from *Lamentations* IV: 20, where it refers to "the Lord's anointed" who "was taken in the pits" of "our pursuers". In this Biblical context, "live" suggests "living among the nations". In the present context of Ibn Gabirol's poem, there is a drastic shift in the implications of these phrases. "His shadow" suggests something like Divine Providence or protection. The phrase "under his shadow" is idiomatic, a dead metaphor; but its juxtaposition with "light's shadow" revives it.

Though in Ibn Gabirol's use, just as in Sidney's, light and shadow have no stable characteristic visual shapes, the unrelated meanings attributed to the images are, nonetheless, less readily fused in Ibn Gabirol's poem. First, because they are not merely unrelated; they are incompatible. The light in Sidney's poem *can* come from afar, break the clouds, shine, give sight and show the right way at the same time, whereas the light and the shadow in Ibn Gabirol's cannot suggest the stages of emanation and protection from heat at the same time. Second, while Sidney's image vaguely evokes a specific scene with a perceiving consciousness walking along the road and looking at the sky, at the light breaking through the clouds, no such specific situation is indicated by Ibn Gabirol's images: they are offered to the reader's contemplation with no background at all; thus, the orientation mechanism is not activated in the processing of the image. Third, the two tokens of "shadow" have incompatible emotional implications, negative and positive: while in the first segment of this excerpt light is perceived as the supreme good and shadow as its opposite, or at least as something considerably less good, in the second segment the shadow is perceived as valuable precisely because it gives protection against light.

Thus, in Ibn Gabirol's image two "most heterogeneous ideas are yoked together by violence" — in Dr. Johnson's phrasing. It presents the "essential paradox of 'the one and the many'"; its elements "enter into a solid unity, while preserving their warring identity" — in James Smith's classic formulation of the metaphysical conceit. In other words, those heterogeneous ideas are accommodated in one linguistic sign, which, pushed to the focus of consciousness, allows consciousness to turn around and examine itself. That is how Ibn Gabirol arouses "a sense of confusion and emotional disorientation", not unlike the feeling aroused by the grotesque; at the same time he provides, by the same image, the means to cope with it. As for the kind of consciousness yielded by the two images, Sidney's image yields a mitigated version of the direct perception of the existence of a transcendental world, beyond the final limit, whereas Ibn Gabirol's yields a different kind of consciousness. If "insight" is correctly characterised as the sudden discovery of unity in complexity, by accommodating incompatible meanings in a single image, such metaphysical conceits as the one by Ibn Gabirol may yield a sense of "insight" into the complexity of the Creator, and the paradoxical nature of human existence — under well-practiced circumstances at least, when one need not consult footnotes for understanding the image. Indeed, in Ibn Gabirol's poetry dealing with the nature of the Creator or the nature of existence, we find not infrequently that where he could achieve an integrated focus by smooth transition, he conspicuously splits the focus of perception by a variety of means. In Chapter 11 I discuss at length another instance from *The Kingly Crown,* violently yoking together, again, the Biblical and the Neo-Platonic conceptions of Creation (involving a personal Creator and light emanation), drastically splitting the focus after having already achieved a smooth transition. These and additional instances strongly suggest that far from being a failure to observe certain Classicist or Romantic norms, split focus is a consistent aesthetic conception in Ibn Gabirol's poetry.

The Paradox of Fire *and* Fire *in Donne and Eliot*

There are good reasons to suppose that the metaphoric identification of heat and emotional arousal has intercultural foundations. Consider the following:

> If the extended uses of the sensation vocabulary in English are historical accidents rather than metaphors then these extensions ought not to be regularly found in other languages so long as these languages have no historical connection with English. Asch drew up a long list of words of this kind and looked at their equivalents in Old Testament Hebrew, Homeric Greek, Chinese, Thai, Malayalam, and Hausa. He found that all these languages have morphemes that are used to name both physical and psychological qualities. They all have morphemes that designate physical-psychological pairings identical with some found in English. These results suggest that the referents have shared attributes which have caused identical metaphors to be independently discovered by different peoples. In addition, Asch found, that a morpheme referring to a given physical property may develop psychological meanings that are not identical in all languages. For example, the morpheme for *hot* stands for rage in Hebrew, enthusiasm in Chinese, sexual arousal in Thai, and energy in Hausa. However, this disagreement does not suggest the operation of accidental factors since there is an undoubted kinship in the range of meanings. All seem to involve heightened activity and emotional arousal. No case has been discovered in which the morpheme for *hot* named a remote, calm (in fact *cool)* manner (Brown, 1968: 145–146).

In our cultural heritage, the identification of intense passions with fire goes back at least to the Old Testament: the *Song of Songs,* and the *Book of Psalms.* Love, jealousy, religious zeal are all like fire. Consider: "For zeal for your house consumed me" *(Psalms* 69. 9), and "For love is strong as death, jealousy is cruel as grave. Its flashes are flashes of fire, a most vehement flame. Many waters cannot quench love" *(Song of Songs* 8. 6–7). Metaphysical poets at least from Ibn Gabirol on took up this partial identification of passions (mainly love) with fire and turned it into a to-tal identification: those passions may literally burn the body. Love could be quenched with many waters, Ibn Gabirol suggests at variance with the verse in Solomon's Song; the trouble is that God has already sworn that Noah's waters will not be exceeded; Donne uses the same conceit about drowning his world in a flood of tears in the sonnet discussed below. He begins one of his Holy Sonnets with the statement "I am a little world"; then he is concerned with the destruction of his world:

> Pour new seas in mine eyes, that so I might
> Drown my world with my weeping earnestly,
> Or wash it if it must be drowned no more:
> But oh it must be burnt! alas the fire
> Of lust and envy have burnt it heretofore,
> And made it fouler; Let their flames retire,
>   And burn me ô Lord, with a fiery zeal
>   Of thee and thy house, which doth in eating heal.
>   John Donne, *Holy Sonnet 5*

Donne here makes use of an elaborate metaphysical conceit and a (concealed) metaphysical pun that lead to an oxymoron. The result is a split focus, a strain of passionate paradoxical reasoning. Passions involve great internal heat, great energy, and may be painful and destructive. Other potentials of fire, such as its ability to destroy huge sections of the physical world, or to smelt and refine ore into pure metals are irrelevant to the identification of passions with fire. But these are, precisely, the meanings attributed to the fire in Donne's poem: the fire of lust and envy will destroy Donne's "little world", unless the "fiery zeal" smelts and purifies — purges — it. Donne uses the verse quoted above from Psalms and inserts it into his poem almost verbatim. The verb "consume" of the English Bible is ambiguous, meaning "to destroy as by burning", or "to eat or drink up". Donne uses straightforward "eating" as in the original Hebrew Bible. The oxymoron "which doth in eating heal" suggests the painful process of purification, and keeps the focus split. I have said that Donne creates here a concealed metaphysical pun as well. The Hebrew Bible uses the same noun קִנְאָה for "jealousy" in the above verse from Solomon's Song ("envy" in the Sonnet), and for "zeal" in the verse from the Psalms. Thus, the Hebrew word denotes a negative and a positive passion at one and the same time. Both passions are partially identified with fire, according to the conventional use of the metaphor. But Donne exploits those features of fire too that are irrelevant to passions, again, a negative and a positive action respectively (I have discussed this sonnet with slightly different emphases in Chapter 6).

From the point of view of Christian Doctrine, there is no great difference between Donne's and Eliot's uses of the fire image. From the stylistic point of view,

too, there is some resemblance between their uses. Consider the following lines
from Eliot's *Four Quartets,* "Little Gidding" IV.

> … The only hope or else despair
> Lies in the choice of pyre or pyre—
> To be redeemed from fire by fire.

> … We only live, only suspire
> Consumed by either fire or fire.

Eliot has recourse to the same technique as Donne: he takes one metaphoric
signifier, fire, and attaches to it two or more *signifieds.* By this he, too, arouses a
sense of unity in multiplicity. But he sharpens Donne's technique for splitting the
focus in two respects. First, Donne clearly indicates the metaphoric identifications
of fire by saying "the fire of lust and envy", or "a fiery zeal", whereas Eliot gives no
indication whatever of his metaphoric identifications. Second, Eliot clearly flouts a
communicational taboo: he uses one word in undoubtedly different meanings, without giving any indication of that. When he says "To be redeemed from fire by fire"
or "Consumed by either fire or fire", there is no formal indication that the various
tokens may refer to different things. Its main purpose appears to be to strike the
reader with its illogicality. Donne, by contrast, offers some dramatic rationalisation
for identifying fire with different passions: He implores that "Let their flames retire"
(of one kind of fire), and asks the Lord to burn him with another kind of fire.

As for the specific meanings of "fire", they may refer to the passions suggested
by Donne, derived from traditional Christian doctrine, such negative ones as "lust",
"envy", or such positive ones as "love" or "fiery zeal". But they may be, also, some
fiery zeals derived from modern life, perhaps reinterpreted in the light of traditional
Christian doctrine. The same may hold true of "Lies in the choice of pyre or pyre",
indicating perhaps such traditional notions as that martyrdom is the only way to escape the fire of Hell; or, perhaps, in modern life, one may choose only between one
martyrdom and another. There is no way of moving smoothly from one term of the
figurative expression to the other; the tautology, or the incompatibility of the terms
is forced upon the reader before he makes any attempt to settle the incompatible
terms. Thus, we may distinguish even *degrees* of split focus.

Neo-Classical poetics would condemn such verse instances as "False Wit". "True
Wit" consists in the resemblance of ideas, "False Wit" in the resemblance of words;
"Mixt Wit" consists partly in the resemblance of ideas, partly in the resemblance of
words (Addison). The assigning of different or even incompatible meanings to the
same image yields "False Wit", or at best "Mixt Wit". The designation of "envy"
and "zeal" as "fire" results in a similarity of words. But insofar as both are human
passions, there is here also a similarity of ideas. Bad Classicism, however, can be
good Mannerism and, as we shall see, even good Romanticism.

The Paradox of Light *and* Light *in Wordsworth*

> Our birth is but a sleep and a forgetting:
> The Soul that rises with us, our life's Star,
>   Hath had elsewhere its setting,
>   And cometh from afar;
>   Not in entire forgetfulness,
>   And not in utter nakedness,
> But trailing clouds of glory do we come
>   From God who is our home:
> Heaven lies about us in our infancy!
> Shades of the prison-house begin to close
>   Upon the growing boy,
> But he beholds the light and whence it flows,
>   He sees it in his joy;
> The Youth who daily further from the east
>   Must travel, still is Nature's priest,
>   And by the vision splendid
>   Is on his way attended;
> At length the Man perceives it die away,
> And fade into the light of common day.

Wordsworth's Ode, and this stanza in particular, is, like so much Romantic po-etry, a secular version of the mystic endeavour to experience the world beyond the absolute limit, and tracing the soul's progress between the two worlds. Much reli-gious-mystic and secular-Romantic poetry begins with a state of utter separation be-tween the two worlds; and the poem attempts to overcome the absolute barrier. In this respect, this stanza is somewhat exceptional. It presents the pre-natal state in which the soul was in intimate relationship with that inaccessible world; birth brings a drastic but not total detachment from that world: the child is still in contact with it but, in the course of "maturation", gradually and imperceptibly this contact is loosened and lost. This narrative may bring to our attention an interesting cognitive and aesthetic problem. Much mystic and Romantic poetry consists of a struggle to overcome the tyranny of conceptual thinking and of conceptual language in order to achieve a non-conceptual experiencing of that world beyond, and convey a verbal imitation thereof. This stanza of Wordsworth's Ode presents some of the crucial stages of the process in straightforward statements whose figurative language can hardly disguise their conceptual nature, such as "From God who is our home: / Heaven lies about us in our infancy!". But some other points of the process are pre-sented with a verbal subtlety that renders its perception "intuitive", "non-concep-tual", "unconscious", or the like. Thus, rather than attempting to give here a verbal imitation of the non-conceptual nature of the experiencing of the world beyond, the stanza provides a verbal imitation of the non-conceptual nature of the transition, of the gradual loss of contact. paradoxically enough, the heightening of this intuitive perception of the subtle, elusive, transition between the two kinds of consciousness, heightens our awareness of that other-worldly consciousness.

Following Coleridge's conception of imagination, Cleanth Brooks insisted in his book *The Well-Wrought Urn* that all good poetry is paradoxical. He had little diffi-culty to show this in seventeenth century poetry, or in Pope's *The Rape of the Lock*. But he insisted that this was true also with reference to such supposedly sin-gle-minded poets as Wordsworth. He demonstrated his contention with reference to Wordsworth's Calais-Beach Sonnet (see above, Chapter 5) and Immortality Ode. I am not entirely happy with some of the details of his analysis; and even where our views overlap, I prefer a formulation that brings out the similarity between Wordsworth's technique on the one hand, and Sidney's, Donne's and Eliot's tech-nique on the other. What is more, I will insist on a further question: if these tech-niques are so similar, why are they so different?

Let us begin with the partial identification of "The Soul that rises with us" and "our life's Star". Unlike Brooks, I am not inclined to interpret "our life's Star" as the sun, but as the individual star that rises with each new-born child and falls with each dying man. Now in this star a variety of potential meanings are encoded. First, its light gives information about a remote, inaccessible reality. Second, this star and remote reality are intimately associated with our soul's origin. Third, its identifica-tion with the soul is only partial. In many respects it behaves like other stars. It rises every night and sets every morning; what is more, it "Hath had elsewhere its setting"—we see it move across the night sky and then disappear. We cannot see the place where it disappears, and it too is inaccessible to us. Thus, the star forcefully indicates to us, and in two different ways, that there is some remote, inaccessible reality, beyond our absolute limits. Fourth, this star behaves in an additional respect like all normal stars. When the day-light comes, its smaller light fades away in the bigger light.

We have seen that Donne and Eliot split the focus by assigning sharply distin-guishable, incompatible referents to the same "fire" image. I will argue that Words-worth does exactly the same with his "light" image, but in a way that blurs the fo-cus of perception and disguises the incompatibility of the referents. Let me begin by presenting the most conspicuous issue in this respect. As I pointed out long ago (Tsur, 1971), the "seeing is knowing" metaphor has two kinds of instantiation in Western thought and literature. Since sight is the most differentiated of the senses (as opposed to the tactile sense, for instance, from which "feeling" is derived) it is used as a metaphor for knowing and understanding. In Chapter 13 below I quote Rudolf Otto who (1959: 15) insists that

> It is essential to every theistic conception of God [...] that it [is] thought of
> by analogy with our human nature of reason and personality; only, whereas
> in ourselves we are aware of this as qualified by restriction and limitation,

as applied to god the attributes we use are [...] thought as absolute and unqualified.

As for the irrational aspect of God,

> We can cooperate in this process by bringing before [one's] notice all that can be found in other regions of the mind, already known and familiar, to resemble, or again afford some special contrast to, the particular experience we wish to elucidate (21).

This holds true regarding the reality beyond our absolute limit as well. Thus, in our case, *seeing* would be used as a metaphor for the perception of the other, suprasensual world. Tradition made the seer Tiresias blind, suggesting that what he was a suprasensual truth. One might say that in this case, blindness conflicts with seeing and deletes the actual sensory feature in the semantic make-up of the verb, thus foregrounding the (nonsensory) information-reception feature. Oedipus', by contrast, whose sensory faculties are flawless, cannot *see* the abomination in which he lives.

Very much in the spirit of Donne and Eliot, Wordsworth refers to both kinds of metaphoric "seeing" by light. But, in addition, he insists on the plain literal meaning of light as well; what is more, that is the meaning that is in the focus of attention in the concluding lines of the stanza: "At length the Man perceives it die away, / And fade into the light of common day." The "light of common day" suggests literal light, in which the smaller lights of the stars fade away. At the same time, "the common day" is a metonymy for certain ways of thinking and understanding. It is the fading away of one light in the other that is in the focus of the reader's attention; the process is smooth, almost imperceptible. The "fading away" of one kind of seeing into another kind of seeing takes place off-focus, and is almost unnoticed. Since light is a thing-free quality that has no stable characteristic visual shape, displays, indeed, no spatio-temporal continuity, it has no identity either, and the smooth fusion of lights takes place unobstructed.

Now consider the following pairs of possible antonyms: pre-natal state ~ birth; sleep ~ awakening; learning ~ forgetting. From the point of view of increasing consciousness one might expect birth–awakening–learning to be analogous and to be used in poetry such that they reinforce each other. One of the central paradoxes Brooks finds in this stanza is that they are presented as acting in opposite directions: "Our birth is but a sleep and a forgetting". The issue here, I suggest, is that rather than transition from non-existence to existence, our birth is a transition from one kind of consciousness to another. Sleep is an altered state of consciousness; forgetting suggests unlearning, whereas birth suggests the beginning of learning. Thus, sleep becomes a state of lowly differentiated consciousness, opposed to the preceding and ensuing more highly differentiated states. Thus we have, at one and the same time, a uniform series of progressions, and an absolute opposition between its extremes. The two differentiated states suggest opposite kinds of perceptions, Tiresias' and Oedipus', related by one continuous process. "Birth, sleep, forgetting" are abstract nouns, and ought to confer a conceptual nature upon the discourse. This ought to be reinforced by the universal background against which the declarative statement of the first line should be understood. Nonetheless, the subtle semantic processes described in this paragraph tend to promote a nonconceptual fusion of the semantic information; this is further enhanced by the absence of stable characteristic visual shapes, and by some additional processes to be discussed later.

"But trailing clouds of glory do we come" is a crucial expression in the process we are considering. "Clouds" may act as a metaphor for blurred memory; it translates temporal into spatial distance, indistinct memories into indistinct light, and remembering into seeing. On the other hand light, or the soul, does not come "in utter nakedness"; it is wrapped, as it were, in "clouds of glory". "Clouds of glory" has about it something of an oxymoron. It can be settled in several ways. For instance, it may refer to an intermediate state of physicalness in the progression of the soul from its origin: from the point of view of our pre-natal state, this substance is perceived as cloud; from our "dull sublunary" existence (to use Donne's expression) it is perceived as glory, splendour, halo. This double nature of "clouds of glory" is emphasised by "trailing": solidity and floating. Clouds of dust may have something of this double nature: they consist of solid particles floating in the air like gas particles. "Clouds of glory" are made up of finer substance — matter, "to airy thinness beat".

This evokes the Neo-Platonic image of light emanating from a distant source — the further it gets from its source, the grosser matter it becomes. This replaces the one progress in space by several. There is the sun's daily progress, as suggested by Brooks, further away from the east; there is the child's progress, further away from the east — the source of his other-worldly light. This motion, however, only continues the other progress, light travelling from its hidden source, gradually materialised as "clouds of glory", as child, as youth, as man.

Now consider the line "Shades of the prison-house begin to close". "Shades" is a physical image, in which several images meet. First, it is the third, relatively gross material stage of the sequence "light–clouds of glory–shades". Second, "shades of the prison-house" suggests that in a prison-house one is deprived of light. Third, "shades [...] *begin* to close" indicates a process of closing more and more. At the same time, "shades" can be conceived as a less substantial prison, which in due course of process, will gradually thicken and solidify — till they become concrete, impenetrable prison-walls. Fourth, this phrase may contain an interesting syntactic manipulation. The predicate "to close" suits a subject like "shades" perfectly well; what is more, the verbal aspect "begins" suits an unstable substance like "shades" much better than stable prison-walls. Nevertheless, the main predicate may refer here to "prison-house" as well. In this respect, we are dealing here with what I have called throughout the present work a "thematised predicate", a transformational device that turns a prenominal or predicative adjective into an abstract noun and places it in a referring position. In this respect, it is a "shadowy prison-house" that begins to close. In this way we obtain a "prison-house" that *is* and *is not* at one and the same time: it is intangible shades that begin to close but, at the same time, they form an impenetrable prison-house. One reason for the softness of focus in the present case is that the verb "to close" suits, in somewhat different senses, both "shades" and "prison-house". A second reason is that the two meanings are difficult to distinguish in the flow or reading: They indicate different stages of the same process of gradual loss of freedom.

"The Light" has in this stanza, then, two different opposites: shades, and the light of common day. Thus, the paradox Cleanth Brooks noticed regarding the first line of the stanza returns in its last two lines. "At length the Man perceives it die away" makes one expect that it lead to darkness. Since, however, light stands for two kinds of vision, the paradoxical outcome is: when light dies away, we have light. In spite of this, the paradox is not felt as in Eliot's "to be redeemed from fire by fire", because the image relies on an additional, physical potential of light, widely experienced in everyday life, namely, that the smaller light tends to "fade into" the greater light. "Common day" is a metonymy (besides light) for everyday life, material needs, etc.

The core of stanza V of Wordsworth's Ode is, then, a paradox — the verbal reconciliation of two incompatible notions, by making a single image (light) stand for both. In this it is like any "metaphysical" poem by Ibn Gabirol, Donne, or Eliot. There are, however, several related motifs in the stanza. Their relationships are diverse. Some motifs are related through the physical attributes of light ("and fade into the light of common day"); some are related by using luminous objects as metaphors ("our life's Star"); or the opposite of light ("shades of the prison-house"). The basic contrast between two kinds of world (implying two kinds of vision) has been reinforced by additional oppositions: contrast between sleep and awakening; between forgetting and recollection (as well as learning and forgetting); between "here" and "there" ("our soul [...] cometh from afar", "our life's Star / Hath had elsewhere its setting", the Youth "daily further from the east / Must travel"); between narrow limits and unlimited space (prison-house—heaven—"cometh from afar"). The blending of various images into one meaning blurs their contours, softens and integrates the focus.

This technique of assigning incompatible meanings to one image would be condemned, as I suggested, by a critic of Neo-Classical inclination, as "false wit", or "mixt wit". As I have pointed out, what is bad Classicism may be excellent Mannerism or Romanticism. This instance of Romantic poetry displays the techniques we have encountered in the instances of Metaphysical poetry. They are only more elusive, and involve a considerably greater number of elements. The wide range of possible meanings of light exploited in this stanza, some in focus, some off-focus, the various near-synonymous (but still different) travellings away from the east, the various images coinciding in "the shades" overburden the reader's mental processing space. As I have suggested elsewhere (Tsur, 1992a: 418), the information conveyed by the succession of images may, under certain conditions, result in a cognitive overload of the reader's processing space; in such a case, one might assume, the reader is compelled to handle this information by collapsing it into an undifferentiated mass (very much in the manner in which perceptual overload is handled by "dumping" the excess of perceptual information into an undifferentiated background mass). These "certain conditions" may include the absence of stable characteristic visual shapes that might obstruct the smooth fusion of such incompatible entities as the ones denoted by *light*. This, in turn, may include the use of a "thematised predicate" (as in "Shades of prison-house"). Consider, for instance, two consecutive lines such as

> Not in entire forgetfulness,
> And not in utter nakedness...

Their way of presentation suggests that "forgetfulness" and "nakedness" should be either parallel or opposite to each other. In either case, the cognitive system could handle them parsimoniously. As a matter of fact, they are neither parallel, nor contrary to one another, thus increasing the load on processing memory.

Allegory, Symbol and Archetype in a 13th Century Mystic Poem

I am going to wind up my argument by examining at considerable length the imagery and archetypal pattern of a whole poem. This poem, like some of Ibn Gabirol's and Milton's, confronts the theological and poetic problem of how to fuse the Biblical personalistic conception of God with a Neo-Platonic conception (cf. Chapter 11). In what follows, I will examine the poetic issues involved in such a fusion, in the short masterpiece "Here Comes the Sun" by the Thirteenth Century Armenian poet, Kostandin of Erznka. My analysis is a by-product of my association with James Russell in 1990, then at Columbia University, and heavily relies on his paper (Russell, 1987).[1]

---

[1] Professor James Russel and myself stumbled into each other at the department samovar when I was a visiting professor at the Department of Near-Eastern Studies, Columbia University, and had a long conversation on religion and literature. On all possible issues we had opposing approaches, then and since, my approach being cognitive, linguistic, structuralist, while his approach might be best described as historical, philological, and "influence-hunting". Nonetheless, we found our encounter most mind-expanding, and he asked me to meet his graduate students so as to expose them to my approach. The discussion of Kostandin's poem, based on Russel's literal translation, is an attempt to sharpen the difference between our two approaches, by directly responding to one of his published papers.

1.

Now this night is past:
The morning's sign has come,
And the shining star rises,
Herald of the light.
The darkness was rejected
And all the world rejoiced,
Calling blessings to each other
That they were worthy of the light.

2.

For them who had been captive
And in the deep dungeon's dark
Now the light is born
In the great light of the Sun.
The earth was cold and frozen
By the icy winter blast,
But Spring has come at last,
In the great light of the Sun.

3.

The earth has come to life,
Mountain and plain are mantled in
green,
And the trees burst into flower
In the great light of the Sun.
Flowers in all the nations
Are adorned in every color.
And the red rose opens
In the great light of the sun.

4.

The fountains of the waters
Burst bubbling forth in laughter,
And the rivers rushing churn
In the great light of the Sun.
All the creatures that are,
And those that lay unsouled and dead
Behold! they are revived
In the great light of the Sun.

5.

How are you not amazed?
Why do you not ask of these things,
About this Sun
Full of its shining light?
This new light for us has dawned,
Far brighter than the Sun,
And to its mighty luminescence
The elder stars are servants.

6.

A beam brimming light was born
Of that light, of that beginning,
Light born from light,
From the great light of the Sun.
This light is of that light
Which is itself lord of all light
And is called king.
And the light of all is from his light.

7.

The arc of heaven stood amazed
Before that Sun,
For it had never seen such light
Nor the Sun from that light.
The earth was happy,
Glad at the tidings that
The duskless great light has dawned,
And the Sun of that light.

8.

Some are soulless, without
understanding,
Blind in their eyes,
Who believe not
In the Sun and its light.
In darkness they drag out their lives,
Asleep in dreams
They share no light
From the Sun, from the great light.

9.   I, Kostandin, who wrote this
I believe not   Long for that light,
In that lying spirit, that it is light   That I may be enlightened
itself   In the Sun, in that great light.
And no beam stretches from the Sun
From the great light.

Allegory and Symbol

The allegoric equivalences lurking behind this and similar Armenian poems have
been stated by Russell:

> Armenian tradition thus regards Christ and God as the Sun of Righteous-
> ness; Mary is Sun-like or else a receptacle of the Sun's fire. The light em-
> anates from, but is not different from, the endless light of the Father (Rus-
> sell, 1987: 123).

I shall argue that in the poem under discussion, such allegoric equivalences are
integrated into an infinitely rich and complex symbolic structure.

The word *symbol* is derived from a Greek word referring to a thing broken into
two, to be used later as a means for mutual identification. Thus, a symbol does not
suggest a this-stands-for-that type of relationship, but rather a relationship in which
the various members complete each other so as to form a *whole*. In other words, the
symbol becomes a node, a point of intersection of two or more planes of reality.[2]

Consider the following example. In a hierarchical conception of the Universe,
one may conceive of a variety of processes as of concentric cycles: the day, the year
and the life-cycle. Thus, the four stages of each of these cycles become analogous to
each other, respectively: MORNING, NOON, EVENING, NIGHT; SPRING, SUMMER,
AUTUMN, WINTER; BIRTH, MATURITY, OLD AGE, DEATH. The stages of the first
two, but not of the external cycle, are more or less rigidly fixed. In the latter we
sometimes find CHILDHOOD, YOUTH, MATURITY, OLD AGE, and other variations as
well. Accordingly, we occasionally encounter what Aristotle called *proportional
metaphors* such as *the evening of his life,* or *the winter of his life* for "old age".
Such metaphors are, then, generated by an intersection of two or more "parallel"
cycles. As I have suggested, in symbols, too, we may find an intersection of three
or more such planes of reality. Thus, one could imagine a case when the three
parallel stages of the three cycles coincide and reinforce each other's effect, as when
one is BORN, in the MORNING, at SPRINGtime. Or, to take another example, in
Chapter 5 I discussed the last but one line of Andreas Gryphius' sonnet "Abend":
"Und wenn der letzte Tag wird mit mir Abend machen" (and, when the last day
brings my evening on). There I spoke of "death as the last evening. In this sense,

---

2   Thus, whereas in *allegory* the sensuous image points away from itself to a different
     plane of reality, in *symbol* the various planes of reality converge in, and thus point
     to, the sensuous image.

the last day and the last evening have a double relationship to life. On the one hand, 'day' is analogous to 'life', and the end of the day analogous to the end of life. On the other hand, the last day completes life, and the last evening completes the last day before death". In Kostandin's poem, the three parallel cycles converge in the APPEARANCE OF LIGHT, lending each other exceptional force indeed. In the first three lines of stanza 1, we have the appearance of the morning, with its morning-star, as opposed to night and darkness: "Now this night is past: / The morning's sign has come, / And the shining star rises". In stanzas 2 and 3 we again have the light, but this time indicating spring and the renewal of the life of the vegetation (as opposed to winter): "The earth was cold and frozen / By the icy winter blast, / But Spring has come at last", and "The earth has come to life, / Mountain and plain are mantled in green, / And the trees burst into flower / In the great light of the Sun". Apparently, birth occurs in this poem only as a metaphoric predication of *light,* as in "Now the light is born" (in stanza 2) or "A beam brimming light was born" (in stanza 6). Thus viewed, these expressions are not very different from e.g. "The earth has come to life", where it serves as a metaphor for, say, "(sudden) appearance". Bearing, however, in mind the allegoric scheme of the poem, *born* has here a rather different status: if *light* stands here for the son, it is Christ who is born (disregarding even the fact that he was born in December). Thus, paradoxically, the various cycles are parallel and intersecting at one and the same time.

LIGHT as a Bundle of Attributes
In the poem under discussion LIGHT is the sustained image in which the various planes of reality converge (i.e., the sustained symbol). It is conceived of as of a bundle of attributes that determine the various meaning potentials of the image. Let us consider, then, briefly, some of these potentials.

LIGHT AS METONYMY. As the foregoing exercise may suggest, then, light is a metonymy of morning (as opposed to night), and a metonymy of spring (as opposed to winter). It may also be regarded as a metonymy of open, unconstrained space (as opposed to caverns, dungeons, graves and other subterranean enclosures; cf. in our poem, "And in the deep dungeon's dark / Now the light is born"). One possible role of *dungeon* in this poem is to reinforce, by way of opposition, *light.*

LIGHT AS SIGHT. The most obvious feature of light is that it affords our sense of sight, which is the most highly differentiated sense of human beings (who, after all, are the users of symbols as we know them).[3] Sight gives us the kind of information about the world with the help of which things appear to remain the same while we go away and return.[4] Thus, light becomes the most important single condition for

---

[3]   Had bats used symbols, presumably the radar would have fulfilled a similar function; with dogs, possibly, their sense of smell.

[4]   This is true, to a lesser extent, of the tactile sense too. But the latter usually gives information concerning a relatively small section of a larger object; and the kind of

affording human activities in the physical world. Consequently, sight is felt to be the most rational of our senses. When human beings immediately experience some supersensuous reality, they don't have a readily available conceptual language to describe their experience. For this end they usually have recourse to some kind of metaphorical or symbolic language. One of the most prominent ways to do this is to indicate some sense-perception proper, and to cancel in a metaphoric or other way, the physical elements in the process. The most readily available and most readily conventionalisable way to do this seems to have recourse to the sense of sight. That is why such archetypal "seers" as Tiresias are traditionally "pictured" as physically blind (physical blindness cancels the visual element in verbs that denote seeing).

THE SOURCE OF LIFE. Light is frequently treated in religion and literature as the symbol of life. This is no mere convention, but the exploitation of one of the natural potentials of light. It is a commonplace that the sun is the source of all life on earth, and the sun is the greatest and most obvious natural source of light on earth. This is most obviously true with respect to vegetation, and is also emphatically reflected in our poem: "The earth has come to life, / Mountain and plain are mantled in green, / And the trees burst into flower / In the great light of the Sun". On the human level, too, it is quite obvious that a continuous deprivation of sun is quite hostile to life. But much more immediately, on mere slight contact, it is intensely perceptible that darkness is hostile, whereas light is favourable to unrestrained life-activities.

PHYSICAL ATTRIBUTES OF LIGHT Light is thing-free energy that spreads ("emanates") in space. It has, as a rule, no stable contours or characteristic shape. It does not even have an identity, that is, what can be identified as the same entity on several occasions. One light can be "swallowed" by another light, and become indistinguishable from it. Thus, light can easily change its "identity" without—paradoxically—really changing it. This "fluidity" may account for some of its major potentials both for the mystic and the poet.

Types of Relationship
Each attribute in this "bundle of attributes" can be developed in a different direction, suggesting different meanings. These are by no means expected to be thoroughly compatible with one another. On the contrary, rather. In true symbolism it is the poetic image rather than the planes of reality suggested that has unity, consistency, and apparently real existence. In allegory it is rather easy to move to the plane of reality suggested, abandoning the physical image itself. Attention is focussed on that aspect of the image that points toward the other plane of reality; the rest of its aspects are easily ignored by the perceiver. In a symbol, as I have suggested, a

---

information it gives is less prone to enable us to uniquely identify objects on slight contact.

considerable number of (incompatible) planes of reality converge in one physical image, related to a variety of its attributes: whenever attention is focussed on one plane of reality and the image's aspect that suggests it, the other aspects of the physical image cannot be "abandoned" because they are anchored, as it were, by the respective planes of reality suggested by them. This multiplicity of potential meanings, based on a multiplicity of attributes, is further complicated by the fact that there may be different kinds of relationships between the image and the plane of reality suggested.

ALLEGORY. The most obvious kind of relationship between the central image of our poem and another plane of reality is, of course, allegorical. Above I have quoted Russell who suggests that "Armenian tradition thus regards Christ and God as the Sun of Righteousness". Apparently, such an identification has a considerable element of arbitrariness in it.[5] All allegory is based on some such "arbitrary" decision; more precisely, it is usually based on the arbitrary isolation and over-emphasis of one of the natural properties of the image.

THE NATURAL BASIS OF SYMBOLISM. Symbolic meanings that have been based on those properties of light which I have mentioned under the heading "LIGHT as a Bundle of Attributes" can be said to have *a natural basis*. For expository purposes, one may distinguish here between those relationships in which light is PART OF (the day, the spring), and those in which the attributes are PART OF the light. Now, why should the sun be identified with either Christ and God or with Righteousness?[6] What is it that facilitates or even encourages "the willing suspension of disbelief" in such an identification? Why is it that God (or the chief god) is identified in so many unrelated cultures with the sun? This last question, if its presupposition is valid, suggests that there must be something in the *natural potentials* of light and the sun that would justify such an identification. I submit that this justification must be sought in what I have said above of the sun as the source of all life, and of light (as opposed to darkness) as one of the most important conditions that are favourable to life. Another aspect of the natural basis of light symbolism concerns certain relationships between the celestial bodies that are not unlike certain relationships between figures in the *New Testament*. Thus, for instance, in stanza 1 we read: "The morning's sign has come, / And the shining star rises, / Herald of the light". Following this natural relationship, the morning star can be taken, in a rather arbitrary manner, to signify Saint John the Baptist, who heralded the birth of Christ.

---

[5] The argument "It is a convention" does not eliminate arbitrariness, merely transfers the "mystery" from one place to another. Now we have to answer the question, "Why did people identify God with light in the first place, and how did this identification become a convention?"

[6] In some Mediaeval paintings God is depicted as radiating light. This may also be the reason for kings and rulers to wear a golden crown into which gems and jewels are inserted: it makes their head luminescent.

Likewise, there are among the celestial bodies "the great light" and "the small light", the light of the latter being derived from the former. This may be one way to explain such verses in stanza 6 as "This light is of that light / [...] And the light of all is from his light": everything, and particularly the moon, receives its light from the sun, just as the Son's light is derived from the Father's. In other words, though the allegorical decision to take one thing as standing for another has an arbitrary conventional element in it, it still has, very frequently, some natural basis that makes it prone to facilitate "the willing suspension of disbelief".

EMANATION. Neo-Platonic Philosophy uses some of the physical attributes of light to account for the creation of the Universe. According to this conception, the Universe was created by light that emanated from a certain source: the nearer the light to its source, the more spiritual its "matter"; the further away from it, the less spiritual it is.

THE TRANSLATION OF A NAME. The name *Lucifer* is derived from Latin *lux*. Russell suggests that the lines "I believe not / In that lying spirit, that it is light itself / And no beam stretches from the Sun / From the great light" *could* at least be interpreted as referring to Lucifer ("that lying spirit"), though this interpretation seems unlikely to him.

LIGHT AS LIGHT. I have earlier suggested that light and sight may serve as metaphors for some supersensuous perception, when a metaphoric contradiction or an allusion to physical blindness cancels the physical element in sight. A rather sophisticated twist occurs in such a conception, when the blind Tiresias accuses Oedipus of blindness. A similar use of blindness occurs in Kostandin's poem too: "Some are soulless, without understanding, / Blind in their eyes, / Who believe not / In the Sun and its light. / In darkness they drag out their lives". Such a conception may corroborate Russell's comment on the last stanza that rather than Lucifer, "the fallen son of the morning", "the 'lying spirit' may be [...] the physical light that is no metaphor" (Russell, 1987: 123). Notice that this reading seems to be applicable, even when omitting (as I have omitted) the noun phrase "the sun-god of the sun worshippers".[7] It might be illuminating to summarise here, what happens to *light* in this respect, throughout the poem. *Light* is introduced as physical light, originated in the rising Sun. *Sun* receives particular emphasis in stanza 5, when **this** *Sun* is substituted for **the Sun,** probably conferring to it some symbolic significance. This possibility is corroborated by the sequel, at the end of the stanza. Perceptually, however, there seems to be a difference between just light and *this light,* that is merely a difference in degree: "This new light for us has dawned, / Far brighter than the Sun". In view of our foregoing discussion of the nature of contours of entities like light and fire, one might even suggest that the two lights (the

---

7   In that case, the passage may be thought of as conveying the Platonic notion of regarding sensuous reality as "lying" as opposed to supersensuous reality.

brighter and the less bright) fuse, so-to-speak: the exact contours of their identities are not observed. Eventually, however, if Russell's or my interpretation is correct, the last stanza "subtracts" as it were *light* in the plain, physical sense, and fosters only *light* in the symbolic sense to be admired and worshipped.

It has been suggested that light in this poem is associated with God and the Son. The act of association is, in a sense, arbitrary. In another sense, it is justified by the natural life-giving potential of light. Once associated, however, this "allegorical" light begins to behave as physical light in many respects that may be irrelevant to the life-giving-aspect of light. Thus, for instance, I suggested earlier that light is thing-free energy that spreads ("emanates") in space. What is more, light has "no stable contours or characteristic shape", so "light-entities" may fuse with one another or be separated one out of the other, in a rather natural way. One should attempt to consider the allegorical identification of God-the-Father and of the Son with Light, as the *encoding* of the identities of the personal Deity in such a way that it can imperceptibly fuse the *many* into *one,* derive the one from the other by way of *emanation.* According to Russell, the following lines (and others) suggest that God creates the Son by emanation: "Light born from light, / From the great light of the Sun. / This light is of that light / Which is itself lord of all light". This technique serves both to enhance the multiplicity-in-oneness of the Trinity, and to telescope this conception of the personal Creator into the Neo-Platonic conception of Creation, without violating the sense of his individual contours. I shall argue later that this encoding of the personal Deity into Light, that has the afore-said physical properties, may also be conducive to the mystical experience associated with this poem.

The present conception will illuminate another prominent feature of this poem (and, in fact, of much mystical poetry). It will be noticed that Light is treated in this poem in a way that would seem to be outrageous by any logical standard. The word *Light* is repeated throughout this poem, without proper indication that the various tokens of the word have different referents. At the same time, they occur in such syntactic positions that they *cannot* be assumed to have the same referent. Such phrases as "Light born from light" may serve as good examples to this. This verbal technique is very wide-spread in religious, and especially in mystical poetry. Its gist appears to be the encoding of different signifieds in the same signifier, thus indicating—or even serving as an icon of—the "essential paradox of the one and the many". In the present instance, however, a special kind of verbal signifier is used, *light,* indicating a thing-free and Gestalt-free quality. To indicate the possible significance of such a signifier to mystical poetry, or mystical experience in general, I wish to remind us of the passage I quoted (in the chapter on oceanic dedifferentiation) from Ehrenzweig who, in turn, quotes Bergson:

> What Bergson calls Metaphysical intuition is a gestalt-free vision, capable of superimposed perception. Let us hear his own masterful description of surface and depth vision:

"When I direct my attention inward to contemplate my own self [...] I perceive at first, as a crust solidified at the surface, all the perceptions which come to it from the material world. These perceptions are clear, distinct, juxtaposed or juxtaposable one with another; they tend to group themselves into objects. [...] But if I draw myself in from the periphery towards the centre [...] I find an altogether different thing. There is beneath these sharply cut crystals and this frozen surface a continuous flux which is not comparable to any flux I have ever seen. There is a succession of states each of which announces that which follows and contains that which precedes it. In reality no one begins or ends, but all extend into each other".

Bergson recognises that juxtaposition is essential for surface perception, but not for depth perception. To achieve intuition he gives a practical recipe; he recommends one to visualise at the same time a diversity of objects in superimposition.

"By choosing images as dissimilar as possible, we shall prevent any one of them from usurping the place of the intuition it is intended to call up, since it would then be driven away at once by its rivals. By providing that, in spite of their differences of aspects, they all require from the mind the same kind of attention [...] we shall gradually accustom consciousness to a particular and clearly defined disposition" (Ehrenzweig, 1965: 34–35).

Ehrenzweig's brilliant analysis of the visual arts amply suggests that such a superimposition has similar effects not only in imaginary visualisation, but also in *seeing* proper, when looking at actual visual designs. In the verbal arts, however, there may be some difficulty to accomplish this. Here, images are conveyed by words and sentences, that are *necessarily* juxtaposed. So, the poet must take some additional, and sometimes rather complex, measures for the fusion of "these sharply cut crystals and this frozen surface" into a thing-free and Gestalt-free mass. One of the simplest and most effective means to achieve this is the verbal technique we have just encountered. The poet uses successive tokens of the same word-type without proper indication that they have different referents; but in such syntactic positions that strongly indicate that they must have different referents. What is more, in the present case, the word used denotes a thing-free and shape-free mass, the instances of which would easily merge without violating the stable contours of their referents.[8]

---

[8]   I have discussed this and additional techniques with reference to what some critics describe as "Whitman's Meditative Catalogue" (Tsur, 1992: 416–428), as part of my discussion of "Poetry and Altered States of Consciousness" (411–470). I have also given a reading of "Kubla Khan" as an ecstatic poem in my book (Tsur, 1987).

The Rebirth Archetype

Finally, I would like to have a closer look at a subset of the elements we discussed in relation to the light and the sun as the source of life or, at least, what affords life. In many mythologies and religions (if there be a difference between them) the god that dies and is resurrected (or reborn) is intimately associated with the yearly cycle of vegetation that dies and is reborn. I shall not get involered here in the dispute whether Jungian archetypes are transmitted in the structure of the brain, or are acquired emotional patterns at best, or nonexistent. I shall only point out that the Rebirth Archetype may turn out to be the final organising principle of the symbolic material condensed in this short poem. In the perspective of this archetype, the various planes of reality among which we have established by now a *partial* identity, may assume a *total* one.

The only image that seems to be only loosely connected to the poem is that of the dungeon, as a possible opposite to light: "For them who had been captive / And in the deep dungeon's dark / Now the light is born". The Rebirth Archetype would tighten its relationship to the dominant imagery of the poem. In her mind-expanding book *Archetypal Patterns in Poetry,* Maud Bodkin examines the nature and structure of Jungian archetypes and their occurrence in some of the major poems of Western Literature. From her illuminating discussions I shall quote only two relatively short passages, from her discussions of Coleridge's "Ancient Mariner" and "Kubla Khan". Bodkin's very notion of *emotional symbolism* suggests that she is not so much interested in what images mean as in what they feel like. By the same token, she suggests how such images assume their power to effect us "on mere slight contact". In discussing the emotional symbolism of caverns and abyss, Bodkin writes:

> Here is the "eternal essence" gathered from experiences of cavern and abyss —an essence of cold, darkness, and stagnant air, from which imagination may fashion a place of punishment, the home of the Evil One (Bodkin, 1963: 101).

One conspicuous thing in this passage is that it does not state merely a simple equation: CAVERN = HELL. It rather abstracts from them such elementary sensations as "cold, darkness, and stagnant air"; these sensations are unpleasant, and in extreme cases unfavourable to life. In Kostandin's poem, Bodkin's *"Archetypal* place of punishment" is turned into the "Archetypal *place of punishment"*. In his stimulating book *God the Problem,* Gordon Kaufman claims that we use "God-language" in dealing with experiences that are beyond the *absolute limit* of our experience, construed by analogy with the relative limits of our every-day life. In this perspective, *dungeon* would be conceived as the most condensed example of the relative limitations of Man, carrying—by the same token—strong overtones of punishment and conditions unfavourable to life.

In discussing the Death-and-Rebirth Archetype in Coleridge's "Rhyme of the Ancient Mariner", Bodkin discusses a wide range of mental events, and then summarises:

I have compared, also, myth and the metaphor of religious confession and of psychological exposition, selecting material in accordance of similarity of imagery, especially of form or pattern. Particular words and images [...] have been examined for their emotional symbolism, but mainly with reference to their capacity to enter into an emotional sequence. Within the image-sequence examined the pattern appears of a movement, downward, or inward, the earth's centre, or a cessation of movement—a physical change which, as we urge a metaphor closer to the impalpable forces of life and soul, appears also a transition toward severed relation with the outer world, and, it may be, toward disintegration and death. This element in the pattern is balanced by a movement upward and outward—an expansion or outburst of activity, a transition toward reintegration and life-renewal (Bodkin, 1963: 54).

Our poem, like so many poems of various ages, styles and cultures, seems to take up the pattern at its pivotal point, at the point of "severed relation with the outer world, disintegration and death", which is, by the same token, the beginning of "an expansion or outburst of activity, a transition toward reintegration and life-renewal". In this sense, the subterranean existence in the dungeon neatly fits both into the emotional pattern of death and rebirth, and into the natural cycle of the vegetation, and even to the state of the water before bursting out in a spring, and thus integrates them into one pattern. In this perspective, the following lines gain enormous significance in the poem: "The earth was cold and frozen / By the icy winter blast, / But Spring has come at last", and "The earth has come to life, / Mountain and plain are mantled in green, / And the trees burst into flower / In the great light of the Sun". The same is true of the following lines: "The fountains of the waters / Burst bubbling forth in laughter, / And the rivers rushing churn / In the great light of the Sun. / All the creatures that are, / And those that lay unsouled and dead / Behold! they are revived / In the great light of the Sun". Vegetation, as well as the fountains of water, and the "unsouled and dead" creatures renew their vitality, are "reborn", burst forth. And all this happens when the "light" (the Son) is born from the "light" (the Father). Now consider this: overtones both of punishment and of conditions unfavourable to life are associated with dungeons, as we have said; but they are also associated with original sin (eating of the Tree of Knowledge), which brought death unto the earth; and it is the appearance of light (the birth of Christ) that redeemed man from this state of "Death", suggested, in terms of the poem's imagery, by the (subterranean) dungeon. Thus, being "soulless, without understanding", and being "unsouled, dead" become various degrees of the same state of "Death", in the perspective of the Death-and-Rebirth Archetype. Here, the *Rebirth* rather than the *Resurrection* of the god fuses with the outburst of energies in the other planes of reality.

I wish, however, to emphasise one all-important thing: the Death-and-Rebirth archetype is not *the meaning,* but the over-all *emotional pattern,* the *organising principle* of the poem's imagery.

Finally, I wish briefly to consider one more issue. Some Soviet Armenian scholars seemed to have difficulties in digesting mystic, religious poetry. Russell mentions some such scholarly attitudes, and also gives the proper answer to them.

> One often hears the suggestion, as in the Introduction to the recent bilingual edition of Kostandin Erznkats'i, that the tenth century St. Grigor Narekats'i was the founder of a kind of secularizing Renaissance. His scenes of natural beauty, and those of Kostandin Erznkats'i and others after him, are considered the product of a poetic inspiration lacking any genuine underlying religious faith; the allegory is disingenuous. According to this view, the expression of religious sentiments should be ignored or derided as primitive, and allegory must in poems of real talent be seen as defensive, as if the poet introduced it only after coming to himself, following a blind, pagan fit of untrammelled creativity [...]. The monolithic power of the church is fooled, and Kostandin and his fellows are emulated; Armenian literature becomes an underground phenomenon of atheist or naturalist subtexts [...]. The theory thus imposes the circumstances of the present time upon a remote age [...]. For Kostandin, as for other medieval Armenian poets, Nature was informed by the reality of the Christian spiritual world and history of salvation, which imposed order upon, and infused meaning, all phenomena and all events, past, present, and future (Russell, 1987, 120–21).

I agree completely with Russell's position. I only want to add here that my foregoing analysis strongly suggests that the poem has a considerable unity and integrity, however conceived by the poet. The only part that makes the impression of a later addition is the last stanza. But this, too, is an *impression,* a perceived quality, derived from the change in the speaker's tone; if the speaker throughout the poem is some unidentified bard, who is speaking on behalf of all believers, or perhaps all humankind, the last stanza speaks on behalf of Kostandin's own person.

The last section of this chapter has been an inquiry into the poetic structure of a thirteenth century mystic poem by an Armenian poet. It also illuminated a wide range of additional issues. In the first place, it had certain things to say about the structure of mystical poetry in general. Secondly, this structure also threw some light on the manner in which mystical poetry in several monotheistic religions, in various periods and poetic traditions may attempt to handle the fusion of the Biblical notion of a personal Creator and the Neo-Platonic notion of light-emanation (cf. also Chapter 11 above). Third and not least, our foregoing reading may suggest that a general understanding of how mystical poems work may facilitate the handling of such poetry by a reader who is not knowledgeable in the specific religious conventions of the particular poem in question.

To Sum up

This chapter has explored the cognitive foundations and the literary applications of spatial imagery. There seem to be several good reasons to have recourse to spatial imagery; this paper has explored two of them. On the one hand, concrete visual images constitute a bundle of features and as such, they allow efficient coding of information. This, in turn, grants the cognitive system great flexibility and efficiency both in creative thinking and in poetry. A single image encoding a variety of meaning units can be regarded as an instance of the aesthetic principle "unity-in-variety". This also can be said to save considerable mental energy, and as Kris and Gombrich (1965) pointed out following Freud, one possible source of pleasure is the saving of mental energy. Or, as Charles Peirce and Umberto Eco would put it in semiotic terms, such a coding substitutes a single predicate for a complicated tangle of predicates, replacing a complicated feeling "by a single feeling of greater intensity" (Eco, 1979: 132). On the other hand, the recoding of information into spatial imagery may help the cognitive system to overcome some of its inherent limitations. Thus, lowly-differentiated information may be recoded into a more differentiated spatial template, as in the case of sound pitch into musical scales; or conceptually presented information may become less differentiated in perception, owing to recoding into Gestalt-free and thing-free imagery. Such lowly-differentiated qualities may be reinforced by the mechanisms of spatial orientation, or the mechanisms for alleviating cognitive overload. From such a perspective, the Lakoffean conception of conceptual metaphor based on spatial imagery appears to be congenial to human cognition, but is still rather simplistic. In the course of the above discussions I attempted to show how religious ideas are turned with the help of figurative language into verbal imitations of religious experience. In this respect, I have pointed out two stylistic modes. Perhaps the most surprising thing about those two modes is the recognition of how similar the techniques are by which the opposite effects are achieved. One of them, the Metaphysical mode, seeks to yield an insight into matters of religious significance or the nature of existence in a flash, through a sudden transition from complexity to unity. The phenomenological quality of this kind of insight is typically witty. The other mode, best described as "Romantic" or "Mystic", seeks to achieve the verbal imitation of some experiential contact, of an intuitive rather than conceptual nature, with a reality that lies beyond the *absolute limit* of our experience. Some poems, at least, are remarkably successful in translating those mystic ideas into verbal imitations of mystic experiences.

Chapter 13

The Asymmetry of Sacred, Sexual and Filial Love
in Figurative Language

Throughout the present work I have appealed (even when not explicitly stated) to the reader's creativity and "poetic competence" in accounting for his response to varieties of religious and mystic poetry. Poetic and religious conventions can facilitate the identification of the relevant elements, but explain very little about the perceptual or emotional dynamics of a poem. In this last chapter I will explore one specific issue in the light of these principles: the asymmetry of sacred, sexual and filial love in figurative language. In Chapter 9 (and *passim*) I drew attention to the commonplace that there is a widespread convention to speak of mystic experiences in terms of sexual love. Some historical approaches account for such conventions by Pavlovian conditioning through culture. Without denying a cultural element in this process, my approach with reference to conventions in general and this specific convention in particular is that they result from the fossilisation of psychological similarities detected by readers in two analogous phenomena. I also quoted Newberg et al., who went one step further, claiming in a neurological and evolutionary perspective that the neurological machinery for "such an apparently impractical talent" for mystic transcendence "may have arisen from the neural circuitry that evolved for mating and sexual experience".

"This is the first century", says Empson (1968: 340), "which has tried to appreciate all art works that ever were, anywhere; and [...] this [...] was bound to produce a kind of traffic jam". One crucial aspect of this "traffic jam" is the amount of "past experience" and the "underlying knowledge" of poetic conventions to be assumed in the "versatile reader", a reader who is able to respond more or less adequately to a wide range of poetic styles. Psychologically—not epistemologically—speaking, there may be some reluctance to concede that such a versatile reader "knows" long lists of specific conventions relevant to the various poetic styles and genres. This might constitute too heavy a burden on his memory, and might well restrict the responding consciousness. Since the versatile reader seems to have some kind of creativity, a more efficient code must be postulated, with the help of which he may meaningfully "process" certain poetic conventions to which he may never have been exposed before. In the preceding chapters, for instance, we have encountered such conventional semantic manipulations as transferred epithet and topicalised predicate, manipulating abstract (instead of concrete) nouns into the referring position; even readers who are not familiar with these rhetoric conventions may respond to the effect of the shift from the concrete to the abstract.

The present chapter is part of an attempt on a larger scale to reclaim perceived effects of literary works from a worship of poetic conventions on the one hand, and from critical impressionism on the other, and to account for them in systematic, non-ad-hoc ways. It assumes that poetic effects cannot be inferred, only directly perceived. It accepts, therefore, poetic structures and reported effects as given, and offers a generalisation or an hypothesis about the structural conditions in which those effects are possible; the reported effects and structural descriptions serve as the basis of generalisations, which, in turn, may corroborate further reported effects.

The basic formula of similae and metaphors is "*a* is similar and dissimilar to *b* at the same time". From this formula an important stylistic principle can be derived. If the *similarity* between *a* and *b* is emphasised in the poetic device, it will be perceived as the "*balance* and *reconcilement* of opposite or discordant qualities"; if the dissimilarity is emphasised, the poetic device will be perceived as "the most heterogeneous ideas yoked by violence together". In the former case, the perceived quality of the trope will tend to be emotional or "sublime"; in the latter case, it will tend to be witty. In the history of Western literature, there are poetic traditions that tend to be witty, and traditions whose dominant effect tends to be emotional. Frequently the difference does not depend on the selection of elements, but on their mode of presentation. Many bundles of discordant elements can be manipulated in either way.

Wellek and Warren (1956: 197) seem to assume that in Donne's figurative language there is a symmetrical relationship between sacred and profane love. "The interchange between spheres of sex and religion recognizes that sex is a religion and religion is a love". The present work claims that as far as the perception of poetic qualities is concerned, this relationship is not quite symmetrical. Love-as-religion is "marked" as compared to religion-as-love, and is likely to occur less frequently in poetry that does not aim at a deliberately witty or hyperbolic effect. Characteristically enough, in those of Donne's poems in which "to sexual love he applies the Catholic concepts of ecstasy, canonization, martyrdom, relics" (ibid.), critics have regularly discovered such qualities as wit and ingenuity—meant, according to some, to "perplex the minds of the fair sex", but had little to do with "genuine emotion"; while those of his Holy Sonnets in which "he addresses God in violent erotic figures", were again and again recognised as poems "in which an individual relationship to God is expressed, debated or described with great personal emotion and much intellectual energy" (Warnke, 1974: 54). The difference may be ascribed, partly, to rhetorical manipulation and poetic structure. I submit that one fundamental difference between ingenuity and genuine emotion is to be traced, in these poems, to the *direction* of metaphoric transfer: from profane to sacred love, or *vice versa* (an issue I consider to be part of "poetic structure").

The same holds true of divine or paternal love. *Our Father in Heaven* for "God" is more readily acceptable than *my god on earth* for "father". When Mephistopheles in Goethe's *Faust* speaks of man as "This little god on earth", readers tend to perceive strong ironic accents. I submit that this difference cannot be explained entirely in terms of "conventions" or "past experience". Certain expressions will sound less natural, some expressions more natural, irrespective of one's familiarity with the relevant conventions. Rather than *inducing* certain poetic qualities, familiarity with conventions may cause habituation and tone down our response to them. Rather than *starting* psychological processes, it may well be the case that some conventions, at least, are the *fossils* of certain vivid psychological processes.

Let us consider the opening verse of a poem by the 11th century Hebrew poet, Ibn Gabirol:

אֲהַבְתִּיךָ כְּאַהֲבַת אִישׁ יְחִידוֹ   בְּכָל לִבּוֹ וְנַפְשׁוֹ וּמְאֹדוֹ

> 1. I love thee with the love of a man for his only one /
>   with all his heart and his soul and his might

Each of the hemistiches contains an allusion to a Biblical verse: "Take your son, your only one, whom you love" (*Genesis* 22. 2), and "Hear, O Israel: the Lord your god is one Lord; and you shall love the Lord your God with all your heart, and with all your soul, and with all your might" (*Deutoronomy* 6.4–5). *His only one* becomes ambiguous in Ibn Gabirol's verse. It is an expression taken from the story of Isaac, but *may* refer here to man's "only Lord", depending on who the addressee is. These allusions bring to the poem the overtones of a father's love to his son, and of human love for God. Since it is the beginning of a poem, it is uncertain whom the speaker is addressing, God or a man. This uncertainty renders the verse particularly apt to demonstrate my point. The first possibility seems to be more available for experienced readers. If one assumes the addressee to be God, who is addressed in terms of man, the verse will sound more natural, less exaggerated, than if one assumes the addressee to be a human being addressed with overtones of love for God. Since the speaker turns out to be a human person addressing a younger man, the theme of the address being the nature of reality discussed in a short philosophical poem, these overtones foreground the lack of congruence between these two kinds of love. In a detailed interpretation of this poem (Tsur, 1985; 1987c), I have shown this lack of congruence to be functional in the poem which has several elements in common with "Metaphysical poetry". It "yokes by violence together" the Biblical notion of personal Creator and the command "you shall love the Lord your God", with the Platonic notion of Eros as an impersonal cosmic principle (very much in harmony with the text discussed above, in Chapter 11).

Let us now consider two possible alternative readings of the following sonnet:

> 2. Most glorious Lord of lyfe, that on this day,
>   Didst make thy triumph ouer death and sin:
>   And hauing harrowd hell, didst bring away
>   Captiuity thence captiue vs to win:
>   This ioyous day, deare Lord, with ioy begin,.
>   And grant that we for whom thou diddest dye
>   Being with thy deare blood clene washt from sin,

> May liue for euer in felicity.
> And that thy loue we weighing worthily,
> May likewise loue thee for the same againe:
> And for thy sake that all lyke deare didst buy,
> With loue may one another entertaine.
>   So let us loue, deare loue, lyke as we ought,
>   Loue is the lesson which the Lord vs taught.

The theme of the three quatrains is sacred love, that of the couplet is love between the sexes. The shift of theme has here a pointed effect, reinforced by prosodic and dramatic shifts. Prosodically, the shift from the quatrains to the couplet has considerable epigrammatic force with a strong "closural quality"; this coincides with a shift of dramatic situations: the addressee in the quatrains being Christ, in the couplet—the speaker's "deare loue".

The sonnet seems to allow two different interpretations, according to whether the religious theme is subordinated to the sexual one, or the other way around. It is quite frequent in the sonnet tradition that there is a sudden shift at the end of the three quatrains, from the ostensible theme to the *real* theme presented in the couplet. A Neo-Platonic view of the world would point in the opposite direction. Love being a central harmonising principle of the universe, which is a universe of correspondences, it is love that may lead men and women, in ever higher and purer forms, to Eternity or Divine Love, above the sensuous world.

One might consider these two readings as changing aspects of the same object, just as Wittgenstein's duck and rabbit are aspects of the same visual design (1976: 194). In one case, the effect is cheerfully licentious; in the other it suggests depth and soberness of attitude. The difference is one of emphasis. In the latter case "we are made to concede likeness" between sacred and profane love; in the former case we are more "strongly conscious of unlikeness". One possible source of this difference derives from the *direction* in which the underlying analogy proceeds.

The sudden shift of dramatic situations arouses a feeling of incongruity between the quatrains and the couplet. The *degree* of incongruity will be determined by the relative congruence felt by the reader between sacred and profane love. This, in turn, is strongly influenced by the direction of metaphoric transfer: whether the theme of the poem is profane love treated in terms of sacred love, or the other way around. This basic difference will have corollaries in several other layers as perceived by the reader. First, in both readings, the prosodic, thematic and dramatic shift will bring about some kind of *shocked recognition:* that sexual "love is the lesson which the Lord us taught", in sharp contrast to what one may have heard from religious preachers. However, the degree of shock may differ in the two readings. This difference of degree may be reinforced by additional factors. In the "libertine" reading, the shocking quality will be amplified by what will be seen as the speaker's false logic in an attempt to persuade his Coy Mistress to yield to his advances. This will be in perfect harmony with the Donne–Marvell line of poetry. In the Neo-Platonic reading, the shock will be mitigated, since the two kinds of love are conceived as parts of one hierarchical philosophical system. Here the shocking revelation will be felt to be founded on some genuine logic. Such a reading would be in harmony with the Spenserian line of love poetry.

Second, according to the Neo-Platonic conception, love purifies the lovers. The reader is therefore inclined to carry over certain attributes from Christ's love to the love between the sexes. Their love is therefore conceived of as one that purifies them, and frees them from the "captivity" of lust and this-worldliness, and is a possible source of felicity for them. In the "libertine" reading, the reader is not motivated to carry over such a meaning to the couplet, and thus it is felt to be more incongruent with the preceding quatrains than in the rival reading.

Third, there is the perceived relationship between the verbal sign and the ideas signified. The eighteenth-century Neo-classic Joseph Addison writes: "As *True Wit* consists in the Resemblance of Ideas, and *false Wit* in the Resemblance of Words [...]; there is another kind of wit which consists partly in the Resemblance of Ideas, and partly in the Resemblance of Words". In the Neo-Platonic reading of this poem one may detect a conspicuous "Resemblance of Ideas" between the two kinds of love, and the verbal sign *love* becomes transparent, barely noticeable. In the "libertine" interpretation, with its "false logic", the "Resemblance of Ideas" diminishes, and the incongruity is felt to be resolved mainly on the verbal level. The verbal sign acquires an existence that is relatively independent of its "incongruent" referents.

The author's intention, and the philosophical doctrine or the poetic conventions embraced by him, can perhaps be resorted to in an attempt to decide which one is the correct reading of this poem. But notice that a well-established convention can be brought in support of each of these two readings. All this, however, is irrelevant to the task at hand, which is to trace the different perceptual qualities of the alternative readings, whether right or wrong. For the present inquiry, one has to regard the two poetic structures and their respective effects as *immediately given*.[1]

We have considered the asymmetry of sacred, sexual and filial love in poetic devices. Transfer in one direction appears to be unmarked, whereas in the opposite direction—marked. The Mädchen-für-alles term *convention* seems to have insufficient explanatory power for this asymmetry. It can be explained, rather, by a structural analysis of these concepts and figures. This structural analysis will be partly Aristotelian, partly componential. I shall have recourse to two issues from Aristotle's discussion of metaphors in Chapter 21 of his *Poetics*, "analogy", and "transference from genus to species". "Analogy or proportion is when the second term is to the first as the fourth to the third. We may then use the fourth for the second, or the second for the fourth". Thus, God is to Humanity as the father is to the family (or the king to the nation). Hence "the Father of Humanity" or "King of the World". However, there is also implied here a transference from genus to species: *family* is included in *nation*, which, in turn, is included in *Humanity*.

---

[1] The author of the sonnet in quote 2 is Spenser.

We have been considering three kinds of love. They have a common core of components: a warm feeling, a drive "towards", a wish to give or get pleasure, a quest for harmony. Beyond this common core, each of the concepts has its own specific components (although the "edges" between these concepts have been blurred through overfamiliarity with their metaphoric attribution to each other). In love between parents and children there are such typical components as a wish to give or receive protection or support; in love between the sexes there are such components as a wish to give and receive sexual pleasure; in love between man and God the components can be called transcendental or "numinous".

The components of the concepts may be considered as the basic components of efficient coding for "poetic competence", making special uses of existing linguistic and psychological mechanisms. Whether a figure is less or more natural, depends on the "amalgam" of components resulting from the transfer of specific components from the source-term to the destination-term. Four kinds of considerations are relevant.

FIRST, THE PSYCHOLOGICAL PRIMACY OF COMPONENTS. The components of protection and support, as well as those of sexual drives are more primary in the individual's experience than the transcendental and the "numinous" ones. I have quoted Newberg et al., who claim in a neurological and evolutionary perspective that the neurological machinery for "such an apparently impractical talent" for mystic transcendence "may have arisen from the neural circuitry that evolved for mating and sexual experience". From a phenomenological perspective, Rudolf Otto (1959: 15), as quoted in the previous chapter, may prove illuminating:

> It is essential to every theistic conception of God [...] that it [is] thought of by analogy with our human nature of reason and personality; only, whereas in ourselves we are aware of this as qualified by restriction and limitation, as applied to god the attributes we use are [...] thought as absolute and unqualified.

As for the irrational aspect of God,

> We can cooperate in this process by bringing before [one's] notice all that can be found in other regions of the mind, already known and familiar, to resemble, or again afford some special contrast to, the particular experience we wish to elucidate (21).

From Otto's description the following principle can be derived. One can make the idea of the transcendental or the numinous *familiar* by using terms that refer to "all that can be found in other regions of the mind", whereas the latter can be made strange by using terms belonging to the sphere of the transcendental or the numinous. In other words, when you are elucidating profane love in terms of sacred love, you are in fact saying that "A is similar to B (about which, in turn, the only thing you know is that it is similar in certain respects to A). Hence the "markedness", the far-fetched quality of metaphors that treat sex as religion, or parental love in terms of divine love. The result is less unnatural when components of protection and support or love between the sexes are transferred to love between men and God, than when "transcendental" components are transferred to love between the sexes or to love between parents and children. Hence, "Our Father in Heaven" for God is less unnatural than "my god on earth" for father. Consequently, the observational fact that the former expression is idiomatic whereas the latter is rare and tends to be perceived as far-fetched or joking, reflects this structural fact; "convention" here is a result rather than a cause. In Mephistopheles' phrase "this little god on earth" for man, the purely proportional analogy has been interfered with: it does not only suggest that man is to the earth as God is to Heaven; it also suggests that he is "little", even though he may be great in his own eyes. The true proportional metaphor would imply that man is as great in relation to earth as God in relation to Heaven.

SECOND, POSSIBLE TABOOS RELATED TO THE AMALGAM OF COMPONENTS. The transfer of components of protection and support from parental love to love between the sexes is less unnatural than transfer in the opposite direction. Hence, when in Alterman's poem-cycle *The Joy of the Poor* the dead husband addresses his living wife as "my daughter", it is fairly natural; as is the request in Bialik's love poem "be a mother and a sister to me" (excerpt 3). If we found, however, a transfer in the opposite direction, such as addressing one's mother or sister "be my beloved and my wife", its stylistic effect would have been found quite unnatural. Likewise, the attribution of divine properties to one's father will violate certain taboos — in our prevalent culture, at least.

THIRD, HABITUATION AND/OR SPECIAL RHETORICAL MANIPULATION. *Habituation* occurs when wide-spread use (literary or extra-literary) continually emphasises certain components and de-emphasises others. In this way, poetic devices become less startling. This is what happened, for instance, to many of the sonnets that celebrate the divinity of the Lady: by now they sound hardly hyperbolic. *Special rhetorical manipulation* may increase the prominence of some meaning-components and decrease the prominence of some others; this may render the figure less or more unnatural. Let us consider the following stanza from one of Bialik's love poems:

הַכְנִיסִינִי תַּחַת כְּנָפֵךְ,

וַהֲיִי לִי אֵם וְאָחוֹת,

וִיהִי חֵיקֵךְ מִקְלַט רֹאשִׁי,

קַן תְּפִלּוֹתַי הַנִּדָּחוֹת.

3. Take me under your wings,
   And be a mother and a sister to me,
   And let your lap be shelter of my head,
   The nest of my rejected [remote] prayers.

According to the considerations of psychological primacy, the application of religious imagery to love between the sexes is perceived as less natural than the other way around, and the last line ought to sound far-fetched. Intuitively, however, the line is passionate rather than witty or hyperbolic. The reason for this seems to be as follows. The tone of the whole stanza is emotional and supplicant. The components of begging and of protection are conspicuous in the first and third lines. According to the foregoing analysis, *mother* and *sister* too contribute components of support and protection. In *prayers* of the fourth line there is, in addition to the religious components, a component of emotional intensity and begging; in *nest* there is a component of protection. The quest for support and protection is so emphasised in this line by the preceding lines, that one is inclined to disregard the religious component in it. Were we to paraphrase the fourth line of the stanza as "The nest of my rejected, devout petitions addressed to your Divinity", the religious component could hardly be ignored, and the resulting quality would be rather witty or hyperbolic. Alternatively, the beloved is not at all addressed here in religious terms; she is to serve as a *substitute* where communication with God failed.

FINALLY, THE LOGICAL RELATIONSHIP BETWEEN THE GENERAL AND THE PARTICULAR. The more extensive the group, the greater generality can be claimed by the ideas and emotions related to its common objects. From what is significant for the extensive group, one may make inferences as to what is significant for the included groups and individuals. Consequently, the validity of inferences from the more to the less general seems to be granted more easily than from the less to the more general.

In a symmetrical analogy, the "Lady" is to the poet as a goddess is to humanity: humanity may *feel love* toward the goddess, just as the individual may *worship* his own lady. Although the analogy *qua* analogy is symmetrical here, there is an asymmetrical relationship too, as in Michael Drayton's sonnet:

> 4. Some Atheist or vile infidel in love,
>   When I do speak of thy divinity,
>   May blaspheme thus, and say I flatter thee,
>   And only write my skill in verse to prove.

In the context of this quatrain the proportional metaphor "thou art *my* goddess" becomes a literal equation "thou art *the* goddess". It is the possessive pronoun that introduces the proportional analogy into what otherwise would have appeared as a literal equation. When the proposition is understood as a literal equation, there arises the sharp asymmetry between genus and species, for one may be expected to feel love toward a goddess, but it would be quite odd to expect humanity to worship the individual's lady. The poet is included in humanity as a group, but not vice versa. The effect here is, indeed, conspicuously hyperbolic. The re-combination of the cited Aristotelian categories to achieve specific poetic effects may serve as a model of productivity in the use of conventions. It is important which conventions you know; but it is no less important what you do with them.

In Donne's love poetry, sacred imagery is sometimes used to *exclude* the extensive group from the emotions of the inner group of the chosen ones, as in

> 5. So let us melt, and make no noise,
>   No tear-floods, nor sigh-tempests move,
>   T'were prophanation of our joyes
>   To tell the layetie our love.

Here the far-fetched quality of the argument relies more on the hyperboles of the second line than on the religious image of the next two lines. In this instance, two aspects of the application of religious imagery to profane love act in opposite directions: the treatment of the psychologically primary experience in terms of the sacred sphere enhances its far-fetched quality, whereas the use of this image to emphasise the privacy of the experience mitigates it. Not so in "Canonization", where the two aspects join forces to render the argument as far-fetched as possible. Here, profane love is treated in sacred terms:

> 6. And by these Hymnes, all shall approve
>   Us Canoniz'd for Love.

At the same time, this private affair claims universal significance, and all will invoke these saints of Love to intercede for them.

To Conclude

One need not check lists of specific conventions in order to know whether a certain metaphor is "far-fetched" or "congruous". There is, rather, a small set of general "rules" which can be creatively applied, so as to account for the perceptual qualities of an indefinite number of specific metaphoric attributions. Frequently we *perceive* that the metaphor is witty or emotional, just as we know that the book is red by looking, or that the tea is sweet by tasting. This chapter attempted to specify the kind of information-processing that underlies such highly sophisticated instances of "direct perception", and broke down the notion of "poetic competence" into sets of operationally definable mediating structures that may systematically relate perceived effects to poetic structures.

References

Addison, Joseph (1951 [1711-12[1]] from "Spectator Papers", in James Harry Smith & Edd Winfield Parks (eds.), *The Great Critics*. New York: Norton. 819-825.

Aristotle (1951) *Poetics*. S.H. Butcher (trans.), in James Harry Smith & Edd Winfield Parks (eds.), *The Great Critics*. New York: Norton. 28-61.

Aristotle (1932) *The Rhetoric of Aristotle,* Lane Cooper, trans. New York & London: Appleton Century.

Arnheim, Rudolf (1957) *Art and Visual Perception*. London: Faber.

Arnold, M.B. and Gasson J. A. (1968 [1954[1]]) "Feelings and Emotions as Dynamic Factors in Personality Integration", in M. B. Arnold (ed.), *The Nature of Emotion*. Harmondsworth: Penguin, 203-221.

Austin, J. L. (1962) *How to Do Things with Words*. London: Oxford UP.

Bakhtin, M. M. (1968) *Rabelais and his World* (trans. Helene Iswolsky). Cambridge, Mass. : MIT Press.

Balaban, Victor (1999) "Religious Metaphor and Cognitive Linguistics: Perceptual Metaphors for Knowledge at a Marian Apparition Site". In Lieven Boeve and Kurt Feyaerts (eds.) *Metaphor and God-Talk*. Bern: Peter Lang.

Beardsley, Monroe C. (1958) *Aesthetics: Problems in the Philosophy of Criticism*. New York & Burlingame: Harcourt, Brace & World.

Beardsley, Monroe C. (1966) *Aesthetics from Classical Greece to the Present*. New York and London: MacMillan.

Beit-Hallahmi B. & Arggle A. (1997) *The Psychology of Religious Behavior, Belief and Experience*. London & New York: Routledge.

Benari Motti (1993) "The Different Functions of Repetitions in Shmuel Hanagids Wisdom Poetry in Ben Kohelet" (in Hebrew), *Mehkarey Yerushalaim Besifrut Ivrit* 14, 81-105.

Benari Motti (2000) *Cognitive Aspects of Metaphorical Phenomena*. Tel Aviv University dissertation (in Hebrew).

Bloom, Harold (1963) *The Visionary Company: A Reading of English Romantic Poetry*. Garden City: Doubleday Anchor.

Bodkin, Maud (1963 [1934[1]]) *Archetypal Patterns in Poetry*. Oxford: Oxford UP.

Boeve, Lieven and Kurt Fayaerts (eds.) (1999) *Metaphor and God-Talk*. Bern: Peter Lang.

Bownds, Deric M. (1999) *The Biology of Mind—Origins and Structures of Mind, Brain, and Consciousness*. Bethesda MD: Fitzgerald Science Press. Available online: http://mind.bocklabs.wisc.edu

Bowra, C. M. (1943) *The History of Symbolism*, London: McMillan.

Bowra, Sir Maurice (1961) *The Romantic Imagination*. London: Oxford UP.

Brady, Susan, Donald Shankweiler & Virginia Mann (1983) "Speech Perception and Memory Coding in Relation to Reading Ability". *Journal of Experimental Child Psychology 35:* 345-367.

Brooke-Rose, Christine (1958) *A Grammar of Metaphor.* London: Secker & Warburg.

Brooks, Cleanth (1968) *The Well-Wrought Urn.* London: Methuen.

Brooks, Cleanth and Robert B. Heilman (1966) *Understanding Drama.* New York: Holt, Rinehart & Winston.

Brown, C. C. and W. P. Ingoldsby (1979) "George Herbert's 'Easter Wings'" in John R. Roberts (ed.), *Essential Articles for the Study of George Herbert's Poetry.* Hamden, Connecticut: Archon Books. 461–472.

Brown, Roger (1968) *Words and Things.* New York: The Free Press.

Brown, Roger (1970) "The 'Tip of the Tongue' Phenomenon", in *Psycholinguistics: Selected Papers,* 274-303. New York: The Free Press.

Budick, Sanford and Wolfgang Iser (eds.) (1989) *Languages of the Unsayable—The Play of Negativity in Literature and Literary Theory.* Stanford, California: Stanford University Press

Burke, Kenneth (1962) *A Grammar of Motives* and *A Rhetoric of Motives.* Cleveland & New York: Meridian Books.

Cohen, J.M. (ed.), 1960. *The Penguin Book of Spanish Verse.* Harmondsworth: Penguin.

Culler, Jonathan (1975) *Structuralist Poetics.* London: Routledge & Kegan Paul.

Dante Alighieri (1980) *The Divine Comedy.* Translated, with a commentary by Charles S. Singleton. *Inferno.* 1: Italian text and translation; 2. Commentary. Princeton, NJ: Princeton University Press (Bollingen Series LXXX).

Davidson, R. J. (1992) "Anterior Cerebral Asymmetry and the Nature of Emotion", *Brain and Cognition* 20(2), 125-151.

Dawson, E. 1963 [1614[1]]. *The Practical Methode of Meditation,* in Louis Martz (ed.) *The Mediative Poem.* Garden City: Anchor Books, 3-23.

Deikman, Arthur (2000) "A Functional Approach to Mysticism" in Jensine Andresen and K.C. Forman (eds.) *Cognitive Models and Spiritual Maps.* Exeter: Imprint Academic. 75–91).

Derrida, J. (1973) "Differance" in J. Derrida *Speech and Phenomena and Other Essays on Husserl's Theory of Signs,* (trans: D. B. Allison & N. Gavner, Evanston). Northwestern UP, 129-160.

Dixon, N.F. (1981) *Preconscious Processing.* Binghamton NY: Vail-Ballou Press.

Doležel, Lubomír (1976) "Narrative Semantics". *PTL* 1: 129–151.

Eco, Umberto (1976) *A Theory of Semiotics.* Bloomington: Indiana UP.

Ehrenzweig, Anton (1965) *The Psychoanalysis of Artistic Vision and Hearing.* New York: Braziller.

Ehrenzweig, Anton (1970) *The Hidden Order of Art.* London: Paladin.

Ekman P. & Davidson R. J. (eds.) (1994) *The Nature of Emotion: Fundamental Questions,* New York: Oxford University Press.

Ellsworth, P.C. (1994) "Levels of Thought and Levels of Emotion". In P. Ekman & R. J. Davidson (Eds.) *The Nature of Emotion: Fundamental Questions.* New York: Oxford University Press. 192-196.

Empson, William (1968) "Rhythm and Imagery in English Poetry", in Harold Osborne (ed.) *Aesthetics in the Modern World.* London: Thames and Hudson. 340-361.

Erlich, Victor (1965) *Russian Formalism* (2nd., revised ed.). Hague: Mouton.

Eynath-Nov, Idith (in preparation) *The Personal Reshuyot: Liturgical Genre and Poetic Category—A Poetic Look at the Poems of the Liturgical Genre and the Like.* Tel Aviv University Dissertation (in Hebrew).

Finke R.A. (1989) *Principles of Mental Imagery.* Cambridge Mass.: MIT Press.

Fónagy, Iván (2001) *Languages within Language—An Evolutive Approach.* Amsterdam/ Philadelphia: John Benjamins.

Fowler, Roger (1974) *Understanding Language.* London: Routledge and Kegan Paul.

Freeman, Rosemary (1979) "George Herbert and the Emblem Books" in John R. Roberts (ed.), *Essential Articles for the Study of George Herbert's Poetry.* Hamden, Connecticut: Archon Books. 215–230.

Frenkel-Brunswick, Else (1968 [1948[1]]) "Intolerance of Ambiguity as an Emotional and Perceptual Variable" in J. S. Bruner and D. Kretch (eds.), *Perception and Personality.* New York: Greenwood Press.

Frijda N.H. (1994) "Emotions Require Cognitions, Even if Simple Ones". in P. Ekman & R. J. Davidson (eds.), *The Nature of Emotion: Fundamental Questions.* New York: Oxford University Press.

Fromkin, Victoria A. (1973) "Slips of the Tongue." *Scientific American* 229, no 6: 110–17.

Gardner, Helen (1972) "Introduction" to *The Metaphysical Poets.* Harmondsworth: Penguin. 15-28.

Genette, Gérard (1966) *Figures.* Paris: Du Seuil ("Tel Quel").

Gibbs, R.W. Jr. 1997. "Taking Metaphor out of Our Heads and Putting it into the Cultural World". In R. W. Gibbs & G. J. Steen (eds.), *Metaphor in Cognitive Linguistics, Selected Papers from the Fifth International Cognitive Linguistics Conference.* Amsterdam: John Benjamins, 145-166.

Gibson, Walter S. (1973) *Hieronymus Bosch.* London: Thames and Hudson.

Gimello R. M. (1978) Mysticism and Meditation, in Steven T. Katz (ed.), *Mysticism and Philosophical Analysis.* 170-199.

Glicksohn, Joseph (1989) *Altered Sensory Environments, Altered States of Consciousness and Meaning.* Unpublished Tel Aviv University Dissertation.

Glicksohn, J., R. Tsur and Ch. Gootblatt (1991) "Absorption and Trance-Inductive Poetry". *Empirical Studies of the Arts 9/2:* 115-122.

Goldman A. (1995) "Emotions in Music (A Postscript)", *The Journal of Aesthetics and Art Criticism* 53(1) 59-69.

Gombrich, E. H. (1963) "Visual Metaphors of Value in Art", in *Meditations on a Hobby Horse—And Other Essays on the Theory of Art.* London: Phaidon.

Gombrich, E. H. (1984). *The Sense of Order: A Study in the Psychology of Decorative Art.* Oxford: Phaidon.

Goodblatt, C. (1990) "Whitman's Catalogs as Literary Gestalts: Illustrative and Meditative Functions". *Style 24:* 45-58.

Greeley A. M. (1975) *The Sociology of the Paranormal.* London: Sage.

Grierson, Herbert J. C. (1965 [1921[1]]) "Introduction" to *Metaphysical Lyrics & Poems of the Seventeenth Century.* Oxford: The Clarendon Press. xiii-lviii.

Gross, Sabine (1997) "The Word Turned Image: Reading Pattern Poems". *Poetics Today* 18:1: 15-32.

Guilford, J.P. 1970 [1959]. "Traits of Creativity". In P. E. Vernon (Ed.) *Creativity,* Harmondsworth: Penguin. 167-188.

Guttmann, Julius (1973) *Philosophies of Judaism—A History of Jewish Philosophy from Biblical Times to Franz Rosenzweig,* David W. Silverman (trans.). New York: Shocken.

Halle, Morris and Samuel Jay Keyser (1966) "Chaucer and the Study of Prosody". *College English* 28: 187–219.

Halle, Morris and Samuel Jay Keyser (1971) *English Stress: Its Growth and Its Role in Verse.* New York: Harper and Row.

Halliday, M.A.K (1970) "Language Structure and Language Function" in Lyons, John (ed.), *New Horizons in Linguistics.* Harmondsworth: Pelican. 140–165.

Hepburn, R. W. (1968) "Emotion and Emotional Qualities", in H. Osborn (Ed.) *Aesthetics in the Modern World,* London: Thames & Hudson. 81-93.

Hirsch, E. D. (1964) *Innocence and Experience: an Introduction to Blake.* New Haven: Yale UP.

Horne, James R. (1978) *Beyond Mysticism.* Ontario: Wilfrid Lawier University Press.

Huxley, Aldous (1972) "Visionary Experience", in John White (ed.) *The Highest State of Consciousness.* Garden City NY: Anchor Books. 34-57.

Isaacs, Jacob (1951) *The Background of Modern Poetry.* London: Bell.

Jakobson, Roman (1956) "Two Aspects of Language and Two Types of Aphasic Disturbances", in Roman Jakobson & Morris Halle, *Fundamentals of Language.* The Hague: Mouton. 55-82.

Jakobson, Roman (1960) "Closing Statement: Linguistics and Poetics", in Thomas A. Sebeok (ed.), *Style in Language.* Cambridge, Mass.: MIT. 350-377.

Jakobson, Roman (1968) *Child Language, Aphasia, and Phonological Universals.* The Hague: Mouton.

James, William (1902) *The Varieties Of Religious Experience—A Study in Human Nature.* New York and Bombay: Longmans, Green and Co.

Jessen, F., Heum, R., Erb, M., Granath, D.-O., Klose, U., Papassotiropoulos, A. & Grodd, W. (2000) "The Concreteness Effect: Evidence for Dual Coding and Context Availability". *Brain and Language* 74(1): 103-112.

Johnson, M.G. 1987. *The Body in the Mind: The Bodily Basis of Meaning, Imagination, and Reason.* Chicago: Chicago University Press.

Johnson, Samuel (1951 [1779[1]] from "Abraham Cowley", in James Harry Smith & Edd Winfield Parks (eds.), *The Great Critics*. New York: Norton. 460-462.

Kahneman D. (1973) *Attention and Effort*. Englewood Cliffs, New Jersey: Prentice-Hall Inc.

Kant, Immanuel (1969) *Critique of Judgement*, (trans.), G. H. Bernard. London: Hafner Press.

Katz, Steven T. (1992) "Mystical Speech and Mystical Meaning" in Steven T. Katz (ed.), *Mysticism and Language*. New York: Oxford UP. 3-41.

Kaufman, Gordon G. (1972) *God, The Problem*. Cambridge, Mass.: Harvard UP.

Kinsbourne, M. (1982) "Hemispheric Specialization and the Growth of Human Understanding". *American Psychologist 37*: 411-420.

Knight, George Wilson (1960[1941[1]]) "Coleridge's Divine Comedy", in M.H. Abrams (ed.), *English Romantic Poets: Modern Essays in Criticism*, 158-169. Oxford & London: Oxford UP.

Knight, Wilson G. (1965) *The Imperial Theme*. London: Methuen.

Knoblauch, Hubert (1999) "Metaphors, Transcendence and Indirect Communication: Alfred Schutz' Phenomenology of the Life-World and the Metaphors of Religion" in Lieven Boeve and Kurt Fayaerts (eds.), *Metaphor and God-Talk*. Bern: Peter Lang. 75-94.

Kris, Ernst (1965) *Psychoanalytic Explorations in Art* (New York: Schocken).

Kris, Ernst and Abraham Kaplan (1965) "Aesthetic Ambiguity", in Ernst Kris, *Psychoanalytic Explorations in Art*. New York: Schocken.

Kris, Ernst, and E. H. Gombrich (1965) "The Principles of Caricature", in Ernst Kris, *Psychoanalytic Explorations in Art*, New York: Schocken.

Lakoff, George (1993) "The Contemporary Theory of Metaphor", in Andrew Ortony (ed.,) *Thought and Metaphor*. Cambridge: Cambridge UP (second ed.). 202-251.

Lancaster, Brian L. (2000) "On the Relationship Between Cognitive Models and Spiritual Maps: Evidence from Hebrew Language Mysticism" in Jensine Andresen and K.C. Forman (eds.) *Cognitive Models and Spiritual Maps*. Exeter: Imprint Academic. 231-250.

Leavis, F.R. (1968 [1945-46[1]]) "Imagery and Movement", in F.R. Leavis (ed.), *A Selection From Scrutiny* Volume 1: 231–248.

Lehner, Ernst and Johanna Lehner (1971) *Devils, Demons, Death and Damnation*. New York: Dover Publications.

Levin, Israel (1986) *Mystical Trends in the Poetry of Solomon Ibn Gabirol*. Lod: Haberman Institute for Literary Research (in Hebrew).

Levinson J. (1997) "Emotion in Response to Art—A Survey of the Terrain", in M. Hjort & S. Laver, *Emotions and the Arts*. Oxford: Oxford University Press. 20-34.

Liberman, A. M. (1992) "Plausibility, Parsimony, and Theories of Speech". *Haskins Laboratories Status Report on Speech Research* SR 109-110: 109-118 [also Liberman, A. M. (1992). "Plausibility, Parsimony, and Theories of

Speech". In J. Alegria, D. Holender, J. Junca de Morais, and M. Radeau (eds.) *Analytic Approaches to Human Cognition* pp. 25-40. Amsterdam: Elsevier Science Publishers B.V.)

Liberman, Isabelle Y., and Virginia A. Mann (1981) "Should Reading Instruction and Remediation Vary with the Sex of the Child?" *Status Report on Speech Research SR-65:* Haskins Laboratories.

"Longinus" (1951) *On the Sublime*. Trans. by W. Rhys Roberts, in J. H. Smith and E. W. Parks (eds.) *The Great Critics*. New York.

Lukács, Georg (1962) "To Narrate or Describe?" in George Steiner and Robert Fagles (eds.) *Homer—A Collection of Critical Essays*. Englewood Cliffs, N. J.: Prentice-Hall. 86–89.

Lyons, John (1977) *Semantics*. Cambridge: Cambridge UP.

Mananzan, Mary-John (1974) *The "Language Game" on Confessing One's Belief: A Wittgensteinian-Austinian Approach to the Linguistic Analysis of Creedal Statements*. Tübingen: Niemeyer.

Mann, Virginia A. (1984) "Reading Skill and Language Skill". *Developmental Review 4:* 1-15.

Martz, Louis (ed.) (1963) *The Meditative Poem*. Garden City: Anchor Books.

Martz, Louis (1962) *The Poetry of Meditation*. New Haven: Yale UP.

Meyer, Leonard B. (1956) *Emotion and Meaning in Music*. Chicago: Chicago UP.

Miller, George A., and Philip N. Johnson-Laird (1976) *Language and Perception*. Cambridge Mass. Harvard UP.

Muecke, D. C. (1970) *Irony*. London: Methuen.

Neisser, U. 1976. *Cognition and Reality*. San Francisco: Freeman.

Neville, Robert Cummings (1999) "A Pragmatic Semiotic Theory of Religious Symbolism" in Lieven Boeve and Kurt Fayaerts (eds.), *Metaphor and God-Talk*. Bern: Peter Lang. 15–32.

Newberg, A., D'Aquili E. & Rause V. (2001) *Why God Won't Go Away: Brain Science and the Biology of Belief*. New York: Ballantine Books.

Ornstein, Robert E. (1975) *The Psychology of Consciousness*. Harmondsworth: Penguin.

Otto, Rudolf (1959) *The Idea of the Holy*, John W. Harvey (trans.). Harmondsworth: Penguin.

Pagis, Dan (1970) *Secular Poetry and Poetic Theory: Moses Ibn Ezra and his Contemporaries*. Jerusalem: Bialik Institute (in Hebrew).

Pagis, Dan (1977) *"Carmina Figurata* in Pre-Modern Hebrew Poetry". *Hasifrut* 25: 13-27 (in Hebrew; English summary: i-iii).

Paley, Morton D. (1969b) "Introduction", in Morton D. Paley (ed.), *Songs Of Innocence and Of Experience—A Collection of Critical Essays*. Englewood Cliffs, N. J.: Prentice-Hall. (1–9)

Paley, Morton D. (1969b) "Tyger of Wrath", in Morton D. Paley (ed.), *Songs Of Innocence and Of Experience—A Collection of Critical Essays*. Englewood Cliffs, N. J.: Prentice-Hall. (68–92)

Peer, Willie van (1993) "Typographic Foregrounding". *Language and Literature* 2: 49-61.

Persinger, Michael A. (1987) *Neuropsychological Bases of God Beliefs*. New York, Westport, Connecticut, London: Praeger.

Plutchik, R. (1968 [1962[1]] "The Evolutionary Basis of Emotional Behaviour", in Magda B. Arnold (ed.), *The Nature of Emotion*. Harmondsworth: Penguin. 67-80.

Polányi, Michael (1967) *The Tacit Dimension*. Garden City, N.Y.: Anchor.

Pratt M.L. 1977. *Toward a Speech-Act Theory of Literary Discourse*. Bloomington, IND:

Preminger, Alex (ed.), (1974) *Princeton Encyclopedia of Poetry and Poetics* (enlarged edition). Princeton, NJ: Princeton University Press.

Ransom, John Crowe (1951) "Poetry: A note in Ontology", in James Harry Smith & Edd Winfield Parks (eds.) *The Great Critics*. New York: Norton. 769-787.

Rickey, Mary Ellen (1979) "Herbert's Technical Development" in John R. Roberts (ed.), *Essential Articles for the Study of George Herbert's Poetry*. Hamden, Connecticut: Archon Books. 311–326.

Riffaterre, Michael (1978) *Semiotics of Poetry*. Bloomington: Indiana UP.

Rosch E. & Mervis C. B. (1975) "Family Resemblances: Studies in the Internal Structure of Categories", *Cognitive Psychology* 7(4), 573-605.

Rothman, David J. (1997) "Verse, Prose, Speech, Counting, and the Problem of Graphic Order". *Versification: an interdisciplinary journal of literary prosody*. Available HTTP: http://www.

Russell, James R. (1987) "Here Comes the Sun: a Poem of Kostandin Erznkats'i". *J. Soc. for Armenian Stud. 3:* 119-127).

Schirmann, Jefim (1961) *Hebrew Poetry in Spain and in Provence*, 4 vols. Jerusalem and Tel Aviv: The Bialik Institute and Dvir (in Hebrew).

Scholem, Gershom G. (1960) *Jewish Gnosticism, Merkabah Mysticism, and Talmudic Tradition*. New York: Jewish Theological Seminary of America

Scholem, Gershom G. (1961) *Major Trends in Jewish Mysticism*. New York: Schocken Books.

Semino, Elena and Jonathan Culpeper eds. (2002) *Cognitive Stylistics—Language and Cognition in Text Analysis*. Amsterdam: John Benjamins.

Shklovsky, Victor (1965) "Art as Technique", in L. T. Lemon and M. J. Reis (eds.), *Russian Formalist Criticism*. Lincoln: Nebraska UP. 3-24.

Sidney, Sir Philip. "An Apologie for Poetrie," in J. H. Smith and E. W. Parks, eds., *The Great Critics*. New York, 1951.

Sinfield, Alan (1971) *The Language of Tennyson's 'In Memoriam'*. Oxford: Blackwell.

Smart N. (1958) *Reasons and Faiths: An Investigation of Religious Discourse, Christian and Non-Christian*. London: Routledge and Kegan Paul.

Smart, J.J.C. (1966) "Theory Construction", in A.G.N. Flew (ed.), *Logic and Language*. 222-242. Oxford: Basil Blackwell.

Smith, James (1934) "Metaphysical Poetry", *Scrutiny 2:* 222-239.

Solomon Ibn Gabirol (1961) *The Kingly Crown*, Bernard Lewis (trans.). London: Vallentine, Mitchell.

Sperber, D. & Wilson, D. 1986. *Relevance: Communication and Cognition*, Oxford: Blackwell.

Spitzer, Leo (1962) *Essays on English and American Literature*. Princeton: Princeton UP.

Spitzer, Leo (1965 [1942[1]]) Speech and Language in Inferno XIII, in John Freccero (ed.) *Dante: A Collection Of Critical Essays*. Englewood Cliffs, N.J.: Prentice-Hall. 78-101.

Spitzer, Leo (1969 [1928[1]] "The Muting Effect of Classical Style in Racine" in R. C. Knight (ed.), *Racine—Modern Judgements*. London: Macmillan. (117-131)

Stace W. T. (1961) *Mysticism and Philosophy*. London: Mcmillan, Chap. 2, 41-133.

Strawson, P.F. 1967. "Singular Terms and Predication". In P.F. Strawson (ed.), *Philosophical Logic*. Oxford: Oxford UP.

Summers, Joseph H. (1954) *George Herbert—His Religion and Art*. London: Chatto and Windus.

Sypher, Wylie (1955) *Four Stages of Renaissance Style*. Garden City, N.Y.: Anchor.

Tellegen 1981. "Practicing the Two Disciplines for Relaxation and Enlightenment: Comment on 'Role of the Feedback Signal in Electromyograph biofeedback: The Relevance of Attention' by Qualls and Sheehan". *Journal of Experimental Psychology: General,* 110 (2): 217-226.

Thomson, Philip (1972) *The Grotesque*. London: Methuen.

Tillyard, E. M. W. (1943) *The Elizabethan World Picture*. London : Chatto & Windus.

Tsur, Reuven (1971) *A Rhetoric of Poetic Qualities*. Unpublished Sussex University Dissertation.

Tsur, Reuven (1972) "Articulateness and Requiredness in Iambic Verse". *Style 6:* 123-148.

Tsur, Reuven (1974) "Poem, Prayer and Meditation: An Exercise in Literary Semantics" (in English). *Style 8:* 405-425.

Tsur, Reuven (1977) *A Perception-Oriented Theory of Metre*. Tel Aviv: The Porter Israeli Institute for Poetics and Semiotics.

Tsur, Reuven (1978) Emotion, Emotional Qualities, and Poetry, *Psychocultural Review* 2: 165-180.

Tsur, Reuven (1983) *What Is Cognitive Poetics*, Tel-Aviv: The Katz Research Institute for Hebrew Literature.

Tsur, Reuven (1985) "'Ahavtikha ...' by Ibn Gabirol—Philosophical Poem, or Rhymed Philosophy?" (in Hebrew), in Zvi Malakhi (ed.), *Essays on Ibn Gabirol*. Tel Aviv: The Katz Research Institute for Hebrew Literature. 23-46.

Tsur, Reuven (1987a). *On Metaphoring*, Tel-Aviv: Israel Science Publishers.

Tsur, Reuven (1987b) *The Road to "Kubla Khan": A Cognitive Approach.* Jerusalem: Israel Science Publishers.

Tsur, Reuven (1987c) *Mediaeval Hebrew Poetry in a Double Perspective: The Versatile Reader and Hebrew Poetry in Spain* (in Hebrew). Tel Aviv: University Publishing Projects.

Tsur, Reuven (1988b) "Oceanic Dedifferentiation and Poetic Metaphor". *Journal of Pragmatics* 12: 711-724.

Tsur, Reuven (1992a) *Toward a Theory of Cognitive Poetics*. Amsterdam: Elsevier (North Holland) Science Publishers.

Tsur, Reuven (1992b) *What Makes Sound Patterns Expressive?—The Poetic Mode of Speech Perception*. Durham, N.C.: Duke UP.

Tsur, Reuven (1997) "Picture Poems: Some Cognitive and Aesthetic Principles" *Psyart—*A Hyperlink Journal for the Psychological Study of the Arts. Available HTTP: http://www.clas.ufl.edu/ipsa/journal.

Tsur, Reuven (1997) "Sound Affects of Poetry—Critical Impressionism, Reductionism, and Cognitive Poetics". *Pragmatics and Cognition* 5: 283-304.

Tsur, Reuven (1998a) *Poetic Rhythm: Structure and Performance—An Empirical Study in Cognitive Poetics*. Bern: Peter Lang.

Tsur, Reuven (2001) "Picture Poetry, Mannerism and Sign Relationships". *Poetics Today*.

Vajda, Georges (1957) *L'Amour de Dieu dans la Théologie Juive du Moyen Age.* Paris:Librairie philosophique J. Vrin.

Verbrugge R.R. 1980. "Transformation in Knowing: A Realist View of Metaphor". In R. P Honeck & R. R. Hoffman (Eds.) *Cognition and Figurative Language*. Hillsdale, New Jersey: Lawrence Earlbaum, 87-125.

Walkup, L.E. (1965) "Creativity in Science through Visualization" *Perceptual and Motor Skills* 21: 35-41.

Warnke, J. Frank (1974) *European Metaphysical Poetry*. New Haven: Yale UP.

Weitz, Morris (1962) "The Role of Theory in Aesthetics", in J. Margolis (ed.), *Philosophy Looks at the Arts*. New York: Scribner. 48-59.

Wellek, René & Austin Warren (1956) *Theory of Literature*. New York: Harcourt, Brace & Co.

Wellek, René (1963) *Concepts of Criticism*. New Haven & London: Yale UP.

Wheelwright, Philip (1968) *The Burning Fountain: a Study in the Language of Symbolism*. 2nd ed., Bloomington: Indiana UP.

Wilson C.L. 1972. "Affect: Feeling, Emotion, and Mood". In *Music and Meaning – A Theoretical Introduction to Musical Aesthetics*, London: Free Press, 214-233.

Wimsatt, W. K. (1954) "The Structure of Romantic Nature Imagery" in *The Verbal Icon*. New York: Noonday.

Winner, Ellen and Howard Gardner (1993) "Metaphor and Irony: Two Levels of Understanding" in Andrew Ortony (ed.,) *Thought and Metaphor*. Cambridge: Cambridge UP (second ed.). 425–443.

Wittgenstein, Ludwig (1976) *Philosophical Investigations*, G. E. M. Anscombe (trans.). Oxford: Blackwell.

Index